CW00938015

Contents

TOTAL
DIRECTING

TOTAL DIRECTING

INTEGRATING CAMERA AND PERFORMANCE
IN FILM AND TELEVISION

TOM KINGDON

SILMAN-JAMES PRESS   LOS ANGELES

First Edition
10 9 8 7 6 5 4 3 2

Library of Congress Cataloging-in-Publication Data

Kingdon, Tom, 1949-
  Total directing: integrating camera and performance in film and
television / by Tom Kingdon
     p. cm.
  Includes bibliographical references and index.
  ISBN 1-879505-71-1 (alk. paper)
  1. Motion pictures—Production and direction. 2. Television—Production
and direction. I. Title.

PN1995.9.P7K543 2004
791.4302'33—dc22

2004048182

Cover design by Wade Lageose

Printed and bound in the United States of America

Silman-James Press
1181 Angelo Drive
Beverly Hills, CA 90210

To Marcella Markham and Harold Lang
for whom energy was eternal delight.

Introduction

This book is an introduction to directing narrative screen drama. It aims to serve the potential feature film director, the independent filmmaker, the director of television series, as well as students making their college (or school) projects. Although an introduction, some practicing directors may also find it an interesting, and occasionally provocative, discussion of their craft.

What distinguishes this book from other texts on the market is that it integrates *both* actor-direction (working with actors) *and* technical-direction (working with camera, audio, and the crew). Almost a century has passed since the principals of modern acting were codified, and still some professional directors have only the sketchiest idea of how to direct actors. For these directors, a movie or a television program is primarily a technical exercise. I believe that if screen drama is to progress beyond its current obsession with mundane reality, if it is to refresh and reinvent itself, it has to empower actors and place the fundamental director-actor relationship at the heart of the process.

I have spent many years in British television, film, and theater, working as a stage manager, an assistant director, and a director. I have also spent years studying the system in the United States. This book describes the successful practices I encountered in both counties, and reflects an approach to film and television programmaking that is primarily industry-oriented. I am not concerned in this book with the fascinating issues that surround experimental work or any work other than narrative drama. Budding Kenneth Angers, Harry Smiths, and Stan Brakhages will find little consolation here. However, the book does try to accommodate the work and concerns of such filmmakers as John Cassavetes, Jean-Luc Godard (in his narrative mode), and Mike Leigh, all of whom are especially preoccupied with performance and how it is captured.

This book also reflects my many years of working with students, trying to discover the best approach to teaching directing. It broadly reflects my classroom approach, which addresses performance issues first and technical matters second. As with students, I encourage readers of this book to learn what the industry considers good practice before evolving their own styles. I offer some very specific suggestions about the way certain things should be done (such as marking the shooting script). Having considered my approach, readers are encouraged to develop their own. A tension between contemporary industry practice and innovation will always exist. I cannot teach innovation, but I can suggest a methodology that may be used as a foundation for creative individuals to build upon, adapt, or thoughtfully reject. One has to learn a discipline in order to unlearn it.

I present topics in this book in the order followed by any film or television project—preproduction, production, and postproduction. Although I have found that a few students adhere to the "big-bang theory of production," whereby a production magically explodes into existence in an act of improvisation on the day of the shoot, nothing could be further from the reality of filmmaking. Even directors known for improvisation, such as Cassavetes and Leigh, spend many weeks refining their scripts and working with their actors before commencing production. I have tried to present preproduction as the most creative stage, full of the research, discovery, and exciting decision-making that will define production and postproduction.

The following pages include examples from my own experience (often presented as sidebars). I hope that these will give readers who may not have worked on a professional project a taste of the realities of production.

Finally, I have tried to define technical terms when they first appear, but please note that they are also collected in the Glossary at the end of the book.

Acknowledgments

I am grateful to a number of individuals and institutions for helping me with this book.

I would like to thank Emerson College for a faculty development grant that enabled me to interview a large number of working professionals in Los Angeles. I am also grateful to the American Academy of Television Arts and Sciences for allowing me to participate in its annual academic seminar. Among the many helpful ATAS members, I'd particularly like to mention Price Hicks for her commitment to the seminar, and Bruce Bilson for sharing a portion of his vast experience of directing in Hollywood with me.

I'd like to thank Silman-James Press for so readily embracing the notion of this book, and Jim Fox for his patience, meticulous editing, and creative suggestions. A number of colleagues have graciously contributed to this manuscript in one way or another, including Robert Todd, Jane Shattuc, and Eric Schaeffer. For several years I have taught a class on directing in conjunction with a class on acting for the camera, and I would like to salute my co-teacher Ken Cheeseman for his inexhaustible energy and commitment to the subject.

I am indebted to Carole Flynt for allowing me unfettered access to the staff and crew of *E.R.* I am also very grateful indeed to the producers of *NYPD Blue*, *General Hospital*, and *The Young and the Restless* for spending precious time with me and allowing me to observe their productions and interview crew members.

I would like to thank the gifted directors whose comments are included in the last chapter of the book for sparing me time in their busy schedules. And I'd like to thank Kevin Bright for explaining the U.S. system of sitcom production to me.

Thanks too to Lauren Byrne, Avani Batra, Aaron Seliquini, and Larry Laska for their help. I am also grateful to the numerous industry professionals and Emerson students from whom I've learned so much. And finally, I would like to express my appreciation to my illustrator, John Lanza, for his talent, patience, and humor.

PART 1
Preproduction

1. Director and Script

"Were the cinema to disappear I would simply accept the inevitable and turn to television; were television to disappear, I would revert to pencil and paper. For there is a clear continuity between all forms of expression. It's all one." — Jean-Luc Godard[1]

"Directing is the sum-total of artistic and technical operations which enables the play as conceived by the author to pass from the abstract, latent state, that of the written script, to concrete and actual life on the stage." — Jacques Copeau, *Encyclopedie Française*, December 1935.

Most of this book is about what a screen director does, but I'd like to start by considering what a screen director *is*. A director is a storyteller who usually works with a script and all the available visual and audio resources to bring a story to life in the most vivid and compelling way. Directors are like orchestra or opera conductors in that they work with performers to realize a work. In so doing, they develop a particular approach to or interpretation of a script, be it a classic such as Shakespeare or an entirely new creation. This is the theatrical element of a screen director's job — achieving a good, interesting, and unique realization — and half of this book is concerned with describing it. However, a screen director controls the recording and editing of a performance too and, although these processes have strong elements of artistry, they also pose technical challenges. The all-important recording and editing of a performance in the most expressive and efficient way is what the other half of this book describes.

---

[1] Tom Milne, ed., *Godard on Godard* (London: Secker & Warburg, 1968).

Texts about documentary filmmaking often start by asking the question, "What is documentary?" If I asked, "What is narrative screen drama?" the answer would require another book as long as the one you are holding in your hands. It would have to describe the big-budget productions of Hollywood, Bollywood (as India's very commercial Hindi movie industry is known), and elsewhere. It would have to include the independent movies of Sundance, Slamdance, and other festivals and screening venues. It would have to examine the made-for-TV movies of HBO, NBC, the BBC, and other networks. It would have to discuss television serials (which have a finite number of episodes, usually between 2 and 12), series (which last longer, but are still finite), and "soaps" (which have multiple weekly episodes showing an ongoing/infinite story). It would also have to include sitcoms, children's drama, "docudrama," and many other forms. It is much easier instead to focus on the role of the one person who is at the heart of almost every narrative screen drama, the director.

The playing field

Screen directors work in a variety of ways. They can shoot on locations far from home, on a soundstage (usually situated in a city), or on a mixture of both. They can find themselves in the solitude of the desert or in a studio with a live audience. They can work slowly and methodically with 75mm film equipment or more handily in 35mm or 16 mm formats. They may shoot with a professional video camera comparable in size to a film camera or on the latest lightweight digital camcorder. They may shoot single-camera (a.k.a. "film style") or with multiple cameras.

The industry is currently divided between those who use celluloid and those who record on videotape. Like feature films, primetime television series and movies-of-the-week have traditionally been shot on film. But there are signs that the rigorous distinction between film and video may be evaporating. This distinction has all but disappeared in postproduction as both methods increasingly use digital nonlinear editing equipment. The development of high-definition television (HDTV), with its enhanced image and the flexibility to record at a variety of frame rates (including the 24 frames per second of film), is making video an increasingly attractive alternative to celluloid. Many films are now produced and edited on video and then distributed on film.

As a director, I am happy to work in either medium. I appreciate the unique quality of the film image and the single-camera concentration on perfecting each shot. I also appreciate the speed of video and multi-camera setups and the convenience of having no time gap between shooting and screening the image.

Getting projects off the ground

The most satisfactory projects are often the ones you originate yourself. The thrill in parenting an idea from inception to completion is considerable. In such cases, the director usually becomes the project's co-producer, with the enhanced status and control that brings. The next best thing, in terms of satisfaction, is joining a project early in its development stage, when you can help to mold it. This really only happens with feature films and, occasionally, pilot episodes of television series. These days, a director entering an established TV series rarely has that kind of defining input.

The process for getting a project off the ground is usually as follows, but there is no absolute rule about how these things are done:

Someone has an idea. The idea is discussed with others in order to flesh it out and assess its strengths and weaknesses and salability. (Ideas are delicate at every stage of their development, but especially during their infancy. Therefore, share them only with those who are honest, discreet, and have your best interests at heart.)

If a director has an idea, she will often go to a writer to develop it and get it on paper. At this stage, an idea should be developed as much as possible without expending unnecessary time and effort. The sad fact is that most ideas do not get funded. The object, therefore, is to do just enough work to allow you to present a concept clearly and compellingly in a pitch (as in "sales pitch") and, subsequently, as a treatment, both of which will be discussed below.

In the United States, and increasingly in Britain, an idea is pitched to a producer. Readers not familiar with the culture of the pitch might watch the virtuoso opening shot of Robert Altman's *The Player* (1992), which shows several professionals actually pitching to a fictional studio executive. Then as now, the "high-concept" pitch was in vogue. This sort of pitch renders a film's central idea as a slogan no longer than a sentence or two in length. "There's something rotten in the state of Denmark," says William Shakespeare to the Vice-President of Development, "and a handsome prince pretends he's mad to exact revenge."

Pitching, like any other form of salesmanship, takes practice. Whoever makes the actual pitch (writer, director, or originating producer) must rehearse her performance and be clear about the strengths of her product (idea) and the tastes of the person to whom she is pitching. A pitch session itself may last ten, five, or even two minutes, so each second counts. The person doing the pitch always tries to leave the session with some form of commitment, be it only a promise from the producer or executive "to think about it."

With luck, a pitch is rewarded with a request for a treatment. A treatment is a detailed working out of a film's concept, prepared by a writer—essentially a screenplay minus the dialogue, which may run from several pages to more than a dozen in length. A director involved in the project may add comments about such factors as production style, possible locations, well-known actors who are interested in appearing in the project, and perhaps even the name of a proposed director of photography. A ballpark budget and some words about the target audience might also be appended. The treatment may not be accepted as submitted, but initial interest can lead to revisions and further meetings, which might eventually produce a firm commitment (or "green light").

Until a director and a writer have a written commitment from a producer, their project is tentative at best. So far, this discussion has assumed a single producer,

Trying to get an idea off the ground is arduous, time-consuming, and above all, unpredictable. In the early 1980s, I had an idea for a three-part television serial. At that time, Northern Ireland was at the height of "the troubles" and I had an insight into how to deal with the subject. One of the oldest Anglo-Saxon poems deals with a warrior who betrays his clan and is outlawed for life. I thought this theme suited the situation in Ireland, with its primitive, local allegiances. I took the idea to a well-known writer from the province who expressed qualified enthusiasm and set to work on a treatment. The treatment was brilliant and filled with the kind of specific insights that only someone who had lived in that country could provide. However, one story incident stood out. He had invented a subplot in which a branch of the IRA plants a bomb in the British territory of Gibraltar. It seemed far-fetched at the time, but I went along with it. I took his treatment, added paperwork about the shoot and budget, and put it in the mail. During the week it languished on our first-choice producer's desk, the IRA actually created havoc in Gibraltar with a bomb—exactly as my writer had predicted. This producer, and all our subsequent ones, read the treatment and wondered why we had blatantly imitated the Gibraltar tragedy! The writer would not go back to the drawing board and rewrite the whole treatment, and the project was never picked up. Oddly, in my experience, that kind of premonition is not uncommon.

such as exists in a studio or a large television company, but projects (especially movies) can be financed by several producers and financial organizations.

With luck, a treatment will lead to the commissioning of a script by a well-financed production company or consortium. A script is the very foundation of a project (be it a feature film or a pilot episode for a TV series) and may take months or even years to complete. The script-writing period is an anxious time for a director, who can only wait and hope that the result will match expectations. During this period, the director must support the writer as much as possible, acknowledging that a writer developing a project is isolated and vulnerable. What transpires between a writer of dramatic fiction and his word-processor can be personal and somewhat mysterious. Sometimes, if the writer has been given a free hand to adapt the treatment, its themes may shift during composition and the result may not be what the director expected. The director should always respect the writing process and, if she is disappointed with the result, should at first attempt to enter into a sympathetic discussion with the author to procure rewrites. In businesslike Hollywood, an author's work is often revised by one, two, or even three more writers at the behest of the director and producers. All this eats up time and can prolong the period a director spends between one production and the next. Rewrite upon rewrite upon rewrite is sometimes called "development hell."

For directors, many projects, especially in television, follow a different path from the one I've just outlined. A producer with a script in hand for a movie, a made-for-TV movie, or, most commonly, an episode of a television series may simply assign that project to a director.

Directors who have been with a project since its inception have the obvious advantage of living with an idea over a period of time—they understand its evolution, its structure, and its nuances. Directors who come to a project afresh have to compensate for this deficit and work hard to bond with a script emotionally and intellectually. It helps if a director can make an instinctual connection. A director who has grown up in Northern Ireland will probably automatically understand the issues in a TV series about the IRA. But a Croatian or Palestinian director will likely be able to empathize with the situation as well. *Fortunately, most of us have points of empathy in our backgrounds and experiences which, when properly tapped, enable us to connect with the varied situations found in screenplays we have to direct.* Of course, this may not true for every scene and every character. When a director has no instinctual connection to a project, connections have to be forged. We will discuss this below and in the next chapter.

Subject matter, character, and plot

Directors, like audiences, react instinctively to a screenplay's subject matter, its characters, and the way it is put together. If you can relate to any or all of these script components, you will be well on your way to generating the enthusiasm necessary to devote time and energy to a project.

Like most directors, I have had to work hard to be inspired by certain scripts. Once, when directing a popular British series, I found I could not relate to either the characters or their humor. Every time I read the scenes, they seemed more and more contrived and unfunny. Finally, in desperation, I asked the producer if he'd consider a rewrite. His reply was frank: "There are seven million viewers who watch this program and find those characters funny," he said. I took the hint, went back to the script, and invented enough "business" (physical tasks for actors to accomplish) to make the scenes work. In this case, the storyline was about two men fighting over what to do with a cupboard infected with deathwatch beetles. I had the characters peer under the cupboard and tap it to see if it would fall apart. I had them empty out its contents and shake powder over the shelves. I had one character press his ear against the wood and listen for the insect. During rehearsal, I found the actors surprisingly charming, cooperative, and creative, and in the end I looked forward to directing their scenes.

For me, character is the single most important ingredient of a plot. If a story's characters are interesting, much of what happens will fall into place. Strong characters make for strong plots. As I will discuss in Part 2, each character should have a direction in which he is going, a direction that will inevitably conflict with another character's. This principal underlies practically all drama in any medium. It is, perhaps, seen most starkly in TV series, which thrive on a set of well-defined and contrasting characters interacting in different ways in every episode.

Character is sometimes considered as separate from plot, but, in fact, the two are closely intertwined: A plot is largely the working out of tendencies inherent within characters. The most satisfying movies, in my opinion, are those in which plot and character are finely poised and almost inseparable. The richness of a film by Bergman, for example, is directly attributable to the subtlety of the characters he creates. And I am happy to indulge the excesses of John Cassavetes and Paul Thomas Anderson for the extraordinary vividness of their characterizations. On the other hand, the adventure film, in which special effects and fast-paced action predominate, often has one-dimensional, unbelievable protagonists.

Alfred Hitchcock was a director who was primarily interested in plot. Like many horror or adventure movie directors after him, he was fascinated by the intellectual challenge of a story—its twists and turns and eventual resolution. But Hitchcock always worked closely with talented writers who created credible characters. The lengthy gestation of his scripts, lasting until every detail of character, dialogue, and circumstance satisfied him and his script-editor wife Alma, is legendary.

As directors, our empathy with a script's characters enables us to overcome our own limited perspectives. (It is a characteristic directors share with novelists and actors who work to create credible, well-rounded, consistent human types.) This empathy is the primary overarching characteristic that good directors must possess. It allows them to tackle situations beyond their immediate experiences. Those of us who have not grown up in war-torn Europe may direct a drama set in Northern Ireland because, at a fundamental level, we can relate to its script's characters. In fact, this mixture of distance and empathy may be a recipe for good direction: It allows a director to bring a fresh perspective to a story while, at the same time, remaining emotionally sympathetic to its characters. (I will discuss ways in which you can connect with characters in Chapter 6.)

The first reading

The first time you open a screenplay is a very important moment. This is the one and only time you will ever come to that script fresh. This is the one and only time you will experience it with few preconceptions—the same way that your audience will experience the finished product on the screen.

It is very easy to rush the first reading. Whenever the poet William Wordsworth received a book in the mail, he would immediately reach for the butter knife and quickly slash open the package. We may experience similar impatience when we get scripts, and it is very tempting to sit down right away and flip through their pages. Resist the urge to do this. Consciously find an apt environment for your first contact with a work that might claim most of your waking life for the next few months or years.

Find a quiet place where you will not be disturbed and read the whole script through at a leisurely pace with a minimum of breaks. You might want a pencil and a notebook at hand to jot down your reactions to the scenes. If some part of the script strikes you as particularly good or bad or attracts your attention in any way—note it.

When you have finished your first reading, write down your reaction to the whole script. Consider the characters too: Who are the major ones? Who are the most appealing? Which ones do not "come off the page" well?

These notes will be by no means definitive. Your initial opinions may change as you get to know the script better, but they maintain a unique value as first reactions. They tell you how someone completely new to the story might see it.

The director who reads a script for the first time can be objective. This, of course, is not so true for directors who have been intimately involved in a script's evolution or who may have penned their own screenplay. I have found, from personal experience and from working with others, that directing a script you have just completed and are too close to is a mistake. It is vital to step back and let the ink dry on the page. If you have written your own screenplay, you need *at least* a month to remove your writer's hat and put on your directorial one. In television, where scripts are produced at great speed and very little time is set aside for authorial reflection, a writer's work is usually revised by the producer or the script editor.

Subsequent readings

A director's *second reading* of a script is very different from her first. The implicit question is no longer "What happens next?" but "How does it happen?" Pencil and paper are used even more at this stage. Note your second impressions and see how they differ from your first. And as you get closer to the structure and themes of the screenplay, more questions will occur to you.

Some of your questions will be for the writer. You will start to wonder about character and motivation. For instance, why did the villain, who is a professional thief, make the elementary mistake of leaving his fingerprints on the telephone? You will have questions about certain scenes that you feel are not working. (What is the conflict in the scene?) You may also notice discrepancies and inconsistencies that have evaded the writer. Why, for instance, is the hero packing his luggage in scene 4, and then arriving at the station several scenes later with only an overnight bag? Why does the heroine's father remark on her Irish-green eyes at the start of the episode, but her lover remark on her "eyes as blue as English porcelain" three-quarters of the way through?

As you continue to read, you will have questions for the designer about the sizes and styles of the sets. You may visualize certain props that are not in the text. You may have suggestions for the location manager about the kind of locations you would like. The script may stipulate a basketball court, but do you see an inside court or an outside one? And you may have questions about the budget that have to be addressed to the unit manager or assistant producer. The script calls for a room in a large house. Can you shoot on location or does the whole thing have to be shot on a soundstage? How many spectators can you afford for the scripted football match?

During the third and subsequent readings of the script your focus becomes increasingly centered on its characters. The mere reading of a script doesn't bring its characters to life, but the daydreaming that goes on during and between readings does. As you consider individual characters, ask yourself about their habits and their backgrounds. What props might they use? (Do they smoke? Do they carry books in their jacket pockets? What kinds of plates do they eat from? What kinds of cars do they drive?) In general terms, what is their appearance? (Are they tall or small, thin or rotund? What are their styles of dress?) What are their backgrounds? What insights can you offer about their psychology?

In gathering this character information, directors rely on two sources. They collect what Konstantin Stanislavski, one of the fathers of modern acting and directing theory (see Part 7, Chapter 37), called "the given circumstances," which are all the details and hints in the script itself, and then they use their imagination to amplify these details. Needless to say, some characters are easy to speculate about, and others take some time to develop. We will discuss this process of bringing characters to life further in Part 2.

I once worked as first assistant on a drama that was set in an elegant English pub during the 1930s. The pub was so important that it was, in effect, a major character. For reasons of logistics, the director settled on a location that was small and in a not particularly attractive setting. Consequently, the viewer was never able to warm to the building or get a sense of it as a whole. It was a flaw from which the movie never recovered. Another director I worked with on a film set in Jacobean times chose exactly the mansion he wanted to shoot in on its production values, not logistics. Luckily, we were able to secure that location, and it cast its beauty over the whole movie.

Every time you read a script you become more familiar with its structure. After several readings you should be able to recount its story in detail, with all its twists and turns. A few more readings and you should be able to recount it scene by scene. Knowing a script inside out is invaluable to you.

As a director's understanding of a script becomes clearer and more focused, she begins to make detailed notes about its sets and locations. Her understanding of its characters can be applied here too, because spaces reflect the characters inhabiting them.

Locations not only dictate how a scene is staged, they also exert an influence on the whole "look" of a film. Each potential location carries a set of advantages and limitations that a director has to assess. *Locations need to be cast with the same care as is given actors.*

At this stage in the reading process, the director should time the script. This is particularly relevant in television, where timing is crucial.

Conventional wisdom holds that a page of script in traditional film screenplay format is equivalent to a minute of screen time.[2] This rule, and rules like it, are accurate four times out of five, but when you have a lot of action or a lengthy monologue or a text is subject to change, the director is the only person who can do the timing accurately. Some directors take the script home and act out the scenes by themselves with a stopwatch in their hands. Others enlist the help of their production team and read the script aloud in the office.

Before moving further into preproduction, the director should read the screenplay *from each character's point of view* in order to clarify exactly what happens to them, and how they react to those events. If each characters' "journey" is not traced in detail, the director may easily overlook subtle yet important moments in their development.

Becoming the author

When a director reads and rereads a script, she is doing more than just familiarizing herself with it, *she is consciously making it her own.* Until the moment a script is handed to a director, the writer is *the* expert who alone has a deep understanding of its structure and characters, and its many details. A

---

[2] When a screenplay typed in standard movie format is broken down by a producer or a member of the production team (for timing, scheduling, or budgetary purposes), single pages are counted and then, if a fraction of a page is left over (a quarter or a half page, for example), it is expressed as eighths of a page. Thus, a scene that is two and a half pages long will be noted as $2^4/_8$ pages. A scene that is just over one page in length, will be noted as $1^1/_8$ pages.

director must acquire that expertise, and she does it by repeated readings of the script and through discussions with its author.

This process of "becoming the author" is the director's first step. Some directors do not make it this far and must rely on the scriptwriter or an expert in the subject matter they are dealing with to help them during shooting. I once worked as assistant to a director who shot an adaptation of a famous novel. The writer/adapter was present for the first week of shooting but then left to pursue his other interests. In his absence, the director became unsure about the text and, therefore, hesitant when directing his actors. I had to ask the producer for permission to recall the writer to the set for the rest of the filming. Another director I worked with shot a movie set in the world of international finance, but had no idea of that world himself and was not allowed time to investigate it. Consequently, many of the scenes lacked conviction and the film itself was not successful.

Stanislavski said that a director's first responsibility is to realize the writer's wishes. When a director receives a script written by someone else, she has a duty to consider what the author tried to achieve before imposing her own interpretation on the work. She should look carefully at the characters, setting, and plot structure, and evaluate them. She should look twice at the dialogue before altering it, because she could easily misconstrue it after only one reading. This evaluation certainly does not mean slavishly implementing every word and stage direction. But it does mean giving the writer the benefit of the doubt in order to appreciate a script's possible strengths.

Television directors generally have less latitude for making script changes than film directors. When directing TV series, I've occasionally been allowed input into the final draft of a script, but usually this is the result of the producer's interest in my opinion about technical matters, such as the running time and the viability of certain locations. The very short preproduction period of TV drama makes director-initiated rewrites problematic because they hold up production.

Directing may be viewed as having two levels: The first is simply "getting the production off the page." A screen director has to understand her characters' motivations and then visualize each scene in its entirety with actor and camera movements. In television series with very little preparation time, this is sometimes all that can be achieved.

The second level is "transcending the written word." It comes into being once a director has a deep understanding of a script and is inspired to add her own insights and experience to it. This is hard to write about because it lies in the

13

intangible field of inspiration. It occurs when you are so in tune with a script that you are able to move it in a direction that the author had not considered, but that is entirely consistent with the author's intention. Look at Kurasawa's re-interpretation of Shakespeare's *Macbeth* in *Throne of Blood* (1957), and Billy Morrissette's interesting reworking of the same play in *Scotland, PA* (2001). Look at Todd Haynes' reworking of 1950s melodrama in *Far From Heaven* (2002). Baz Luhrman (*Romeo & Juliet*, 1996, and *Moulin Rouge*, 2001) is concerned with realizing texts in a lavish yet very personal way. Many of the directors I admire have produced results that are grounded in a text, which they then transcend.

The director and the writer

A production is only as good as its script. A great script can make for a great film but it does not guarantee it.

The writer and the director are mutually dependent. Most directors realize this and go out of their way to work closely with their writers. The writer can offer inspiration by leading the director into a story's themes. The writer can offer important character and plot insights that will shape the director's approach. And the writer can act as an excellent sounding board when the director begins to evolve her own ideas. Eventually, however, the director has to shed dependency upon the writer, who still remains a valuable resource for rewrites and consultation.

If you are lucky enough to have rehearsals, you may find that the writer can make valuable contributions to them. Invite the writer to the read-through and, possibly, ask him to remain for the first few rehearsal sessions while the cast is getting to grips with the text. The writer, hearing the actors speak their lines, may be prompted to make creative improvements. Additionally, the actors themselves almost always have queries about lines that the director can refer straight to the author.

If you choose to improvise your film's dialogue, you may need someone on hand with strong authorial skills to pull the dialogue together, rendering it taut and effective. You may also need someone with a gift for narrative to lay down the scenario for each improvisation. I have seen films in which the author has provided a very detailed description of the scenes but not actually written all the dialogue. The director then worked with the actors to create the staging and flesh out the lines. Filmmaker Mike Leigh works for a long time with his actors, discovering the details of their characters before beginning to piece the script together through improvisation. Directionless improv leads to unstructured and self-indulgent results. Given the time constraints on most projects, defining, conducting, and sifting the results of an improvisation may be very difficult for the director alone. A writer may be a valuable addition. (Improvisation is discussed in more detail in Part 3, Chapter 15.)

The script editor

The film director usually deals with the writer (or writers) face to face. The more assembly-line organization of television drama alters that relationship. A soap opera producer may work with a *story editor*[3] to create the show's overall plot direction, and then delegate the job of working on the details of each individual episode to a *script editor*. The script editor then works with the writer of each episode to ensure that every script follows and advances the overall plot.[4] Authorship of a soap opera script thus lies somewhere amid the work of the story editor, producer, script editor, and writer.

Script editors have varying powers, depending on the production. In some shows, they have the power to extensively rework the script, while in others they act as judicious editors, suggesting rewrites. Regardless of their methods, the result is that television directors work closely with producers and script editors and have little opportunity to explore the individual nuances and intentions of individual scripts with their writers. On the other hand, in the producer or script editor, the director has someone who knows the grand sweep of the storyline and exactly how the individual episodes are linked together. In a formal meeting that usually occurs early in preproduction, a sensitive script editor will draw a director's attention to important plot points and character moments.

Script editors occasionally write scripts. If you are fortunate enough to direct one of these scripts, make sure you take advantage of this rare access to a living, breathing author. Talk to him about character and motivation, and try to discover the themes he is dealing with. Having script editor and writer in one body also improves the quality of rewrites, as well as the time it takes to turn them around. Writer/script editors are usually pleased to cooperate closely with a director, sensing that a close working relationship will improve the final product.

---

[3] A story editor plots the storyline of a series many months into the future, whereas a script editor works with writers to produce individual episodes.

[4] This is the most common scenario. Alternatives do exist. The popular British series *EastEnders*, for example, invited its writers to sit down with the script editor and "break down" the story arc into separate episodes.

2. Research and Vision

"...the nature of directing is questions. But the person asking the questions doesn't know if they're going to distract me or not. Only I know that when I get the question. And so there's that state of anxiety."—Martin Scorsese

The first part of this chapter discusses the importance of research and how it leads to a "directorial vision." The second part describes how research is actually carried out by the director and crew.

Research and creativity

If we are lucky, creativity is spontaneous and happens in ways that are unique to the creator. For instance, the screenwriter Alan Bennet is often inspired by snippets of overheard conversations. Dreams were a fruitful source of creativity for Luis Buñuel and other surrealist filmmakers. Music—especially Mozart—galvanized the writer George Bernard Shaw. Drugs have assisted pop musicians and beat poets. Unfortunately, such inspirations are a little too haphazard for a director facing a deadline. Directors need a more reliable method to help them make day-to-day decisions.

No single activity encourages creativity more than research. The mind requires raw material to work on in order to produce something new. Ideas need to rub against other ideas to produce the sparks that generate originality. In this sense, pure originality doesn't exist. What we consider creativity is usually the imaginative reworking of ideas to produce new configurations or show off facets that have been unexplored or hidden. For most directors, especially those working from a script written by another hand, research offers one of the most practical methods of stimulating creativity. It connects us with the work that has been done on a given subject and encourages new interpretations and syntheses of this work to take place in our minds.

Research is an open-ended activity that is only limited by the director's available time. The director will discuss a script with its author, visit the locations where the action is set, and gather background material from books, magazines, the web, and other sources. In setting the project's style, he will discuss paintings and related works of art with the designer and director of photography. If the project is based on real, contemporary events, the director will try to confer with the story's living participants. A director may also watch movies and television shows dealing with similar subjects in order to evolve a distinct and new approach.

Research introduces new perspectives, broadens our knowledge, and helps us think around and behind our subjects. And the more we meditate on a subject, the more connected to it we become. This seems to have a lot to do with the actual energy expended on research. As we grow more fascinated by and committed to a subject, we forge a deeper connection with it and see it in a new light.

Through research, directors can become experts in the subject matter of their dramas. Research can be gathered in two ways—from *primary sources* and from *secondary sources*. Primary sources are the reports on events made by the participants themselves, or by others who directly witnessed them or interviewed the participants at the time (such as journalists). Secondary sources are accounts, such as those found in history books, written at a later date by people who have collected and studied primary sources. If your project deals with recent historical events, going to the participants involved (primary sources) is invaluable. If your drama concerns a medical procedure, contact a hospital and try to observe that procedure. If your drama is set in a particular town, go there, walk the streets, and note how the residents interact and behave. These and similar research activities will give you additional authority with regard to your story and help you control the process of creation on the set.

By deepening the understanding of a story, research can contribute to a director's overall approach—which is often called "the director's vision." Yes, oh dear, yes, the director must have a vision! A director must create a world that is unique to each project. It may be a world as excruciatingly realistic as those portrayed in *The Pianist* (2003) and *Schindler's List* (1993) or as fantastic as those of *Star Wars* (1977) and *Star Trek: The Motion Picture* (1979) or as seemingly ordinary as those of *Tape* (2001) and *In the Bedroom* (2002), but it is always an artificial dramatic construction. Unless a director personally responds to a screenplay's subject matter, a project can be neutral and bland.

Formulating a director's vision

Some directors have very strong personal visions that inform most of their works. One can tell a film by Godard, Greenaway, or Fellini at a glance. Hitchcock was a master at constructing intricate and distinct worlds. A strong vision executed at every level—performance, visuals, audio, and design—is obvious in every picture that Joel and Ethan Coen direct. I would guess that the vision behind the television series *E.R.* is the portrayal of a busy city hospital in as immediate and realistic a way as possible. Implementing this vision naturally leads to the use of large, busy sets with natural overhead lighting, elaborate scenes in operating rooms, a fluid camera style, and quick edits between multiple storylines.

Research will help you identify themes. Talking to people with firsthand experience of the story's subject or to experts will sharpen your awareness of the implications of the subject matter. A medical authority says, "You know, the trauma your hero is undergoing is very common in wartime," and suddenly you realize that the drama you have been working on about an urban gang is a metaphor for war.

Sometimes a story's themes announce themselves clearly: The screenplays *Norma Rae* (1978) and *The China Syndrome* (1978), for example, were unambiguously political. Not every film has such a clear message, but all projects (even daytime series) reflect, to some extent, the preoccupations and experiences of their authors. Talking to the writer about her intentions can be very rewarding —especially if she is passionate, articulate, and knowledgeable about her subject. If you are unable to meet the writer, then ask yourself what impelled her to write the screenplay in the first place. Was there a clear issue that motivated her? Was she fascinated by certain characters? What aspects of her own experience do you think she brought to the script? A director can easily become fascinated by the preoccupations of a particular author—especially when they resonate with his own experience.

You can look for parallels between the script and your own experience. What parts of the plot do you really appreciate? Are there any issues that you can relate to? I imagine most of us can relate to the hardships of a love story or the anger of a revenge-thriller. Sometimes we need to extend our empathy even further. Peter Mullen cannot have experienced the horrors of internment in a church reformatory for "fallen" women that he depicted in *The Magdalen Sisters* (2003), but he must have experienced powerful feelings of shame and frustration that he could channel into the project.

You can also look at the characters you are especially drawn to. The characters who stand out for us (as either good or bad) are the ones who most contain elements of ourselves. *So, examine your feelings, experiences, and memories in relation to these characters and see where it leads.* Here is an example: You find you are drawn to a script's leading character, who is the mother of a wayward girl. As you examine your attraction, you realize that she reminds you of your own mother, which immediately gives you insights into her character and behavior. You also realize that this mother is passionate about holding her family together. This is an emotion you immediately recognize because you are equally passionate about, perhaps, your own current personal relationship or about getting the movie itself made. Suddenly, the story becomes one about obsession — the mother's obsession with holding her family together, the daughter's obsession with breaking away, and the obsessive desires of some of the other main characters. Beginning to emerge is the seed of a vision, which you will have to nurture and extend to casting, shooting, lighting, design, and all other areas.

A vision may suddenly arrive as an epiphany and transform your approach to the whole project. More often, it will announce itself as an insight that will need further pondering. *As you progress through preproduction, try to articulate your personal approach to the project.* You should be able to write it down in a sentence or a short paragraph. Then, revisit this statement from time to time to check if you still feel the same way, because a vision can change and develop over time.

A director with a vision will use the preproduction, production, and editing periods to develop and implement his vision with great attention to detail. Martin Scorsese, for example, is especially adept at this. His detailed representation of different worlds (often criminal ones) is consistently rich and fascinating.

On the other hand, the vision behind the episodic television program is usually that of the executive producer and the original screenwriter, assisted by the director of the pilot episode. Thereafter, directors of individual episodes usually must accept the well-established style handed down via the associate or line producer (who is responsible for overseeing individual episodes) and the script editor. But this does not mean that television directors cannot have visions.

19

In fact, they *must* forge individual connections with the material if their work is to have any spark at all.

Let's look at the ways research is done during preproduction.

Research done by others

Traditional documentary-making is almost entirely about research: researching facts, environments, and people. But research is just as important for narrative drama. And most drama directors have a great advantage over most independent documentary makers—they have a number of people helping them do research.

A large part of the drama director's job during preproduction is processing information presented by others. This can amount to a vast amount of information and require hundreds of directorial decisions about casting, set design and props, costume, makeup and hair, and locations. When information in all these areas floods in, you may find difficulty processing it. Sometimes numerous decisions have to be made on the spur of the moment, so you must have a firm vision in place if your decisions are to have consistency.

Production design

"In work with a designer, a sympathy of tempo is what matters most."—Peter Brook.[1]

The person most responsible for the overall look of a production is the *production designer* (a.k.a. *art director*). She is its urban planner, architect, and interior decorator rolled into one. The size of the design department varies according to the project. A small independent film may only employ one designer and, perhaps, a couple of *grips*—who move and arrange the props on location. The designer's staff on a larger-scale movie might include one or more assistants, painters, carpenters, prop men, stagehands, drivers, and others. On a production of this size, she may also have a set designer who is responsible for drawing plans and overseeing the construction of the sets, and an art designer who creates and selects the interior design elements.

The production designer works closely with the director to create a project's overall design concept—the coordination of all physical elements, producing a certain intended look. She is often the first creative crew member the director talks to during preproduction, and their conversations are highly significant. The production designer may join the initial search for locations or help the director

---

[1] Peter Brook, *The Empty Space* (New York: Touchstone Books, 1995), p. 101.

select sites from a shortlist. As a creative individual in her own right, a good production designer will take the director's vision and really run with it, applying it to her work in her own way. Directors should allow designers their freedom, but at the same time hold regular meetings and check plans and prop lists to make sure both individuals are seeing eye-to-eye.

All projects require design research. Directors and designers will examine where and when the script is set and then decide on the style they want to impose on that place and period. If it's a contemporary piece set in a particular city, they will most likely visit the area to look at various buildings and interiors. If the drama is set in the past, they will discuss the look found in photographs and paintings and other documents from the period. The designer will visit museums, libraries, and other collections to research all appropriate objects. Dante Ferreti, the designer of *The Gangs of New York* (2002), a film set in the second half of the nineteenth century, described his approach: "I want to know every single detail. I try to be like an architect living in that period, so if something needs to be changed, I can change it with the same kind of mentality."[2]

Good production designers work at the level of character. This work has to be not only accurate historically and architecturally, but it must also reflect the characters that will inhabit it. There is no such thing, for instance, as a "standard" office set. Offices reflect the people who work in them. My cluttered workspace, with its papers strewn all over the floor, stands in stark contrast to my neighbor's, which is neat and uncluttered. Even the buildings we inhabit comment on or reflect our characters—he lives in a large studio on the top floor of an apartment block, I live in a ramshackle brownstone.

Costume and makeup

The costume (or wardrobe) designer also works closely with the director. Based on her discussions with the director, she submits a series of options. She strives to realize the director's vision and to express each character's personality through her designs. Costume makes an enormous statement about a character and helps actors step into their roles. How much easier it is to play a successful businessman once you've put on a well-tailored suit and knotted an Italian silk tie. And how much easier it is to cross the centuries and play Queen Elizabeth I once you are wearing the starched ruff and the crown.

The costume designer and the wardrobe department play a valuable role that goes beyond simply supplying the appropriate costumes. Because they are often

---

[2] "Mean Streets," *American Cinematographer*, January 2003, p. 52.

When I was directing a production set in the nineteenth century, I had to become something of an expert on an item of female attire called the bustle. This was the enormous attachment to the rear of the dress that made a woman's existence, already complicated by the corset, even more uncomfortable because now not only could she not bend but she also had difficulty maneuvering through doors and up stairs. There were, I learned, two styles of bustle—the one that went straight out from the waist like a shelf, and the one that was more rounded and looked like the backside of a horse. This information will go with me to the grave.

the personnel most frequently in contact with the actors while they are in their dressing rooms or caravans between scenes, they can create a supportive and friendly atmosphere. A wardrobe assistant who has a nervous actor's clothes ready when he appears, and is willing to provide a cup of coffee and a cheery word, can be of incalculable value to a production.

The lives of all types of designers are made easier when directors are specific. If you can detail your vision by pinpointing a specific house or a photograph or, in the case of period drama, a specific year, designers can carry out their research and produce remarkable results. Of course, a literal approach to design can have its limitations when historical accuracy is not the director's most important storytelling criterion. I once worked with a director who wanted to set a seventeenth-century drama in an indeterminate mid-Victorian period. This caused the costume designer considerable anguish, but she eventually worked out a way to solve the problem.

Here are two final observations on working with wardrobe and makeup designers:

The first is that wardrobe is so integral to performance that a director should do everything within his power to help an actor become accustomed to her costume before shooting begins. If rehearsals are held, unusual items of wardrobe (such as special jewelry or uniforms) might be worn at that time. This is especially important in period drama in which actors often have to discover how to wear old-fashioned items like corsets and trailing dresses. In such cases, the wardrobe supervisor will often supply stand-in costumes if the real costumes are unavailable.

The second piece of advice is more sanguine. Blood, particularly when it appears on an actor's face, is the concern of the makeup department. As anyone who has tried to dilute bottles of ketchup will attest, blood, with its distinct color and consistency, is a difficult substance to imitate. (A number of companies manufacture coagulated blood gel, artificial blood capsules, and other products in The United States. The type most frequently used by professionals in England goes by the gruesome name of "Kensington Gore.") Blood can be a very tricky effect to control, and directors have varied in their approaches to it. The Sam Peckinpah/Quentin Tarantino school may be said to hold that the more blood there is the better. Other directors opt for a more minimalist approach, on the grounds that too much blood can become distracting. Whatever your approach, you should discuss fight scenes with the makeup supervisor (and the fight arranger) during preproduction, and then work closely with a makeup artist during shooting to ensure that the appropriate amount of blood is applied.

If you are considering using blood squibs—small pouches of blood, detonated by explosives—to simulate the impact of bullets, you should include a *special effects supervisor*[3] in your discussions well in advance of the shooting day. (A special makeup effects artist may also be required.) Bear in mind that where you actually position the blood squibs on a body may have continuity implications if the wounded character reappears in subsequent scenes. Blood squibs may be popular in action movies, but they are also potentially dangerous to the actor, the camera, and anyone within ten feet of the effect, and should always be used under professional supervision.

The director's own research

While a great deal of research information comes in from many different sources, directors also carry out their own research.

There are two areas for a director to research: the on-screen and the off-screen. One concerns *people and things* that actually appear on the screen, such as costume, makeup, locations, and props (especially such telltale items as cars and furnishings). This is the area in which designers and other crew members will be most helpful, either offering suggestions themselves or recommending sources of reference. Auditions—research into the available pool of actors—may be considered part of this on-screen research too. (Auditions are discussed in Chapter 4.)

The other area is the *ideas* that underpin the story. This is research into the philosophy and values of your characters or the period and place in which they live. It usually involves reading books that deal with your subject and watching

---

[3] An experienced (and, usually, licensed) special effects operator, who assumes responsibility for the effects during shooting.

programs or videos that are similar to yours in theme or setting. By immersing yourself in all this material and creating time to think about it, your personal approach evolves.

People are by far the most important research resource: They supply information directly about a subject or point you toward other people or resources that do. Unlike books, people are interactive. And unlike CDs or DVDs, they also can convey the emotional quality of an event. They can serve as models for the characters in a drama as well.

In the late 1970s, I worked as assistant director on a "docudrama" about a disabled boy who was adopted by unusual parents. The fact that the whole family happily cooperated with the production gave the director (and, later, the actors) enormous insights into the drama. The film was based on a book that implied that the boy's school had not supported his disability. When I was looking for locations, I toyed with the idea of visiting the school but backed away because of what I'd read. Finally, I had to make an appointment to visit the headmaster to see if we could shoot there. "I'm glad you've come," he said when I met him, "I think that there are certain details that are wrong in the book." He was right. It turned out that the school had tried its very best to accommodate the boy, and we were able to put the record straight in the film.

Experts can be important research sources for most types of drama production. People who have spent their lives working in the areas you are representing in your film will always have an interesting point of view or an illuminating anecdote. I have consulted academics when I needed to be pointed toward essential research articles. I've also talked to doctors about medical procedures, lawyers about points of law, and farmers about crop rotation. If you interview an army lieutenant about military maneuver, he becomes a potential model for certain characters in your story. You note the details of his uniform, his bearing, and how he speaks. Your questions gradually become more personal until you end up talking about his quarters and his relationship with his wife and children.

Choosing locations

Soaking up the atmosphere of the site where the narrative takes place can be vital to your research. If your drama is set in the center of Manhattan or in the bayous of Louisiana, go to these places if you can, and observe the houses, the people, the customs, and the lay of the land. Some odd detail will sink in and enrich your storytelling and, occasionally, you will make a discovery that will transform your whole approach.

The director refines his approach to a project as he travels around with the location manager and designer, looking at possible shooting locations. Different locations suggest different ways of staging a scene. When I visit a location, I ask myself, "Does it say yes?" Sometimes I walk into a location and it instantly feels right. The location says, "yes." Sometimes it says, "no," equally emphatically. Often the answer is less clear cut and you have to size up a location's practical and stylistic advantages and disadvantages and compare them with those offered by alternative locations.

Practical factors, such as a location's distance from the production's base or from the other locations, and its ability to fit into the shooting schedule, are important. Indeed, for the members of your production team responsible for the budget and the logistics (the unit manager and the location manager, for instance), these factors may be decisive. On low-budget TV productions, where the shooting schedule is very tight, the director may have little or no control over the choice of locations. On larger-scale productions, he may have considerable freedom of choice.

A good location offers you all, or most, of what you are looking for. An ideal location offers you more than you expected. It suggests ways of shooting that you had not considered, and provides a powerful atmosphere. The right location is worth holding out for.

From time to time, I've directed long-running television series set in small English country villages. As these villages become known to the general public, large crowds turn up to observe the shooting. These television tourists not only destroy the villages' peace and quiet, but hinder the unit's freedom of movement, turning the shoot into an exercise in crowd control. One solution might be moving to villages that are even more remote, but transporting a television crew to distant locations would take more time and severely reduce the length of the shooting day. We have become, in a sense, the victims of our own success.

Three phases of preproduction and the tech scout

Sometimes, you seem to only have time to read the script once before you are asked to make decisions that will affect the entire production. This is particularly true in TV, and it can be a terrifying experience. Directors should try to get their scripts as far in advance of the start of preproduction as possible. The Directors Guild mandates that directors receive scripts at least three days before they join a production. As soon as a director sits down in an office he will be asked questions by his production team (as will be discussed in the next chapter). He should be prepared.

Preproduction, as far as the director is concerned, is divided into three phases.

The first deals with the major design elements and auditions. It involves deciding on locations and talking to the designer about sets that have to be built. It also involves making the main casting decisions: casting both leading players and leading members of the crew, such as the director of photography and sound recordist. Since these are early decisions, they often occur at a time when the director's vision is not complete, so he has to make decisions on the basis of very little knowledge. If a director is suddenly forced to make a decision about a leading player or an important location, his available options are instantly reduced, short-circuiting his decision-making process, and committing the production to a particular direction. On the other hand, sometimes making crucial decisions early on can be liberating.

The second preproduction phase involves working on the smaller details that arise after the major decisions have been made. Once the primary locations have been found and the set designs agreed upon, the production designer is free to concentrate on the details of prop selection and set construction. Once casting is underway, costume and makeup departments can contact the actors and begin fittings. The production team can now start putting actors and locations together in the shooting schedule. The director is required to make important decisions throughout this phase, but the decisions tend to be less far-reaching. "Do you want a sofa or two more chairs?" "We've come up with a charming little vest for her to wear in Scene 8. What do you think?" "Is this the kind of person you want as an extra in the police station?" During this phase, the director's attention is also focused on finding the secondary locations and casting the remaining "day players" (actors with small roles, who will probably only be required for a short period). Gradually, his attention turns to the individual scenes and how to shoot them.

The third preproduction phase, which falls immediately prior to production, involves the director working hard on how the individual scenes are to be staged and shot. Rehearsals, if they're to be held, will take place at this time, as will meetings with important members of the crew, such as the director of photography. If locations are involved, there will be a *tech scout.* The tech scout (which is discussed in more detail in Part 5, Chapter 27) brings the director, production designer, director of photography, chief electrician (known as the *gaffer*), and certain members of the production team (notably the first assistant and location manager) together on site to discuss the forthcoming shoot.[4]

Preproduction is a time when plans are laid, but it is also a time when relationships are forged with important personnel—relationships that have to endure the strains of shooting.

---

[4] Other crew members may be invited if they have important contributions to make.

3. The Director's Team and Controlling the Budget

The director's team—the small group working immediately around the director during preproduction and supporting her during the shoot—is enormously important. It forms the director's intimate circle of advisors during preproduction. It is her communication system, disseminating information to the other departments. It also organizes everything from the first breakdown of the script (to ascertain technical requirements, and logistical and budgetary implications) to the end-of-shoot party. During production it runs the set and everything that goes on around it, ideally leaving the director free to concentrate on the actors and the camera.

The director's team is usually assembled at the very start of preproduction (before the DP and other technical crew members come aboard) and continues on the payroll till shooting is complete. Different directors approach their teams in different ways. Some see their team as a close-knit family and strive to keep it near them. These directors tend to eat with their teams and invite them to view rushes in the evening. Other directors work closely with their teams during preproduction but then turn their attention to crew and actors during production. I know of one director who used to start preproduction by allocating army ranks to his team members, hoping to encourage military efficiency. This ploy had mixed results: Directors' teams tend to be very efficient, but not in a military way, and those of us lower down the pecking order resented being told we were mere corporals.

A note on terminology: The term *production team* usually describes all the members of a crew engaged in shooting a project, from the first assistant director to the carpenter. However, occasionally it is used to describe the same group as the director's team. On a large-scale production, the producer may refer to the *directing unit*, which includes just those people who direct or are assistant directors (director, first assistant director, second assistant director, dialogue director, and second unit director). This is a slightly artificial category created for mainly budgetary purposes. On such a production there may also be a separate production management unit as well as a locations department.

Here are the members of the director's team and their responsibilities.

PRODUCTION MANAGER (PM): A senior member of the team. This person will look after production (including hiring members of the crew) and implement the budget. On smaller productions, he may double as first assistant director or location manager.

A production manager is different from a *unit production manager* (UPM), who works closely with the producer to monitor the budget and administer certain productions.

FIRST ASSISTANT DIRECTOR (AD): This person is the director's right arm. He usually takes the lead in scheduling the shoot. He is responsible for making sure that everything happens in the most efficient way on the set. He will coordinate actors, extras, and crew, call the meal breaks, and make sure that everyone is on the same page. He arrives on the set before the director and leaves once arrangements for the following day have been finalized. During the shooting period, he will be thinking ahead, trying to forestall problems. He will also be constantly communicating with the director about the details of the shoot. ("Do you want another extra in this scene?" "Is it all right to break for lunch after this shot?" "Wardrobe says it needs another ten minutes to get the actor ready.") An ability to be efficient without being authoritarian helps.

SECOND ASSISTANT DIRECTOR: Because the first assistant is somewhat tied to the director and the camera, the second assistant is the first assistant's eyes, arms, and legs. She carries information from the first assistant to the various departments, such as wardrobe and makeup, and back again. She has particular responsibility for actors and extras, and keeps track of their hours (on *call sheets*). First assistants often delegate the responsibility of placing extras on the set to their seconds. Often, a resourceful second assistant can help a director out by, for example, conveying an important message to a member of the cast or crew. Eagerness and efficiency come in handy.

LOCATION MANAGER: This person is responsible for the infrastructure of the shoot. He will take an active part in searching for locations, negotiating the rights to use them, and arranging for permits to be issued by the authorities.

He also assists in drawing up the shooting schedule. The location manager is usually one of the first people on location, making sure that everything is ready for shooting to take place. He will be particularly concerned with access to the site, parking, catering, and toilet facilities. He will also be working ahead of the shoot to make sure that the next location is available to the designer and whomever else needs to be preparing it. He is, in effect, the production's liaison with much of the world outside the set. The director is most involved with the location manager during preproduction, when they choose the locations together. During the shoot itself, the location manager tends to work outside the director's immediate circle of attention, although he will frequently discuss logistics with the first assistant. ("The next location will be ready by four o'clock." "The designer is taking three of the grips to unload props at the next location." "What time do you expect to 'wrap' (finish shooting) here?") An ability to go without sleep is an asset.

SCRIPT SUPERVISOR OR CONTINUITY ASSISTANT: This member of the director's team is responsible for logging (i.e., noting down on a form) all the shots, communicating the director's preferences to the editor, and helping the director keep track of the many on-screen details (about character movement, prop placement, and the like) that ensure a smooth flow from shot to shot and scene to scene (i.e., its "continuity"). During shooting, she is always near the camera and an arm's length away from the director. (Her role is discussed more fully in Part 5, Chapter 29, in the context of continuity.)

PRODUCTION SECRETARY (DIRECTOR'S ASSISTANT): This person assists the director and production manager with paperwork. He is knowledgeable about all the forms that have to completed, and is prepared to type out last-minute revisions to the script and the schedule. On some small-scale productions, he doubles as script supervisor (or continuity assistant). An eye for detail and patience in dealing with the other members of the team are essential to his work.

PRODUCTION ASSISTANT (RUNNER OR "GOFER"): This is a low-paid but essential position. A production assistant may be given many diverse assignments, including stopping traffic during a take, escorting actors onto the set, carrying messages, and running errands. It is an entry-level position that gives people the opportunity to learn how a shoot works and a chance to impress a producer or production manager, who will, hopefully, hire them in the future as second assistants. A willingness to place themselves at the end of the lunch line is helpful.

30

Since members of the director's team work with the director but are paid by the producer, there is the potential for conflicts of loyalties. Sometimes a first assistant feels bound to let the producer know what is in the director's mind—especially if the director insists on a hopelessly ambitious schedule. And a location manager who is faced with a soaring budget, due to a director's costly location choices, will have to bring the matter to the producer's attention. Fortunately, these occasions are rare and members of the director's team understand that their first loyalty is to the director.

(For examples of directorial management techniques, especially as they relate to the director's team, see the description of three directors in Part 9, Chapter 43.)

Once when I was working as a first assistant, the director began to scream uncontrollably on the set, and I had to threaten to wrap the day's shoot if he did not pull himself together. Mercifully, this does not happen often. Successful directors know that if the shoot is to go smoothly, they must maintain excellent working relationships with each member of their team and the crew as a whole.

Watching the budget

Making a movie or a television show is not cheap. Most, if not all, of a director's choices are constrained by the money allocated to a project. A project's financial resources are organized in the budget. If a director wants to understand what she can achieve, she had better consult the budget.

Many employers insert a clause in the director's contract requiring her to deliver the finished project within budget. And, even if not explicitly stated in the contract, a director is expected *not* to exceed the available funds. Word spreads fast in the film world, so going over budget may imperil your career.

The unit production manager, or whoever is responsible for drafting a particular movie's budget, will allocate resources to certain areas according to his own interpretation of the filmscript. Budgets for television programs, on the other hand, tend to be somewhat standardized, which means that they may not reflect the particular requirements of your episode. Studying the budget can help you allocate resources. A director may increase her budget allocation in one area if she knows she will not need the money in another. If your project takes place predominantly in one house, for example, you may be able to transfer funds from the location budget to the cast budget, in order to afford more extras.

A budget is a complicated document, and you will probably need the UPM's or production manager's assistance to decipher it. If you haven't got time to go through the whole budget, line by line, at least make sure you understand the general areas discussed below.

1. Make sure you understand the lengths of time you have been allocated for preproduction, production, and postproduction.

    The complexity of a project has to be weighed against the time allocated to complete it. It is not uncommon for directors to decline potentially interesting projects because there is not enough time to do them justice.

    Preproduction on a film may vary from one to six months, depending on the size, the budget, and the complexity of the shoot. Preproduction on a primetime television series is approximately eleven days.

    Production can vary from a few weeks on a low-budget independent movie to six months or more on a major production. It takes ten days or less to shoot an average episode of a primetime television series.

    Postproduction can last between six months (or more) on a large-scale movie and six weeks on a low-budget one. The director of an episode of a primetime TV series may only get a few days in the editing room. (See Part 6 for a detailed discussion of postproduction.)

2. Ensure you have sufficient funds to consult experts and to carry out research, if required.

    Directorial research is not an item that appears on every drama budget, so make sure that there are funds available for travel, and for gratuities to helpful individuals and experts.

3. The cast: Check how much money has been allocated. Can you afford all the actors and extras you need?

    Creating miracles on a shoestring budget is part of a director's job, but you cannot create a crowd scene without a minimum number of extras (even if the producer says it can all be done digitally in postproduction). Weighing the high cost of well-known actors against a limited cast budget is another calculation directors and producers have to make. It is important to come to an understanding about these matters early on.

4. The director's team: How long will the various members be working with you? Do you have enough production assistants to control traffic in busy

locations? Most members of the director's team leave after the shooting period is over. Make sure that you have adequate support during the lengthy period of postproduction. Will the director's assistant (production secretary) stay with you part way or all the way through editing?

5. The technical scout: Check that sufficient money has been allocated for a decent tour of the locations with the DP, chief electrician, designer, and whoever else you would like to attend, prior to the shoot.

6. Equipment: Check that a generous amount been allocated to lighting. Do you have enough time and grip equipment to do all the camera moves you want? Do you need special camera lenses?

7. Crew: Check that you will be able to afford talented department heads (DP, designer, sound mixer, wardrobe, makeup, etc.). Can you afford all the grips, storyboarders, Steadicam operators, special effects crew, and others that you require?

   Naturally, the larger the production, the more specialists are required. Directors of productions with limited budgets are sometimes asked to provide action sequences and visual effects that are more appropriate to big-budget movies. Make sure you are not being asked to do without essential personnel.

8. The shoot: Check that overtime pay has been included. If you have night shoots, has sufficient money been allocated to cover them? Does the budget assume a particular "shooting ratio" (the amount of footage shot compared with the actual footage appearing in the finished project— usually in the region of 10-to-1 for an average drama production)? If it does, is that ratio too generous or too restrictive?

9. Check to see if there is anything in the script that might require additional expenditure.

   Corporate employers, such as television companies and large studios, often use standardized budget forms that may not reflect the special needs of your particular project. A director may need supplementary funds for aerial or underwater shots, animal training, fight arranging, and so on. Sometimes directors invent business that is not included in the script and is, therefore, not budgeted for.

10. Locations and props: Is the allocated money sufficient for all the locations you require? Do you need any particularly expensive props (such as period items)?

11. Transport: Check that the budget for trucks, coaches, and other production vehicles is sufficient. Have you been allocated a car?

If you have a lot of separate locations, you will need to move efficiently from one to the next in order not to lose shooting time. If you foresee numerous location changes, make sure that the unit has the resources it needs (in terms of manpower and vehicles) to achieve them.

If some scenes have a large cast or a large number of extras, make sure that coaches, caravans, and other vehicles have been hired to accommodate them. For instance, if you are shooting on a remote beach or mountainside, transporting your cast to and from the caterer and the toilets will be a time-consuming activity.

12. Special/optical and other effects: Has enough money been allocated for visual and digital effects? Do you need a fight or a stunt arranger?

Directors of low-budget films sometimes make the mistake of not hiring the kind of specialized crew members mentioned above. A good, licensed, visual effects supervisor, for example, saves the production time and money. He also reduces the likelihood of injuries.

Hiring a fight or stunt arranger does not mean handing over the choreography of a scene to someone else. These experts start by discussing the director's ideas with her, and then work with the actors (or stunt crew) to achieve them.

13. Editing: Check that enough time has been allotted to complete both visual and audio editing.

Every project has its own unique requirements. Once you are familiar with the stages of postproduction outlined in Part 6, check that you have the time and resources you require. For instance, if you know your project will involve actors rerecording their dialogue (automatic dialogue replacement), make sure that sufficient funds have been set aside. Do you have enough money for music and Foley, and other audio effects? (See discussion of these in Part 6, Chapter 35.)

14. Prints: If you are working in film, has enough money been allocated to enable you to obtain the quality of print you require? (See discussion in Part 6, Chapter 32.)

When I was young director working on large-scale projects, there were times I wished I had been more inquisitive about the budget. If you don't know the resources that are available, you tend to think any additional requests are causing an over-spend—which places you at the mercy of the accountants.

4. Casting

"Ursula was one of the first athletic sex symbols, or at least that's how I remembered her. I remember the strength of her shoulders in *Dr. No*, and thinking how her ears were higher than her eyes. She had a kind of . . . the way you think of automotive design, where the rear end is higher than the front, to make it look like it's moving faster. There was a sort of violence to her physicality that I always felt was very attractive." — Matthew Barney on why he cast Ursula Andress

If, as Sidney Lumet has said, there are no small decisions in moviemaking, then there are only big ones. Choosing actors, especially leading actors, are among the very biggest. Actors define a movie. They are the embodiment of the director's vision: statements about the way he or she sees the characters.

The director casts by appearance, certainly, but also by the entire impression an actor makes. This impact or "presence" is difficult to describe. It is essentially what an actor brings to a role before he starts rehearsing it—an amalgam of personality, experience, and training. Great theater actors tend to have considerable presence—they dominate a space and have commanding voices. But this is not always an asset when cameras and microphones are being used. Casting directors will use words such as "strength" and "lightness," "humor" and "seriousness," "subtlety" and "quirkiness" to try to convey a particular actor's quality, but these adjectives seldom pinpoint the visceral impression an actor actually creates. Different actors will, by their looks and personalities, produce different trajectories for the same character. One will be light and flirtatious in a certain scene, another more straightforwardly comic. One will tend to play a scene with emotion, another will hold emotion in check. Some actors like to make an immediate and appealing statement about their characters, others prefer to let the characters emerge slowly, a glint here and there, over the whole course of a film. This may sound complicated, but actors are naturally so different from each other, and they are generally willing to make such strong decisions during their audition readings, that gauging their distinct qualities is not hard.

Beyond making a directorial statement about a particular character, casting makes a statement about the production itself. For instance, the presence of a star implies a certain level of commerciality, so we will expect high production values and a strong narrative featuring a dominant central figure.

Will you choose mainstream or independent actors? Theater or film actors? Pier Paolo Pasolini (following the example of Italian neo-realist filmmakers like Roberto Rossellini) cast non-actors in *The Gospel According to St. Matthew* (1964) because he wanted an entirely fresh cast with realistic, non-filmic looks. In reality, unless your movie is a commercial Hollywood production in which star names are almost obligatory, your cast will consist of a mixture of well-known and lesser-known actors. But the balance you strike is critical.

"Bankable" stars (those few extremely hot stars whose names guarantee a profit at the box office) will commend a production to studio executives, but they can also complicate the casting equation. Stars bring two separate identities to a film: that of the character bring portrayed as well as their own manufactured persona. Although a wonderful actor like Meryl Streep can lose herself in a role, the audience will always be aware of her identity beyond the character and think, "Isn't she doing a great job? How different from the last movie we saw her in!" This dual perception may be interesting for some moviegoers, but it can be frustrating for directors who experience their films becoming star vehicles.[1]

In recent years, high-profile film projects are "packaged" increasingly by agencies or producers and then offered to directors with the stars already on board. In television, directors usually join a series with all its main characters in place and only get to make decisions about short-term players, and even then they are likely to find the producer sitting in on their casting sessions. Whenever I have had the opportunity to cast a major character in a TV series (because his first appearance was in an episode I was directing), the decision was always ultimately made by a group that included the executive producer.

---

[1] Bankable stars may complicate a production in other ways as well: They may tip the budget out of balance. They may request approval of other members of the cast. They may demand approval of the script. They may have expensive off-camera requirements, etc.

Mounting the classic Edwardian play ***Trelawny of the Wells*** for BBC Television, I was under some pressure from the producer to cast stars. Since it was a play about a troupe of nineteenth-century thespians, I decided to select actors with a good deal of theater experience, some of whom were familiar to the television audience, and then asked a few relatively unknown younger actors to join the cast. It's important to give actors breaks. Star presence was provided by a knight of the theater, Sir Michael Hordern. [2]

For a successful TV series, on the other hand, I once had to direct a star who was heading toward the end of his contract and what he (mistakenly) thought was going to be a successful career in another series. He caused considerable problems by insisting on special treatment in front of the rest of the cast and rejecting all ideas about staging, except his own. Sadly, at this point in his career, celebrity, tension, and personal problems beyond the studio had combined to make him almost impossible to work with.

An actor has to look the part, has to bring a unique presence *to* the part, and, ideally, should contribute positively to the working environment.

Two approaches to casting

In general, casting takes two alternative approaches: The first involves casting the net very wide and choosing the actor who stands out. It might be called "trawling" and is perfectly exemplified by the theatrical "cattle call," that open house when a large number of actors are auditioned in rapid succession. Sometimes, you might use this approach in film or television casting as well. If, for instance, you're looking for a special, as-yet-unknown young actress to star in your movie, you may have to see hundreds of hopefuls before making your choice. When you are casting a character like Scarlett O'Hara in *Gone With the Wind* (1939), you have to audition all the young actresses in Hollywood.

The second approach to casting requires the director to have a clear notion of the way he wants to cast—a notion consistent with his overall interpretation of the film—*before* starting auditions. In this approach, the director looks for actors who fit his conception of the role, rather than casting his net widely and accepting the best applicants. "I see Sean Penn in this role" says the director, instead of, "Call all the agents in town and have them send me their best actors between 35 and 45." The advantages of this method for the film or television director:

---

[2] Sir Michael Hordern (1915-1996) was equally at home in modern and classical plays and on screen.

(1) It narrows the field at the outset and makes for a less protracted audition period. In those genres where time is at a premium (TV series, TV movies, independent features, etc.), casting often overlaps with other duties like script-review and research, and must, therefore, be kept as short as possible.

(2) A more focused approach means that you are giving the casting director a very specific direction in which to work, instead of simply responding to her suggestions. This tends to result in fewer, more productive, auditions.

(3) Casting in line with a firm directorial vision will often produce stronger character choices, since you are selecting actors to embody *your particular interpretation* of the script. Casting becomes a process of developing the ideas inside your head.

Not surprisingly, in light of the above, film and television casting is prone to "type-casting."

Typecasting

The proximity of the camera in film and television requires an actor to do more than act the part, she must to a certain extent *be* that part. Looks are important, and particular actors tend to get cast repeatedly in similar roles (that is, "typecast"). However, there are degrees of typecasting.

Directors have to consider whether they are going to cast *with* or *against* type. Casting *with* type is merely finding an actor who matches the character description. In contemporary dramatic genres, it generally indicates a director has not thought beyond the first layer of characterization, has not discovered the one or two contrary characteristics that bring a particular character to life.[3] Typecasting "telegraphs" a character's behavior—tells us in advance how that person is going to act. It ignores the ambiguity that can contribute to dramatic tension and leaves little to the imagination. On the other hand, as Harold Clurman, co-founder of The Group Theater and a noted director, points out, typecasting makes life easier for directors with brief or nonexistent rehearsal periods.[4] At least you know what you are getting!

Casting *against* type acknowledges that characters may act out of contrary motives. It allows an actor to bring something more to the role than what is

---

[3] Early post-revolutionary filmmakers in Russia, including Eisenstein, adopted an extreme form of typecasting that has become known as "typage." In this style, lean, intelligent-looking actors would portray the proletariat and overweight actors the capitalists. The intent was not to present psychological realism but to support the class struggle.

[4] Harold Clurman, *On Directing* (New York: Collier, 1972), p. 69.

obvious at first sight. You can cast radically against type for shock value, playing with and reversing audience expectation—as Mel Brooks did in *Blazing Saddles* (1974), casting a black actor as the cowboy hero. Also shocking, though dramatically very interesting, was Sergio Leone's casting of archetypal hero Henry Fonda as the villain in *Once Upon A Time in the West* (1968).

With the right script and a good director, some actors are capable of giving finely shaded performances that defy easy description—Tommy Lee Jones in *Blue Sky* (1994), Geoffrey Rush in *Shine* (1996), Brendan Gleeson in *The General* (1998), Judy Dench in *Iris* (2001), Sissy Spacek in *In the Bedroom* (2001), Brian Cox in *L.I.E.* (2002), and Isabelle Hupert in *The Piano Teacher* (2002) are all high on my list of favorites. A strong performance and complex characters are hallmarks of an Altman movie. The director, when in the process of envisioning a film's roles and subsequently during auditions, should constantly strive for *a strong yet unsuperficial interpretation*.

Analyzing the casting strategies of directors you admire can be a very worthwhile activity.

The casting director, agents, and headshots

Many talented, decision-oriented people will accept responsibility for various aspects of the production—the camera operator will frame the shot, the continuity person will correct the actor, the designer will go ahead and furnish the set. The casting director is potentially one of these people. He or she is, in a sense, someone who can design your cast for you. Some directors are happy relinquishing casting decisions to a casting director, but these are usually not directors who are particularly interested in finely shaded performances.

Although Central Casting was created in the early 1920s to handle the large number of freelance extras applying to the studios for work, the position of the modern casting director did not develop until after the break up of the studio system in the 1950s. Until then, the major studios had their own "contract players" (actors who were under exclusive contract to them), and casting was done by either picking from these employees or, occasionally, hiring players from another studio. The available pool of talent and the number of actors' agents are now so large in centers like Los Angeles, New York, and London that it requires a specialist—the casting director—to handle them.

A few directors are so focused on the technical aspects of their jobs that they do not to keep themselves current about actors. This is unfortunate. The discussion between director and casting director is much more fruitful if the director can suggest names and knowledgeably respond to some of the casting director's suggestions. Knowledge of movie, television, *and* theater actors raises the level of discussion and encourages the casting director to look beyond first choices. Good casting directors are creative, energetic, sympathetic, and supportive. They can be your advisor, sounding board, and confidante. They can nurse you through the long process of auditioning and relieve you of having to talk to agents and do paperwork (and they invariably have excellent taste in champagne). But, like everyone else on the crew, they need to be challenged.

In the United States, directors and casting directors are assisted by the *Academy Players Directory*, a publication that features photographs of over fifteen thousand professional actors, mainly from the Los Angeles area. It is actually four tomes that separate actors into Leading Women/Ingenues, Leading Men/Younger Leading Men, Characters and Comediennes/Comedians, and Children. Another publication, the *Players Guide*, serves the New York area. The nearest equivalent in Britain is the *Spotlight* directory. These are all fascinating resources that jog the memory and supply the name of an actor's agent. But, be warned: Thumbing through these directories is a time-consuming business!

Producers are always concerned about casting, and it is important to find out early on how involved in the process they wish to be. Do they want to be present at all the auditions for a leading role or just at the call-backs (when the most suitable candidates are re-auditioned) or not at all? There are producers with strong suggestions about casting, and others with none. An experienced producer can be a valuable sounding-board for your ideas, and will help you find the balance between hiring stars and lesser-known actors. Whatever your producer's attitude toward casting, it is always wise to keep her informed of both your intentions and your actual progress.

When casting begins, the casting director will want *breakdowns* (character descriptions) of each part to circulate to agents. These could be extracted straight from the script, but it is better to have the director's spin on it. The script might read, "Red Riding-Hood: a pretty young girl in her early teens." The director should be able to refine that. Perhaps he wants a blue-collar Red Riding-Hood. Or one with a Midwestern accent. Or a non-Caucasian. The director's particular interpretation of the script will guide these decisions.

Upon reading a production's breakdowns, a casting director may have some immediate suggestions, but often will need a day or two to think, talk to agents, and gather some *headshots* and/or videotapes. Headshots are the standard

8x10-inch photographs of actors. On the backs of these photographs are details of the actors' ages, heights, eye colors, etc. Actors supply headshots to their agents who in turn pass them on to anyone who might be interested. Headshots cause much anguish for actors who, understandably, do not like being reduced to one particular image. The director must not rely entirely on these shots; they only serve to illustrate whether the actor is generally the physical type required for the role. With the aid of headshots and, increasingly, videotapes, the director and casting director decide whom to invite to the audition.

> Directors sometimes receive dozens of headshots either from the casting director or directly from agents, in which case they simply pass them all back to the casting director to be filed at the end of the casting process. If I am casting a small production and have only received a couple of dozen headshots, I do the actors the courtesy of returning them with a short note of thanks. But actors do not expect their headshots to be returned.

If your project cannot afford a casting director, you and your assistant must contact actors' agents. This is simpler in smaller cities, where there are only a few agents and everyone knows everyone else, than in the major film centers like Los Angeles and New York. In Los Angeles, the Breakdown Service will distribute breakdowns to agents, and it now has combined with The Academy of Motion Picture Arts and Sciences to produce an on-line breakdown service called The Link. But even small-scale producers would be better off working with a casting director to handle contracts, insurance, and related matters than on their own. Student filmmakers who want to use professional actors should contact their local Screen Actors Guild/American Federation of Television and Radio Artists (SAG/AFTRA) office to check the special student agreement. This agreement does not waive actors' fees altogether, it simply postpones them until the project begins to earn money.

Auditions: an opportunity, not a cattle-call

Auditioning, like almost everything else in preproduction, is a time of discovery for a director. You can use it to observe different character interpretations. You can discuss roles with talented professionals and benefit from their opinions. You can also work with them on a scene, making suggestions and asking them to interpret it in different ways. Indeed, in productions without a rehearsal period, the audition is often as close to a rehearsal as you get. Overall, you will find that as auditions progress, and you outline and discuss your film with each new applicant, your own views of the characters and the film itself mysteriously deepen. By the end of the audition period directors are usually much more certain about their visions than before.

An audition is a highly charged event. It is usually the first meeting between a particular actor and a particular director—and, sadly, often the last. A casting director possesses the power of suggestion, but it is the director (and producer, if she is present) who actually makes the decision. Strangely, directors, who may have just been unemployed themselves, often forget what it's like to apply for a job. It's tough. It's especially tough for actors, who give their all at auditions and are then rejected. No wonder some veteran actors resent auditions and are reluctant to "read" (read a scene out loud) for a part.

Most film roles are cast by audition, though, as just mentioned, certain star performers will not condescend to read. When I cast Sir Michael Hordern, he did not read. We went out to lunch instead, and, based on that meeting, he decided whether or not he felt comfortable doing the production. (It was a good restaurant but I was too nervous to enjoy the food.) I've cast other, less famous, actors without inviting them to read because I was very familiar with their work. On the few occasions when I have actually asked well-known actors to read, they have graciously agreed to do so.

When a student filmmaker considers casting local professionals, should he ask a senior actor with considerable experience in professional theater, and a few film credits, to read? The answer is probably yes, as long as the request is phrased respectfully.

Casting is, in effect, a continuation of directorial research and, like all good research, it can yield exciting results. It requires the skills of listening and being open to suggestions. Principal casting usually occurs fairly early in preproduction, when ideas about interpretation are not yet fully worked through. A director can afford to be playful during auditions, reading the same scene with a variety of actors and observing how they interpret it. Sometimes an actor will walk in and read the scene exactly as you envisage it. Very occasionally, an actor does something so totally original and sensational that it bowls you over. (I was once casting the role of an old servant in a Victorian mystery when an actor walked in with a loose set of false teeth that made a whistling sound every time he spoke.

His poor dental work made him perfect for the role.) Usually, you will hear the same interpretation time after time until, out of the blue, someone walks in and does it differently.

Often, two or three actors can play a given part equally well. Then your choice becomes a matter of considering whose personality and interpretation you prefer. If you have time, you can meet the actors on your shortlist again. Call-backs are common in the industry.

There are other casting concerns beyond the initial impression an actor makes during an audition. One has to consider how certain actors might interact in particular scenes and imagine what the effect of that interaction might be on the film or project as a whole. (Obviously, lovers have to be cast especially carefully.) You might or you might not want your two leading characters to look similar. A difference in height might be a factor if one character must intimidate another.

If you sense that one actor is just more talented than the other with whom she is competing for a role, go with the talent even if you have some reservations in other areas.

I almost talked myself out of casting a brilliant elderly actress in a TV series because her style of acting was so different from that of the "regular" with whom she would have to play her scenes. Luckily, the producer insisted we hire her and she lifted the performance level of the other actress.

Experienced actors have their own audition strategies, ranging from disarming modesty to stunning bravado. Some actors, a minority, are actually better at auditions than performances.

A director should be aware that a polished audition does not necessarily guarantee a good performance. If a director is casting a principal player with whom he intends to work on a role during rehearsals, an audition reading strongly committed to one interpretation may not be a good sign. Theatrical audition technique has received a good deal of attention in the past few years and there are books and videos about it. Where it has been applied to film and television, an actor is encouraged to find out all he can about what the director is looking for in order to give as plausible a reading as possible. The actor is also encouraged to get as much time with the script as she can to learn the lines (at least the key ones) so that she feels free giving a performance in the audition room. An actor who has memorized her lines is better able to look her reading-partner in the eye when she reads and give a more convincing performance.

I once worked as first assistant to a director who was casting the lead role of a cantankerous nineteenth-century *paterfamilias* in a film. I happened to be present when the actor who got the part arrived for his audition. He had memorized his lines, found a convincing accent, and had even dressed for the part. Unfortunately, he failed to deepen his understanding of the character during rehearsals, and the performance he gave at the audition remained his very best.

Two casting scenarios

I. You are about to cast a film and the script describes one of the characters in this way: "'Tophy': Short for Christopher. A charming young man in his mid-twenties."

This is a character description that leaves considerable latitude for the director. How do you see this role? How does the character fit into your tentative vision or interpretation of the wider script?

"Charming" is the only concrete character clue here: The fact that there is no other adjective (endearing, devious, hard-working, etc.) implies that Tophy might be a little weak and one-dimensional. The fact that he uses the diminutive "Tophy" also suggests a certain informality. Do you try to cast just on the basis of that simple description—or do you have your own interpretation, which adds another layer to the character? (Perhaps you see him as mother-dominated or as someone who is avoiding reality by becoming obsessed with gadgets or computers.) Or is this an opportunity to cast against type, to look for someone who is charming but strong?

You go to the script and analyze the given circumstances: everything he says and does, and all the references to him by other characters.

Now you must ask yourself how your view of this character compares with the characters you have been casting in other roles. More specifically, how will this particular actor work with the other actors with whom he will be playing most of his scenes? What will the "chemistry" be like? If there is conflict, are the characters sufficiently different? On the other hand, perhaps you want to cast actors who are superficially similar in order to make a point—to imply a sibling relationship, for example. Casting all characters, but especially leading ones, involves consideration of all these issues.

One further point: Tophy has a scene in which he rides a horse. So one of the criteria you stipulate when contacting agents is "ability to ride a horse." Unfortunately, it is one of the endearing peculiarities of actors that, in order to get a job, some of them will stretch the truth. ("Sure, I've been riding horses all my life!") They will assume that between being cast and turning up on set they can take a few riding lessons. Sometimes you can shoot around these shortcomings—how many close-ups of hands on piano keyboards have not been those of the actor in the wide shot! But if you cannot "cheat" a shot, you'd be wise to insert a clause into the contract stipulating that Tophy really has to be able to ride (or do whatever else the role demands) to the standard you require.

II. In a production about left-wing politics in the 1960s, you are looking for an actress to play "Lillian Hellman, late in life."[5]

The description is so specific that it would seem to narrow your choice. Surely only a finite pool of actresses are physically suitable, so casting consists of mechanically interviewing each of them, right? This is not so. The look-alike approach to casting seldom works.

Lillian Hellman had such firm political ideals that surely it would be advisable to cast an actress with strong political convictions. Again, not necessarily. You do not have to be a neo-Nazi to play Hitler, and you do not need to be a socialist to play Hellman. Of course, if you do have an excellent actress who also happens to be a political animal, it may facilitate self-identification—as it did in the film *Julia* (1977), in which Jane Fonda played the younger Lillian Hellman.

Superficial physical similarities might be convenient for the makeup and wardrobe departments, but capturing the emotional and intellectual qualities of the character is likely to be more important to the success of the film as a whole. Talented actors can transform themselves physically once they understand the character. Oliver Stone made the unlikely choice of a British actor, Anthony Hopkins, to play the President in his film *Nixon* (1995), and the result was a *tour de force*. Similarly, Nicole Kidman turned in a sensitive

---

[5] Lillian Hellman (1905-1989), dramatist and social critic. Her plays include *The Children's Hour* (1934), *The Little Foxes* (1939), and *Toys in the Attic* (1960).

and technically brilliant impersonation of the English novelist Virginia Wolf in *The Hours* (2003). Casting has few easy solutions. The director has to audition thoroughly and assess what each individual actor brings to the role.

Conducting an audition

There is no single way to conduct an audition. Methods will vary according to the nature of the production and the personality of the director. A performance space with a piano and an accompanist is necessary when auditioning singers and dancers. Auditioning for a sitcom for which the director is looking for an actor with a strong personality that will make an immediate impact on a studio audience may differ in tone from a movie audition, where an actor's chameleon qualities are more in demand. Mike Leigh, the English director who constructs films through improvisation, often asks actors to come to auditions as a defined character. The audition then consists of extended improvisatory work. Other directors may incorporate some improvisation into straightforward reading and interviewing.

I have worked with directors who have auditioned actors in their offices with the entire director's team working at their desks. I believe that is not the way it should be done. Auditions require privacy, informality, and the freedom to be intimate. So much is important: first impressions, the nuance of performance, the development of director-actor relationship, and the director's indefinable intuition. Both parties need time to assess each other.

Some directors like to videotape auditions. This makes sense if you have a large number of applicants and you have to submit your choice to a producer. A video can also serve as a form of "screen test" for less experienced actors. I have heard directors argue that "the camera loves" certain actors who can only be appreciated through a lens.[6] These are compelling reasons for auditioning with a camera, but I personally find taping an intrusive process and still tend to rely most heavily on my own notes scribbled down immediately after an actor has left the audition room. A full screen test at a later date (for which actors who are not subsequently hired have to be paid a fee) remains an option, particularly on big-budget productions.

Here is a common audition scenario.

The casting director, who organizes the audition, has contacted agents and allocated an audition time to each actor. The director has selected

---

[6] The experienced editor and filmmaker Walter Murch has said, "There is a chemistry between each actor and a certain lens." Michael Ondaatje, *Conversations* (New York: Knopf, 1002), p. 196.

certain scenes from the screenplay to be read. If he has not sent them in advance to the actors' agents, the casting director will leave scenes (known as *sides*) with the receptionist for actors to peruse before they audition. Generally, actors require at least twenty minutes to become familiar with a two- or three-page scene.

Before calling an actor, the casting director makes sure the director has a copy of his or her résumé (furnished by the agent). The director and casting director will also take a few seconds to agree who is going to read with the actor. Directors usually appreciate being in the position of objective observer, though there are times when they will choose to read a scene with an auditioning actor in order to emphasize or explore a particular aspect of the scene. Reading with an actor can sometimes afford insights that solitary script analysis cannot. If the director and casting director prefer not to read, then a professional actor may be hired to do that.

The auditioning actor is usually met at the elevator or in the hallway by the casting director, who tries to make her feel welcome and relaxed. (For some reason, casting directors don't trust directors to do this.) The casting director introduces the actor to the director, invites her to sit down, and then gets the conversation rolling. The conversation soon turns toward work, and the director asks the actor if she would read a scene.

At the end of the reading there is invariably a pause while the director decides how to proceed. If the first reading has been interesting, he may ask the actor to read the scene again with a different approach, in order to gauge the actor's adaptability and range. If the reading has lacked a particular quality, the director may try to elicit that quality during the second reading.

In my experience, two readings is the norm, but a director might want to make further changes and go for a third. Or, if he wants to try out an improvisation (when the actor is warmed up and "in character"), this might the time to do it.

The most awkward moment in an audition comes after the final reading or improv. It has been an intense ten, fifteen, or twenty minutes, and the actor has given her best. What is there left to say? The director and casting director must now ask her to leave in a way that preserves her dignity and acknowledges the inevitable post-audition letdown. The director compliments the actress on her reading and says how nice it was to meet her, while the casting director says something to the effect of, "Don't call us, we'll call you"—though hopefully not in so many words.

The director and casting director (and producer, if he is present) briefly discuss the actor they have just seen. Then, while the casting director leaves the room to collect the next candidate, the director jots down a few notes next to the name of the actor on the audition list supplied by the casting director. By the end of the day he may have seen dozens of actors for different roles and these notes will be invaluable.

Making the offer

It is important *not* to commit during an audition. Though it is sometimes tempting to offer a distinguished or powerful actor the part there and then, this is a mistake. "I would seriously like to consider you for this part" is preferable to "The part is yours." Wait till you have seen all the candidates and reserve your final decision till you have weighed all the factors. Impulsiveness can lead to error. Twenty-four hours can provide a precious respite.

Once you (or you and the producer) have chosen an actor, the casting director contacts the actor's agent and makes an offer. Although the casting director, as the producer's representative, is in a strong bargaining position, delays and slip-ups can occur. An actor may want more money than has been budgeted for the part. An actor may be negotiating a role in another movie and, therefore, postpone a decision about your offer for a number of days. The actor may have availability problems (e.g., she is not free till a week after your scheduled shooting starts). Then, there's the unexpected. A well-known actor once spent a long time considering a role I had offered her and then turned it down a week before production started. She said she had recently played in another production by the same author and did not want to be typecast. There was no time to set up new casting sessions, so I reviewed the list of actors I had already auditioned and chose the one I thought most talented. Contract negotiations were swift, and I was very relieved indeed when my new leading lady turned up for her first costume fitting.

PART 2
Preparing the Script for Rehearsal

5. Basic Structures

"It's what you *don't* say in a film that matters."
— Kevin Spacey

The story may not originate with the director, but it is his job to tell it well. For this reason, he has to be very aware of how stories are structured. A television script or a screenplay is comprised of two elements: What is said—the text—and what is thought—the *subtext*. Both are different and both are equally important.

The text comprises the printed words on the page. There are styles of acting primarily concerned with simply speaking the lines, as Hamlet put it, "trippingly on the tongue" – i.e., in a clear and melodious way. However, almost all modern acting schools in the western world now advocate penetrating beyond the text itself.

Subtext

Joan is a tennis player who has reached the U.S. Open semi-finals. She is scheduled to play an opponent to whom she has never lost, and she woke up that morning feeling very confident. She arrives at the court an hour before her match to find the weather changing. She gasps, "It's starting to rain!"

Bill is a middle-aged resident of a suburban town whose pride and joy is his lawn. It is high summer and there is a water restriction in force that has prevented him using the sprinkler. His once-green grass is gradually turning brown. Then, miraculously, the sky darkens and there is a cloudburst. He says, "It's starting to rain!"

The same spoken text in both cases, but very different subtexts. If we verbalized Joan's subtext, it might be: "Oh no! Everything was going so well and now it's spoiled!" If we verbalized Bill's it might be: "Thank God! My lawn's going to be rescued!" The difference in subtext depends on who is speaking, as well as on the circumstances they find themselves in.

Words tell the plot and describe things, but they also point to the psychological and emotional states of the people who utter them. Directors and actors have to study a script's characters, the circumstances in which those characters find themselves, their relationships with other characters, and their spoken dialogue in order to understand a screenplay's non-verbal level—its subtext.

A script's subtext often emerges most clearly during rehearsal. By working on subtext, a director can alter the meaning of individual lines as well as a whole performance. Subtext, therefore, is one of a director's most valuable tools and a key to meaningful rehearsals. As Clint Eastwood says, "For every character, you play an inner monologue as you play your outer."[1] "Make my day!" says the gun-toting cop. The words themselves appear inoffensive, and if one just read them off a page one might be tempted to reply, "Why thank you, officer. I'll try." It's the addition of subtext—"I'm going to kill you"—that makes them threatening.

The most important thing for actors is to bring their characters to life, and to do this they have to connect with their emotions. Emotions largely exist in the subtext. The American "method" actor sees subtext as all-important.[2] A method actor might change the text if it stands in the way of expressing subtextual emotion. It may be a little unfair to single out method actors in this regard because there is a tradition, extending at least as far back as Stanislavski's pupil Boleslavski, which asserts the primacy of emotion over text. This school of acting would agree with the late actor/teacher Sanford Meisner that "the subtext is the river and words are the boats floating on the river."[3] James Dean was an actor who constantly broke up the smooth delivery of his lines and used bodily movement and gesture to convey subtext. Another example of subtext triumphing over text is Marlon Brando's Don Corleone in the first *Godfather* where many of his words are lost in his deliberately mumbled delivery.

On the opposite side of the coin are European classical actors who regard the text as sacrosanct. Their approach stems from working on the acknowledged masterpieces of Shakespeare, Molière, Lope DeVega, and others. But even in America, some producers and directors insist that actors strictly adhere to the text. They do this for two reasons:

(1) Variant readings from take to take can cause errors in continuity. (2) Some

---

[1] Radio interview on *Fresh Air*, 1996.

[2] See Part 7, Chapter 39.

[3] Dennis Longwell, *Sanford Meisner on Acting* (New York: Vintage Books, 1987), p. 142.

texts are the product of a long and often costly process of composition, involving rewrites and—in TV—script editing. Some contemporary filmmakers, including David Mamet, argue that a well-written screenplay conveys emotion and characterization, and that actors must use their technique to bring the written lines to life. "When the actual courage of the actor is coupled with the lines of the playwright, the illusion of character is created."[4] Great movie actors of the past, like Cary Grant, Mamet argues, "played the lines"—that is, they were primarily concerned with articulating the text.

Despite these reservations, subtext is very helpful in constructing a performance. When actors are experiencing difficulty with a text, it often stems from their not appreciating its subtext.

Example: An actor enters and says his lines angrily. "Oh, it's you. I didn't expect to find you here." It is not the effect you want. You ask him about his state of mind as he enters and discover that he is still playing the leftover rage from a scene that took place the day before. One way to change this would be to say: "You are not angry with Pearl. You've had a day to cool off. Your lines are said tentatively, like a naughty child watching to see if he's been forgiven." At the very least, a subtextual change such as this can lead to a discussion of an actor's underlying character, objective, and relational choices. In this way, subtext enables meaningful rehearsal to take place.

When you watch a well-acted and well-written film, look out for subtextual moments. Look for occasions when the actor's emotion seems to contradict or be more important than the words he's speaking. Also look for moments when a point is made non-verbally by a look or another kind of physical movement or by an expressive silence. Rod Steiger's brooding central performance in *The Pawnbroker* (1964) offers many good examples of this.

Acts

Many great movies and television shows have been mystery stories. *Citizen Kane* (1941), *The Maltese Falcon* (1931), *The Fugitive* (the 1960s TV series), and *The Usual Suspects* (1999) might start a list that could easily run on for pages. Mystery movies are carefully plotted, highly artificial constructions that release significant bits of information at precise moments. In a sense, every good movie is a mystery, because the element of the unknown arouses our curiosity and hooks us into a film's unfolding events. Therefore, directors must

---

[4] David Mamet, *True and False* (New York: Vintage Books, 1999), p. 21. Interestingly, great writers like Harold Pinter and David Mamet himself frequently write in a way that implies meaning beyond the words on the page.

appreciate a project's structure—the way it releases information—in order to work with it, occasionally improve it, or at least not stand in its way.

The dramatic work as a whole is, of course, called the film or the episode. It is a project's largest single unit—the total drama shown at one sitting, from start to finish. It encompasses all the other divisions and subdivisions that are discussed in this chapter—acts, scenes, sequences, and beats. Let us look at the way a dramatic piece is built.

Shakespeare (or his printer), following the conventions of his time, divided his stories into acts and scenes, and so do we. It is amazing that the formal elements of dramatic construction have remained substantially the same for four hundred years.

The act is the largest story division, and it is not easy to describe. It is a block that has a broad narrative direction. Shakespeare's plays had five of them, each consisting of scenes with often very loose temporal or thematic relationships. Contemporary Hollywood movies usually have three. According to influential author Syd Field, the first act presents a dramatic situation, "the set up"; the second act, usually the longest, represents a series of initiatives by the hero (or heroes) that meet with resistance, "confrontation"; and the third act works toward a "resolution" of events. Ideally, toward the ends of acts one and two are "plot points"—plot turns that take the story in another direction.

This simple three-act model is still widely accepted, and a director wanting to work in Hollywood should be familiar with it. However, recently there has been a reaction against this rigid three-act structure, often in favor of a looser organization of multiple storylines. For example, *Traffic* (2000), which garnered many Academy Awards, had several intertwining plots. Parallel storytelling has long been a feature of television drama, so it is significant that *Traffic* itself was an adaptation of a British TV series. Three popular examples (among many others) of complex, parallel storytelling are *Pulp Fiction* (1994), *American Beauty* (1999), and *The Hours* (2003).[5]

Some movies have an underlying mythological narrative structure in which the hero has to be sought out or discovered and is subsequently subjected to certain tests that establish his credentials. He then metaphorically descends into an "underworld" where he undergoes a process of "rebirth." This model is apparent in some science fiction movies—notably the *Star Wars* sequence, but also exists in more humble films like the remarkable New Zealand-made *Whale Rider* (2004).

When you watch a film, look for significant dramatic moments that are a

---

[5] The originality of parallel storytelling should not be exaggerated. D.W. Griffith used this device in *Intolerance* (1916).

culmination of a series of events and that take the story in a new direction. These pivotal points will often mark the division between acts. See if you can break its story structure into acts.

Appreciating the underlying organization of a film or TV drama enables the director to place emphasis in the right places and control the tempo of a production. It also allows her to become more sensitive to the rhythm of the piece as a whole and more conscious of climaxes and those periods following climaxes when tension and momentum have to be built up again.

Television shows are divided into acts as well, these divisions being largely dictated by commercial breaks. A half-hour sitcom with a break in the middle will have two acts. The first act will initiate events and begin to develop them, and the second act will develop them further and then bring them to a resolution. Some sitcoms have another break—a coda—after the second act, before a final short gag and the end titles.

Primetime series often have four acts (not including a short "teaser"—a short dramatic event at the very start). In a series like E.R. or NYPD Blue, multiple storylines impact the arrangement of the scenes. During each act, the individual stories will rotate (for example, story A – story B – story A – story C – story A – story D and so on), setting up the commercial break after a particularly dramatic moment that "hooks" the viewer.

The "hook" is an important concept in television. Here's an example: We have a hospital drama in which a patient in the operating theater suddenly goes into cardiac arrest. This provides an immediate increase in tension. The surgeon tries to rescue her but a nurse notices failing vital signs. "We're losing her," she says. Then the surgeon's assistant brushes the surgeon aside and carries out some unusual and controversial medical procedure that resuscitates the patient. There is a tangible sense of shock. We go into the break on this wave of excitement. We can't wait to come back and find out how events will play out (the hook). When we do return, it is to the same set several moments later. The surgeon tears his mask from his face and walks out. His assistant knows she has broken protocol but cannot help being elated. "Make sure the patient remains under observation for the next twenty-four hours," she says with authority. "I'll be on Ward Four if anyone wants me."

The four acts of primetime TV drama will usually form a pattern in which the first act initiates all the storylines. The second develops them and may lead up to some kind of climactic moment—a confrontation, an explosion, a murder, an arrest or some other dramatic event that will set yet more conflicting events in motion. The third act continues the development, and the fourth proceeds toward resolution.

A typical hour-long daytime drama (or soap opera) has six acts. Directors need to be aware of these acts in order to work with the script to provide dramatic "hooks" that lead into commercial breaks and offer strong visual or dramatic statements coming out of them. All of this dramatic manipulation encourages the audience to keep watching the show.

Scenes

A scene is an uninterrupted event that takes place in one location. *The rule is when the time or the location changes, the scene also changes.* A scene can be one line of stage direction—"Joe goes into his room and picks up his comb"— or it can last much longer, as in *My Dinner With Andre* (1981), in which a single scene takes place over the course of an evening at a restaurant.

Scenes generally move a narrative forward by concentrating on a particular dramatic event. A scene almost always has some form of conflict, either overt or implied, and it is the director's job to identify that conflict and bring it out. This is not too difficult in a well-written film or primetime series in which the story is so well structured that its characters usually come together in order to create some kind of dramatic point. But the situation is not always clear-cut in soap operas, where the text can be so bland and the characters so unassertive that it's hard to manufacture conflict.

Ted
It's a beautiful day.

Sue
It sure is. It reminds me of the day
we first met.

Ted
Yes, there wasn't a cloud in the sky
then, either.

Soap producers I have known fall into two schools of thought about this kind of scene. The first believes that the director's business is to find subtextual conflict and persuade the actors to play it. (Perhaps Ted is really nervous in this scene, and is talking about the weather to try to calm himself down.) The other school believes that soap fans are just so pleased to see their favorite actors on screen that they don't care if a scene's dramatic or not. All my instincts as a director rebel against the second approach (but sometimes it's just not worth going to battle with producer and cast).

Sequences

Occasionally, a scene that's limited to one location does not make a satisfactory, workable unit. A couple is having an argument, for instance, which starts in the living room, develops into the hallway, and ends in the kitchen. Director and actors will want to rehearse this argument as a unit and not think of it as three separate scenes. A chase is another example of a series of scenes that form a unit connected by a common event or idea. These propulsively grouped scenes are called sequences. In the case of the argument sequence, an experienced production manager drawing up a shooting schedule will help the director by treating it as a single unit and scheduling all three scenes to be shot on the same day.

In a sequence, an actor often has to vary his performance across the whole group of scenes rather than trying to look for variation within each individual scene. Here is an example:

You are asked to direct a driving sequence comprised of three short scenes. In scene 1 newlyweds Jay and Lauren are driving happily along the coast. In scene 2, they pull up at a traffic light and witness a gang of bank robbers driving away from a crime. Jay steps on the gas, runs the light, and gives chase. In scene 3, Jay plus Lauren chase the robbers down the highway.

In each of the above scenes, which may be shot at different times and in separate locations, Lauren has varying emotions. The key to her giving a convincing performance will be to know what she is doing in the scene that is currently being shot, and how that scene relates to the whole sequence. Her change of emotion occurs in scene 2, so if she were to shoot scene 3 right after scene 1, she would have to be aware of the change. Directors can help actors in sequences like this by discussing exactly where in the sequence they are emotionally.

Arcs

Ever since Homer's *Odyssey*, literature has used the story of the journey—people going from one point to another (and then perhaps to another)—as one of its favorite narrative devices. "Picaresque" is the word used to describe this kind of tale, and examples from literature include Cervantes' *Don Quixote*, Fielding's

Tom Jones, Voltaire's *Candide*, Joyce's *Ulysses*, and Kerouac's *On the Road*. There have been many great picaresque movies too. My list would include *The African Queen* (1951), *Easy Rider* (1969), *Apocalypse Now* (1979), *Fitzcarraldo* (1982), *Thelma and Louise* (1991), *Saving Private Ryan* (1998), and *O Brother, Where Art Thou?* (2000). And, in a sense, all narratives are journeys, because the main characters in them move from one physical location to another, and/or from one state of mind to another.

The narrative comes prepackaged in various ways. Acts, scenes, and sequences offer ways of compartmentalizing elements of the narrative, but not all story developments fall conveniently into these divisions.

Any unit of a film or show in which there occurs some change or development can be viewed as an *arc* (sometimes also called a "trajectory"). I think of an arc as a journey. The television story editor creates the "story arc" of a whole TV series—the overall direction in which the narrative travels and which all episodes must follow. A screenwriter is concerned with the story arc of his main plot. He will also be interested in the "act arc"—how the story develops throughout each act—and the "scene arc"—the development within each scene.

Writers and actors are concerned with "character arcs"—personal journeys of self-discovery—which are how characters develop during the course of a drama. Playing Queen Elizabeth in *Elizabeth* (1998), Kate Blanchett started out as a somewhat naïve and susceptible teenager and grew into a haughty, isolated, and calculating queen. All the leading characters in the several plot lines of Steven Sodebergh's *Traffic* (2001) have distinct arcs. There is the crusading judge who comes to a deeper understanding of the problems of drug use; the pampered middle-class housewife who develops into a Lady Macbeth; and the posturing Mexican policeman who undergoes rebirth to become a hero. These are arcs that take place over the course of the whole movie, but in just one scene the would-be drug czar goes from reluctant acceptance to complete rejection of his appointment (a character's scene arc).

A director must be aware of all these overlapping and interweaving arcs: They propel the story. They are also a roadmap for production. One of the first questions a director should ask herself is, "What are the characters' arcs?"

Almost all stories are inherently about change, and arcs are a means of thinking about change. A director thinking in these terms will automatically have a dynamic view of a script's characters. When she talks to actors she'll be able to discuss how their roles develop – which is an approach that enriches performances. The developments of principal characters are important, but don't forget that minor characters can develop as well. Even a waitress or a hotel porter can change a little bit in the course of a scene. For example, waitresses often give a performance when they first come to a table.

```
                    WAITRESS
          (In an overly perky and slightly
          drawn-out manner.)

          Hi, my name's Gaynor and I'll be your
          waitress this evening. Our specials
          today are Cajun lobster, catfish with
          almonds, and scallops in a creamy
          white wine sauce. Would you folks
          like to order now or should I come
          back in a few minutes?
```

How is that performance received? How does she feel when she walks away from the table? Giving day players an arc to accomplish can keep their interactions with the principals alive. Paul Thomas Anderson, director of *Boogey Nights* (1997) and *Magnolia* (1999), is someone who obviously thinks in this way. All roles in those films, even the most minor, have developed (and developing) characters with defined attitudes.

6. Connecting with Characters

"The techniques of the actor and the director are
... indistinguishable, since the director ... is also,
to some extent, an actor." — Sergei Eisenstein[1]

Characters in films are usually defined by their actions, so considering their arcs is an important initial step. But to envisage a character completely, and to communicate at a meaningful level with the actor, the director has to dig deeper.

Examine a particular character by looking at everything in the screenplay that pertains to her (the given circumstances). Look closely at what that character says and the way she says it. Look at what others say about her. Accumulate every available scrap of evidence about that character's background, social circumstances, and mental states provided by the script. This hunt for information is important. It makes you expert in the text. It is similar to a conductor of a symphony orchestra familiarizing himself with a score. It enables you to work with complete confidence, which is the bottom line for a director.

Backstory

An actor uses her imagination to create a life prior to her appearance in a script. Writers often do this too in order to get to know their creations fully. Soap operas frequently keep a book, called a "bible," in which they chronicle the histories of each character, which serves as a reference for new writers, producers, directors, and story editors. These descriptions not only contain important

---

[1] Sergei Eisenstein, *The Film Sense* (New York: Harcourt Brace, 1947), p. 37.

background information, such as date of birth, number of marriages, and so on, but the essential personality elements of character as well. I still remember the wonderfully succinct description of "Dirty Den," the raffish pub-owner, in the original *EastEnders* bible: "He is a man who changes his shirt twice a day." Somehow that said it all.

Now, you must go beyond the script's given circumstances. Confining your knowledge of a character simply to what the author writes only gives you information about the immediate world of the script. To become better acquainted with a character, you must ask yourself about her background and, based upon what the writer provided, create all the little details not mentioned in the screenplay. It's imperative to use the given circumstances to start *imagining* the character's life before the script begins. In short, you have to create a *backstory*—the history leading up to the events covered in the screenplay.

Choices made in the past determine the way we behave here and now. Try to imagine the events that have led up to the start of the story. Perhaps a screenplay has a scene in which a man hears a gunshot and runs in the opposite direction. The actor who plays the scene as a traumatized Vietnam War veteran will do it very differently from the actor who plays it as someone who is merely timid by nature. Create a rich backstory for each character, being as vivid and imaginative as possible. The shaping of a character's backstory is one of the strongest weapons in a director's arsenal. Writer/director John Sayles often writes a very detailed backstory for each of his leading characters, which he and his actors use to create subtle, credible performances. (We will return to this important point.)

Connecting with a character

To really get under a character's skin, a director can compare him to the one person he knows inside out—himself. Directors, like actors, need to make an emotional investment in their characters to bring them vividly to life. If directors can relate to aspects of the characters or to their means of dealing with a situation or even to the situations in which the characters find themselves, then the whole production becomes more deeply felt. If you really understand a scene at an emotional level, you are more likely to make the specific, detailed choices (about design elements and character behavior) that will bring it to life.

Stanislavski had a simple way of relating to a character. He called it "the magic *if.*" Just ask yourself, "If I were in the same situation as this character, how would I behave?" If I worked for a company that had hard, scientific evidence it was producing a lethal substance but went out of its way to suppress that information, what would I do? (This is, of course, the situation faced by the ex-cigarette executive played by Russell Crowe in *The Insider*, 1999.)

Find parallels between your experiences and those of the character you are working on. It is amazing how we possess other people's characteristics (even the bad ones). Sometimes we're so like a character that it is more profitable to concentrate on our differences. For example, take a character who sits at the same table in a restaurant day after day and becomes very upset when he finds it occupied by someone else (*As Good As It Gets*, 1997). This exact situation may not have happened to you, but there must have been analogous events in your past. I can remember lining up for meals when I was at school and, through a quirk of school regulation, always being placed at the head of the line. Then, one day, the regulation changed and I found myself near the back. How angry and exasperated that made me feel! A director who can connect with a character's pain and discuss it with the actor is likely to produce a more intriguing scene than one who simply plays it for superficial comic or dramatic effect. He will help the actor by creating an atmosphere that supports whatever collaborative interpretation they choose.

The director uses his sympathetic imagination to begin to understand a character's emotional landscape. But be careful about identifying *completely* with a character. Student directors who strongly take the side of their leading characters and construct scenes entirely from these characters' points of view tend to make two mistakes. They produce scenes that lack balance—because they so strongly skew their scenes in favor of one person. And their product is often sentimental— because they over-indulge their own feelings. Asking how a character is similar to you is only half the process. Equally important is asking how a character is *different*. Being aware of the differences between yourself and a character helps you to objectify that character. This knowledge will tend to make that character more independent and strongly delineated. You will appreciate her as a unique and compelling being with an independent life of her own.

A director and an actor can work on a character in two ways. They can work from the inside outward, trying to understand the character's mental/emotional traits by personally identifying with them. Or they can work from the outside in, building up an objective picture of the character first, and then stepping into it. "His method was to work from the outside in, to establish a sequence of actions in the hope that they would stimulate the right mood and emotion," writes Jean Benedetti of Stanislavski during the period when he was trying to come to terms with Chekhov's characters.[2] (Later in his career, Stanislavski experimented with the opposite approach.) An actor or a director may prefer one method to the other, but both methods actually complement each other. You should try to merge one with the other.

An example: You are about to direct the latest adaptation of Shakespeare's *Hamlet*. You work on the script and discover, as people have throughout the centuries, that you can identify with quite a lot in the hero's character (he has such a contemporary, questioning, psychological way of thinking). If you are a man, perhaps you can draw on memories of your own relationship with your mother to help you understand Hamlet's feelings toward Gertrude. And if you are a woman, you may have some emotional memories of your mother that can help you understand the ambivalence of this relationship. This emotional identification leads you to more specific ideas about how you want to produce it. But, on the other hand, Hamlet is *not* you, and too much self-identification with him will lead you to overlook some of his important characteristics. He is, after all, an early seventeenth-century prince who lives in the public gaze. As royalty, he can indulge his emotions and be callous with subjects who cross him in ways that most modern people cannot appreciate. Any purely personal interpretation of this role will reduce it to the emotions of the director (or the actor playing it).

Asking questions

Here is a list of questions you can ask about characters. If the answers are in the script, fine. If they are not, create your own answers. I like to ask questions that deal with important moments in a character's childhood, because that's when personality, morals, and character traits are formed.

- Where was she born?
  (Did she stay close to the nest all her life? Did she move away?)
- What was her relationship with her father and mother?
  (Was she dominated by her parents? Did she have a nurturing relationship?)
- What was her relationship with the rest of her family?
  (Did she have siblings? Was she the only child? Was she part of an extended family?)

---

[2] Jean Benedetti, *Stanislavski* (London: Methven Publishing Ltd., 1988), p. 97.

- What were her schooldays like?
  (We tend to either love or hate our schooldays. In either case they have a great impact on us.)
- What was her first important relationship outside her family?
  (First relationships, whether they are love, mentoring, or of a different kind, can have a long-lasting effect.)
- What was her first sexual relationship?
  (This can set a pattern of future behavior. What is her sexual orientation? Was she sexually active at an early age or did she wait till much later?)
- Did she rebel against her parents?
  (Did she accept parental values? Has she spent her life trying to rebel? Did she rebel against her mother or her father or both?)

These are powerful questions that most actors will relate to. However, if they do not provide enough substantial insights and the characterization remains one-dimensional, another exercise can produce results. It's called "finding the trauma." You ask, "What was the one incident in her youth that made her the way she is today?" This deepens a characterization by emphasizing vulnerability. It also gives an actor something specific to relate to in a scene. Choose a character's trauma carefully, because an inappropriate choice can lead to a confusing interpretation.

Here is an example of looking for a character's trauma. You are working with an actor who is playing someone who seduces a married man and compulsively attempts to destroy his marriage (the kind of role memorably played by Glenn Close in *Fatal Attraction*, 1987, and Uma Thurman in *The Golden Bowl*, 2001). Suggesting a traumatic incident, such as the character as a young girl witnessing her father walk out on his family, may supply the actress with a motivation that is powerful enough to feed her character's sense of present-day desperation.

Another way to burrow deeply into a character is simply to work with the actor on the question, "What were the two or three most decisive events in your character's past?" Once again, choose carefully—the answers will strongly influence the way the actor plays the role.

You can test whether you've gotten under a character's skin by asking yourself questions about her likes and dislikes. The more detail you instinctively bring to these answers, the more successful the characterization will be. For example,

1. What kind of car does he drive? Answer: "A family car."
   This is a very generalized answer. It's a start, but you can be much more specific. "A second-hand blue Dodge Caravan" is better. "He drives a

second-hand blue Dodge Caravan chosen by his wife, though he would secretly like a Ferrari. When she is away he goes into the garage and soups-up the engine," is better still because it tells us so much more about the character.

2. What kind of food does she like? "Wine and hot-dogs" is a start. "Riesling and frankfurters bought from an up-market delicatessen" gives us a much more specific picture.

(Suggestion: Think of three different characters from three different movies, and speculate about what their favorite foods might be.)

3. What kind of clothes does he wear? "He likes to wear comfortable clothes, especially on weekends" is a superficial answer. If you really know the character you might say, "He buys most of his clothes from on-line catalogs because he's too lazy to go to a store. But he insists on buying silk boxer shorts in person from Versace."

(The great American actress Laurette Taylor believed her preparation was not complete till she was "wearing the underpants of the character."[3])

4. What kind of holiday does she like?

5. What kind of music does she enjoy?

6. What kind of pet, if any, does she have?

7. What television shows does she watch?

The list can go on forever. It is important to think in these terms, though, because sooner or later the designer, wardrobe designer, make-up supervisor or someone else may want to know the answers to these and many similar questions.

One more question :

8. What kind of animal is she like?

This is an exercise associated with the actor and teacher Stella Adler (though many others have used it). Actors can imagine themselves as animals to make their performances more physical. Again, detail is essential. If I'm playing a solitary agent on a dangerous, secret mission, I might envision myself as a wolf. But what kind of wolf? A lone wolf? A wolf starving and separated from the pack? A pack leader?

Occasionally, when a character is so evil that questions about her first date or where she went to school or even what childhood trauma she experienced seem woefully inadequate. This is often the case, for instance, with psychopaths in horror movies. Turning to animals for inspiration can be helpful here. For instance, there is more than a trace of snake in Anthony Hopkins' portrayal of

---

[3] Uta Hagen, *A Challenge for the Actor* (New York: Scribner, 1991), p. 48.

Hannibal Lechter in *The Silence of the Lambs* (1990).[4]

When you have accumulated enough detail to know a character, you should be able to provide a single, succinct statement about his or her behavior. So, after you have answered the questions listed above, try to compose a sentence beginning with the phrase "He/she is the kind of person who ..." At the start of this chapter I quoted the illuminating description of Dirty Den in the original *EastEnder*'s bible — "He is the kind of man who changes his shirt twice a day." Bette Davis recalled Joseph Mankiewicz telling her that the character she was about to play in *All About Eve* (1950) "was the kind of dame who would treat her mink coat like a poncho."[5] Helpful, penetrating insights such as these can only be produced by people who intimately understand the characters.

Objectives

As I sit at my desk working, a black cat is trying to jump onto my lap. I'm busy, so I block its path with my hand. The cat prowls round to the other side of the chair, but I block it again. I lift my hand to the keyboard and it immediately places its paws on my knee preparatory to jumping. I brush the paws off but it puts them right back up. This is a determined cat. It has a very strong objective — to get onto my lap.

We all have wants or desires that shape our lives. For example, a high school student may want to be on the sports team or to get good grades. And these desires may, in turn, be prompted by the desire to be liked by peers or approved of by parents. Another example: The lawyer wants to win the case to earn her fee, but at another level, she craves the affirmation that victory brings.

All characters in drama have definable objectives — things they strive toward. Without these objectives they would have no reason to do anything. Characters are like vehicles that need fuel to move. Objectives are that fuel. They provide the reasons — the *motivations* — for actions. In real life, our objectives may not always be as clear cut as they are in drama (though they often are). In the fictional world, Bill is an ordinary guy who would not normally break the law. But he has fallen in love with Jean, and she likes a bit of excitement. So to make her happy he agrees to rob a bank. Bill's objective (to make Jean happy) takes his life in a whole new narrative direction.

Characters in drama frequently have very strong wants or objectives. We usually meet these characters at a crossroads in their lives, when they face

---

[4] I'm grateful to my colleague Ken Cheeseman for drawing my attention to this.

[5] Bette Davis, *The Lonely Life* (New York: Berklee Books, 1990), p. 217.

choices. They must choose to continue or to escape, to possess or to relinquish, to free themselves or to free somebody else. Ultimately, these choices are so important to them that they have a life-or-death quality. The energy they expend to attain their goals makes them attractive and exciting. At the same time, the ever-present threat of failure makes them vulnerable and potentially tragic.

There are as many objectives as there are characters, and wherever characters with contrary objectives meet, drama ensues. If a film's genre is comedy, the conflict will be funny. If it's a drama, the conflict is likely to be serious. If it's an action movie, the result may be violent. If it's a horror flic, the result may be frightening.

In every scene that has two or more characters, there is the potential for conflict. Even love scenes possess an undercurrent of tension if both parties want something different from the encounter.

In *The Fugitive* (1993), Harrison Ford's character's primary objective is to find his wife's murderer. Tommy Lee Jones, as the pursuing law enforcement officer, wants to capture Ford. These two characters' objectives are strong and simple, to the point of obsession. Most of the movie is, in fact, an extended chase sequence based on these cross-purpose objectives. Action movies with characters who have strong objectives that vary little (or not at all) are comparatively easy to play—which is why so many action films with stars far less talented than Harrison Ford or Tommy Lee Jones have been successful.

A word of warning: Actors live in the present moment of the scene and are primarily interested in objectives. Stanislavski did *not* use the term arc, and writers and directors tend to find the concept more helpful than actors. When directing an actor, concentrate on objectives, not arcs.

We will return to objectives, and also discuss how they can be strung together, in the next chapter.

Resistance

Resistance, like gravity, is always present. Drama wouldn't exist if there weren't obstacles. The cat that was trying to climb onto my lap met the resistance of my hand sweeping away its paws. Some force has to attempt to stop people from achieving their goals; otherwise a story would not be compelling. How monotonous it would be if our favorite football team consistently walked over its opponents. Even Michael Jordan had days when he was stopped on his way to the basket.

Stanislavski believed that the director's principal task was to provide actors with their objectives. But objectives and obstacles go hand in hand. (There is no point in Michael Jordan leaping for the basket if no one is trying to stop him.) So, your hero may want to rescue his girlfriend, but his objective is constantly frustrated by her kidnappers, who provide the obstacle or resistance. Classically, films end with harmony in the third act, when resistance is overcome and the hero achieves his objective and, thus, the narrative arc is completed. But many dramas have more ambiguous endings, where resistance endures and objectives are not always achieved. (The prosecutors in *Law and Order* don't win every case; and the characters in *A Simple Plan* (1998) have their objectives perverted in the course of the film.)

In a good, interesting story, characters constantly encounter resistance. Something almost always interposes itself between them and the completion of their objectives, causing them either to change objectives or struggle harder to achieve them. For instance, Frances wants to get home quickly from the shop to cook dinner but is delayed by a gossipy neighbor. An airman wants to drop a bomb on a target but encounters resistance from enemy aircraft. *By making an objective hard to achieve, resistance intensifies that objective.*

Resistance is present at all levels of human activity, including the personal level. Internal resistance—psychological or moral considerations—may prevent a character from achieving his goal. Len has been hired to assassinate Belle, but he complicates matters by falling in love with her. Think of the conflicted characters Russell Crowe portrays so well in films like *L.A. Confidential* (1997), *The Insider* (1999), and *A Beautiful Mind* (2001)— characters who battle inner demons.

In the theater, actors may use physical resistance to magnify their actions, so that they can be visible throughout the auditorium: an actor crossing the stage in the teeth of an imaginary gale; an actress simulating arthritis in order to portray an old woman; an actor making his way across an imaginary bog. Magnifying gestures tends to make them theatrical. This is obviously not the effect we want in a naturalistic movie, but a subtle application of resistance can be beneficial. When directing romantic scenes taking place outdoors in a park or the countryside, I sometimes have a stranger pass by and distract the couple. I think this emphasizes a relationship's vulnerability and also stops a scene from becoming indulgent. At the end of *When Harry Met Sally* (1989), Billy Crystal runs across New York City to declare his love to Meg Ryan. The moment could be clichéd and sentimental, but Rob Reiner has Crystal fight to get himself heard above the noisy background of New Year's Eve revelers.

Example: A screenplay's stage direction reads, "HE ENTERS THE VAULT AND UNLOCKS THE SAFE." But what if the character encounters some difficulty opening it? Wouldn't it be more interesting if he had to struggle to find the combination or almost tripped the alarm? Such resistance might tell us something about the character. It would also humanize the action—after all, only Jedi Knights never have any trouble accomplishing objectives.

What's the story?

Stories are interesting when their characters engage us and then take us from one conflict to another. As a storyteller, the director must be aware of every change— of every twist in the plot and every subtle character development. When evaluating a script, look for arcs, conflicts, objectives, and resistance. They exist at every level. If you come across a scene (or a sequence) that appears to have no development, question the writer or her representative. This may require a re-write.

As you envision a screenplay at the scene level, bear arcs, conflicts, objectives, resistance, relationships, and character analysis in mind. These tools will reveal the screenplay's structure, as well as its characters' points of view.

As you read, keep asking yourself, "What's the story?" Over time, as your appreciation of the script, the characters, and the issues deepens, the story will grow more complex and fascinating. A scene that started with the simple stage direction: "George enters the room and sits down" could expand in your telling into one that is much more detailed, layered, and interesting. You could start by adding *backstory*: "George, a cub reporter who has just had an argument with his girlfriend, enters the office where they have spent so much time together."

Then you might add your *knowledge of his character*: "He takes rejection badly."

You might include an *obstacle*: "He can still smell her perfume in the air and tears well up in his eyes."

You might also include his *objective*: "He desperately wants to regain his self-control before his colleagues come back from lunch." And the action that stems from that objective: "So, he sits down at a table and tries to concentrate on the draft of an article he is writing."

7. Blocking and Beats

*B*locking is at the heart of the rehearsal process. It is the process of analyzing a scene in detail from all the relevant perspectives (themes, story, character, relationship, rhythm, production style, etc.) and then assigning positions and physical moves to the actors within the set. It is a term that derives from painting. When artists "block" a picture, they divide it up into its constituent surfaces and then decide how much light and color to assign to each of them. Some early painter/director must have seen the similarity with dividing up the stage and placing actors on it.

After a few years' practice, most television and film directors can block a scene quickly with actors so that it works superficially. This is a blessing for directors in high-pressure, tight-deadline situations (such as daytime drama), but the results of instant blocking are rarely artistically satisfying.

Very occasionally, more by accident than anything else, instant direction produces a satisfactory result. A director may take advantage of some beautiful natural light to shoot a short scene, and the resulting visual effect compensates for the lack of considered blocking. There are some charming improvised scenes in Jean-Luc Godard's early movies—especially *Pierrot le Fou* (1965)—that have this quality. Once in a while a quickly blocked scene works because it somehow strikes a specific chord with the actors who invest it with real emotion, which is why a scene in a soap opera will occasionally take wing. Aside from these anomalies, the more time spent on preproduction and rehearsal, the better the result. Guaranteed.

The director's most creative hours are spent alone, sitting at a table, bent over a script, pencil in hand. A well-known director once told me his young daughter called him "Erasercrumbs," because his desk was always strewn with shavings from his well-used eraser. A director considers the script as a whole, and then considers the characters, and then works on individual scenes. A

Once, in a raging storm, when a crew and I were at the end of a pier overlooking a Scottish loch, I was handed a brand new scene and asked to shoot it at once. This kind of challenge concentrates the mind but does nothing for program quality. I spent a few minutes reading the soaking pages, shouted a few basic instructions to the actors (who were frantically learning their lines), and we managed to produce a gray, awkward scene. In the editing room we were horrified to discover that one of the actors had forgotten to say the crucial word "not" in the sentence, "I did *not* meet Mrs. Smith"– an omission that rendered the whole scene meaningless.

conscientious director will devote as long as it takes—two, three, four or even more hours—to considering each scene. It is important not to rush this step. In a sense, the whole of the rest of the process—the shooting and editing—is merely the implementation of this plan.

A director in Los Angeles preparing a primetime episodic drama such as *E.R.* or *The Practice* has between seven and ten days to read the final script, cast incidental characters, confer with the design departments, and then come up with a shooting plan for every scene. In a feature film, on the other hand, where only one or two scenes are shot each day, directors may have the luxury of working with the actors informally or in rehearsals and then reconsidering their plans the evening before the shoot. No matter what the medium, though, a blocking plan is necessary, and the earlier it can be formulated the more opportunity there is for revision and improvement.

On the other hand, simply foisting an elaborate directorial plan on crew and actors can have an adverse effect. Room must be left for inspiration and improvisation during production. Many of the great movies of the late 1940s and early 1950s seem leaden to us now because their directors were so inflexible about implementing their shooting plans. Leon Becker, sound man on the Academy Award-winning *The Best Years of Our Lives* (1946), told me how William Wyler and his team constructed the whole movie down to the smallest detail during preproduction, and then simply executed the blueprint. To me, these films often lack the sense of vitality that results from obstacles being wrestled with and overcome during shooting.

A film is born when a writer creates it. It is re-imagined when a director works on it. And it is re-imagined again at various points, such as when shooting begins and the director's abstract ideas are converted into reality, and when the individual shots are assembled during editing. Rehearsal is one of these moments when re-imagining can occur. Actors, who enter the process after preproduction, can literally breathe fresh life into a scene. Directors must understand that there is never just one, definitive, interpretation. Scenes will change naturally according to atmosphere on the set and the personalities of the actors. Scenes change from day to day, between rehearsal and shoot, and from take to take. Actors introduce an element of uncertainty that constantly threatens the integrity of the director's plan. When the unpredictable relationship between actor and director works well, the result can be very exhilarating. But both parties must be prepared to put their personal visions and preferences on the table for the sake of respectful collaboration.

This discussion and modification of the director's plan makes preparation more essential. A scene that has *not* been thoroughly considered will always be superficial (unless the actors somehow manage to rescue it by themselves). Preparation empowers a director, giving her the knowledge and the confidence to make alterations. Oddly enough, the longer you work on a scene the more you are able to adapt to new ideas, whereas hasty preparation makes you cling desperately to the only workable solution you've found. The English director Alan Clarke used to say that he shot his best scenes when he threw out his initial plans.

In the early days of the popular BBC series *EastEnders*, Dirty Den and his wife Angie used to have a raging argument about once a month—which was one of the reasons why half the population, including Princess Diana, tuned in to every episode (though the Queen thought there was too much shouting). When I was lucky enough to direct one of these scenes, I sat down with the actors (Leslie Grantham and Anita Dobson) and tried to keep up as they frantically rewrote the script, line by line, and pretty much invented their own moves. It was a case of tearing up hours of homework and starting again from scratch, but the results were worth it.

This is an experience that other directors of television series will probably recognize, and is partly the result of the familiarity that actors on these shows have with their characters. On a period drama, I was having a hard time staging a fight and was on the verge of hiring a professional fight-arranger when a member of the cast suggested a solution that worked very well. One of the advantages of adopting suggestions made by actors is that they commit to them instantly and wholeheartedly.

In reality, a competent film or TV director usually does not have to make drastic compromises in every scene. But experienced directors know the excitement of abandoning a plan of action in response to a challenging new interpretation.

Starting to block

Planning a scene starts with reading it through by yourself several times. Resist the temptation to start assigning positions to characters immediately—you can easily get locked into an interpretation leading to a dead-end. You should be able to imagine the whole scene, moves and all, in your head before you pick up your pencil. Once you have jotted down your blocking plan, double-check it to make sure it really works. Then you might want to check it once again to see if there's a better way to accomplish your intentions. (See Fig. 7.1 for an example of a script page with director's notes about blocking. I'll explain how to mark a script in this way in Part 3, Chapters 13 and 14.)

Here are two tricks I use: I think of a director I admire and ask myself if this would be a solution she might adopt. If my chosen director is Jane Campion, for instance, it might lead me to reconsider the visual elements, as well as prompt me to think again about my handling of the female characters. The second trick is to think of a director I don't admire, and ask if I'm committing any of her mistakes. Am I making obvious choices? Am I doing things in a lazy, convenient way? Am I moving characters in the wrong directions?

Blocking a scene is a kind of a game. It has rules, but it also has an infinite variety of solutions. The object is to choose the most elegant one.

In Part 1, I have discussed the director's first readings of the script, in which she starts searching for the identity of the characters. After her second reading, she has begun to form a strong impression of the principal characters, though it may take another reading to begin to understand secondary and minor characters. Occasionally, it is not until she starts working with the actors in rehearsal or on the set that she realizes she has missed the nuance of a relationship or even the whole point of a scene. This is not uncommon in television series, where a scene can be about something that has occurred on the show months or years previously. An actor can point out, "This is the first time I've met Sally since she threw a plate of spaghetti at me three months ago," and an encounter that had seemed mundane suddenly has dramatic potential. (Perhaps the two characters start the scene wary of each other, and the scene is about whether or not they can overcome their distrust.)

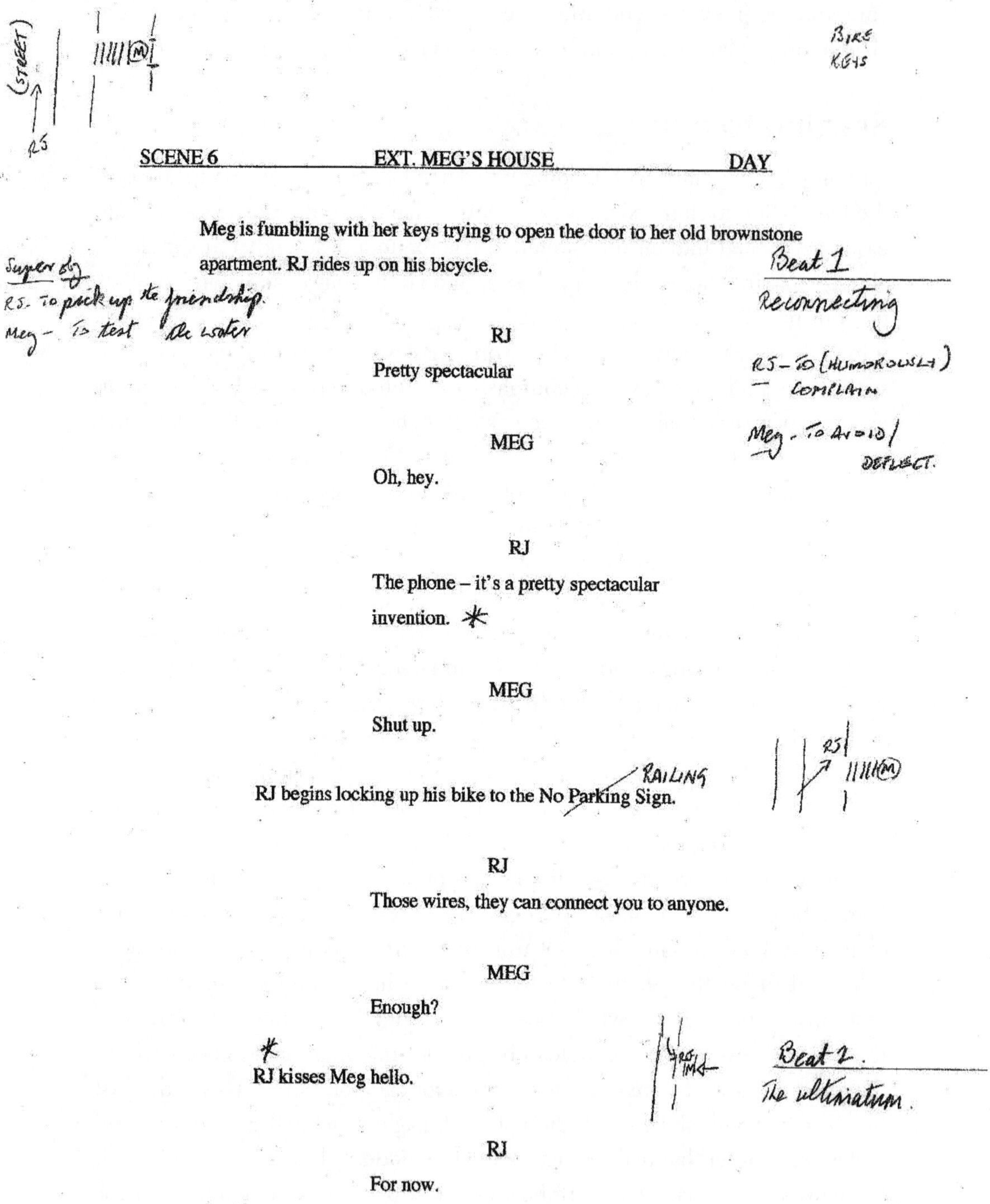

(STREET) →

RS

BIKE
KEYS

SCENE 6   EXT. MEG'S HOUSE   DAY

Meg is fumbling with her keys trying to open the door to her old brownstone
apartment. RJ rides up on his bicycle.

Super dry
RS. To pick up the friendship.
Meg — To test the water

Beat 1
Reconnecting

                    RJ

Pretty spectacular

RS — To (HUMOROUSLY)
— COMPLAIN

                    MEG

Oh, hey.

Meg. To AVOID/
DEFLECT.

                    RJ

The phone – it's a pretty spectacular
invention. ✳

                    MEG

Shut up.

RJ begins locking up his bike to the No Parking Sign.   *RAILING*

RS
IIIIIIM

                    RJ

Those wires, they can connect you to anyone.

                    MEG

Enough?

✳
RJ kisses Meg hello.

Beat 2.
The ultimatum.

                    RJ

For now.

Fig. 7.1: Script page with director's blocking notes.

In Chapters 5 and 6, I covered analyzing a script and understanding its characters in general terms. What is required now is a more systematic approach to preparing a script for rehearsal—one that can be applied at the scene level.

Beats

To analyze a scene, it is usually divided up into smaller sections, which are called beats (or, occasionally, *units*). But before I discuss this use of the word, let me clear up a possible misunderstanding.

The term "beat" sometimes occurs in a script.

Helen
Barry, you're so disgusting! I've never seen anybody as repulsive as you!

Barry
(Beat) I guess that means you don't want to get engaged?

In this usage, "beat" means a short pause. The writer does not want Barry to reply immediately. He wants to give the impression that Barry is taking in what Helen has said. This has the effect of momentarily restraining the flow of the dialogue so that Barry's reply carries a little more weight.

This is *not* the kind of beat that concerns us here. If a scene is longer than three-quarters of a page of dialogue or consists of several lines of complicated stage directions, it may be useful to divide it up and tackle each section separately. Directors are not the only people who do this. Writers and actors also chop scenes up into similar bite-sized chunks. Each of these people uses the term "beat" slightly differently, and so we need to be aware of its various applications.

When Stanislavski originated the term "beats," its English translation was simply "bits"—as in, "Let's divide the scene up into bits." Apparently, it was the ex-Moscow Arts Theatre actress Mme. Ouspenskaya's Russian pronunciation of the word in her acting classes that turned it into "beats."

Writers' beats

A self-conscious writer constructs a scene from beats. The best description of writers' beats I know occurs in David Mamet's *On Directing*. Mamet describes how a scene is not simply one event but a series of smaller actions that accomplish that event.

Let's look at an example. A writer has to create a scene about a man murdering his wife. He does not just sit down at his word-processor and write "Joel picks up a gun and shoots Muriel." The scene should be carefully constructed to lead up to this climax. The writer first considers where the characters are physically located at the opening of a scene and realizes he has to start by bringing the murderer into the apartment.

Writer's beat 1—preparation. Joel enters the hallway and sees Muriel's still-wet coat hanging in the closet. He takes this as confirmation that she has been out with her lover. (He has been thinking about confronting her and this is the final stimulus.) He next notices that the bedroom door is ajar. (A closed door might have offered some resistance but, unfortunately for Muriel, the open door draws him in.)

Writer's beat 2—almost relenting. Joel enters the bedroom. Muriel, who is not quite asleep, opens her eyes and smiles. She asks him about his day at work. He begins talking and the act of communication makes him start to relent.

Writer's beat 3—forcing himself to confront her. Joel, sensing his own equivocation, forces himself to remember her betrayal. His anger is instantly rekindled. He blurts out that she has been unfaithful. At first she denies it but then, after he shows her the private investigator's photographs, admits it.

Writer's beat 4—the murder. He immediately crosses the room to his dresser, opens a drawer, and takes out a gun. His back is to her and she is too busy apologizing to notice what he is doing. His hand shakes, but he manages to load the gun. He turns and pulls the trigger. She falls back on the bed.

Writer's beat 5—the consequence. He throws the gun into the corner, enters the little bathroom adjoining the bedroom, and washes his hands. He is emotionally exhausted. He looks in the mirror and a haggard face peers back. Then he staggers into the room and passes out on the bed alongside his victim.

For a writer, beats are the steps that take him through a scene. Having this structure in place allows him to proceed to the next stage, which is to add dialogue.

Actors' beats

Actors are less concerned with story structure. They tend to see a scene from the perspective of the character they are playing. They are concerned with the way their own roles develop, so they divide up a scene on that basis.

A change in an actor's beat usually coincides with a change in objective — usually his own, though a change in another character's objective may also affect him. It may or may not coincide with a writer's beat. The actor playing Joel divides the scene up as follows. (Remember, he is only looking for changes that occur to his own character.)

Actor's beat 1 — He comes in wanting "to confront" Muriel, sees the coat (which reinforces his intention), and wanders into the bedroom.

Actor's beat 2 — He listens to her and then has "to harden his heart" — a definite change of attitude for him, which results in his producing the photograph.

Actor's beat 3 — It is only after Muriel has admitted her adultery that his objective becomes explicitly "to murder her." This would be the second major change in gear for the actor, and he would call it his third beat (even though it is Writer beat 4).

Actor's beat 4 — After the shooting, his objective changes again and he wants to forget.

A director has to be aware of actors' beats in order to be able to understand a scene from their perspective.

Directors' beats

Although directors take writers' and actors' beats into consideration, they are not primarily concerned with either constructing a scene or seeing it myopically from just one character's point of view (unless it is a one-character scene).

Directors need to be able to divide up a scene into smaller pieces for two reasons: first, to analyze it more closely. By looking at a scene as a series of smaller units, the director can focus intently on details. Second, to facilitate its rehearsal and recording. If a scene is longer than three-quarters of a page, it usually helps to break it up into beats for discussion with actors. The key here is to find sections that are long enough to warrant being rehearsed on their own, but not so long that the cast loses focus. Ideally, in film and TV, a beat should be no shorter than half a page and no longer than a full page.[2] I

---

[2] Beats are used in the theater as well, but because theater scripts tend to be less concise than screenplays, beats tend to be between one and two script pages.

find that the ideal length is three-quarters of a page. So, the challenge is to create beats that are approximately three-quarters of a page long, and are at the same time definite, self-contained units.

The director, when dividing up a scene, will look for moments when it changes direction in a number of ways. She will look for small shifts in emphasis and mood. She will identify the writer's structure and the actors' objectives. Then she will draw the line for the start of each of her director's beats.

This sounds like a tall order, but in practice it is almost always achievable. In our two-and-a-quarter-page murder scenario above, for example, a director might create the following beats:

Director's beat 1—"Entering". ($^6/_8$ of a page)[3]

Joel enters the apartment and makes his way into the bedroom. Muriel wakes up and starts speaking to him.

Director's beat 2—"Arguing" ($^7/_8$ of a page)

Joel starts talking to Muriel and then decides to pick a quarrel.

Director's beat 3—"Murder and its aftermath" ($^4/_8$ page, including extensive stage directions)

Joel takes out his gun and shoots Muriel. He wanders into the bathroom and then comes back and collapses on the bed.

As you can see, there is a moment when the director's beats coincide with the screenwriter's and a moment when they coincide with the actor's. The important thing is, however, that we have three manageable sections. The director can sit down with her actors and discuss the scene in terms of these beats. (Note: Giving each beat a distinct name helps director and cast to understand them.) She can then rehearse each of the beats separately. When it comes to shooting the scene, she will also have definite sections whence to commence each take. When picking up a shot half way through a scene, it's important to give actors enough of a lead-in so that they are completely in character and up to speed when it comes to their "on-shot" line. Beats often give directors convenient starting points.

Scene analysis

Here is a short scene. How would you divide it up into director's beats? And what name would you give to each beat?

---

[3] I have divided the page into eighths, as described in Chapter 1.

Int. Office   Day

Hector, 65 years old and of Greek origin, is a
salesman and Eleanor, age 24, is his niece. They
have recently met for the first time. Hector was
separated from his sister, Eleanor's mother, during
the war.

He is studying a family photograph she has given
him.

                    Eleanor
          It was taken a few years ago. You can
          see my brother. They named him
          Hector, after you.

                    Hector
          (Touched) And he lives in Greece
          too …?

          (Eleanor nods)

                    Hector
          You must miss them.

                    Eleanor
          I met my husband in a village in
          Thessalonika—it took a long time for
          him to persuade me to come and try
          living here.

                    Hector
          If you hadn't …

                    Eleanor
          But I did. And now I know I have some
          family here, it might make it a
          little easier for me …

                    Hector
          (Staring at her) You are so like your
          mother.

(They sit smiling at each other for a
moment)

                    Eleanor
I should be getting back.

                    Hector
Of course.

(They get up)

                    Eleanor
There's just one thing we haven't
talked about—how are we going to
break the news to Mama? Do you want
to be the one to call her?

                    Hector
(Excited but nervous) The thought of
it! Just picking up the phone and
hearing her voice! I don't know if
I'd be able to get the words out.

Maybe you'd better prepare her first?

                    Eleanor
I'll do it as soon as I get back. I'm
sure she'll call you straight away.

                    Hector
I'll be waiting. Though I don't know
where we'll begin, there's so much to
talk about.

                    Eleanor
The first thing she'll want to know
is when you're coming over for a
visit.

                    Hector
You try and stop me!

(He smiles at the thought)

I would suggest that this scene is made up of two beats. The first beat is slow and somewhat sentimental. Hector, in particular, seems lost in reminiscence as he looks at the pictures and then at his niece. I might call the first beat, which includes the moment they sit and smile at each other, "Rediscovering the Past." The second beat is quicker. It has a sense of urgency, as it is introduced by Eleanor's announcement, "I should be getting back." There are still questions to be asked and arrangements to be made, but time is now at a premium. Under this pressure Eleanor goes straight to the central issue and asks about breaking the news to her mother. I might call this second beat "Breaking the News."

The start of this second beat coincides with new objectives. Eleanor's initial objective is "to inform." But then she changes the mood by saying, "I should be getting back." You might characterize her objective in the second beat as "to move things along."

Consideration of the beats has already brought us quite far in the analysis of the scene. Here are two more points you should consider:

(1) I think Hector's objective for the scene as a whole is "to find himself." This may sound a little dramatic, but I think he has been living an unfulfilled life, separated from his family and his country. Eleanor gives him the opportunity to rediscover himself.

What is Eleanor's scene objective? We have already considered her beat objectives—but what does she want in the scene as a whole? (Note: I *don't* think her scene objective is as dramatic as Hector's.)

(2) How should we describe Eleanor's character? We get a strong sense of Hector's character in this scene. We know he is in his mid-60s and still working as a salesman. We also know that he was born in Greece and became separated from his sister during the Second World War. If I had to describe his character on the basis of this one scene, I might say: Hector is an unsuccessful businessman trying to hold onto his job long enough to afford retirement. He is a dapper man who would not dream of going to work (to sell ladies' handbags) without a clean white shirt and silk tie. He has been married, but he has no children. He is lonely and haunted by the past. On the dresser in his bedroom is a photograph of his family, taken in Greece in 1940, when he was a young boy. He looks at the picture most nights and wonders what has become of his mother and elder sister.

8. Putting Together Beats, Objectives, Actions, and Transitions

This chapter takes many of the concepts that have been introduced in this book and discusses them in more detail. Acting theory is a very practical subject, and I hope I have not presented it in too abstract a way. You might regard these concepts as a tool kit designed for a wide variety of projects.

Beats and objectives

If, as Stanislavski said, the director's job is to give actors their objectives, then directors should to be aware of each character's objectives as they exist at every level—story, act, scene, and beat.

As we have seen in the Eleanor/Hector scene (in the previous chapter), at least two levels of objectives exist at any one time. Characters have immediate, short-term objectives, which will eventually lead (they hope) to the attainment of their longer-term objective. The short-term objective is the beat objective. The longer-term one, which frames it at the scene or sequence level, is often called the *super-objective*. We can all only do one thing at a time, so actors tend to play their beat objectives. But the super-objective is always there in the background, acting as a strong reference point, framing everything. Losing sight of it will cause a performance to lose focus.

As we saw in the previous chapter, all characters have an over-arching objective that defines them. This overall objective is sometimes referred to as a character's *spine*. Spine is actually a very good term for it because it is the central supporting structure from which all the other objectives spring. The spine gives meaning to everything the character does. It is her underlying motive and provides her purpose.

In a narrative with a clear structure, like the traditional Hollywood three-act movie, characters may have different objectives in different acts. (They will also have an objective in every scene and in every beat.)

Let's take an example. A man wants to be loved by a woman—this is his overall objective or spine. In Act 2, he might try to get her attention in all sorts of different ways, many of which will be frustrated. (His Act 2 objective is "to get her attention.") In one scene he steals some flowers to present to her. (His scene objective is "to steal.") In order to steal the flowers, he first has to distract the salesperson. (The objective of the first beat in the scene is "to distract.")

When you give an actor an objective, it's very important to keep it active and concise. A succinct objective makes the actor's job easier. It enables her to

I was once working on a variety program with a producer/director who had hired professional actors for a comedy sketch. This was a novelty for him because he usually worked with stand-up comedians and puppeteers. Inevitably, after several rehearsals, one of the actors approached him and asked, "What's my motivation?" The producer had not thought about the scene in this way. He became embarrassed and left the room. What the actor wanted to know was, "Why should my character do this?" Or, put a different way, "What is my objective?" Suggesting "motivation" is straightforward if you have considered the character and worked out her objectives.

focus clearly on one idea. If the idea is powerful and active, the performance will tend to be powerful and active too. An objective always starts with the word "to." The best objectives are usually two-, three-, or four-word phrases: "to protect," "to contradict," "to annoy Joan," "to punish her enemy."

Imagine you are an actor about to play a love scene. Your director says to you, "Your objective here is to bring all your passion and longing to this one man (or woman)." How do you start? You work hard on evoking the character's passion and then equally hard on imagining her (or his) longing. At the end of the scene you have no idea if you have achieved what the director wanted because the instruction was phrased in such a generalized way. Had the director said, "Your objective is to smother him with love," how much simpler it would have been. "To smother with love" is a playable objective.

Actors who have strong objectives and implement them imaginatively stand out. Jack Nicholson at his vintage best (*Five Easy Pieces*,1970, *One Flew Over the Cuckoo's Nest*, 1975) must have used active and graphic objectives. Antony Sher, the South African actor working in Britain (*Alive & Kicking*, 1997, *Mrs. Brown*, 1997, *Shakespeare In Love*, 1998), is another actor who gives vivid, single-minded, energetic performances. The clarity Anthony Hopkins brings to a role is evidence of well-thought-out objectives. The same goes for Joan Allen (*Nixon*, 1995, *The Crucible*, 1996, *Pleasantville*, 1998).

While a scene may have multiple beats, an actor's objective does not have to change with each one. An actor may maintain the same objective, from beat to beat, throughout the scene. One would expect, however, that another actor's beat objective would change in order for the scene to have some life. Let's imagine you are playing a scene in which you are a teenager asking your Dad for pocket money. Your super-objective in the scene is "to collect" the money. You start off asking nicely ("to charm"), then get angry ("to bully"), and finally end up on your knees ("to plead"). On the other hand, your father's objective ("to resist") remains exactly the same throughout.

For an actor, a scene becomes a series of objectives. As I noted in the last chapter, a character's objective changes when he encounters resistance. The teenager above changes from charm to anger in response to the resistance provided by his father. For an actor, a scene or a sequence of scenes or the whole drama is a series of objectives formed in response to obstacles.

Emotions, those essential characteristics of a performance, simply happen as a result of the process I've been describing. Most actors do not decide to play "love" or "anger" or "hate" or any other emotion. To play generalized "anger" will inevitably lead to a clichéd performance. Emotions arise as a result of choices about character and relationship being played out in the context of objectives and resistance. So, when you are directing, do not ask your actors to be upset or happy. Give them specific objectives instead. ("Your objective here is to understand why she insulted you" or "You really want to enjoy being with him.")

Actions and objectives

An *action*, at its most basic level, is something that an actor does—e.g., picks up a glass, signs a paper, slugs a villain. *It is a physical activity*. It is what a character actually does to carry out an objective. If my objective is to punish, my action might be to throw a punch. If my objective is to land a business deal, my action might be to telephone the client.

One way we can arrive at an objective is by submitting an action to the simple question "why?"

During the fencing scene at the end of *Hamlet*, the King executes the action of dropping poison into a chalice. Why does he drop the poison in the cup? To poison Hamlet. His objective is "to poison."

So, there are two different levels in a performance.

1. Physical activity   (e.g., dropping the poison in the cup)
2. Objective   (e.g., to poison)

It is possible in many cases to continue to ask "why?" and obtain fruitful responses. We can ask why The King (Claudius) wants to poison Hamlet. The answer will vary according to who is playing that role, but one answer might be, "Because Hamlet knows his secret." This suggests another, different objective: "To keep his secret." But, *why* does Claudius have to keep his secret? Answer: "To protect himself." Our hierarchy now looks like this:

1. Physical activity: Dropping the poison in the cup.
2. Objective: To poison.
3. Objective: To keep his secret.
4. Objective: To protect himself.

An actor playing a major role in a drama may, at a given point, find herself with several possible objectives. It is up to the actor and director to choose the strongest and most important.

Objectives should always be simple, succinct, and, as the great actor/teacher Michael Checkhov put it, "primitive"—effective at a gut level. Which of Claudius's three objectives listed above would be the most "primitive?"

We can reach still another objective by asking why: Why does Claudius want to protect himself? The answer is "to survive." Behind all objectives, super-objectives, and spines is the ultimate urgency to survive. Without it, a performance becomes, in Hamlet's words, "weary, stale, flat, and unprofitable." If an actor is giving an insipid, uncommitted performance, the director may have to remind her that, at a fundamental level, her existence is at stake.

A note on terminology: I have used the word "objective" because it seems to be the one in most common usage. In Britain some people use the word "want," which is a very expressive alternative. In America and elsewhere, the word "action" is frequently used in a number of contexts and with a number of meanings. Some people will distinguish between the physical *activity* (which is what the actor is physically doing), the *action* (her immediate objective), and the *objective* (her long-term goal).

One of my first jobs as a theater stage manager was working with the influential English actor/director Harold Lang. He said the actor had to continually ask three questions: "What am I doing? In order to do what? Against what resistance?" By asking these questions the actor was forced to consider (a) his physical action (b) his objective (c) his obstacle or resistance.

Example:

Let's look at the start of the Hector and Eleanor scene.

```
Hector is studying a family photograph Eleanor has
given him.
```

Eleanor

Objective: to introduce Hector to the family. Physical action: holding a stack of photographs. Resistance: having to tread carefully because she does not know him.

```
        It was taken a few years ago. You can
        see my brother.

        They named him Hector, after you.
```

Hector

Objective: to learn as much as possible. Physical action: looking closely at the picture. Resistance: the emotion that threatens to overwhelm him.

```
        (Touched) And he lives in Greece too ...?

        (Eleanor nods)
```

Hector

Returning the picture.

```
        You must miss them.
```

Eleanor

Placing the picture in the pile. Resistance: physically trying to keep the photographs in order.

```
        I met my husband in a village in
        Thessalonika—it took a long time for
        him to persuade me to come and try
        living here.
```

Adjustments

An "adjustment," in this context, is a new action that is carried out to overcome an obstacle, and achieve an objective.

This can be seen in its plainest form in the early silent comedies of Chaplin, Keaton, Harold Loyd, and Laurel and Hardy—comedians whose characters all want to achieve something simple and extremely important to them, but are continually frustrated. Chaplin, for instance, falls in love and then has to figure out how to spirit the girl away from under the nose of her brutish father. The father confounds Chaplin's objective (to elope) and Chaplin has to try a new way to achieve it (i.e., has to make an adjustment). In one particular beat, Chaplin's objective may be "to distract" the heroine's father while the girl makes an exit through the window, and the way he does this is to invite him to drink. When the father declines the drink, Chaplin quickly *adjusts* by trying to tell him a story, and when that does not work, he adjusts again by stomping on the man's foot.

Please note that in the above example Chaplin's objective (to distract) did not change, he simply had to adjust three times in order to achieve it.

Many of the Coen brothers' films concern characters who have to adjust to obstacles thrown in their paths (the obstacles are often the unforeseen consequences of their own actions). In a long scene near the end of *Blood Simple* (1987), the heroine has to adjust to each new strategy of her assailant in order to survive. He enters the hotel room and she flees to the bathroom. He tries to enter through the window and she impales his hand, and so on.

Putting actions and objectives together

The director's job is to suggest, not *impose*, actions and objectives. Ideally, physical actions should express, complement, or comment on objectives.

A scene is a series of physical actions and objectives. Stringing all of them together so they become a sustained performance is a large part of an actor's task. It is not easy. It requires intellectual energy as well as emotional stamina and control. Activities and objectives not only have to be perfectly judged, they must also fit into the shape of the performance as a whole. To achieve all this in a challenging role is a remarkable feat. When an actor, either by insight or by logical analysis, finds the key that pieces together all her actions and obstacles so that they are meaningful and *playable*[1], it is referred to as finding the *through-line of action* or simply finding the *through-line*. Stated another way, the through-

---

[1] An action or a role becomes playable when it makes sense to the actor. (The physical activity and the actor's understanding of her character must both be compatible.)

line is a choice an actor makes that unites everything she does and says in a sturdy chain, which supports her objectives.

Stanislavski said, "Carrying out the logic of a physical action will bring you to the logic of emotions … " So, meaningful and playable actions, organized by a strong through-line, stimulates an emotional response from an actor.

Example of a through-line

You are working on an emotional scene between a man and his ex-wife with an actor who keeps stopping half way through. He says he is having trouble justifying the anger at the end of the scene and does not want to express a forced, unreal emotion. It may that be his real problem is finding the through-line. You both may have to sit down and find those moments in the scene that would provoke his character: the line when she denigrates his carpentry skills, for example, or calls him by a pet name he has always abhorred. The actor has to use these moments to start getting riled up. Looking closely at these moments is helpful, but the actor still lacks a satisfactory emotional explanation for his behavior that will bring all these individual moments into focus. In this case, the director might suggest that he is insecure about his role as a husband. Such insecurity would certainly explain his acute sensitivity, and would justify his over-reactions. It might provide the actor with his through-line.

It would help to bring the actor playing the ex-wife into the discussion as well. No performance is given in a vacuum, and the ex-wife's relationship with the man must be considered. Working on their *relationship* might bring out her vindictiveness. If, for example, she played the scene with the intention of deliberately evoking his insecurity, then he would probably find it easier to respond with anger. Were she to adopt this tactic in the scene, she would be playing the "counter through-line"—the through-line that exists in opposition to her husband's. Villains, whose ambitions are to thwart the wishes of main characters, often play the counter through-line.

Considering beats, objectives, and physical actions in the context of the characters' relationships helps a director helps an actor arrive at a through-line.

Transitions

I'd like to introduce one more term that is related to objectives, which will help during rehearsal.

In all performances, but especially on film, where the camera offers us a privileged viewpoint, we savor watching another person under pressure. And among the moments we enjoy most are those when a character changes direction. It may be a change in an objective or an adjustment when we see someone switch from one way of doing things to another (e.g., Chaplin switching from telling the father a story to suddenly stomping on his foot). It may be a change of emotion as something happens to alter the emotional state (a character learns she has won the lottery). It may be a sudden, surprising event that stops the character in their tracks (the burglar rounds a corner and finds an angry dog in his path). Whatever the cause, the actor has changed his train of thought before our eyes. These changes are called *transitions*.

Examples: In the following examples, the moments of transition are shown by the bracketed word "transition."

1. Int.   Living Room   Afternoon

Jack enters the room whistling a current pop tune.

Suddenly he sees Mr. Dewey, the neighbor, lying unconscious on the floor. [Transition]

2. Int.   Study   Evening

                    Mother
          Alice, darling, where have you been
          all day?

                     Alice
          Oh Mummy! I've been with Jeff. He
          proposed and I accepted!

                    Mother
          (Beat) [Transition]

          How very nice for you, dear.

3. Ext   Park   Day

Reggie and his dad are walking their dog.

                    Reggie
          Dad, I'm going to a party tonight.
          Please can you lend me the car? I'll

> be very careful with it—I'll even
> wash it.

>   Dad
> Not tonight, I've got to pick up your
> sister from the station.

>   Reggie
> [Transition] Damn it, Dad! I never get to
> drive it!

4.Int   Principal's Office   Day

Jeremy knocks nervously on the door.

>   Principal
> Come in!

>   Jeremy
> You wanted to see me?

>   Principal
> Yes, I have some very important news.

>   Jeremy
> (Almost losing his voice) For me?

>   Principal
> Yes. You've been accepted by the
> college of your first choice. [Transition
> for Jeremy] And they want to offer you a
> scholarship.

A director would probably cut to Jeremy for his reaction to "You've been accepted by the college of your first choice." (Non-verbal reactions are used frequently—especially in horror movies, where victims are constantly reacting to the unexpected.)

Transitions are moments when the drama comes alive. A characteristic of good acting is the ability to find them and convey them convincingly. They are a scene's jewels, and almost every well-written scene has them. At least a couple of transitions will be found in a two-page dramatic scene, and probably more in a comic scene where a character's response frequently provides the humor.

All characters, unless they are completely incapable of being surprised and are therefore inhuman (Jedi Knights, for example), have transitions.

One of the most memorable transitions I know occurs in the middle of Sam Raimi's A *Simple Plan* (1998). I won't give away the plot, but the scene involves the shifting loyalties in a group of thieves in which one, played by Billy Bob Thornton, changes allegiance. Transitions usually occur quickly, but this one takes almost half a minute and turns the plot around one hundred and eighty degrees. With mesmerizing deliberation, Thornton's character gradually makes his decision. Credit goes to the director for recognizing the importance of this moment, and to the stunning technique of the actor for achieving it.

Jessica Lange's dazzling performance in *Blue Sky* (1994) contains so many transitions that it is hard to single out one. Her ethereal character is constantly changing mood before our eyes. Only in the last act, when she has to rescue her husband, do the transitions somewhat abate and a fixed determination overtake her.

Transitions on screen do not have to be obvious. Peter Fonda in *Ulee's Gold* (1997) deliberately suppresses them in his portrayal of a somber bee-keeper. Judi Dench in *Mrs. Brown* (1997) delivers a marvelously still performance with transitions often only conveyed by a flick of the eyes. Robin Williams gives an interesting technical performance in *Good Will Hunting* (1997), where he starts off hardly registering transitions at all and then, as his character relaxes, allows them to become more pronounced.

PART 3
Toward the First Rehearsal

9. Working With Set and Location Plans

"Two days before I began, I had nothing, absolutely nothing. Oh well, I did have the book. And a certain number of locations. What helps to give me ideas are locations." — Jean-Luc Godard on *Pierre Le Fou*

Blocking without a plan would be like building a house without a plan: The project would grind to a halt as soon as you got to the details.

Strictly speaking, plans are the designer's territory. The production designer (or her assistant) will measure the set or location and draw up scale plans. The scale is generally half an inch equals one foot (1mm = 50cm in Britain). These plans, which are revised as specific props and other design elements are agreed upon, are the basis of discussions between the director and the designer. It is important to keep in touch with the designer and communicate any alterations you require as soon as possible. If the designer is creating a new set, he might provide a scale model (see Fig. 23.1). From these small, cardboard replicas, the director can get a very good idea of how the set will look in three dimensions. However, two-dimensional plans still remain the best aid to working out actors' positions.

Designers create various kinds of plans. There are "elevations"—drawings of the walls—which are used when creating a set for a studio or a soundstage. They contain information primarily for those who will do the construction—the carpenters and painters.

There are "section plans," which are a cross-section of a set—a side view with the front wall taken out. If your designer is a good draftsman, he may also produce other sketches to illustrate his design concepts.

And there are "architectural-style plans." These are flat, two-dimensional diagrams of the set or location from a bird's eye view. (See Figs. 9.1 and 9.2). They are basically maps of the location. As with a map, any attempt to suggest a third dimension confuses the issue. If you have to draw an architectural-style plan, keep it simple. A table is a square, oval, or circle—do not try to draw its legs. Walls are simple lines, chairs are three-sided boxes with the front edge of the cushion marked on them, and trees are crenellated circles.

A director should know how to draw a plan. First of all, a designer is a luxury on student-scale productions. Secondly, directors often scout locations ahead of the designer and need to have a plan to start working from. If I am shown a number of potential locations, I always make a rough plan of each one so that, when I get home, I can compare them.

To draw a plan, you need a sharpened pencil and an eraser. (A sharp pencil or a decent mechanical pencil really does make a difference: Clear lines help avoid confusion.) A ruler is also handy if you are going to turn your rough plan into a working one.

Obtaining accurate measurements is very important. You may get the drawing wrong in your initial location sketch, but as long as you have the measurements, you can correct it. The most accurate method of measuring is to use a retractable measuring tape, but other, less scientific, methods may be used in a pinch. If you know the length of your shoe in inches, you can pace out a room. (My own shoes are conveniently twelve inches long.) If you know your span—the length of your horizontally raised arms from fingertip to fingertip—you can measure with that. (Your span is usually equivalent to your height.)

When you draw your plan make sure you include:

- All the walls and their lengths. (You need not calculate their height unless they are particularly tall or low.)
- All the windows. (A window is drawn on a plan by adding an extra line along the outside of the wall.)
- All the doors. (Doors are drawn to show the direction in which they open—the way a door opens can be very important when blocking a scene for the camera.)
- Include all important permanent features such as cupboards, fireplaces, kitchen counters, ovens, etc.
- Include all the movable features you want to use, such as tables, chairs, sofas, beds, mirrors, etc. But if you don't plan to use them, don't draw

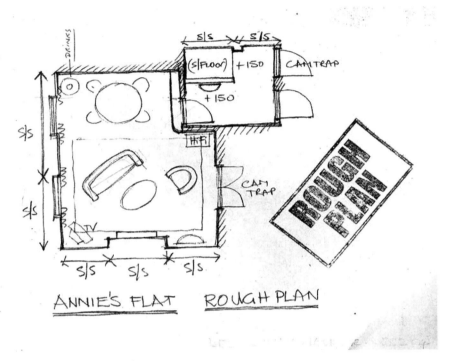

Fig. 9.1: Interior location plan

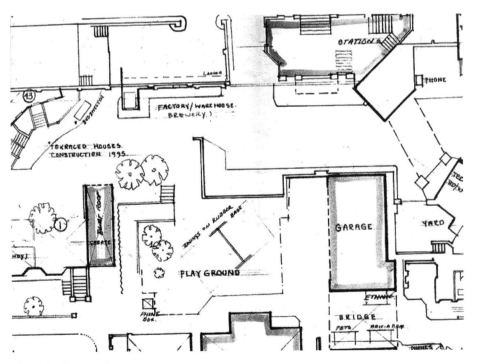

Fig. 9.2: Exterior location plan

them—they can be removed before you start shooting. Sometimes, a location is chosen for its size or its "feel" and the designer changes all its furniture.

- All electrical outlets.
- If you can, note which direction the room faces: north, south, east, or west. The position of the sun my affect your shooting.

On the rare occasion when you have to start planning your shots before discussing the set with the designer, draw in the main furnishings in the positions that suit you. A cooperative designer will provide *design props* (furnishings) that will approximate those you have drawn, and precisely where they are placed is largely up to you.

If most or all of the elements of a location are going to be used, be careful to note all the important details: If you are shooting in a bar, for instance, where is the cash register located? Where are the glasses and bottles stored? Where are the beer pumps placed? Are there any mirrors? Where is the sink? Is there a bar-flap? Are the stools movable? All these items may affect where you position actors and the camera.

Working from a plan

Someone faced with a script and an architectural set plan for the first time is entitled to ask, "How do I use them together?" The answer is imagination. The director gradually imagines the characters on the architectural plan—imagines them sitting, standing, and moving about. Specific techniques for starting a scene, and for moving actors in relation to each other and the camera, will be discussed in the next few chapters.

When you start working on a scene you don't immediately see the complete, three-dimensional picture as it might appear on the screen, because you are primarily concerned with inventing logical and believable actions for your characters. When ideas about moving the actors occur to you, you test them out on the architectural plan. You may need to revise your ideas three or four times before you are satisfied. Gradually, the characters and the set come increasingly into focus, until you are actually capable of visualizing them in three dimensions.

Robert Wilson, an artist and experimental director who has produced theatrical events with blind performers, evolved the concept of "internal" and "external" screens. The internal screen is the image as it is projected inside the head (as in a dream or as a sightless person might imagine it). The external screen is the objectified image as perceived by the eyes and ears during normal waking life. As directors, we first create our images on our internal screens through the use of imagination, and then try to turn those visions into reality for our external screens.

An experienced TV director once suggested an exercise that helps me transfer the image from the interior to the exterior screen. He advised me to sit in front of a blank television screen and project my imaginary images onto that. It was hard work at first, but eventually I saw whole sequences as if they were being transmitted.

Every director has his own way of taking the next step and working out the details of the actors' moves in relation to the camera. Pencil and eraser are generally invaluable: The director can mark various positions on the plan and later erase them if need be. One of the aids I use, especially for television series (for which literally hundreds of scenes must be prepared), is the humble thumbtack. A decent-sized thumbtack occupies about as much space as a person on most plans. I have two sizes, large and small, and use the small ones for children. The great thing about thumbtacks, as opposed to buttons or coins, is that the sharp point sticks up and you can use that to slide it around the paper. My long eraser frequently stands in for a car, and I have a large coin that becomes my camera. Using these props allows me to prepare without making messy pencil marks on the plan itself.

Storyboards and other visualization tools, which are discussed in Part 4, Chapter 23, also help to clarify the overall picture.

Two places to work on a scene

Directors traditionally work in a quiet room with a copy of the script and the location or set plans. Initially, there is something appealingly abstract about this—it is like playing a board game. In private, without a stream of questions from the crew, without lighting instruments, makeup boxes, trays of half-finished food and all the other detritus that accumulates on a set, the scene takes shape and you capture it in notes on your script. John crosses to the table. Paula stands up. John opens the will. Paula crosses to the door. John runs over and stops her. The process is clean, intellectual, and a little unreal.

A cure for this sense of unreality is to work in the actual set or on the location. This is not always possible, of course. Locations often don't become available till the last minute, and then designers have to prepare them. Television studios or soundstages are in use all the time, and the production noise from a nearby set may prevent you from concentrating. But working in the actual room where you are going to shoot can be an advantage. You get a feeling for the space that you cannot get from an architectural plan. You also notice details that are not apparent on the plan—the inkstand on the desk, the row of books on the shelf, the design of the clock, the figurine by the couch. Standing up and walking through the scene like one of the actors, you find you can use these props. You also notice that the door is not as big as you thought, and that John's entrance with the wheelbarrow may have to be rethought. Finally, you stand where you are going to position the camera, and you get a very clear idea of what the shot will look like.

Both solitary work away from the set and on-set planning are valid and valuable. The best approach is one that mixes the clarity of the first with the detail of the second.

10. Finding the Characters' Opening Positions

Scenario: You are in your room. A sharpened pencil and eraser lie by the script on your desk. Rehearsals start in a couple of days, so its time to get to work. You open your script to Act 1, Scene 1, but you hesitate. You are about to make decisions concerning the placement of actors and cameras—important decisions that will define the whole project—and the sheer magnitude of the task intimidates you.

But then you remember that you have already been thinking about the scenes and characters for a long time. You're an expert in the script, and this fact bolsters your confidence. You have already thought a great deal about the characters, so you have a pretty good idea how they'll behave in any given situation. You have divided the scene up into beats, so you understand its structure and can approach it section by section. You even know where the character transitions occur and, thus, which characters the camera should be favoring at those moments. You may not have a fully developed idea of how all the scenes will look, but you certainly have imagined some moments in detail. So, allocating positions to actors and the camera(s) is not a new phase but the logical continuation of all the good work you've done up to this point.

This chapter and the next will take you through the process of blocking, step by step. (Then in Chapter 13 we will apply these elements to a specimen script.) By following these steps, you will thoroughly consider the scene, and you will (at the very minimum) do a good job. Finally, I should reemphasize that my methods are only *suggested* modes of operation. Take from my suggestions whatever you need. There is no standard directing procedure.

Stage directions

Broadly speaking, there are two script formats. The most annoying, from a director's point of view, is the one that describes the action shot by shot.

```
Shot 53. Angle on Jenny.
She picks up a rock and throws it.

Shot 54. Medium on Harry.
He ducks and the rock flies over his head.
```

Writing this way makes it difficult for directors to visualize a script afresh. They have to disentangle the story from the way it has been put down on paper. Fortunately, this style is increasingly out of fashion today.

The most common style, and the one used in this book, rarely includes specific shot descriptions. Nevertheless, it does contain stage directions. Here is an example of a scene consisting entirely of stage directions.

```
Laraby, a mild-mannered, 30-year-old engineer with a
slight lisp, is thrown into a dark, windowless room.

He pats his pockets and finally extracts a packet of
matches.

He lights the match and looks around.

The room is bare except for some trash and several
spiders' webs.

He tries the door but it's locked.

The match burns his fingers and goes out.
```

There are different kinds of stage directions, and some are more helpful than others. The direction that introduces you to characters is certainly useful.

```
Laraby, a mild-mannered, 30-year-old engineer with a
slight lisp …
```

All this information is pertinent. It is the springboard from which the director and actor will create an expanded character.

Also very useful is the stage direction that describes action: "Laraby … is thrown into a dark, windowless room." This is a strong image and helpful to the director and designer. However, some elements here need to be questioned.

Does the room have to be "windowless"? And how dark is "dark"? What if the designer or location manager finds a room that is perfect but has a barred window? Directors must not treat stage directions like these as sacrosanct. They are *suggestions* only. They are ways an author tries to evoke a visual mood that the director is free to expand upon. The author's area of expertise is words and story; the director's is visualization.

```
He pats his pockets and finally extracts a packet of
matches.

He lights the match and looks around.

The room is bare except for some trash and several
spiders' webs.
```

This whole "business" with the match is a little cliché: The director might try to come up with something better. He might keep the trash and spiders' web idea, or maybe he'll think of something more striking.

Here is another example: You are working on a scene with a character you know enjoys cycling. In the stage directions it suggests that she is making a cup of coffee during the scene. However, as director, you might substitute some activity that expresses her character better. So maybe you have her checking an inner tube for a puncture or have her oiling the bike, which sits upside down on newspapers on the floor.

Many directors do not read stage directions at all. They go through their script crossing them all out or applying "white-out." I do not suggest this. I think stage directions are interesting because they provide insights into the writer's intentions. I think directors should look at them critically and decide if they are worth preserving. In a sense, they challenge a director to come up with something better.

The best scripts I've worked with had very few stage directions but a strong sense of movement in the dialogue. The writer had visualized the scene so clearly that, somehow, you could tell from the dialogue alone whether the character was standing or sitting, moving or stationary.

Opening positions

So much depends on the start of a scene that getting it right can be the most important element of blocking. Give yourself time to consider it. It's like high-diving: If you can get the right lift-off, then the dive itself, with all its embellishments, will follow naturally.

Stage directions can set a scene—though, as we've just suggested, they must be approached with caution. The dialogue can also indicate what's happening: At the start of a breakfast scene a character comments, "It says here the Yankees lost …" and you can assume he is reading the newspaper.

The best way to approach the start of a scene is not to think of it as a beginning. The lives of the characters extend backward in time before a scene's opening. What happened in the minutes immediately preceding their first lines? If the director can establish that, then the opening will flow from it.

Example:

Scene 12   Int. Kitchen   Morning.

Baby is in his high chair, being fed by Sherry.

> GARY
> If you feed him too much, he'll get
> fat.

> SHERRY
> But he's still hungry. Aren't you,
> Sammy?

What was happening before the scene started? If Gary is on his way to work, then maybe he's putting his plates in the sink or standing and gulping down his coffee.

If it's a weekend and Gary has slept in, then perhaps he's just entered in his dressing gown and is getting his breakfast. Or maybe they've been sitting across the table from one another for a while, and Gary's been watching Sherry feed Sam.

Use your knowledge of the characters to help you imagine appropriate opening positions for them. Different characters tend to gravitate to different places in the room. Grandma has her chair that no one else would dare sit in (and if they do, she glares at them till they get out of it!). Dad likes to sit in the easy chair by the fire. Daughter likes to stretch out on the couch, and so on. Where people position themselves in a room often reflects their states of mind. Confident people tend to occupy center stage. Nervous people hover at the edges.

Example: Where might this person be at the start of the scene?

```
SCENE 26.          INT. LIVING ROOM         NIGHT

Wendy has her head in her arms. She has stayed up
waiting for Mick to arrive. She hears his car pull
up and tentatively pats the bruises on her cheek.
```

It looks like this character has been assaulted. She is probably scared, depressed, vulnerable. It would be wrong to place her at a desk in the middle of the room or on a sofa watching the TV, because these positions are too exposed and make the character too prominent. A more appropriate opening position might be off to the side, perhaps sitting curled up defensively on the floor with her back to the wall. If you are working with a single actor in a tense beat like this, it can be helpful to ask her where she feels her character would be at the start, and adjust your plan accordingly. Most actors will appreciate this approach. But, be warned, some people have bizarre imaginations. When I asked an actor this question once, he chose to crouch under the dining-room table.

Blocking is like doing a puzzle. You have to keep at it, testing your solutions, until the whole scene falls into place. The solution can come immediately, or it can take hours to work out. Once you have settled on an approach, keep revising and adapting it till it works in every detail.

Sometimes, you come to a scene with a clear idea of one particular moment in it. Perhaps you see the climax very clearly, or you imagine a character saying a line while in a particular position in the set. In such cases, working backward from the moment you envision clearly can be very helpful. For instance, you want a character called Judy to stand in the doorway for her line, "I'll be back when you pull yourself together." So you use the half page leading up to that line to get her to the door. Perhaps you have Judy picking up her handbag from a table and crossing to the door. Then you can ask yourself, "What was she doing *before* she went to the table?" The answer to that question will take you still farther back into the scene.

This approach can be fruitful when you are having difficulty envisioning a scene, but it is also easy to lose track of the emotional line of the characters when you are working backward. When you feel you have finished, always go back and check your blocking from the beginning of the scene to the end from each character's perspective.

Visual transitions between scenes

Whenever you start to block a scene, you should know two things:

(1) What the last shot of the preceding scene was. *The outgoing shot (from the previous scene) and the incoming shot (from the present one) should not be the same.* A new scene is a fresh start in a different location, and usually there should be no ambiguity about this in the audience's mind. The transition between scenes is an opportunity for a directorial statement, and some directors plan them elaborately. At the very least, the incoming shot should be substantially different from the previous scene's outgoing shot. If the last scene ended on a closeup, for example, the new scene might start on a wide shot. And the directions in which the actors are looking or moving should also be different. Thus, if the previous scene ended with a closeup of an actor looking left of frame, the new shot should have the new actor looking right. If the previous scene ended with actors exiting left of frame, the new scene might start with actors entering right. (See Fig. 10.1)

The only exception to this rule that I'm aware of occurs when a director deliberately cuts (or dissolves) from one character to an almost identical shot of another character in order to suggest a strong link between them, as Hitchcock occasionally did. Unless handled adroitly, the effect can be jarring.

(2) When and where the character in the present scene last appeared. If the last time we saw one of the characters was ten scenes ago, when he was caught in the rain, maybe he's now beginning to sneeze or is sipping a cold remedy. In a show or a movie with a large cast of characters, losing track of a single character's thread is surprisingly easy.

With out-of-sequence shooting, actors appreciate a director who can help them find their place. A quiet word to an actor—"The last time we saw you was in that scene where you insulted George"—can suddenly bring a performance into focus (especially in a television series, where scenes are being shot in quick succession).

Having looked at the factors involved in starting a scene, the next chapter will discuss the ways you can develop a scene, especially with regard to movement.

Difference in screen direction

Last shot of scene 1   First shot of scene 2

Difference in screen direction and shot size

Last shot of scene 2   First shot of scene 3

Fig. 10.1: Screen direction and shot size

11. Movement

"Ah, now I know what you truly are," said Martha [Graham] to someone who had just walked across the floor. "You have revealed yourself to me."[1]

Words are a limited means of expression. They appeal primarily to the intellect. They are sometimes ambiguous and may be craftily arranged to give an erroneous point of view. People who manipulate words well and slyly can very often also control or subdue their facial gestures in order to conceal the meaning of what they say. If we limit ourselves to recording words and to filming faces, we omit a great deal of human expressiveness.

A girl tells a boy she loves him, but at the same time she backs away and her eyes do not rise to his face. A bully circles his victim. A family sits at a table while the mother constantly moves to and from the stove, serving them. Movement is the vehicle of subtext and relationship. This means that directors are not only composers of shots, they are also choreographers.

Seeing a character's body movements is important in order to get a total picture of that character. Dancers know this, and modern dance has been concerned with expanding the expressive potential of the human body. The dance-theorist Rudolf Laban broke down human motion into a group of eight basic gestures—pressing, flicking, punching, floating, dabbing, wringing, slashing, and gliding—each of which can be experienced in different ways. Some drama schools use Laban's theories to encourage their students to think in physical terms. The great Polish theater director Jerzy Grotowski also explored creative physical movement. And the contemporary American theater director Anne Bogart has borrowed concepts from modern dance to make performances more physical.

---

[1] Agnes De Mille, *Martha: The Life and Work of Martha Graham* (New York: Random House, 1991), p. 103.

As we will see, every scene (except, perhaps, the most fleeting of them) should have some element of movement in it. Some movie purists argue that a beautifully lit image, captured on the silvery medium of 35mm film, and projected at a magical twenty-four frames per second onto a wide screen, is in itself sufficient. This may be aesthetically satisfying, but directors who deal primarily in still images are limited , denying themselves the expressive power of movement.

In a dramatic scene, either the actors move or the camera moves, or both. It is almost always more satisfying to have the actors move, but if they cannot, then the camera should move instead. Let's look into this further.

Actor movement

Actors move for two reasons: to physically vary the shot and to express their characters and relationships. A director must therefore motivate actors at both the psychological and the physical levels.

The psychological level

In life, our movements and gestures are often produced by psychological or emotional factors—by how we feel about ourselves and other people. A father stands up to scold his son. The son slumps defensively in a chair, his arms folded in front of him. A girl sits in a bus with her shoulder turned away from the stranger in the next seat. A junior executive walks a deferential half step behind her boss. A monarch strides freely to and fro, dictating to his secretary. The secretary sits still, only his hand moving frantically across the page. An element of psychology manifests itself in almost everything we do. Anthropologists coined the term "body language" to describe exactly this form of non-verbal communication.

When we choose to move an actor, we must have a psychological or emotional reason to do so. Person A moves because she wants to adjust her position in relation to Person B.

Toward and away

The space between two actors on a set is filled with an adjustable volume of empty air. Usually, we watch the actor so intently that we pay no heed to this dramatic equivalent of what artists call "negative space"—the "empty" space that surrounds objects. If we start noticing this space, we soon see it has a constantly changing volume, altering as actors walk forward or back or lean in or away from each other.

Changes in the space between a pair of people indicate changes in relationships. Movements toward another person tend to heat up a relationship, and movements away tend to cool it down.

A scene becomes increasingly tense as people begin to invade each other's personal spaces. Extreme closeness suggests love or the threat of physical violence. People who are close together tend to talk softly about matters that are important to them.

On the other hand, distance suggests estrangement—it is difficult to play a love scene at opposite ends of a room. It also suggests formality and non-communication. The structure of many scenes can be seen as either a movement toward or a movement away from a person or thing. A couple falling in love will move toward each other. A couple splitting up will move apart. A bickering couple might maintain their distance until one of them becomes heated and edges threateningly closer. In a courtroom scene, the enforced distance between a tearful wife in the witness stand and her husband on the opposite side of the room adds poignancy.

I once worked on a television series with a director who always got this wrong. When his characters said, "I love you," they walked away from each other. When they said, "I have to go now," they got closer!

Moving and still

Scenes, in essence, are about opposition and resistance, and movement (that of the actors and that of the cameras) is a way of expressing this.

Where there is opposition, one person is usually initiating movement and another blocking or deflecting it. This can be expressed by having one person in motion and the other still. The lawyer in a courtroom paces back and forth, trying to draw out information from a hostile witness. He moves closer as he attacks and then, if foiled, moves back to his table to gather his thoughts before attacking once more.

Stillness often conveys strength and the potential to harm (not unlike the concept of potential energy in physics). Movement, especially frenetic movement, suggests mental turbulence and possible loss of control. A surgeon displays control by being the concentrated, still center of a hive of activity. In a domestic argument, one person tends to attack while the other defends: The husband paces the bedroom accusing his wife of being profligate while she sits on the bed, waiting for the moment to strike back. On the other hand, the confident detective interrogates a suspect until the suspect finally gets up and either retreats guiltily to the back of the room or slumps into the back of the chair. When one character completes a circle around another character he is, in a sense, "encompassing" him or "surrounding" him. Circling with a deliberate, constant radius often indicates control by the person who is moving. The smaller the radius, the more ostentatious the control. (The scolding principal walks round the stationary student.) On the other hand, maintaining a larger radius may indicate fear of getting too close. (The wary peasants respectfully circle the seated samurai. But even as they circle him they are assessing him, perhaps weaving an invisible web.)

It is easy to be too categorical about the meaning of certain movements and positions. Where power resides in any physical relationship, and especially those in which one character is moving and the other is still, largely depends on the intentions of the characters. A character with a strong intention can make either motion or stillness seem powerful, and a character with weak intent will always seem weaker, even when still. However, in the case of two strong opposing characters, the one who is still will inevitably appear more in control. (Compare Jodie Foster's questing FBI agent with Anthony Hopkins' incarcerated murderer in *Silence of the Lambs*, 1991.) Perhaps something about the need to display superiority through movement simultaneously undermines it. We appreciate the languorous, kinetic stillness of the lion more than the snarling activity of the hyena. The reader might compare two formidable representations of evil: Marlon Brando's monk-like Kurtz in the final act of *Apocalypse Now* (1979) and Dennis Hopper's frenetic Frank Booth in *Blue Velvet* (1986).

Knights of the British theatre, I have found, like to take strong, static positions in the center of the set. So do actors playing presidents, generals, and monarchs. Actors playing salesmen, would-be lovers, frightened maidens, and petty criminals tend to move around.

Status

In drama, as in life, there are two levels of relationship: equal to equal and superior to inferior. When relationships work well, people relate to each other as equals: They accept and respect each other's point of view, and there is no power play between them. One occasionally sees scenes like this in "professional

Here is a guideline about movement in front of the camera: *Actors move when we can see them doing so. They should not move off-shot.* If you have a wide shot of two people strolling through a garden or walking down a street, we experience no continuity problem provided both people are in the shot all the time. But, once you start shooting characters individually, be careful: If one of them suddenly appears in a different place the next time we see her, the viewer won't understand how she got there. It will look like she's "jumped" from one position to the other. On the other hand, if we have seen a character *begin to move* and then cut back to her later, we accept the fact that she has continued moving during the interim (see Fig. 11.1).

2 people in shot

Cut to 3rd person

Cut back after person 2 has moved.
(She appears to have "jumped" to another position.)

Fig. 11.1: Changing position off-shot

dramas" on television, in which two doctors sit down to discuss a case or two cops work out a plan. But, for the most part, drama is not about perfectly functioning relationships. The upsetting of hierarchy or status is a very common theme in movies. Here are three examples: *Good Will Hunting* (1997) is about the floor-sweeper who usurps the professor. *L.A. Confidential* (1997) is about detectives who uncover their boss. And *The Green Mile* (1999) is about a prisoner who is superior to his guards. A concern with people's status is not only an aspect of many films, it is present in one degree or another in almost every scene in almost every movie.

Scenes can start off with equal relationships that become unequal. Relationships can be unequal to one character's advantage from the start and continue that way. They can start as unequal in favor of one character and then become unequal in favor of the other. There are many permutations.

Rule of thumb: When blocking a scene, the dominating character should try to assume a higher physical level. This occurs naturally in certain circumstances. The teacher stands to teach while the students remain seated. The monarch confers a knighthood on a kneeling subject. A minister climbs into a pulpit to address his congregation. It is a law of nature that people dominate by height.

Over the years I've directed many arguments between couples. These scenes usually start with both people being in an equal position—lying in bed or sitting at a table together. Then the one who starts the argument stands up. Sooner or later, the other person will also rise in order not to be dominated. With both on their feet, the argument escalates until someone gives in and sits down or flees. I once tried to invert this formula and have the actor who was starting the row remain seated. But actors are trained to stand up when their characters are to dominate, so I had to change my plan.

I know of just one exception to this guideline: Occasionally, you meet characters who are so powerful that they don't have to stand up to dominate. Popes and medieval royalty did not have to stand up. By the same logic, in *The Godfather*, Brando (the head of the Corleone family) does not rise to give orders or receive guests.

The concepts and guidelines I've discussed above are designed to start you thinking about finding expressive movements. You will discover that every scene is different and few fall into easily delineated patterns. You may start out thinking that one character is dominant, only to realize half way through that it's the other.

Characters move for psychological and emotional reasons. But *psychological and emotional movement has to be tied firmly to appropriate concrete actions.* Otherwise movement can look unconvincing, as on daytime drama where actors often float around each other, settling to deliver a few lines before floating back in the opposite direction.

The physical level

One of the great advantages of film and television for an actor is the sense of physical reality they usually provide. In traditional theater, actors have to vocally project, cope with the gaping fourth wall of the proscenium, and halloo each other across the wide-open expanse of the stage. Problems of gaping space and vocal projection all but disappear on film. Instead of the auditorium, the actor faces the more intimate presence of the camera and crew. Even more helpful to the actor, everything on a film set is designed to duplicate the real thing. An actor performing surgery in the television series *E.R.* works in a very credible setting, which means that he does not have to make a great effort imagining his environment. All the surgical machinery is there; the realistically appointed room itself is not too large, and a medical advisor is on hand to ensure that the actions are authentic. If the same actor were to appear in a theatrical revival of *Men in White*, the 1930s hospital drama that set new standards in theatrical realism, he would have to call on his powers of imagination a lot more. *Television designers are masters of realism, and that makes the director's and actors' jobs easier.*

Of course, some productions deprive actors of a realistic performance environment. Movies involving electronic special effects, like in *The Lord of the Rings* series (2001-2003) and *Spiderman* (2002), to name but two, demand that actors perform against nothing more than a green wall[2] (onto which images are subsequently projected). Much *green screen* work involves stunts that occupy an actor's attention and pose a real physical challenge. Being swung across a studio in a harness in front of a green background may not be the same as flying over New York, but it concentrates an actor's mind in a similar way. Despite the proliferation of optical and digital special effects, naturalism remains the dominant mode in film and television drama, and as long as this is so, most actors will benefit from realistic props and sets.

When planning movement for your characters, use the physical reality of the set. Give them concrete tasks to perform.

---

[2] In green screen work, an actor performs in front of an evenly lit green background. The green background is then electronically replaced by selected footage or digital images during postproduction.

114

Business

Directors work hard in television and film to provide actors with appropriate physical activity, or *business* as it is often called. *Finding the right business places the characters in their environment and makes them credible.* The formidable Julia Smith, producer of several major BBC series, told me on my first job for her, "Directing in television is all about business." She was right. Sometimes, the business is obvious: If the scene is set in a hospital admissions cubicle, the doctor will be examining the patient. If it's set in a grocery store, the character will be shopping. But sometimes, if the location does not prompt you, you really have to use your imagination to invent business.

When I block a scene, I try to find something original for the actors to do. I try to discover the activity that will add something to the characterization. I scour the script for hints. Where is the scene set? What props might be handy? When absolutely nothing comes to mind, character notes can help. What are the character's interests? If she is a fanatical housekeeper, might she be sewing up a pillowcase or polishing the silver? If he is a schoolteacher, might he be correcting schoolwork? If she likes wine, could she be decanting a bottle? Then there are always the old standbys of making tea/coffee or pouring a drink. I used to think they were too obvious, but I'm now more prepared to use them. They have the advantage of not drawing attention to themselves: Compared to, say, washing the windows or arranging a butterfly collection, they are practically invisible. Different characters will also do these mundane tasks in different ways, and how a person performs business can be as telling as the business itself.

Having chosen the business, the director has to make it work. If she chooses serving coffee as the primary activity for a three-page scene, then it's no good having the character just pour the beverage once. Business has to be stretched out so that it becomes a series of mini-businesses that punctuate the scene. The great thing about making tea or coffee is that it involves many smaller actions, such as filling the kettle, turning on the stove, getting out the leaves or the grains, putting them in the pot, collecting the cups and saucers, finding the sugar, fetching the milk, and so on. These actions involve a whole series of potential moves that can take your character toward and away from another character.

Once you have established some business, encourage the actors to exploit it. If you've gone to the trouble of ordering cookies and cakes for a tea party scene, make sure the actors eat some of them! If the designer has put dolls on the bed, ask the actress to pick one of them up during the scene. If you've furnished a desk with pencils and pens, suggest that the actor starts the scene with a pen in hand, and then comes back to the desk later to put it away.

Over-doing good business is a danger. I was once directing a scene between two gossips in a remote village. The business I chose was for one of them to practice first aid on the other—bandaging a wrist. That was appropriate business and I should have left it there. But as we rehearsed this undistinguished scene, it occurred me that the first-aider should get carried away and not stop at the wrist but continue bandaging up the arm and over the head, turning her friend into a kind of Egyptian mummy. When they left the room at the end of the scene, the blind mummy got up and banged against everything on the way out. It seemed really inspired at the time, but—not surprisingly—it was cut at the producer's insistence.

Action and activity

So far, I have been using the words "action" and "activity" to mean the same thing—any business or other physical task an actor performs. However, a very useful distinction can be drawn between them.

There are two kinds of physical tasks you can give an actor to help her get through a scene. The first is the kind of everyday task that is almost invisible. If your character is a secretary, you might ask her to work at her computer. If your character is a bartender, you might ask him to polish some beer mugs. These tasks are generic—you could give them to almost any actor playing a secretary or a barkeep—and we see them on screens all the time. These tasks are sometimes called "activities."

The other kind of task expresses an *individual* character. It takes a little longer to conceive, and is often created by an actor and director working together. This is sometimes called an "action." Actions are often unusual physical tasks that work because they are perfectly justified by the character.

Hitchcock's *Spellbound* (1942) is a psychological thriller that contains a bizarre dream sequence designed by the surrealist painter Salvador Dali. One of its other delights, however, is a ten-minute scene involving Ingrid Bergman, Gregory Peck, and the legendary Russian actor Michael Chekhov. Chekhov's performance is a "tour de force" in which he demonstrates exactly how actions can be achieved in film. Every one of his physical tasks serves both to reveal the character he is playing *and* to illuminate the story. When he gets up in the morning, having sedated the potentially harmful Peck during the night, he raises the shades on the windows. As a bright, clear-thinking scientist who is at his best in the morning, this is the right action from a character standpoint. But in opening the blinds and letting the sun stream in, he is also metaphorically letting in the bright rays of reason, and dispelling the horror of the night before. Chekhov proceeds to pick up his pipe and attempt to light it (of course, a character such as the one he is playing would smoke a pipe), but becomes frustrated by Bergman's irrationality and spills his box of matches. Again, from a metaphorical standpoint, the spilled matches represent disorder being introduced into his fragile, ordered world.

Directors aspire to discover actions. Occasionally, they are assisted by actors who have the ability to elevate everyday activities into actions. A talented actor will transform as mundane an activity as preparing tea into an event that expresses his unique character.

Restricted movement

Sometimes only restricted movements are possible. What can you do with a scene that occurs halfway through dinner in a swanky restaurant? You can't have one of the diners get up to collect the dishes or serve the next course as they might at home. In this case, a number of alternatives are possible. First of all, in an intimate scene like this, where the shots are going to be quite tight—mid-shots and medium closeups mainly—the smallest movement will register.[3] So, just leaning across the table will have impact, and possibly change the shot from a single to a 2-shot (see Fig. 11.2).

Single of character talking   Character leans across table and shot now includes person 2

Fig. 11.2: How leaning in can change a shot

---

[3] Shot sizes are described in Part 4, Chapter 18.

In this situation, lean-ins, lean-outs, and the adjusting of a chair replace more exaggerated physical moves. Secondly, you can introduce movement around the characters so that the frame looks busy. Waiters and diners can create the effect of constant activity. A third option is to cut away to movement. In *The Green Mile* (1999) is a scene in which the prison officer (Tom Hanks) visits a lawyer (Gary Sinise), and the two of them sit talking on a veranda. Here, movement is introduced by cutting away to the lawyer's children playing on a swing in the garden.

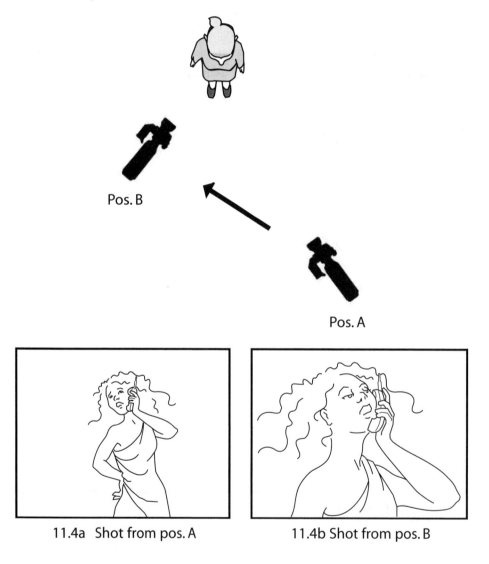

Pos. B

Pos. A

| 11.4a Shot from pos. A | 11.4b Shot from pos. B |

Figs. 11.3 and 11.4: One-sided telephone conversation

You can also introduce movement by moving the camera. For instance, one of the ways to shoot the screen's most boring scene—the one-sided telephone conversation—is to have the camera truck in and around the speaker (see Fig. 11.3). (We will discuss camera movement in Part 4, Chapter 24.)

This need to motivate movement on both the physical and the psychological levels has been emphasized in this chapter. Directors can help actors achieve this by the way they address them. *A good directorial instruction to an actor should always contain these two elements: the physical and the psychological.* "He turns on the TV to distract himself." "She moves over to the table and picks up a napkin in order to avoid his glances." "He sits down on the window ledge to be able to watch her work." "She goes to the table and picks up the knife to defend herself." Get into the habit of thinking on both levels at once.

12. Blocking Actors to Camera

Screen drama is a curious mixture of working with actors to create realistic and vivid performances and also drawing back from them to view their performances from the camera's point of view. The director starts off in rehearsal emphasizing the acting process, but, as shooting commences and the demands of production become more urgent, must take care not to let the technical process dominate. Directors should resist this natural inclination toward the camera.

The assumption of this chapter is that we are shooting with one camera. Most film drama is shot with a single camera—attention to one shot at a time allows film to achieve high production values. Occasionally, a second camera is introduced to cross-shoot in situations where two characters are arranged opposite each other, or to shoot a loose shot and a tighter shot of the same character at the same time. Having a second camera speeds up the shoot and can allow a pair of actors to give a performance together rather than have their lines recorded at different times. Sometimes, second or third cameras are introduced in sequences that can only happen once, especially action sequences such as car crashes. Television drama, particularly sitcoms and soap operas, may be recorded multi-camera in a studio. (Multi-camera shooting is discussed in Part 8.)

Some basic concepts

1. A director divides a scene up into a variety of shots. A shot is a particular piece that may be fitted together into the mosaic of a scene. (Shots have descriptions,

like "Mid-shot Marjory" or "Closeup Nat." We will discuss shots in more detail in Part 4, Chapter 18.)

2. The camera has to be in a particular place for each shot. This place is called the *camera position* or *setup*. The camera may remain in the same position for several shots. It might take a mid-shot, a medium closeup, and a closeup of an actor from more or less the same spot. When a camera changes position (creating a new setup), a certain amount of time is spent moving things around, adjusting the lighting, and rehearsing the new shot. There's a saying, "It's not the time it takes to take the takes, but the time it takes *between* the takes that takes the time to take the takes." In other words, moving to a new camera position is time-consuming (see Fig. 12.1).

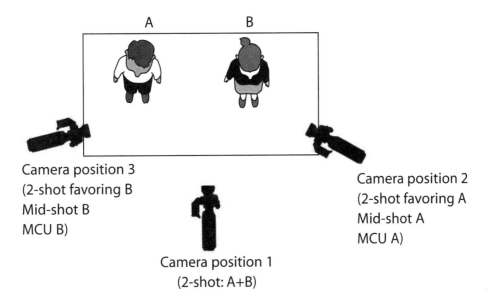

Fig. 12.1: Three camera positions (or setups)

3. A shot may be taken once or a number of times. The director usually decides if and when to "go again," though outside factors will influence his decision, such as the opinion of the camera operator and the sound recordist. When each shot is photographed (on film) or taped (on videotape), it is called a *take*. Someone, usually a camera assistant, introduces each take by reciting the shot and the take numbers: "Shot 53, Take 1" (or Take 2 or 3 or 4, and so on).

One of the keys to effective blocking is seeing both individual characters and groupings of characters as units that act as a single subject in front of the camera. These units can either remain separate or they can merge with others. Let's start with two actors.

Working with two actors

If you have only two actors, they can be placed either together or apart. This sounds obvious, but a common mistake is to block them too close to each other, causing difficulty when trying to get a shot of just one character (a *single*) without a portion of the other character impinging on the frame. A single without any trace of another actor is called a *clean single*. When a little bit of the other actor appears (an arm, or shoulder, or nose), the shot is *dirty*, and dirty shots are generally considered less visually appealing. A director working with two actors has to be definite about when they are together and when they are apart (see Fig. 12.2).

A "dirty" medium closeup   "Clean" medium closeup.   "Clean" tight 2-shot.

Fig.12.2: "Clean" and "dirty" shots

An invisible straight line always exists between two actors, connecting their noses (even if they are not facing each other). It is referred to as *the eyeline,* or simply as *the line.* Two things happen when a camera taking a single approaches shooting directly down the eyeline:

(1) The shot begins to include the back of the second character's head.

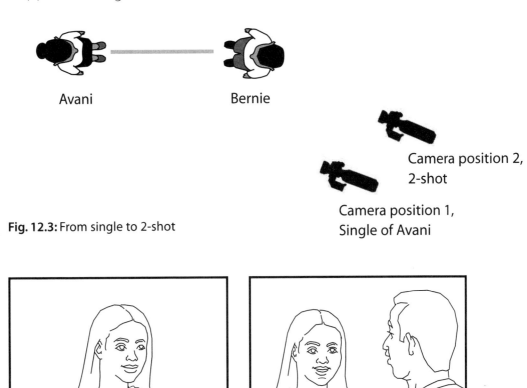

Fig. 12.3: From single to 2-shot

Camera position 2,
2-shot

Camera position 1,
Single of Avani

Single of Avani.

2-shot, favoring Avani.

Fig. 12.4: Shots from position 1 and position 2

(2) The second thing that happens when the camera gets close to shooting down the line is that we see more of the full face of the favored actor. The further away the camera is from the line, the more the actor appears in profile. This is why, when camera operators shoot closeups, they tend to move the camera toward the line.

Shots taken from close to the line emphasize one character more than the other and are called "subjective." Shots taken perpendicular to the line tend to be wider and more in profile and are called "objective." Subjective shots allow us to read a character's expressions and emotions, objective shots tend to illustrate the characters' positions relative to each other and the environment. (We will look more closely at the implication of this in Part 5, Chapter 28.)

Although I have been quite specific about actors' positions relative to one another, an enormous amount of latitude exists within these positions. Actors don't have to stand stiffly upright, looking straight ahead: They can alter their stance so that the body faces the camera (in the "open" position). (See Fig. 12.5.) They can also alter their height by sitting, leaning, or even standing on a rostrum or *apple box* (a sturdy wooden box used for raising people and objects).

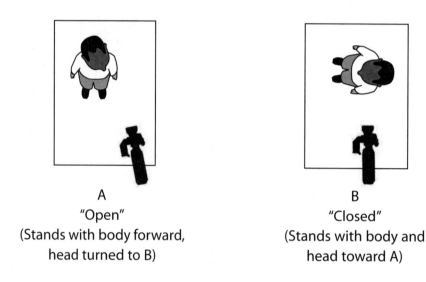

A
"Open"
(Stands with body forward,
head turned to B)

B
"Closed"
(Stands with body and
head toward A)

Fig. 12.5: Open versus closed stance

Similarly, the camera itself can be adjusted to offer different angles. Camera height can be altered. Low angles often suggest respect (literally "looking up to" a character); very low angles tend to elongate the face and are common in horror movies. High angles can show the physical relationships between people, but they can also diminish the subjects and sometimes produce a slightly comical effect.

Instead of being placed on the obvious, open side, favoring the front of an actor, the camera can also be placed on the closed side that emphasizes the character's back. In Fig. 12.6, two people are sitting on a bench. The open position allows us to see Barry's chest and gives us a good shot of his face. The closed position favors their backs and the back of the bench. It is also slightly harder to get a good shot of the face because the head just cannot turn so far round.

Fig. 12.6: "Open" and "Closed" camera positions

Working with three actors

There are three common groupings when working with three actors.

(1) Keeping all three actors separate. One arrangement is shown in Fig. 12.7.

These three characters might be seated at different desks in an office or working separately in a field.

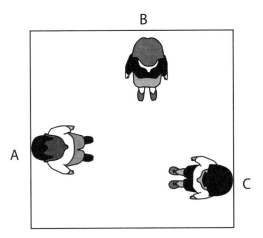

Fig. 12.7: Separate characters

(2) Group them two versus one.

In Fig. 12.8 below we have a couple of "two versus one" arrangements.

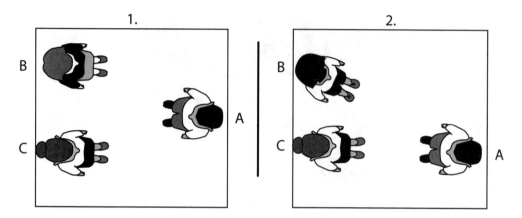

Fig. 12.8: Two versus one arrangements

In both these examples, B and C are grouped together and may be regarded as a unit for shooting purposes. These positions encourage the director to alternate between a 2-shot of B and C, and a single of A. This arrangement is very suitable for situations in which two people are opposing a third (e.g., trying to intimidate him) or a single person (A) is dealing with two others (e.g., interviewing them, giving them instructions, etc.).

Note that example 1 encourages the director to shoot A from between B and C, whereas example 2 encourages him to shoot A from below C.

3. Arrange them in a straight line.

This is probably the least interesting of the three options. It occurs most often when people are waiting in line—in a post office or a cafeteria, for instance.

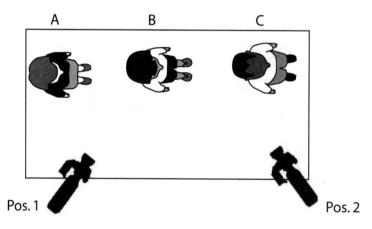

Fig. 12.9: Waiting in line

One danger with this setup (as represented in Fig. 12.9) is if you shoot a 2-shot of A and B (from camera position 2), and follow it with a 2-shot of B and C (from camera position 1), then B will be perceived to "jump" from the right side of the screen to the left.

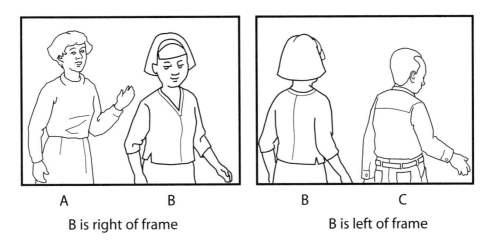

A B	B C
B is right of frame	B is left of frame

Fig.12.10: The jumping nurse in the middle

The director must either shoot all three in a group shot or cut between singles and 2-shots. Cutting from a 2-shot to a 2-shot will cause the "jumping" problem.

Working with four or more actors

When blocking larger numbers of actors, grouping becomes very important. And how you place the actors within the group is also critical. Let's look, once again, at some common arrangements.

(1) Separate positions.

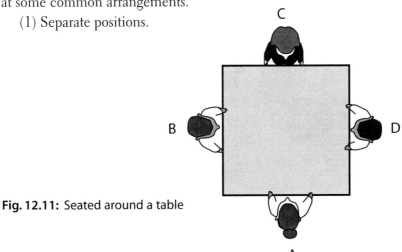

Fig. 12.11: Seated around a table

Four people are seated around a table. This can become very difficult to shoot. A large number of camera positions may be required if each addresses comments to the others. A better solution might be:

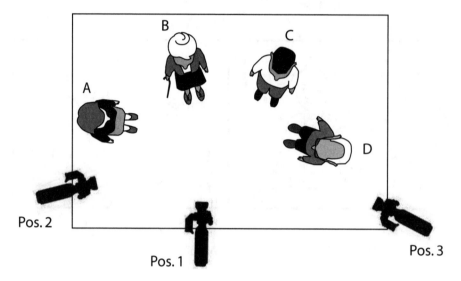

Fig. 12.12: Open fourth-wall placement

The benefit of the arrangement in Fig. 12.12 is that it provides an open side, or "fourth wall," from which to shoot. The drawback is that people don't usually sit like this in real life. If the first arrangement (in Fig. 12.11) is to work, we have to look closely at the script and see who the main characters are. We would then place them in the most convenient positions for shooting. The diagram below (Fig.12.13), assumes that B and D have the most lines, that C has something to say, and that A (who is in the most awkward position for shooting) has very little to say.

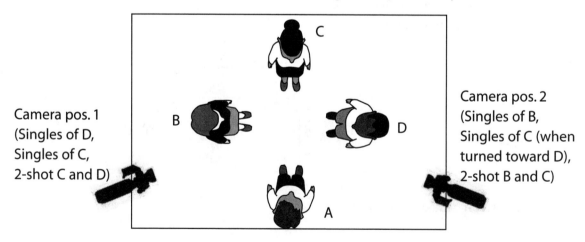

Camera pos. 1
(Singles of D,
Singles of C,
2-shot C and D)

Camera pos. 2
(Singles of B,
Singles of C (when
turned toward D),
2-shot B and C)

Fig. 12.13

(2) An easier arrangement would be 2 versus 2.

Here, two couples meet in the street or sit across from each other at a long table.

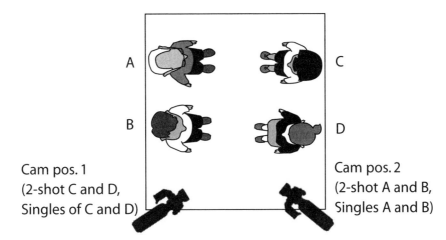

Cam pos. 1
(2-shot C and D,
Singles of C and D)

Cam pos. 2
(2-shot A and B,
Singles A and B)

Fig. 12.14

Again, placement of actors is important. Camera positions 1 and 2 work well for a conversation between B and D. They also work well when A and C address the downstage pair (B and D). But more upstage (i.e., toward the back of the set) camera positions would be needed if B and D were to turn upstage and talk to A and C (as in Fig. 12.15). So, assuming B and D do not have substantial exchanges with A and C, the arrangement in Fig.12.14 works well.

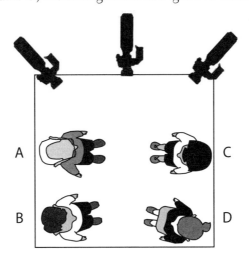

Fig. 12.15: Possible extra camera positions to cover B and D when they address A and C

129

(3) Three versus one.

Three people are ganging up on one or one person is lecturing a small group. It is almost always simplest to place the main speaker(s) downstage (i.e., nearest the camera positions).

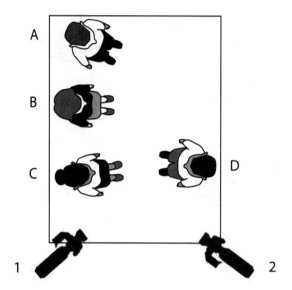

Fig. 12.16: 3 versus 1

In Fig. 12.16, the main speakers are C and D and there is also a great eyeline from A to D from camera position 2.

Again, I must emphasize that all these are general positions and you should use your imagination to vary them subtly. Unless they happen to be doing military drill, lining actors up in perfectly straight lines is usually a sign of hasty blocking.

Example:

Here is a design for a scene that uses some of the guidelines we've been discussing.

The scene is set in an open-air cafe. The principal players (*principals*) are Bill, Charlie, Peter, and Sandra, and the non-speaking actors (*extras*) are denoted by Xs. (See Fig.12.17.)

Camera positions 2 and 3 are used for the discussion between Sandra and Charlie at the table. (Peter has only one line, which is picked up separately from position 3.) Halfway through the scene, Bill leans across the counter and asks

Sandra a question. He is shot from position 3 (with 2 extras in the frame). A 3-shot of Charlie, Peter, and Sandra (with extras in the background), as they turn and face Bill, is taken from position 1.

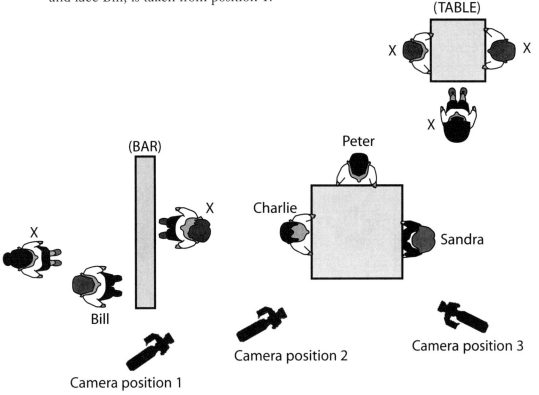

Fig. 12.17: Outdoor café

Toward the end of the scene, the extra at the counter takes his food and leaves frame. Her place is taken by Ellen (see Fig.12.18), who orders a drink (shot from camera position 1) and then turns, leans against the counter, and talks to the group at the table (shot from position 3).

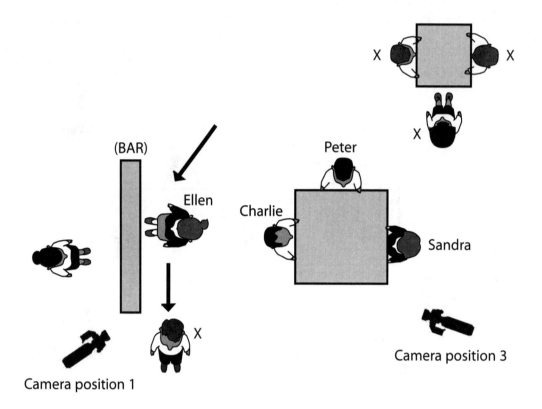

(BAR)

Ellen

Peter

Charlie

Sandra

Camera position 1

Camera position 3

Fig. 12.18: Outdoor café continued

13. Marking the Rehearsal Script (Part 1)

We now have enough information to start marking up a script for rehearsal. Our knowledge is somewhat theoretical, but we can start the important background work on character that informs everything else. Can you block a scene without considering background? Yes, you can. But if you don't want your work to be superficial, and if you want the respect of your actors, do the preparation.

What follows is a two-person scene (a *two-for*). I have chosen it because it is an acting scene rather than an action scene, which means that character and relationship play an important part in it. At two-and-a-half pages ($2^4/_8$) in standard script format, it is long enough to raise a number of issues.

There are no rules for marking up a script, but if you approach the scene using the following eleven steps, you will have a solid foundation from which to start annotating the blocking of almost any scene. (When you work on a full-length drama, you won't have to do all this work for each scene. Character descriptions, for instance, will only have to be done once.) Doing the following exercise thoughtfully should take between one and two hours.

First step

1. Read the following scene, bearing in mind what was said in Part 1 of this book about taking your time. (Spend a few minutes letting your first reactions form in your mind, and then proceed to step 2.)

INT. COFFEE SHOP   DAY

Maura and Paul, both in their mid-30s, are recovering alcoholics who are about to go to a 12-step meeting. Paul, who is married, owns a small construction company. Maura manages a branch of a temp agency.

Paul has just told her they have to end their affair.

> Paul
> You're not angry?

> Maura
> It might make you feel better, but it wouldn't stop you going, would it?

> Paul
> (He's suffering.) Look, I'm sorry. This shouldn't have started in the first place …

> Maura
> Yes it should.

> Paul
> (He stops, looks at her.)

> Maura
> This is the best thing that's happened to me in a long time. I'm not going to wish it never started.

> Paul
> (Beat) Doesn't feel so great right now, does it?

> Maura
> No.

> Paul
> It's not ….

> (Paul trails off.)

> ### Maura
> What? That you don't like me?

> ### Paul
> (Shakes his head vigorously)
>
> No. I like you a lot. That's the problem.

> ### Maura
> (Smiling) That's not a problem. Look, I've only known you for a few days, but I wish it could go on a lot longer.

> ### Paul
> I'm sorry.

> ### Maura
> We could have really hit the big time, Paul Jameson, believe me. If you were footloose and fancy-free.

Maura stands, unable to hide her upset any longer.

> ### Paul
> Where are you going?

> ### Maura
> Home. Not really in the mood for the meeting any more.

> ### Paul
> (Beat) No.

> ### Maura
> (Hesitates) Don't suppose I'll see you again. You'll find another group to go to from now on?

> ### Paul
> (Another beat) Yeah. Yeah, I guess so.

```
She hesitates a moment, then leans over and kisses
him, softly, gently.

                        Maura
            So long.

On Paul watching as Maura makes for the door. He's
completely torn apart by this. As Maura actually
gets to the door, he calls out.

                        Paul
            Maura —

Maura turns, looks back at him, tears on her cheeks.

Out on Paul.
```

Subsequent steps

2. Write down your first reactions. What was interesting about it? (Did you like the characters? Did it have a mood?) Were there any problems? (Any bits that didn't make sense? Any section you didn't like?)

3. Read it through a second time. Have you had second thoughts about anything you just wrote? Read it once again.

4. Start breaking it down into director's beats. Try to find beats that are between half a page and a page long. There should be a definite change of subject or direction between beats.

When you have identified the beats, take a **pencil** (all markings on the actual script should be done in pencil, so they can be erased) and draw a short horizontal line on the right hand side of the page, where the beats start and finish.

Next, make up a short title for each beat and write it above the line. A good title identifies the beat, making it clear to everyone exactly what it's about.

5. On a separate sheet of paper, or the back of a script page, write down each character's super objective (their objective through the whole scene).

Keep objectives active.

Use an infinitive: "To …"

Keep them short.

Make them "primitive" or gutsy.

6. Write down their objectives for each beat, using the same system. Not every character has to change his objective with each new beat, but almost certainly one will, because changes of beats often coincide with changes of objective.

7. What is the climax of the scene? What is the moment (or the moments) you must emphasize in your staging?

8. On the script, in pencil, mark where transitions occur with the symbol (**T**). Avoid the temptation to put in too many transitions. If, after you've read the scene a few times, almost every speech seems like a new thought, then just mark the major ones. Check the characters' reactions to see if you can find any non-verbal transitions too.

9. Write character descriptions for everyone in the scene. They should be a minimum of 150 words for a major character, but they can be longer. Keep your descriptions pithy and lively.

If you are in trouble, think about the list of questions under "Connecting with Characters" in Part 2, Chapter 6.

Think in terms of "He or she is the kind of person who …"

Although a certain amount of relevant backstory is helpful, a character description is not a description of what they do in the scene.

10. What is the relationship between the characters in this scene? (This is a complex yet fruitful inquiry in this case.)
    How far back does it go?
    Is it a relationship of equals, or is one person dominating the other?

11. What further research would help you understand the scene better? What research would help you direct the actors? What research might benefit the actors? What kind of research can you use: People, library, movie, TV, Internet, or other forms of research?

14. Marking the Rehearsal Script (Part 2)

H ere is the Maura and Paul scene as I might mark it. Your character objectives and other notes should be written on a separate piece of paper.

```
INT. COFFEE SHOP     DAY
```

Maura and Paul, both in their mid-30s, are recovering alcoholics who are about to go to a 12-step meeting. Paul, who is married, owns a small construction company. Maura manages a branch of a temp agency.

Paul has just told her they have to end their affair.

Beat 1
Maura's honest reaction

↓

```
              PAUL
      You're not angry?

              MAURA
      It might make you feel better, but it
      wouldn't stop you going, would it?

              PAUL
      (He's suffering.)

      Look, I'm sorry. This shouldn't have
      started in the first place—
```

                           MAURA

Yes it should.

                           PAUL

(T) (He stops, looks at her.)

                           MAURA

This is the best thing that's
happened to me in a long time. I'm
not going to wish it never started.

                           PAUL

(Beat)

Doesn't feel so great right now, does
it?

Beat 2
What might have been
↓

                           MAURA

No.

                           PAUL

It's not ….

(Paul trails off.)

                           MAURA

What? That you don't like me?

                           PAUL

(Shakes his head vigorously)

No. I like you a lot. That's the
problem.

                           MAURA

(Smiling)

That's not a problem. Look, I've only
known you for a few days, but I wish
it could go on a lot longer.

                           PAUL

I'm sorry.

MAURA

We could have really hit the big
time, Paul Jameson, believe me. If
you were footloose and fancy-free.

(T) Maura stands, unable to hide her upset any
longer.

Beat 3
Maura's farewell

PAUL

Where are you going?

MAURA

Home. Not really in the mood for the
meeting any more.

PAUL

(Beat) No.

MAURA

(Hesitates)

Don't suppose I'll see you again.
You'll find another group to go to
from now on?

PAUL

(Another beat)

Yeah. Yeah, I guess so.

She hesitates a moment, then leans over and kisses
him, softly, gently.

MAURA

So long.

Beat 4
Paul can't let go

On Paul watching as Maura makes for the door.
He's completely torn apart by this. As Maura
actually gets to the door, he calls out.

PAUL

(T) Maura—

Maura turns, looks back at him, tears on her cheeks.

Out on Paul.

Plan

The next thing we need is a plan to work from, and in order to have a plan, we have to have a set or location. This may be an opportunity for your first location scout. Find a suitable coffee shop where Paul and Maura might meet and draw a plan of it. If you know two possible contenders, draw both and think about which one might be best—which one says, "Yes!"

- Measure the location.
- Include on the plan all the furnishings you think you will need.
- Make a note of the positions of important objects (such as the coffee machine and the cash register).
- Draw the door and show which way it opens.
- Go home and make a fair copy of the plan.

For a complete location checklist of items to include in your plan, see Chapter 9.

If you do not have a coffee shop handy, then you must become your own designer and create one. This is also an interesting exercise. At the very least, you will begin to appreciate how hard it is to be a good set designer.

Here are some suggestions about how to proceed.

- What kind of coffee shop would Paul and Maura choose to meet in? Try to remember cafés you have been in. Make a quick sketch of two of the most suitable ones. Which layout is preferable?
- Does the design you favor allow you to move the actors and camera and get the shots?
- Draw the plan in detail.
- Note all the design props you'll need—tables, chairs, counter, coffee machine, etc. Draw them in.
- Be precise. Include measurements and draw in features like windows and doors.

Marking moves

Next, using your coffee shop plan and your knowledge of the characters and the scene, imagine the action.

The moves in the scene with Paul and Maura are fairly straightforward and indicated in the stage directions. Do you agree with the stage directions? The first half of the scene takes place at a table and is therefore quite static. Do you see any small moves there? (Perhaps the best course of action would be to rehearse it with the actors and notice where they tend to lean forward and back.)

When you have thought it through, quickly mark the moves on the script in pencil. Put in directions like "stands" and "crosses to door" so you don't forget them as you proceed. In the example below, I have noted the moves I've chosen. I've also placed two lines under the places where I've decided to go with the stage directions.

Gradually, you will learn what abbreviations work for you. In theatre, television, and film, the term *cross* (an actor's move) is commonly shortened into "x." Other common abbreviation are "l" (left), "rt" (right), "u's" ("upstage," the area of the set in the background of the shot), and "d's" ("downstage," the area of the set nearest to the camera). Thus an actor can "x d's rt," which means he "crosses downstage right"—a diagonal move (left to right) from the background to the foreground.

Note: The theatrical terms "stage left" and "stage right," meaning left and right as perceived by an actor standing on the stage looking at the audience, do not exist in film and television—all directions are in relation to the camera. Thus "left" is "camera left," unless otherwise stated.

Paul has just told her they have to end their affair.

> **They start separated**
> **Beat 1**
> **Maura's honest reaction**

                    PAUL
        You're not angry?

                    MAURA
        It might make you feel better, but it
        wouldn't stop you going, would it?

        _____

                    MAURA
        We could have really hit the big
        time, Paul Jameson, believe me. If
        you were footloose and fancy-free.

> **Beat 3**
> **Maura's farewell**

(T) [**Maura stands**, unable to hide her upset any longer.]

                    PAUL
        Where are you going?

        _____

Beat 4

Paul can't let go

MAURA

So long.

M xs to door

On Paul watching as Maura makes for the door. He's
completely torn apart by this.

Turning to the plan once again, go back over the moves. At this point it's important to ensure:

- That the moves work in the set. That there is enough room for the actions to occur smoothly and without obstruction.
- That you know exactly where in the script the moves occur.
- That the moves work from an emotional and psychological point of view. Are they consistent with the characters? Would the characters do that?
- That there are good physical reasons for the moves. That people are moving in order to do something definite.
- That there are enough moves to make it interesting. Should you add moves? Have you put in too many?

This is when I use my thumbtacks to plot out the actors' moves. Using a thumbtack (or button or coin) for each character, go slowly through the scene, examining all the moves. Go over it at least three times, being as critical as you can. Ask yourself, "Is there anything I can improve?" If you had to change one thing, what would it be? Think of your favorite director and ask yourself how he/she would approach the scene.

Add the camera

We will concentrate more on shots and camera placement in Part 4. For now, just make sure that what you have plotted can be covered with a camera. If you have visualized certain shots, where would you place the camera to get them? If you do not have specific visuals yet, think about where your camera positions might be.

Go over the scene once again and begin to imagine what it might look like. Pay special attention to the moments when an actor's movement begins— the start of the cross, the precise moment Maura does her rise. Is it still working exactly as you had planned?

Noting moves in the script

When you are satisfied with your solution, add the moves to your script in diagram form. Once again, use pencil. If you make marks on your script in ink and then have to change them, the script rapidly becomes indecipherable. (When I started directing, I used to keep all my old, discarded, notes on the page because I was scared of losing any information. I soon realized a better and less-confusing method was to erase and start afresh.)

The first things that have to be marked are the characters' opening positions. This is the one and only time that the set plan has to be drawn on the script, and only its most important features need to be included.

• On the top left-hand side of the page, under the "Int. Coffee Shop" line (known as *the slug line*), draw a reduced version of the set plan. Keep the diagram small, only about 2 or $2^1/_2$ inches on its longest side. Mark on it the table where your characters are sitting, the door, the positions of the other tables, and the serving counter (if there is one).

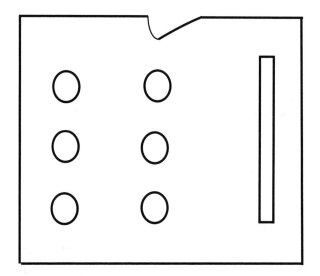

Fig. 14.1: Coffee shop

• Now draw your characters on the reduced version of the set plan on your script. Just use a single letter to denote them. Maura is "M," and Paul is "P." (The square bracket behind them indicates that they are seated in chairs.)

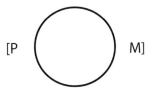

Fig. 14.2: Marking seated figures

- Consider whether any other characters are on the set. The presence of other people will obviously affect the way Maura and Paul play their scene. Someone is probably serving behind the counter. Add extras as necessary, using an "X" to represent them.

  From now on, every time a character moves you will draw a diagram in the script opposite where the move occurs. Some directors mark all the moves on a single master diagram and number them. The numbers then go into the script where the move occurs (see Fig. 14.3). The trouble with this method is that it is very easy to get confused. In a scene with several moves, valuable shooting time is lost finding the original diagram and then working out the numbers.

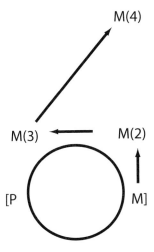

Fig. 14.3: Noting moves on a master plan

The much simpler method is to mark each move in the script as it happens.

In the section from the script below, Maura's new position is marked and an arrow shows new movement. There is also an asterisk in the text to show exactly where the move occurs. As we will see when discussing continuity, in film and television (as opposed to theater) knowing *exactly* when a move takes place is very important. If during the rehearsal, the actor moves at a different point from the one marked in the script, then the director needs to clarify this with her.

MAURA

We could have really hit the big
time, Paul Jameson, believe me. If
you were footloose and fancy-free.*

(T) [<u>MAURA STANDS</u>, UNABLE TO HIDE HER UPSET ANY
LONGER.]

Beat 3

<u>Maura's farewell</u>

M]

PAUL

Where are you going?

On Paul watching as Maura makes for the door. He's
completely torn apart by this. As Maura actually
gets to the door, he calls out

PAUL

(T) Maura –

<u>Maura turns</u>,* looks back at him, tears on her
cheeks.

(He gets up.) * Wait a minute …

Out on Paul.

M

[P

All these moves will be discussed with the actors. In this case, they are very straightforward and should present no problem. Do not get obsessive about actor positions at this stage. Once you have blocked the scene, check it and then go on to the next one. If you rehearse, you will have time to come back and reconsider. If rehearsal has to take place on the set, make sure you start plotting the scene as early as possible and leave time to return to it a few days before you shoot it. It is much better to come back to a scene with a clear head than to try and get it absolutely perfect in one pass.

Props

Note down the *action props* (those objects the actors actually handle) that are going to be used in the scene. Write a list of them at the top of the script page, above the slug line. Having it in that visible position enables you to tell the prop person exactly what you need when you start rehearsing.

The action props needed in this scene will include: Coffee cups and saucers, teaspoons, a sugar bowl, coffee, milk, and Maura's coat and handbag.

The script is now ready for rehearsal. However, it is not yet a shooting script. We will address shooting considerations in Part 4, at which time we will return to the script and mark it for shooting. You might want to look at my completed version of the script in Part 4, Chapter 25, to see how all the elements have been incorporated.

Blocking during rehearsal

Directing, at its most basic level, is about not making a fool of yourself in front of a crowd of people. What actors and crew dislike most is a director who is unprepared. The time pressure most directors are under nowadays makes it imperative for them to take charge on the set.

This does not mean that they impose their will on everyone else. It means that they present a well-thought-out plan for discussion— a plan that, by virtue of its clear logic, brings everyone on board. Directors who have done their homework have nothing to fear. They know they have considered every angle. They are able to adapt if need be. When a member of the cast or crew has a better idea, they recognize it, change direction, and run with it.

However, there is one situation in which blocking a scene in advance may not be the best option. If you have the luxury of rehearsal, or you have set aside enough time on the set, it is sometimes advisable to block a two-person scene with the actors themselves. A freshly blocked scene can have spontaneity. It can draw commitment from actors who create the scene with you. Actors who are used to working this way in the theater will appreciate it. It is also healthy for directors (that species of control-freak!) to occasionally experience the excitement of surrendering control. However, to do this well you must have a very solid grasp of the scene so that you will immediately recognize when moves or actions are inappropriate. Ergo, your essential homework on the characters and the script must still be done.

If you work out the blocking of a scene with the actors, make sure you note down the actors' positions on your script before they leave so you can add the camera positions later. Also, at the end of the rehearsal, warn the actors that some positions might change once you have considered where to place the cameras. I've always enjoyed blocking scenes afresh, but I would not try it with more than two actors. The potential for complication greatly increases each time you add another character.

15. Improvisation

"To relax our attention into the present moment is extraordinarily simple, but, for most of us, it demands a lifetime of practice." — Ruth Zaporah (founder of "Action Theater")

There are two opposite approaches to creating a performance. The first is textual. At one extreme, this is exemplified by the works of classical authors, such as Shakespeare, Racine, Molière, Chekhov, and others, to which we accord great respect. A textual approach often places faithfulness to the author's words above other production values.

The second and opposite approach is that of creating a performance on the spur of the moment. This is exemplified by seventeenth-century Italian Commedia del'Arte, Russian circus clowns, and certain mime artists. The work of the best improvisers is not produced by inspiration alone, it is also the product of prolonged physical and technical training.

Most modern theatrical performance aspires to combine both approaches.

Should a rehearsal include improv? Almost always. Especially if the scene is a page or more in length. To achieve an expressive performance, an actor has to do more than simply recite a text. Improvisation is an infusion of energy. It elicits a whole-body response from actors and stops them acting "from the neck up." It also deepens characterization, enriches relationships, focuses objectives and is truly fascinating to perform. The influential American director Harold Clurman wrote, "There should always be a degree of improvisation in the making of a production. No matter how traditional the rehearsal methods. If such a margin of freedom were not allowed, [the production] would be reduced to mere recitation of lines in conjunction with the most primitive sort of illustration."[1]

---

[1] Harold Clurman, *On Directing* (New York/London: Touchstone Books, 1972), p. 101.

Improvisation requires a lack of self-consciousness on the part of the improviser. I have worked with actors who have declined my invitation to improvise. When I told one actor that I liked to do improvs, he looked at me quizzically and said, "You're not going to ask me to be a tree are you?" I directed a production once with three main characters, a middle-aged man, a young girl, and a young man. The middle-aged character was played by an actor of considerable technical ability whom I admired, but he refused to do improvs. The two younger actors were happy to improvise. The result was a production with two distinct styles: The scenes with the senior actor were workmanlike and effective, while the scenes between the younger actors were astonishingly realistic and powerful. If you intend to use improv (as I hope you will), make sure you cast actors who are willing to engage in the process.

For many people, improvisation is synonymous with the game-playing that goes on in high school drama programs, and is seen on television in the show *Who's Line Is It Anyway?* These "theater games" (promoted by Viola Spolin, Keith Johnstone, Howard Barker, and others) are certainly one aspect of improv. They emphasize the fun side of the technique and teach important lessons about storytelling, relaxation, mental and physical agility, and about being responsive to others. Many of these games derive directly from established acting techniques (which we have already discussed), such as considering "status" and making different types of transitions. I have used exercises like these in children's drama to help kids overcome nervousness and start relating to each other. They really work. But I also discovered that it's no good just doing it once or twice with children—it has to be done every day before rehearsal and during shooting as well.

Structure and rules

Improvisation is spontaneous and unpredictable and, therefore, works best if you have a definite structure to contain it (who, what, where, and why). As with any scene, your improv requires *a setting*, which the director should describe: "You are in the company board room. It's formal and slightly imposing, with pictures of past CEOs on the walls. There is a long table in front of you. The door is over there. There's a window behind you. There are glasses of water on the table."

To work effectively, improv also requires *defined characters*: "You are a dedicated, hard-bitten, union negotiator who has been doing it for twenty years." It also often helps to give actors general *character objectives*: "Your objective is to get the best possible deal from this boss."

To propel them, actors need to know *the basic story leading up to this moment*: "Your members have been striking for two weeks. They can't go on much longer without suffering real hardship. It looks like the owners might be willing to compromise. This is your last chance."

Improv has two rules, which a director must enforce. The first is that no one should get so carried away that someone gets hurt—physically or emotionally. This is very important. It engenders confidence in the process itself and allays the fears of actors who might be nervous.

The second rule is that there should be no denial. If, during the improv, I tell you that I'm a bus driver, you cannot say, "No, you're not. You're a nuclear scientist." If you tell me you have a sister called Marge, I have to accept it (even though I know your real sister is called Pru). If I say, "I feel seasick," you should not say, "No, it's only the oysters you had for lunch."

Directors must *not* let an improv *exceed its natural length*. When an improv is flagging, the director should have no hesitation bringing it to an end. A three-minute improv is quite long enough for those who are inexperienced. I find eight minutes is a long improv, even for more experienced actors. Sometimes, if it's a group doing the improv, it can last longer, because others pick up the thread when one person drops it. The more experienced the group, the longer it is able to sustain an improv.

Some directors ask their actors to stay in character (improvising) as they go shopping or interact with strangers on the street. Extended improvisation requires longer rehearsal periods. Some actors automatically do it as part of their preparation.

Opportunities to use improvisation

Here are some situations in which improvisation might be useful.

When no sense of a strong relationship exists between two characters: either they are not relating to each other physically or you sense that their relationship is superficial

One way to deepen two characters' interaction is to create some important event they have in common. The Maura and Paul scene we've been looking at in the previous chapters assumes a strong relationship. It would be very hard for any actor to come to this scene for the first time and produce the required intensity. The director can help the actors by suggesting they improvise some important event in the past. Possible scenes might be the moment they met at Alcoholics Anonymous or their first post-AA meeting in the café, which ends with their agreeing to see each other again. If we chose to do the AA meeting, we might set it up as follows:

> "Paul, this is your second AA meeting, but the first time you actually stand up and confess to being an alcoholic. It's a big moment. It will take a lot of courage to get up there and admit it. It will be painful to talk about your addiction and the pain you've caused your family and others.

> "Maura, you have been attending for three months. You noticed Paul the last time he came, but he was very quiet then. This is the first time you will hear him speak. As someone facing similar problems, and fighting addiction, you are in a very vulnerable state.

> "Here is the table Paul is sitting at, alongside the person who is conducting the meeting. There are about fifteen other sympathetic people in the room to hear you. Maura, how about sitting here?"

If the improv is successful, it will give the performers emotions and feelings about each other that they can bring to the scene. One good improv can enliven a whole interaction between characters. If this happens, there is no need to create other incidents—which would only tend to dilute the effect. However, if the director feels a specific quality is still missing in the characters' relationship, then another improv might be in order. Thus, in the scene above, if the director wanted more physical tension between Paul and Maura, he might improvise a scene in the café where they find themselves physically attracted to each other.

Directors often get ideas for improvisations during rehearsal. Nevertheless, I tend to have one or two possible ones up my sleeve in case inspiration deserts me.

When a group of actors are working together and their relationships are superficial

When working with a group of actors, some of whom might have small roles, helping them create performable characters is important. A sentence or two to day players is often enough to help them bring their characters to life. But, when acting in concert, they may not be convincing. The group may be portraying a team of firemen or radical '60's students or workers who share the same open-plan office. The social interactions within these groups can be very complicated, so it is important to give the audience a sense of that. The director can improvise a social event that brings the whole group together—an office party, for example, or a workplace award ceremony or a crisis to which they all react in different ways. In this case, either the director must assign objectives or, if the actors already have a strong grasp of their characters, allow them to invent their own.

John Cassavetes improvised extensively in his movies. A memorable scene near the beginning of A *Woman Under the Influence* (1974) is the one in which a large group of workmen unexpectedly drops in on Gena Rowlands' character for dinner. There is a tremendous sense of individuality among all the workmen, but, at the same time, there is the sense that they have been working together professionally as a unit.

When working with individual actors on deepening their involvement with their characters

Have you ever watched a performance and felt, "It was interesting, but I didn't believe he was really a policeman" (or steel-worker or schoolmaster or symphony conductor)? An improvisation can help remedy that problem. The actor playing a police detective can experience (through improvisation) a boring stakeout; the actor playing the workman can enact a demanding physical task; the actor playing the schoolmaster can attend middle school and re-experience the highs and lows of a school day, and so on. Then they can bring the results to their performances.

Here is a slightly different situation. An actress is playing a very nervous young girl who loves going to parties. There is something untrue about her performance —she is playing all the obvious choices (false laughter, mannered gestures, rushed speech). The next day the director calls her in early and suggests an improv. The improv deals with what is *not* written in the screenplay—what happens to her character when she is alone in her apartment *between* parties. The actress discovers that she is separated from her parents, depressed, and listens to the radio to stop herself crying. She comes to realize that going to parties enables her to create a new identity, one in which she feels glamorous and in control.

Working on the physicality of a role

Actors, especially in their first performances on screen, often choose to play a scene safely. This way, even if they do nothing memorable, at least they won't do anything embarrassing. The director has to work with such actors to loosen them up and make them feel physically at ease on the set. Harold Lang, the 1960s English experimental theater director, used to get his actors to compose a dance that expressed their characters. (Lee Strasberg also had a "song and dance" exercise that helped actors break their verbal and physical habits.) This might be considered too outlandish for some movie actors, but a director can certainly suggest animal-types as models for movement. (To an actor whose portrayal of an inn-keeper may lack sufficient weight: "Make the character more like a bulldog." To an actor whose performance needs to be lighter: "Try to make her more bird-like." The metaphors we use every day support this way of thinking. Sleuths are said to "ferret" out information, and the pirates in *HMS Pinafore* imagine they have a "cat-like" tread.)

I have used Michael Chekhov's "moving center" exercise with actors who have had difficulty finding a physical approach to their roles. The actor stands in a relaxed manner, feet slightly apart, while the director suggests that he imagine a small, circular metal weight in his chest. The actor then moves that weight around till he thinks he's found where the character might have it—in the left arm, the shoulder, the knee, wherever. The slight accentuation this gives to one part of the body often helps a character come to life physically.

When clarifying the opening of a scene

Scenes can open in the middle of an activity such as a conversation or while a character is watching television or with a scream of anger and frustration about something that has just occurred. To have a leisurely opening to a scene with two characters wandering onto a set and gradually getting acquainted is unusual, especially in film, where time is condensed and the story is told in shorthand. The pace of movies is generally so staccato that we often cut to or from scenes just as something is about to happen, has happened, or is in the process of happening. This means that actors have to start their performances at a somewhat elevated level, with their emotions already engaged. This is not easy. Consequently, actors sometimes begin scenes on a false note. Directors can start to remedy this problem by improvising the beat prior to the opening of the scene, so the actors have a chance to get into stride.

Improvising the previous beat is quite a common practice, and actors appreciate it. It involves finding a few moves and usually inventing a few lines of dialogue. This work will not appear on screen (unless it's so wonderful that the director decides to keep it), so the director and the actors can be as bold as they like—especially if they are working up to a particularly emotional opening. If you improvise prior to a take, ask the actors to pause briefly before saying the first scripted words of the scene you are shooting. This will enable the editor to cut into it cleanly.

For scenes that start on a lower emotional level, have a character improvise her pre-screen life when she's on the set. Thus, if a scene starts with someone slumped in front of the TV, that person can enact some of the mundane activities leading up to switching it on. Exciting stuff! But this helps the actor feel at home, and sometimes something positive emerges. For instance, instead of just slumping in a chair, the actor may discover that she has just finished dinner, has her tray on the floor, and is sipping wine. This in turn helps to motivate her boyfriend, a teetotaler, who is about to knock on the door and tell her he's ending their affair.

If the scene were to start with two characters, instead of one, watching television, the director might explore how both characters arrived there. Who chose the program? Did they battle over the choice? Are they watching TV to avoid conversation? Answering questions like these would indicate not only their physical relationship to each other (how they are sitting), but also the atmosphere in the room in which the scene develops.

Filling in an omitted scene

Not all the action in a film or program takes place in front of the camera. People meet and events occur that are only referred to on screen. They may, however, be significant moments for the characters involved and, therefore, well worth improvising.

The Paul and Maura scene is a case in point. The declaration that they must stop seeing each other happens off screen, and we are only privy to its repercussions. A director might improvise this off-screen scene. As it so happens, the omitted scene in this case is also the preceding beat, which doubles the case for an improv.

When a scene seems too wordy

In some movies and television series, the words get in the way. This is a particular problem with soap operas and even some comedy shows. When conflict occurs in such shows, it is often more verbal than physical. To correct this, the director can try improvising the scene he is working on without using the scripted words. Before the scene starts, the actors are reminded of the beats and their objectives. Then they improvise the scene in a physical way before going straight back to the scripted dialogue. This encourages actors to concentrate more on objectives, physical actions, and subtext, and it helps highlight the real conflicts in the scene. Hopefully, when the actors return to the text they will be less confined by it.

Harold Lang used to adopt this attitude toward Shakespeare. "We have to earn the right to speak the verse," he said. When he eventually added the words, his actors knew exactly what they were intended to achieve. Lang also believed in paraphrasing—looking at difficult lines and putting them into your own words. Paraphrasing is a very useful tool for clarifying lines and uncovering subtext. Of course, Lang's company always returned to Shakespeare's text for the actual performance.

When creating a scene through improv

Authors shape a script and put elegant phrases into characters' mouths. Directors and actors, though equally creative, do different things.

Some directors dream of improvising their projects, and thus controlling the whole process from inception to completion. The problem with improvised drama is that, unless it is ruthlessly controlled, it can easily become self-indulgent. Not all directors who improvise are aware of the guidelines cited at the start of this chapter: Improvisation works when there are strong, well-defined characters. It works when actors know what they have to achieve in the story and how they are to achieve it. (Plot and objective.) It works when the director exerts control over pacing, so not all the scenes are played with the same intensity.

One way to create improvised drama is for an author to write a detailed treatment that omits the dialogue. With a strong, well-thought-out scenario, the director and the actors can produce startling results. If possible, the author should be present during the improv, helping to incorporate the actors' insights and dialogue into a finished scene.

This approach can be applied to television series and soaps. When I was working on my second TV series, instead of "wrapping"[2] when I finished early, I would keep the cast and crew and improvise scenes. The scenes were often delightful because, freed from the specificity of the script, we could go wherever the sunlight and scenery invited us. When I took these back to the script editors and producers, they mumbled, "We can't have this. It does away with writers."

---

[2] To "wrap" is to end a day's shooting. Crews also "wrap a location" in order to go on to the next one—a process that is repeated until the last day when the "final wrap" is called.

On the other hand, not all the scenes worked. Without some sort of script to improvise from, many of the situations did not advance the story. After a while, I realized that an early finish was an opportunity for hard-working people to go home and see their families, so I stopped my improvs. However, I have always felt that there is room for a few semi-scripted improv scenes in TV series because: (1) They can inject an element of freshness and unpredictability into a tired format. (2) No one knows the characters better than the actors themselves, who have, in some cases, been portraying them for five, ten, or twenty years. (3) Actors on these programs are always complaining about their lines, and this gives them an opportunity to co-create them. (4) It would raise the aesthetic values of the show by breaking the rigid format and providing new creative opportunities. Of course, the problem is that every time you improvise a scene, it adds at least half an hour to the shooting schedule. It takes a very brave producer in today's climate to support such an expensive proposition.

Directing an improv

The director sets the guidelines for an improvisation and gets it underway. The atmosphere should be as informal and relaxed as possible. Improvisation is not an intellectual exercise. It is physical, emotional, and very often sheer fun. The director's attitude should always be encouraging and supportive. She watches carefully, noticing what the actors are coming up with and how that might be applied to the scene. With luck, the improv will turn up some exciting new moments (some discoveries) that will clarify the individual characters' attitudes and relationships. The director is looking for "real" moments—moments of vulnerability or honesty—on which she can build.

Directors should be wary of a couple of improv's common pitfalls. If the actors are self-conscious, the improv will be clever but superficial, and of no real help to the scene being considered. And an improv can also become unfocused. If it wanders off-track and inappropriate material is introduced, the director should bring it to an end.

Some questions to bear in mind while watching an improv:

- What particular moments were successful?
- What particular piece of acting was truthful and effective?
- What is the tone of the improv? And does it differ from the scene?
- What new information is surfacing about the characters?
- What new information is surfacing about their relationships? How would I describe the resulting changes to the relationships?

When an improv is over, the director usually thanks the actors and finds something encouraging to say. Then, she will bring up the one or two most important points she noticed and discuss them. The actors will also want to say something. The director can sum up the improv by suggesting the application of certain specific discoveries to the scene at hand (e.g., "Let's keep that moment when you were frightened by what you thought he was going to say."). Always strike while the iron is hot—go straight back to the scene itself and apply the lessons learned.

Improvs present actors with a double challenge: To respond freshly and spontaneously to an improv exercise, and then to incorporate its discoveries into the performance itself without losing that precious sense of freshness. Actors—especially those with little experience at improvisation—may take a little while to fully and successfully assimilate the discoveries they make during an improv. A director helps an actor by reminding him of what he has done and encouraging him to commit to it.

16. Gauging a Performance in Rehearsal

"The correct theatrical means, when discovered, gives the author's work a true reality on the stage. One can study these means, but the form must be created, must be the product of the artist's great imagination—fantasy. This is why I call it 'fantastic realism.' It exists in every art."—Eugene Vakhtangov.[1]

Assessing a performance, whether a rehearsal or a take, is fundamental to directing. So much directing depends upon a director's individual tastes and vision, because one man's catharsis is another man's melodrama. So here I'll confine myself to suggesting criteria and procedures for use during rehearsal. (I will return to this subject again in Part 5, Chapter 30, where we discuss a director's focus during shooting.)

I think what a director looks for above all in a performance is "truth." One interpretation of truth is the sense that what we are seeing is thoroughly lifelike. We have come to expect characters in movies to behave outwardly like our acquaintances and ourselves. This way of judging a performance is a great asset for Hollywood because both filmmakers and audiences can agree on it. As we will see when discussing the history of film acting (in Part 7), the dominant Hollywood acting style for the past fifty years has been Stanislavskian naturalism, especially as interpreted by the American Method school. It is a style that emphasizes personal experience and psychological realism.

There are degrees of truth. A distinction is often made in the performing arts between naturalism and realism. Naturalism portrays real objects and events,

---

[1] Rubin Simonov, *Stanislavsky's Protégé: Eugene Vakhtangov* (New York: DBS Publication, Inc., 1969), p. 147.

but it tends to glamorize them. Realism shows reality with its warts and all. American soap operas are naturalistic. I once directed episodes of a British soap opera that were set in an abortion clinic—and those episodes were realistic. The difference has to do with the treatment of subject matter, but it also has to do with mood. *Friends* is somewhat naturalistic. The HBO TV series *Oz* tends to be realistic. Most Hollywood movies are naturalistic. The work of the European Dogme[2] filmmakers tends to be realistic.

Most Hollywood productions are naturalistic, but not all. Some abandon verisimilitude altogether. Musicals, science fiction, and horror movies are genres where the laws of verisimilitude are not always strictly applied. (Though, when events in the *X Files* were at their most bizarre, Molder and Scully still maintained extraordinary, naturalistic composure.) There have also always been a handful of directors and producers willing to challenge the status quo. In recent years, movies like *Edward Scissorhands* (1990), *The Truman Show* (1998), and *Pleasantville* (1999) have been stylistically refreshing. Non-American filmmakers are less constrained by the standard of naturalism. When we made *Tartuffe* and *Moliere* for the BBC and RKO in 1982, we experimented with transferring a theatrical style to television. In a sense, what makes a performance convincing is not its degree of realism, but the degree to which the actors believe in what they are doing. The great Russian director Eugene Vakhtangov strove for a style that combined the free play of an actor's imagination (fantasy) with the discipline of truth (realism). He coined the phrase "fantastic realism" to describe it, and it has generally been considered one of the touchstones of great acting.

There are signs that the American theater, which has also been heavily influenced by Method acting, is becoming more open to alternatives. For instance, the theater director Anne Bogart has been evolving a style that draws on Asian, European, and American theater traditions (as well as dance) to produce works that are more physically expressive and less dominated by the text. Sooner or later, a reformation in theater acting could influence screen performance as well.

Watching a performance

As I watch a performance, I relax and empty my mind of preconceptions. I look for the slightest false note. Stanislavski once commented on a performance, "It was truthfully done. But you added something to the truth, a scarcely perceptible

---

[2] Dogme is the name chosen by a group of filmmakers, including Lars von Trier and Thomas Vinterberg, who advocated a rejection of special effects, special lighting, and all such "gimmicks," in favor of directness and simplicity.

extra touch, obviously to get a laugh."[3] It's that "scarcely perceptible extra touch" that directors try to catch and correct. As soon as I sense (and sometimes it is a sensation more than a rational thought) anything is unbelievable, I try to correct it. Turning my sensation into a coherent observation requires knowledge of the techniques discussed in earlier chapters of this book. My comments usually start, "I did not believe you when you said …" Then I tentatively suggest, "Maybe your objective is not clear enough there" or "Let's look at what you actually mean when you say that" or something else that addresses the problem.

Sometimes I sense a genuine problem but prescribe the wrong remedy. If so, at least the problem has been identified, and the actors and I can work on it together. Directors should have no hesitation admitting they are wrong—actors and crew will support people whose critical eye extends to themselves. Anne Bogart concurs, "A director's job is not to supply answers but rather to provide interest.… If you already have the answers, then what is the point of being in rehearsal? But you certainly need to know what you are looking for."[4]

- Ask yourself, "Do I believe this character?" and "Do I believe this relationship?"
- Don't feel bad about running the same scene two or three times while you analyze it.
- Use your eyes, but don't forget to use your ears too—they can detect uncertainty. Inexperienced directors often miss small hesitations and "fluffs" —slight mispronunciations or erroneous word choices.
- Don't stand too far back. Get at least as close as the camera will be. And you don't have to stand in one position. You can move around the actors looking for the best camera positions.
- Support actors by responding to their performances. (Some comedy directors are so serious they never laugh at a line.) With the exception of sitcoms, which are generally taped in front of an audience, the director is the actors' only opportunity for live feedback.

Credibility (or verisimilitude) is the basic criteria for almost all screen performances. But performances should be more than merely real. Reality is often monotonous. Drama demands *heightened* reality. It demands that actors pursue objectives, encounter conflict, and make interesting transitions. So directors should ask themselves other questions as well.

- Are the big moments in the scene definite enough?
- Are the actors' choices too passive?
- Are the actors' choices too obvious?

---

[3] Vasili Torpokov, *Stanislavski in Rehearsal*, p. 23.

[4] Anne Bogart, *A Director Prepares*, p. 131.

Be aware that one version of Method acting (apparently not one endorsed by Lee Strasberg) holds that deliberately incorporating fluffs and slips into a performance makes it more real. Some actors who adhere to such thinking will preface lines with extraneous sounds or sighs. Sometimes they will even intentionally say a wrong word and correct themselves—on the grounds that it happens all the time in real life. I find this kind of acting confusing, and I think it draws attention to the actor at the expense of the role. Will Smith does it in *Enemy of the State* (1999), whereas his co-star, the entirely credible Gene Hackman, does not. I once cast an apparently sane actor who inexplicably manufactured a stutter on the day we started shooting—"I ... I ... I want a glass of water." We cured his stutter by simply cutting it out in editing.

Directorial adjustments

The way directors work with actors has always varied. The great Federico Fellini would stand in front of his actors miming the roles and expect them to imitate him. There is what Simon Callow has called "the Otto Preminger school of direction," which believes in purposefully demeaning actors. And most common of all is the hands-off school of directing that lets actors pretty much do what they want as long as they hit their camera *marks* (marks on the floor indicating where actors should stand to be correctly in frame and in focus). When it comes down to it, on a set, with the lights blazing and a producer in a lather, giving coherent directions is hard. A lot of directorial comment takes the form of "louder," "softer," "faster," "slower." The kind of direction advocated in this book, however, changes performances by giving actors *adjustments*.

A directorial adjustment is an alteration to one of an actor's *choices*.

Choices

For most actors, acting is a very intuitive and visceral craft. Yet everything an actor does can be seen as the effect of (conscious or unconscious) choices that she makes. Directors who are very involved with performances are attuned to these actors' choices. When there is a problem, directors can pinpoint a particular choice associated with it and discuss that choice with the actor. Very often these choices are about background, objectives, actions, subtext, and the relationships between characters. If you change any of these underlying choices, you have changed the performance. This is a directorial adjustment.

Adjusting actors' choices

A director will discuss character with an actor early in the proceedings. A character's spine will most likely not change during rehearsal (though that is possible), but the smaller details of a character might. For instance, a director can work on *external* details, such as how a character appears. I was once casting a production against severe time pressure and, instead of matching the character to the part, I cast an actor I knew was chameleon-like and would be able to adapt to almost anything. Little did I realize how much he'd have to adapt to be physically credible! By completely altering his external appearance—giving him a wig and a beard, a limp, and a pair of glasses—we at least got within range. This is an extreme example. Often simply altering someone's tie or makeup will make a difference.

The director can also work on the *internal* level, adjusting a character's traits. Each character will have several defining characteristics, such as humor, intelligence, romantic impulses, stern morality, etc. These basic elements may be substantially changed or it might be more effective just to change their degree. For example, Oscar is a scholarship boy who has started a relationship with Gloria. The actor plays Oscar as rather distant and superior, but that interpretation is not working. We need to qualify Oscar's intelligence and introduce more emotion. "He's the kind of guy who is an owl when it comes to books, but a puppy as far as emotions are concerned." (As always, animal imagery is helpful.) An adjustment can be a change made to the imaginary identity or feelings of a character. It can also be an adjustment to one character's relationship with another ("You have used up all your anger toward her, and now you're exhausted") or with an environment ("You've spent time in this room and feel very at home here") or simply, "You don't like the color of the walls."

A director might also adjust objectives. Usually, though not always, a director suggests stronger objectives. "You seem to want to placate him. Why don't you try to challenge him instead?"

Transitions may be adjusted. Directors can usually find new transitions that bring a performance alive. "I think there's a transition when she tells you she likes your collection of beer mats. Up till that point you've been ignoring her, but suddenly you begin to get interested, you take notice of her." Or, "When he mentions dollars, I think you begin to perk up. After all, we know your character is very interested in money."

The director may make a subtextual adjustment to add interest to an exchange. "When she asks him what movies he likes, it's not a casual question. Movies are very important to her. She's really asking, 'What kind of person are you?'" Or, "When he says, 'Close the door, please,' it's not the first time he's asked her. So he's beginning to get irritated."

As we have noted when discussing improvisation, openings always require careful attention. A character's state of mind or emotion at the very start of a scene has an exaggerated effect on what follows. This can be addressed either through a previous-beat improv or an adjustment or both. "Let's not make her quite so angry with him at the start. I think she's willing to give him one last chance. If she's furious from the get-go, then she can't build her anger during the scene."

Playing against

One of Stanislavski's earliest recorded insights into acting was, "When you play a good man, try to find out where he is bad, and when you play a villain, try to find out where he is good."[5]

Some emotions and actions are so powerful that they can lead to self-indulgence. Think of the melodramatic breast-beating emotions portrayed in some early silent films or the over-played pantomime drunk lurching about the stage. *Playing against* stereotype counters this tendency by suggesting that characters on the verge of losing control cling dearly to whatever control they have left. The drunk fights against stumbling, and the widow who has lost her only child tries to hold on to her sanity. Look at Mae Marsh's reaction to the frenzied mob attacking her house in Griffith's *Birth of a Nation* (1915). Instead of playing conventional silent movie terror (wide eyes, screaming, etc.) she chose the far more interesting response of nervous laughter.

There is a scene in the movie *Independence* (1983) in which Al Pacino makes one of his rare emotional miscalculations. He sits in a boat, clutching his young son, weeping uncontrollably. It is a moment of indulgence that the director should have encouraged him to play against. In *Biloxi Blues* (1988), Christopher Walken plays a domineering military sergeant. The obvious way of playing the role would have been to strut and bark, but Walken plays against this stereotype by being superficially soft-spoken and mild.

An actress was performing a scene in which she told her husband she was dying of cancer. It so happened that the actress's own father had cancer at the

---

[5] David Magarshack, *Stanislavsky: A Life*, p. 68.

time, so she brought all her personal feelings of loss to the part. But using her own "personal truth" was not working—the character she was playing became sad and self-pitying. The director had, first of all, to acknowledge the actress's own experience with her father, and then convince her to play against the emotions. "She won't give in to emotions. She knows if she once does that, she'll completely lose control." The effect eventually achieved was that of a character bravely controlling her grief.

Playing against obvious ways of interpreting scenes or roles helps avoid clichés. It also prompts the director's creativity by encouraging him to think twice. It can lead to new interpretations of scenes and roles. In Asia, some schools of performance have fully embraced this way of thinking. An actor in Japanese Noh theater, for instance, sometimes initially moves in the opposite direction to the one he eventually intends to take, so that the movement contains a small element of surprise. This logic can be adapted to film and television as well. For example, the murderer seems on the point of putting down his revolver before he suddenly raises it and fires. The landlord appears to be rude and ill-tempered but then generously lets the young artist stay on free of charge. In this sense, "playing against" is a principal of good storytelling and something a director should constantly bear in mind. It is particularly worth considering in all moments of high emotion or loss of control. (As we shall see, in Part 6. Chapter 36, this principle can be applied to musical underscoring as well.)

Over-directing

Some directors like to dictate every detail of their actors' performances. This may well be a sign of brilliance (as with Fellini), or it may be a sign of a director's desire to exert inappropriate control. I have seen young directors approach rehearsal with instructions for their actors on how to deliver every line. Over-control on this scale is sometimes called "mapping."

The object of rehearsal is to nurture and focus the actors' creativity, not extinguish it. Actors must be given freedom—freedom to experiment, to make mistakes, to approach their roles by whatever routes they wish (within reason). The director who presents an overly detailed map curtails this freedom. This director also stifles alternative interpretations that might improve and energize a scene. The influential French theater director Jacques Copeau recommended, "The more [the director] can leave initiative to the actors the better. And, when he cannot, let him emulate the diplomat rather than the drill sergeant, hint and coax and flatter and cajole, do anything rather than give orders; let them if possible still be persuaded that the initiative is theirs, not his."[6]

A variation on mapping is the verbal assault. Some directors have too much to say. The purpose of doing the amount of preparation suggested in this book is to be able to make the just-right comment at the just-right time. Too much directorial chatter during rehearsal produces a glazed expression in an actor's eyes. The best directors talk very little and still communicate everything that needs to be said. Indeed, advice is not always what is required from a director. Frequently the greatest service a director can perform for an actor is simply to listen attentively without preconception to what the actor is doing. Such attention empowers the actor and fosters a creative bond between her and the director. It can lead to an open, honest and fruitful discussion.

Result-oriented direction

Most actors do not *choose* emotions. As we noted in Part 2, emotions happen as a result of a character responding to the circumstances of a drama. An actor should not say, "I am going to play sad" or "excited" or "in love." These are imprecise words we spectators use to express what we have seen. Actors playing an emotion will tend to be unbelievable and superficial because they are playing a *result* instead of playing an action.

An actor plays a character *within* the specific circumstances of a scene. How might an actor respond to the direction, "I want you to be happy in this scene"? She might smile a lot and even skip about, but the effect will be superficial. The director needs to be more specific about what the actor is doing within the world of the drama. "It's the day she plays bingo. She's looking forward to it so much that she rushes her breakfast and forgets to feed the cat." A specific direction like this would certainly result in the actress appearing happy, but her performance might have a little more detail and depth.

Result-oriented direction ("be happier," "be faster," "be sparkly," "be annoyed," etc.) thrives in an environment where priority is given to technical issues and not to acting. Sometimes a director has to stand up to his producer and crew in order to give his cast the attention it deserves. On the other hand, once you have been working with a group of actors for a long time and they are perfectly secure in their roles, the *occasional* exhortation to "speed up" or "slow down" is acceptable.

---

[6] "Dramatic Economy," *Directors on Directing*, ed. Cole and Chinoy (New York: Bobbs Merrill Co, Inc., 1963), pp. 218-19. Copeau is quoting the English director Harley Granville-Barker.

17. Conducting the First Rehearsal

What follows is an outline of how rehearsals *might* proceed. Every rehearsal follows its own particular route, so this chapter simply provides something akin to a checklist rather than a precise formula.

Preliminary arrangements

Rehearsals are scheduled, just like the shoot itself. The director, as always, has the last word, but the details are usually worked out by the first or second assistant director. Often the second assistant looks after the rehearsals in order to leave the first free to plan the shoot.

The director will want to rehearse scenes in the most convenient order, and will need to know which scenes to prepare for the next day. The actors want to know when rehearsals are scheduled so that they can start (hopefully) learning their lines and attending makeup trials and costume fittings. Unless rehearsals take place in an isolated setting, many actors will also pursue their personal business-related activities, such as personal appearances and voice-over recordings, in their spare time. (I was once bluntly told by an actor that his advertising jobs supported him and allowed him to work for me.)

The second assistant, or whoever is responsible for organizing the rehearsal, will ask the director what she would like in terms of rehearsal props. Will stand-in props do, or are certain *action props* (props the actors handle during a scene) needed? (An actor whose character uses a very personal item like a snuff box or a cane will want to rehearse with the actual prop.) What does the director want to do about coffee breaks? How would she like the sets arranged? Would she like the actors to arrive before their scenes are scheduled, just in case she gets ahead of schedule?

Any rehearsal period is valuable, even if it is only a few days. Theater rehearsals generally take two, three, or four weeks, of which the last week is largely devoted to run-throughs and technical rehearsals. A minimum rehearsal period these days for a ninety-minute film that relies on good performances (as opposed to constant action) would be five or six days. If you have the luxury of a week's rehearsal, you should aim to go over each scene at least twice.

First meetings take more time than subsequent ones. When actors arrive for their first rehearsal, fifteen or twenty minutes will be spent becoming acquainted and discussing their characters before getting down to the scene at hand. As a rule of thumb, allow at least forty-five minutes (and more if you plan to do several improvs) for a two-page scene's first time round. You should also leave yourself a few minutes at the end of each session to make notes.

In the good old days of British television series (prior to the mid-1990s), when episodes were rehearsed before they were recorded, we were allocated about twenty minutes a scene. This meant that, with careful planning, and if the actors were not required for shooting elsewhere, a few of the more important scenes could receive additional attention. Twenty minutes allows an experienced director to block a scene and run it twice. It does not allow for serious consideration of performance or for improvisation.

Rehearsal techniques differ greatly from director to director. Some directors are satisfied with table readings—that is, just sitting round a table with the actors reading the script and discussing their characters and the structure of the scenes. Some directors, like Francis Ford Coppola, like to spirit their actors away to the location or an isolated spot where they can improvise. Sidney Pollack prefers not to rehearse at all—"I'm not as happy with an actor who's grown roots in the performance as I am with an actor who's just a teeny bit not quite sure"—though he will rehearse with stars like Al Pacino and Paul Newman if they request it. Sidney Lumet, on the other hand, prefers to work in a rehearsal room for two weeks or more, going over each scene in detail.

Most directors who choose to rehearse prefer to do it in story order—the order in which scenes appear in the script (which, in films with flashbacks, is not always the same as chronological order). This method allows them to see each scene in its proper place, so they can consider continuity and pacing. On the other hand, working in story order often means keeping people waiting around for long periods of time between appearances. To ease this situation, a compromise order is usually worked out.

The read-through

Theater rehearsals start with a read-through. Movie rehearsals, as opposed to those for TV series, tend to start that way too. Getting everybody around a table serves as a good way of breaking the ice. It may well be the only time the entire cast, along with the designers, producers, and the production team, are in the same place at the same time. It can be an intimidating event, especially for actors who are reading the script in public without the benefit of rehearsal. (The actor Simon Callow says, "It's like the worst party we've ever been to in our lives."[1]) On the other hand, at least it gives everyone a chance to see who is involved. For the director, it is an opportunity to see how the actors are approaching their roles. It also allows her (or an assistant) to take out the stopwatch and get a rough timing of the movie.

The director, the cast, the producer, and anyone else who's been invited meet in a large room and sit around a big table or in a circle. The director and producer welcome the participants and make a few introductory remarks. When it's your turn to speak, bear in mind that these will be your first words to the cast as a whole and your tone is important. I tend to keep my remarks brief and businesslike, and proceed quickly to the read-through.

The director then picks up the script and the reading commences. At this point, I emphasize that I do not expect polished performances because people will be feeling their way through the script. But at the same time, I ask everyone to speak up so that we can all hear what is being said. During the reading, the director usually announces the stage directions when they are pertinent. Sometimes an actor cannot make it to the reading and a member of the production team has to read that person's part. If this happens, try to give the stand-in enough time to prepare. A director once asked a production manager colleague of mine to read a major role at the last minute. The character he was reading was thoroughly English but had a French name. My poor friend read the whole part with a ghastly French accent, and everyone else was so nervous that they giggled but did not correct him.

Actors vary in their approaches to a first reading. Some seem to have their characters in place and read their lines with conviction. Others are still feeling

---

[1] Simon Callow, *Being an Actor* (New York: St. Martin's Press, 1984), p. 133.

their way into their roles and are reluctant to commit to an interpretation. The director observes the dynamics and begins to see where her energies will be focused, though it is still too early to draw conclusions about the kinds of performances that will be given. As Simon Callow says, "Simply to *hear* it through, to hear the balance of voices, and to begin to sense the shape of the whole thing is exhilarating."[2]

If the script breaks equally into two sections, the director might take a short coffee break halfway through. When the read-through has finished, the director usually thanks everyone, and the production personnel make announcements about such matters as costume fittings and the rehearsal schedule. Sometimes models of the sets are brought out for the actors to examine, and the director or the designer says a few words about the project's design concept. The completion of the first reading frequently coincides with lunch, and it is always advisable to take a good, refreshing break before reconvening.

Scenework

Work now begins on the script scene by scene or, if there are a number of short interrelated scenes, sequence by sequence. The director chooses how private the rehearsals will be. Many directors prefer to work with only the second assistant in attendance to set out the furniture and props, call the actors, and be "on-book" (i.e., ready to prompt). Others don't mind a small audience. When I was working my way up the production ladder, I was always grateful to directors who allowed me to observe rehearsals. Consequently, I've never objected to my own assistants being present.

Rehearsals commonly begin at a table with a reading of the scene. Questions immediately arise. Are the actors comfortable with the lines? Are the relationships clear? Does everyone understand the point of the scene? Discussing these issues inevitably leads to a discussion of character, and one is very soon in the thick of it.

A director listens carefully when actors want to change lines. Line alterations should not be undertaken lightly. The author or authors have worked hard on the script and the director will also have spent time on it. Changes should be discussed and only implemented if there is good reason. Actors, especially at first rehearsals, often express their overall insecurity by second-guessing their lines.

---

[2] *Being an Actor*, loc. cit. p. 133.

A director soon realizes that actors, like musicians in a symphony orchestra, see the whole performance from their own perspectives. Therefore, the director has to explain the significance of the scene and everyone's contribution to it.

The director must sense how the actors want to work. There are two types of actors: those who are happy discussing a scene in detail and those who want to get up and start blocking it. My own preference is to get up and start "moving it around" as soon as the fundamentals are in place—though I am always careful to reassure the cast that we will sit down again if there's something to talk about.

During rehearsals, directors can either refer to the characters by character names ("I think Pandro would stand up at this point") or by the actors' own names ("Harry, I think *you* would stand up at this point"). There is a subtle difference. The first approach assumes that the character is an entity that the director and actor are creating together. The second assumes that the performer is merging the identity of the character with his own. Choose the approach that works best for you.

Blocking

When it's time to get up and start blocking the scene, the director suggests the positions from which the actors should start. These *opening positions* are important because the rest of the scene flows from them, so the director might explain why they were chosen. "I think you've just had dinner and you are sitting at the table finishing your coffee" or "I've got you chopping wood because I figure he (the character) does that every morning to watch her as she passes by on her way to school."

A very fine line exists between imposing moves and letting the actors find their own. I wait till the actors have gone well past executing the move I have in mind before I stop them. I want to see if they will do my move unbidden (which sometimes happens) or move of their own accord at about the same point. If nothing has happened, I stop the rehearsal and say, "I think we need a move around this point in the scene." If there is no objection, I will describe my move and try to justify it. Occasionally, an actor will have another suggestion, which I will consider and adopt if it's an improvement. If we are heading toward an impasse (which rarely happens), I'll ask the actor to try my move on the understanding that if at the end of the scene she is still unhappy, we will reconsider it.

Blocking need not take long, but it is important not to rush it. Once you have reached the end of the scene, ask if everyone is happy with their moves. If the actors have questions, sit down, either in the set or at the table, and address them. Then, as soon as this discussion ends, invite the actors to get up and run the scene again while the moves are fresh in their minds.

You cannot give an actor an adjustment or change his moves or introduce new business without giving him the chance to put it into effect. Abstract "notes" (the comments a director offers an actor on his performance, usually at the end of a rehearsal) are all but useless. If you give a note at the end of a rehearsal session (e.g., "I'd like you to think about how you might relate to him more as a father"), then remember to bring it up again when the scene is next rehearsed.

Timing needs to be rehearsed as well. A director might say, "Wait a beat (or a second) before you answer the door." But when actors are performing, their inner tempo is racing and a beat may go by artificially fast. If an actor is not getting a critical piece of timing right, the only way to precisely communicate its duration is to touch him on the arm for the required length of time. This is the only circumstance when there need be physical contact between an actor and director.

As I mentioned in the previous chapter, when observing a run of a scene, do not sit politely at a distance as though you were in a theater. The director should be at least as close as the camera. The director should also feel free to wander around the set observing from different potential camera angles. Sitting in one place encourages the actors to play to you, and the performance becomes "out-front" and theatrical.

Feel free to react to the performance by laughing or crying if you feel like it. Most film and TV actors appreciate genuine feedback. Creative differences may arise between director and actors, but outright antagonism is rare. The only times I have ever been annoyed with actors was when they turned up late or refused to learn their lines or indulged in some other form of unprofessional behavior.

One problem for directors is that they have to consider so many things at once—performance, moves, and camera positions. Since it's difficult to do more than one thing at a time, use the first run-through to go over the moves and cement them. If changes occur during the run-through, then run it again. Once the moves have been established, ask your actors to go through the scene again so you can concentrate specifically on their performance.

Evaluating

As I suggested in the previous chapter, when evaluating a performance, empty your mind and watch the scene as if for the first time. Put the script aside, along with all your accumulated expectations and concerns. Like an actor about to step onto a set, the director has to consciously relax. In this state of quiet receptivity, she picks up on anything that is awkward, unconvincing, or unreal. Some directors make quick notes on a piece of paper. But even scrawling something in shorthand can take your mind off the action for a few seconds. Usually, scenes are so short that you can easily remember the two or three main points you will want to make.

As the director, the choice is yours whether to stop a scene to address a problem or wait till the scene ends. Running a long scene in its entirety if there is a problem in its first beat is certainly a waste of time. On the other hand, actors don't appreciate being constantly reigned in when they are in full gallop. With a little experience you will be able to distinguish the problems that have to be immediately addressed (because there is no point running the scene any farther) from the ones that can be postponed till the scene's end.

When you do notice something that is not working, you may not automatically have a solution for it. So you may wish just to raise it and invite others to examine it with you: "What seems to be going on here?" As you start mastering the concepts discussed in this part of the book, you will gradually be able to make specific recommendations and adjustments. This might also be the time, as you begin to analyze performance and character relationships, to introduce an improvisation.

In subsequent run-throughs, encourage the cast to put down their scripts. Your assistant will be there to prompt, if need be. And as you incorporate the discoveries from an improv or as the actors implement your adjustments, be sure to encourage and reassure them. Invite their reactions to the way the scene is going and be prepared to enter into a discussion. Actors tend to want to stop after a few runs. This is understandable—they know they have reached a point where they need to consolidate what they have absorbed by studying their lines and thinking the scene over. I usually find that I want one more run than my actors—probably because of all those things a screen director has to consider.

As you observe the final run-through, be conscious of where your attention is drawn. You are the audience, and what you find interesting is what will intrigue the viewer as well. (Make sure that you well cover those moments when you shoot.) If two characters are having a conversation, it is very easy to slip into a pattern of simply cutting back and forth between them for their lines. Listening carefully to the way lines are delivered and observing the nuances of performance frequently helps you break this pattern. Perhaps you realize you can cut to a character for his reaction or to a prop that a character is nervously handling or to an object elsewhere in the room at which a character glances.

As the first rehearsal winds down, try to leave the actors on a positive note. Congratulate them on their work and say something encouraging about the scene. If you'd like them to work on their roles or do any research into their characters' backgrounds, don't forget to mention it. If you will be meeting to go over the scene again, ask them to have their lines memorized for the next time.

Once the rehearsal is over and the actors are checking their next call time with the assistant, go back to your script. With the rehearsal still fresh in your mind, make sure you have noted down all the changes you've made to the scene during rehearsal. You will need a very accurate record when you start considering exactly how to shoot it.

PART 4
Some Principles of Shooting

18. The Hollywood Continuity Style

"I play
You play
We play
At cinema
You think there are
Rules for the game"
— Jean-Luc Godard, from "Letter to my Friends to
Learn how to Make Films Together"[1]

This book began addressing shooting issues when I discussed blocking actors for the camera. Performance and shooting cannot be considered entirely separately.

Film and television directors work on two levels—the theatrical (or performance) level and the technical level—and constantly oscillate between the two. During rehearsal, the emphasis tends to be more on performance, but that does not mean the technical is not being considered at the same time.

This chapter is designed to provide enough information to produce a fully marked-up shooting script. Some of the subjects introduced here, such as continuity, will be developed further in Part 5 when I describe the production process.

Over the past century, a series of rules has emerged that influence how drama should be shot. Taken together, they have been called The Hollywood Continuity Style. The HCS is so widely accepted that it is hard to say if this style is arbitrary (one of a number of possible styles) or if it actually reflects a natural film logic. Perhaps we have simply become so used to this film language

---

[1] Jean-Luc Godard, *Godard on Godard* (London: Secker & Warburg, 1972), p. 242.

that we cannot conceive of speaking another. And perhaps the handful of people who react against it (such as John Cassavetes, Pier Pasolini, Jean-Luc Godard, Derek Jarman, and other avant-garde filmmakers) develop dialects rather than entirely new tongues. If you want to create your own non-HCS style, at least you should know what you are reacting against.

The HCS has two fundamental goals. The first is invisibility. It is designed to efface the production process and propel the story to the forefront. The HCS director wants to do nothing that will hold up the flow of events and draw attention to the artificiality of the film process. In his book *Conversation With Wilder*, Cameron Crowe praised the director for a body of work "without one overly complicated shot." Wilder replied, "If it does not follow the story, why? It's phoniness. The phoniness of the director." In a sense, the great achievement of the HCS is that it has taken something as technically complex as moviemaking and made it invisible. It is an industrial achievement comparable to a modernist skyscraper, which hides all the beams, drains, ventilation ducts and wiring under a smooth skin of steel and glass.

The second HCS goal is to combine two opposites: variety and continuity. The Hollywood movie plays with time and place. It varies long scenes with short ones; it darts about from location to location and from one time of day to another. Its accelerated tempo, exotic settings, (comparatively) unpredictable storylines, are all part of its appeal. So too are its mixture of action sequences, interpersonal drama, special effects, and naturalism. The HCS can take diverse material and weld it together into an acceptable whole, so that incongruities that could shatter the structure are neatly contained within it.

Let us see how it works.

Shot sizes and their applications

Until around 1904, films consisted of a single static shot lasting the whole length of a film magazine, which was twelve minutes.[2] Then, like single-celled entities, films evolved by subdividing. An insert shot was added, then a mid-shot, and then a closeup, until five years later, when something appeared that looked very much like a movie as we know it today.[3] Varying the shot necessitated a huge advance in technology. Different lenses were required for different shots, lighting had to be moved and adjusted, and suddenly editing was born. The technological potential of the medium increased exponentially. As we watch groundbreaking

---

[2] Edwin S. Porter, considered to be the father of modern editing, began using edits in 1903.
[3] D. W. Griffith began cutting shots of different sizes together in about 1908.

early films, we sense the excitement of a master like D.W. Griffith, yoking together disparate elements in *Intolerance* (1916), and the contagious bug spreading to Russia where Sergei Eisenstein and others developed a radical theory of how shots should be edited together (*montage*).

The shot remains film's basic element—it is the building block that, by itself or combined with others, creates a scene or sequence. The director plans it during preproduction. During production, a number of other people—the lighting director, camera operator, sound recordist and boom operator, production designer, special effects designer, and actors—lavish substantial attention upon it. As a single, independent entity, it should be as perfectly achieved as possible. Single-camera shooting emphasizes this by forcing all crew members to focus on only one shot at a time. In postproduction, the single shot is examined, trimmed, and physically combined with other shots. At this final stage, the director is not so much concerned with altering shot content (because, unless visual effects are to be added, it is more or less unalterable) as with finding its optimum place within a scene or sequence. The director considers a shot's ability to stand alone during production, and also its ability to be combined with other shots during editing.

Let's look at standard shots and see how they can be applied to narrative fiction.

Varieties of wide shot

The establishing shot

The traditional use of a wide shot (WS) is to establish (visually introduce) a location. It used to be assumed that every time you changed location, you had to remind audiences where you were by planting an establishing shot at the top of the scene or sequence. Refinement in cinematic technique is often a response to the audience's increased sophistication. Now it is more common to establish a location the first time you encounter it and only re-establish it when the audience has not seen it for a while. (This shot may be considered drama's equivalent of a TV news "ident"—those names on the bottom third of the screen that periodically identify the journalist or the expert who is speaking.)

Establishing shots in sitcoms such as *Seinfeld* and TV dramas like *NYPD Blue* have a dual function. They serve to inform viewers where the ensuing scene is located, as well as to offer the visual relief of an exterior shot during an otherwise unbroken succession of interior scenes.

Establishing shots in films that are projected on large screens often carry detailed information that might pass unnoticed on a standard television screen. When a movie shot in widescreen is shown on standard TV, the image is altered in various ways (see Chapter 23). Consequently, the viewer no longer feels encompassed and engulfed by the images. HDTV and widescreen receivers mitigate this effect, but are still not quite the same as viewing a movie on a large cinema screen.

How the establishing shot is handled depends upon the director. Sometimes, for the sake of change, a director will postpone the establishing shot till later in the scene and start with a tight shot. I first noticed this in Ridley Scott's *Blade Runner* (1982. director's cut, 1991). The effect plunges viewers straight into the conflict and, at the same time, deliberately disorients them. It is a device well suited to a film like *Blade Runner*, which is about uncertainty.

Once, attending the screening of a movie I'd worked on as a first assistant, I noticed an establishing shot of a house I'd never seen before. It had been picked up after the shoot by a separate camera crew. (A crew that picks up additional footage is called a second unit.) While editing, the director realized that he had to slow the momentum down at that particular point, and an establishing shot did the trick.

Sometimes, directors have chosen to have two establishing shots, one after the other. In *Vertigo* (1958), for example, Hitchcock establishes the exterior of a restaurant. Then, as James Stewart enters it, Hitchcock establishes its opulent interior. This has the effect of greatly slowing down the pace of the action, and most contemporary directors would think twice about doing it. An alternative might be the astonishing opening shot of *Boogey Nights* (1997) in which the camera starts on a busy boulevard, swoops down, and follows the characters all the way into a nightclub.

The master shot

A wide shot can also be used as a "master shot." In the 1950s and early '60s, films were shot very methodically. The whole scene was first shot in wide shot. Then, mid-shots were taken—both singles and 2-shots. Then, medium closeups were shot, followed by closeups. Directors who observed this unalterable sequence knew they had good "coverage"—that is to say, they knew they had shot the scene thoroughly and would not be short of material when editing. If worse came to worst, they always had that wide shot to fall back on. Also, as far as most were concerned, they did not have to really plan their shots in detail beforehand because everything was shot the same way. I once assisted a director who worked in this manner. He was well known at the time and a complete professional. The film we worked on was excellent and won many awards, including an International Emmy. But the shooting process was dull and time-consuming.

Although it is occasionally taught in film schools today, the old-fashioned master shot was effectively discredited by the "new wave" (a.k.a. Nouvelle Vague). In the late 1950s, this group of excited, committed, and brilliant filmmakers was in a hurry. French filmmakers Truffaut, Godard, Rohmer, Chabrol, Rivette, and others did not have Hollywood's resources, but they had studied the techniques of a few favorite filmmakers, particularly Hitchcock and Hawkes.

When the new-wave directors started shooting, they knew exactly what shots they wanted and did not waste time playing it safe. In other words, they visualized their shots ahead of time. Instead of being an inflexible element, the shot became capable of making a variety of visual statements. There were long hand-held camera shots (a style hitherto more associated with documentary than drama), 360° panning shots, and a multitude of tracking shots. ("Your camera movements are bad because your subjects are bad," Godard once told a group of established filmmakers.) Godard also often edited shots together in a way that emphasized their discontinuity and differences. Shot design and manipulation are now considered as expressive as performance, scene design, and other creative aspects. *We now expect directors to manipulate the shot expressively to suit the individual scene.*

When directors shoot a scene, they sometimes start in tried-and-true fashion with a master shot, which they keep filming till its composition breaks down and the characters' movements can no longer be aesthetically contained within the frame. Directors who work this way employ the master shot as a "safety" (i.e., a shot they can fall back on), but will also use it as an opportunity to allow the actors to run through the scene. If the director decides to shoot another slightly less wide shot at a later point in the scene, the subsequent shot is sometimes referred to as a "mini-master."

Master shots are still used by Woody Allen and others who often shoot whole scenes in a single shot without *cut-ins*—additional shots of characters or objects within the scene. (We will look more closely at this style in Chapter 24.) Traditionally, masters tend to be used less in television, where time constraints inhibit directors from choreographing developing shots. However, the increasing use of the Steadicam in the nineties has changed that. Many scenes in *E.R.*, for instance, consist entirely of a single developing master shot that starts wide and then changes size as the camera moves with the characters around the set.

Occasionally, a director just needs a wide shot for its own sake. Sometimes the beauty of the landscape or the location calls for it. Godard frequently cuts to a shot of the sky for no apparent reason except that it is beautiful. Landscape shots are often "point-of-view shots" (a.k.a. POV shots): A cowboy climbs to the top of a rock and looks out across the valley—we then cut to a wide shot of the valley from his point of view. An interesting twist on this practice used by Hitchcock, among others, allows characters to enter their own point-of-view shots. Thus, in *Psycho* (1960), we are shown Lila's POV of Mother Bates' bedroom, before she enters it in the same framing.

Wide shot as group shot

A wide shot is often required for groups of people. It is difficult, especially on a traditional TV screen or academy format with a 4x3 aspect ratio, to show groups without going wide—especially if they are positioned horizontally across the screen. You generally have to go pretty wide to shoot the jury in a trial scene (even if the shot is taken at an oblique angle) or the line of policemen about to advance on a crowd. On the other hand, no matter what format you are shooting in, if you want to shoot epic moments, such as the battle for Mogadishu (*Black Hawk Down*, 2002) or the Scottish army charging the British (*Braveheart*, 1995), the shots have to be wide to contain all the action. Perhaps the greatest wide shots in this category are those of Akiro Kurasawa that integrate shots of armies with dramatic landscapes.

The full-length shot

The full-length shot (FL), or full shot, includes the entire person from head to toe, allowing headroom (the space between the top of the head and the top of the frame) and some space below the feet. It shows the person in relation to the environment. It is also convenient for shooting movement.

When shooting interiors on location, where it is often impossible to get the camera far enough back to achieve a genuine wide shot, the full shot is as wide as you will get. Thus, it is often the equivalent of an establishing shot.

When two characters are shot in a depth relationship, such as at different ends of a corridor, it is not uncommon for the one farthest away to be in full-length (especially if a wide-angle lens is used). (See Fig.18.1.)

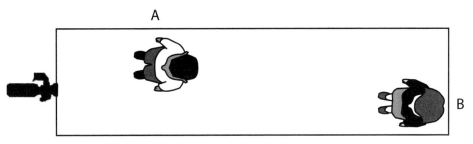

Character A is in mid-shot. Character B is full-length.

Fig. 18.1: Deep 2-shot.

The full-length is not a shot used very often on television because, when shown on a small screen, it diminishes features like the eyes, the mouth, and the hands. This shot is more effective when projected onto a fourteen-foot screen. It is often used at the start of a tracking shot, when a person or persons appear and walk toward camera. In this case, the camera often first shows the whole person, then waits till the shot tightens before tracking out with the subject. If you have Richard Gere dressed collar to toe by Armani (*American Gigolo*, 1980) or Chaplin tapping his boots with his cane, the full-length shot is a necessity.

Tightening the shot

The three-quarters shot

The three-quarters shot (3/4s)—sometimes called a knee shot or medium full shot—cuts at the subject's knee or thereabouts. Its function is similar to the full-length shot. It is also useful for moving characters, especially in a large set or location.

One of the very first innovations in early film was to tighten the single static wide shot to a three-quarters shot. It brought the viewers closer to the action—effectively moving them from the rear of the upper balcony to the front of the middle balcony. No one seemed to mind the absence of the lower leg except the French, who disclaimed the shot, calling it the "plan Americain" (the American shot).

The mid-shot

The mid-shot (MS) shows its subject from around waist level on up. Since it is considered aesthetically unacceptable to cut at the waist itself (after all, only magicians cut people exactly in half), it is subdivided. The tight mid-shot (TMS)—sometimes called medium close shot—starts above the waist, and the loose mid-shot (LMS)—sometimes called the medium shot—starts below. When planning a scene, you can just think in terms of mid-shot and adjust the size when you start shooting.

The mid-shot is the workhorse of shots. It is very common in film, where it combines the intimacy of a tight shot with the freedom of a looser one. A filmic mid-shot, especially a tight mid-shot, allows facial expressions to be clearly seen. It is also very common in comedy, especially sitcoms, where it clearly shows the face, arms, and body—the physical comedian's utensils. Comedies seldom go to a tighter shot unless there is an emotional moment.

The qualities of a mid-shot lend it to movement. It is loose enough that when people start to move they do not immediately disappear out of frame. The mid-shot allows sufficient *lead room* to allow a camera operator to pan or track without losing the performer. Lead room (see Fig. 18.2) is the space between a subject and the edge of frame. Directors often cut to a mid-shot in the middle of a sequence of tighter shots to accommodate a move.

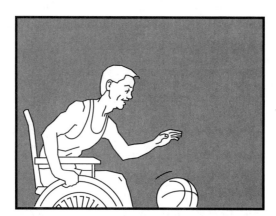

Fig 18.2: Lead-room

The mid-shot is also commonly used to show two people (mid-two-shot, M2s). The subjects can be standing apart, one behind the other (a deep mid-two-shot, DM2), or side-by-side, either in an open arrangement or a profile one. (See Figs. 18.3 and 18.4.)

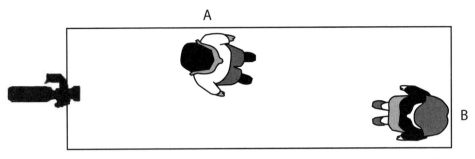

In the above deep mid-2-shot, character A would be in tight mid-shot and B in a loose mid-shot.

Fig. 18.3: Deep mid-2-shot

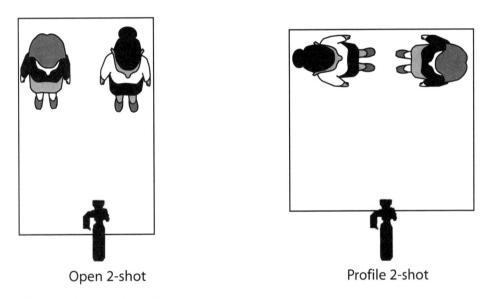

Open 2-shot   Profile 2-shot

Fig. 18.4: Open and profile two-shots

When actors are blocked in M2s (or tighter), they may have to stand closer together than they would in real life. Average Westerners feel their privacy is invaded when someone comes to within three feet. Actors who are used to accommodating the cramped demands of a TV screen adjust automatically, but inexperienced actors have to be coaxed.

The MS works well as a group shot in wider formats, such as widescreen and anamorphic (see Chapter 23). Group mid-shots are less effective on the traditional television monitor/academy format, where the mid-four shot rarely occurs. Anything greater than a 2-shot on a 4x3 screen is usually considered a group shot. To create a mid-four shot, a TV director would have to block the characters with at least one person standing behind the others.

The medium closeup and tight 2-shot

The medium closeup (MCU) is sometimes also known as a close shot. In the silent movie era, when filmmakers were less inhibited, it was called the bust shot (and some directors still use that term). The prim BBC used to define it as "cutting at the top of the breast pocket."

This shot is common in television, particularly for static shots. The old adage says "television is a closeup medium," and the MCU is the most frequently used closeup. Its strength is that it presents the landscape of the face and yet relates it to its environment. In film, where details are exaggerated by projection onto a large screen, the MCU is considered a very tight shot.

It is tricky to move characters in an MCU because, as soon as they set off, they tend to disappear (or half-disappear) out of the side of the frame. To shoot movement in an MCU you either have to give your camera operator plenty of rehearsal, or you have to make sure your actor moves relatively slowly. To have to ask actors to slow down artificially is unfortunate, but occasionally it cannot be helped. The more experienced the actor, the more she will accommodate such a request. I once had an irate actor complain to me about another director who had asked her to cut down the speed with which she crossed the set. When she showed me how she originally did the move, she went like greased lightning. I think the director was within his rights to make the request, but, knowing the actress, I would probably have accommodated her move in a wider shot.

The MCU is really a "single" (a shot with one person in it). If you add a second actor to an MCU, it becomes a "tight 2-shot" (T2s). The tight 2-shot works in widescreen formats, but on standard television, getting tight 2-shots when the subjects are standing in open or profile relationships is difficult—there just is not the width. So, on TV, tight 2-shots tend to be arranged with one person in front of the other. When two people stand face to face, and the camera shoots past the back of one head onto the face of the other—the shot is said to "favor" the person we see clearly.

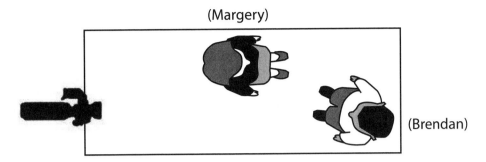

Fig.18.5: Tight 2-shot favoring Brendan (T2s fav Bren)

The tight 2-shot, with all the space in the frame occupied by the two heads, is an intense shot. It is most commonly used for scenes in which people are arguing, making love, or going to the dentist.

The over-the-shoulder shot

The over the shoulder shot (O/S) is halfway between a single and a strongly favoring 2-shot. Although it serves to relate one person to another, its main virtue may be aesthetic. It provides foreground for what would otherwise be a medium closeup or mid-shot.

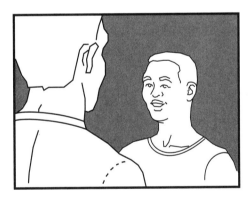

Fig. 18.6: Over-the-shoulder shot

A couple of potential problems exist with the over-the-shoulder shot. As we will see, continuity problems may arise if the foreground head is moving. And, because it is such a heavily accented shot (accenting the side of frame with the larger, foreground head), cutting back and forth between two consecutive over-the-shoulder shots can be very distracting.

When describing an over-the-shoulder shot, just mention the person the shot is favoring: An over-the-shoulder shot of Zac is "O/S Zac."

Occasionally, objects other than heads enter the foreground of a shot. Muriel is seated and Reginald is standing in front of her. If you are shooting Muriel and want to include Reginald's waist in the foreground, the shot can be described as an "MCU (or MS or whatever the shot size is) Muriel *past* Reginald." If you replace Reginald with a tree, then the shot would simply be "MCU Muriel, past tree," and the exact details of the framing would be discussed with the cameraperson.

The implications of the over-the-shoulder and other shots as far as film continuity are concerned are discussed in Part 5, Chapter 29.

The closeup

The closeup (CU), or head shot, starts below the chin. Unlike the shots discussed above, which leave space between the top of the head and the top of the frame (headroom), the closeup cuts off the top of the head.

A closeup that includes *both* the chin and the top of the head just does not look right. The head tends to resemble a disembodied, floating, balloon-like object. By cutting the shot at or around the hairline and including the neck, the head seems connected to the body.

The closeup is a powerful shot in both television and film. It brings us into considerable intimacy with the subject and maximizes the voyeuristic quality of screen drama—allowing us to gaze closely and unseen at someone who may be undergoing extreme pressure.

The closeup can be tightened still further to the big closeup (BCU)[4] or extreme closeup (ECU), which cut above the chin. However, when a shot becomes so tight that it just shows a single feature—an eye or mouth or ear—it becomes a detail shot.[5]

Shot sequence and when to use a closeup

The traditional sequence of shots in a scene is from wide shot to mid-shot to closeup. There is a good reason for this: Most scenes are constructed to work toward a climax. The opening of a scene establishes the characters within a setting.

---

[4] For some directors—especially film directors—a big closeup (BCU) is the equivalent of what I have called a closeup (CU). They may also use closeup to describe what I have called a medium closeup (MCU).

[5] Some directors call a shot of a single facial feature (such as an eye) an extreme closeup (ECU).

As it progresses, we begin to focus more specifically on the characters themselves and their issues. And then, as the conflict intensifies and will meets will, we expect to see what people are thinking and how they are reacting. Far from being tedious, this repetitive pattern reassures audiences. It contains a built-in mechanism of tension and release as the action moves from the intensity of a closeup at the end of a scene to the release of a wide shot at the beginning of the next.

This pattern is not rigidly the same in scene after scene. What prevents it from becoming totally predictable is the movement of the actors. Movement, as we have seen, tends to require looser shots. A well-designed scene with movement in the right places will seemingly naturally build toward tight shots, relax to looser shots, and then build to tight shots again.

Dramatic tension can be controlled, to a degree, by the size of the shot. For instance, tension is sustained if a movement is taken in a tight mid-shot. Tension is released if the move is taken on a wider shot. However, it is usually more effective to release tension and then tighten it up again than to keep it constantly sustained. As the French say, you sometimes have to retreat in order to advance again.

A wide shot distances us from characters and cools a scene down. A close shot, which seems to take us into their thoughts, warms it up. One of the challenges of working on TV series is deciding how to introduce new regular characters and how to shoot the final scenes of characters who have been around a very long time. One producer used to insist that new characters be introduced in a medium closeup—a sudden infusion of heat. It was a way of telegraphing to the audience, "This character is important!" I think a better way is to let characters gradually establish themselves and have the audience wonder, "Is this person going to stay?"

I once had to shoot the final scene of a long-standing character in a television series. He was a much-loved minister, and his final scene was a farewell address to his congregation. I had planned a dramatic truck out, leaving him poignantly isolated. However, as we rehearsed the move, I realized I'd got it wrong. What was needed was the exact opposite—a gradual track into an MCU in order to read his feelings.

When I was starting out, a cameraman gave me the following piece of advice. "Who is the pressure on?" he asked. "Dorothy," I answered. "Then she should have the first MCU," he declared. At the time, I was suspicious of this overly neat formulation, but I've since found it very helpful. When considering when to tighten the shot, ask yourself, *"Who is the pressure on?"*

How would you shoot this scene?

<u>INT. HEADMASTER'S OFFICE   DAY</u>

<u>PRINCIPAL</u>
Beth, why did you do it? Why did you
take the money? Don't you know it's
wrong to steal? Was the handbag too
much of a temptation for you? Do I
have to tell my teachers not to take
their private property into the
classroom? Do I have to run this
school like a prison and frisk pupils
as they come in and out? Why did you
do it? Tell me. Were you put up to
it? Tell me!

Asking the question, "Who is the pressure on?" suggests that, although he has all the lines, the principal is not the focus of the scene. Beth is the one under pressure, and when you came to shoot this scene you will probably (a) tighten the shot on her first, and (b) give her more screen time than the principal. Dramatic focus can be indicated by duration. By spending more time on Beth's reaction to the principal than on the principal himself, Beth becomes the focus.

Here is a rule. Like all rules in this business, it's made to be broken, but here it is anyway: *Once you have tightened or loosened a shot on one character, the next shot of the other character should match it.* Thus, if you tighten your shot of Beth to an MCU, the ensuing shot of the principal should also be an MCU. A series of four or more shots unmatched in size tends to look ragged. Some young directors resist "matching" because they feel they can focus the scene on one character by consistently shooting her in a tighter shot. But the director indicates focus or pressure by tightening the shot *on one character first.* The initial tightening of the screw is what counts.

This rule has two exceptions. One is, as you might suspect, when a character is moving. Thus, if the headmaster is pacing the room as he castigates Beth, he might be shot in a mid-shot while she is in MCU. Doing this would further increase the focus on Beth. The other exception is the "reaction shot." Reactions, because the point is made by the expression in the eyes and not by words, have to be tight shots. Since we only see her reacting to the principal's speech, Beth would be in an MCU or CU all the time.

Some experienced actors deliberately restrain their reactions and suppress their vocal levels. Many of these actors are extremely successful on screen because the camera and the microphone manage to pick up the smallest delivery. The problem, from a director's point of view, is that their performances have to be shot in closeup to be appreciated. John Travolta is an actor with a phenomenally subtle film technique that often has to be captured in a tight shot. When a director does not tighten the shot sufficiently, the result can be frustrating for the viewer, who may have difficulty understanding what the actor is saying. This problem is compounded in cinemas with poor speakers or when viewing on a low-quality VHS cassette.

The line of intimacy

All moments in a scene are important—but some are more important than others. We have already identified the opening as one such important moment. Another is the moment of the first closeup (MCU or CU). This is when the point of the scene becomes overt, and we see on one person the effect of what is happening. Going to closeup takes the audience beyond a cool, objective view of events to a point of view that is unnaturally subjective. *It is the crossing of a line into intimacy.* Use the closeup too early and the scene degenerates into melodrama. Use the shot too late and it draws attention to itself. The closeup should occur at exactly the point at which the audience wants it to. In most cases (horror flics apart), it should go almost unnoticed. Some directors resist using it because they resist its intimacy. But, in most dramatic scenes between two or more characters there is a place for the MCU. Sometimes, as we've noted, physical comedy avoids using closeups, and some filmmakers also limit themselves to the tight mid-shot because the CU can be so overwhelming on the big screen.

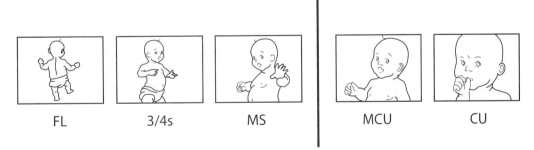

| FL | 3/4s | MS | | MCU | CU |

Fig. 18.7: The line of intimacy and intrusion

The closeup is a delicate and tricky shot. Once employed, it can set up a pattern of closeups that is difficult to break. Young directors commonly make the following three errors with the CU: (1) They jump the shot sequence and introduce it before the mid-shot. It takes practice to understand when the traditional shot sequence can be broken. (2) They use it prematurely in the scene. If a director introduces a closeup on page two of a four-page confrontation, where will he go for the rest of the scene? (3) They get caught in long runs of MCUs and CUs—ping-ponging back and forth between similar shots. Few things are as monotonous as these long sequences of closeups. Julia Smith, the original producer of BBC's *EastEnders,* had strong thoughts on this (as on most things). "Never have more than six successive shots of the same size," she declared. She was right. Her directors were forced to come up with movement and to think very carefully about their shot progression. Nothing is more testing for a director than a four-page scene between a couple at a table in a restaurant when he cannot use the same size shot more than six times in succession. Sergio Leoni, who used closeup after closeup in the showdown sequences of his "spaghetti westerns," nevertheless varied the size of the closeups or occasionally cut away to a wider shot in order to break the repetitive pattern.

The discussion of shot sequence will be resumed in Chapter 21.

19. Framing And Lenses

F raming is such a personal element of a director's vision that I hesitate to write about it. Yet certain rules of visual composition have been handed down from as far back as Ancient Greece, and we would be foolish to ignore them. (Thinking of innovative framing brings to mind the Italian filmmaker Michelangelo Antonioni, whose extraordinary perspectives were the result of his obsession with composition.)

The fact that films are sometimes called motion pictures reminds us that they have evolved from still photography and painting. Film motion certainly has its own aesthetic (to be discussed in later chapters), but we can start here by considering static composition.

Composition

As I noted when discussing camera shots in the previous chapter, shot composition is concerned with objects within a space, and care must be taken in the placement of both elements.

The simplest composition places an object in the dead center of the frame. A news anchor reading the headlines from a teleprompter is usually placed squarely in the center of frame. This framing announces that he should command our entire attention. The eyes, as they read the teleprompter, are directed straight into the camera and, hence, at us. The centered person certainly dominates the screen, yet, perhaps because we are so used to this framing, he is not quite as dominant as the position suggests. The space, which is evenly distributed around the figure, balances the composition and also makes it a little formal. So the effect is intimate and yet formal, dominant and yet neutral. Heads of state are always shot like this when addressing their nations, precisely because it is neutral. If you placed the president anywhere else but dead center you would be implying a lack of balance.

Drama rarely adopts this framing because characters do not usually talk directly into the camera. When this convention is broken, the effect can be momentarily startling. I still remember how effective Iago's soliloquies were when Frank Finlay delivered them straight at the camera in Stuart Burge's production of *Othello* (1965, with Lawrence Olivier in the title role).

Most commonly, characters deliver their lines to someone who is just off-screen. As we have seen, it is important that the camera is positioned close enough to the line between the two actors to get a clear, two-eyed shot. And the tighter the shot, the closer to the line (discussed in Chapter 12) the camera should be. In this situation, space is not equally distributed around the character. A character looking camera-right will be offset to the left of frame. The further the character looks to the side of the camera, the more space (or *looking room*) will be in front of his nose. If you shoot someone in profile, the back of the head might almost touch the side of the frame.

The rule of thirds

The Ancient Greeks divided a composition according to a mathematical formula to produce areas called "golden sections," which they believed had almost magical properties. It so happens that if you divide up a canvas or screen by drawing lines a third of the way across it (both vertically and horizontally), you achieve approximately this same ratio. Figures placed on these lines, or where the lines intersect, seem to have particular prominence and aesthetic value. This is known as *the rule of thirds*. If you look at a classical painting or an artistic photograph, you may well find this method of composition. (See Fig. 19.1.) In fact, most artists seem to either consciously or intuitively adopt it. Of course, it can be applied to film and television as well.

Fig.19.1: The rule of thirds

The strongest position for an actor on a theater stage is said to be "downstage right," and characters or objects prominently placed on the right-hand side of a screen also seem to have particular weight. This may be due to the way the eye in Occidental cultures is said to scan the screen from left to right, momentarily resting on the right-hand side before darting out again. Directors from the black-and-white era of Hollywood movie production seem to have been aware of this, and tended to place their heroines on the right of the screen at climactic moments.

Horizontals, verticals, and diagonals

According to the classical rules of composition, drawings consist of lines and points. Lines are continuous movements of the brush or pencil, and points are either small individual marks (dots and small circles) or those places where two or more lines intersect.

Many intersecting lines tend to fill a composition and make it feel busy. Intersecting lines also give the impression of space, because objects appear to be placed either in front or behind one another. (If the trunks of two trees intersect, then our brains automatically place one in front of the other.) Many points also make a composition busy, and moving points (such as a filmed crowd) give the impression of energy.

Lines can also suggest mood. Horizontal lines, for example, suggest calmness and repose. Many eighteenth century landscapes (as in Fig. 19.1), which emphasize the horizontal lie of parks and fields, seem to have a timeless quality. This was a mood Stanley Kubrick exploited in his sumptuous historical film *Barry Lyndon* (1975). In this respect, the arrival of the prince (played by Omar Sharif) across the level desert plain in *Lawrence of Arabia* (1962) — a scene of considerable tranquility and beauty — contrasts with the movie's other, more restless, desert scenes featuring high, rolling sand dunes.

Vertical lines often suggest aspiration and power. *Patton* (1969) opens with the arresting image of the general gradually ascending a huge stage. In compositional terms, this is a solitary vertical appearing on a strong horizontal — aspiration superimposed upon order. (This effect is heightened by the symbol of the American flag, with its many horizontals, in the background.) A composition of many vertical parallel lines strengthens the effect. The skyline of Manhattan is a perennial symbol of aspiration and power because of its cluster of parallel-thrusting skyscrapers. A movie that consciously employed verticals to denote power was King Vidor's *The Fountainhead* (1949). Ridley Scott also employed verticals in *The Gladiator* (2000), in which he consciously referenced the documentaries of Leni Riefenstahl, which had employed low angles and strong verticals to celebrate the power of the Third Reich.

The rising, falling, plunging quality of diagonals often suggest disequilibrium and unrest. German Expressionist films of the 1930s contain many stylized diagonal lines. Diagonals were also used to great effect by Carole Reed in *The Third Man* (1949), in which certain shots were *canted* (shot at a slanted angle). I also think of the transition in Jane Campion's *Portrait of a Lady* (1996) in which the vertical lines of Florence Cathedral were shot at a canted angle and then slowly rotated to the horizontal. Many high-angle shots (shot at seventy or eighty degrees above their subjects) are also diagonals and suggest disequilibrium. Consider the dizzying, high-angle shots of the Five Points area of New York in *The Gangs of New York* (2002).

Analysis of two paintings

The following analysis of two paintings is designed to illustrate compositional elements, as well as to encourage the aspiring director to look at art books and visit museums. Directors, designers, and cinematographers frequently discuss the look and mood of their movies by referring to paintings and photographs.

The eye requires time to scan a painting, and many painters can (to a certain extent) control where the eye first lands and the journey it subsequently makes across the canvas. This is especially true of classical paintings in which artists controlled the viewer's eye by manipulating color, light, and composition. Here are two examples—one fairly simple and one more sophisticated—of how meaning is conveyed through the elements of composition.

In Fig. 19.2, the viewer's eye lands somewhere in the group of courtiers on the left, or perhaps in the lighter area above them. It is subsequently drawn to the bowing cleric (in a bright red jacket) and the courtier (in a white jacket). Then attention is dragged across the painting to the right till it rests on the solitary, descending figure in brown, who is reading a book.

The courtiers, gathered round the banister, form the shape of an arrowhead pointing directly at the solitary figure. (In design terms, they form a "vector.")

Fig.19.2: *L'Eminence Grise* by Jean Leon Gerome (painted circa1874)

The figure on the right occupies a powerful position in the picture—he is placed halfway down the canvas and on the right-hand horizontal third of the picture. It is an effective, though somewhat simple, arrangement. A director should note the interesting placement of the crowd (one group bowing, the other group looking back down the stairs), and the placement of the guard with the halberd behind the balustrade. The shaded foreground pillar on the left-hand side also gives the composition added depth.

For me, this composition conveys the sense that the courtiers, for all their ostentatious affluence, exist to magnify the power of the single, spiritual, man with a book.

Fig.19.3: *The Daughters of Edward D. Bolt* by John Singer Sargent (painted circa 1882)

In Fig. 19.3, I think the eye is immediately drawn to the figure of the child sitting in the light, in the mid-lower foreground of the painting. We are also attracted by her slightly curious, seated posture (because all the other figures are standing) and by the doll she's holding.

Our gaze then flows naturally to the second girl on the left (who is also prominently lit) across corner of the carpet, which forms a vector (or arrow shape) similar to the painting discussed above.

Our attention tends to be attracted by light and therefore moves on to the two girls standing in the center, whose white pinafores reflect the light. From there, perhaps, it moves on to the window in the upper background.

There are clearly two areas in the composition: The area in the foreground and then the darker area behind it, which is framed by the wall on the left and the brown screen on the right-hand side. This "frame-within-a-frame" is a common and very effective visual device. Many movies have shots framed through doors or windows, separating foreground from background.

What would you say the mood of the picture was? I think there is a superficial balance as the strong horizontal line of the carpet complements the vertical line of the wall. I think the slightly off-center framing, which places the four girls to the center and left of the picture, is a little disturbing. And so is the darkness of the background, which occupies so much of the painting's space. The vertical lines of the three standing girls are emphasized by the large jar (placed on a vertical third), which almost seems to be another figure. The brown screen (on the right hand side) is also disturbingly crooked. This subtle unbalancing of the composition suggests a particular "reading" of the picture. For me, the picture implies the journey from the innocence of youth (represented by the two younger daughters in the light) to the murkier regions of adolescence and maturity (represented by the older girls standing on the threshold of darkness).

Illustrations 19.4–19.8 show static (single-frame) compositions by filmmakers that illustrate some of the points mentioned above.

Fig. 19.4: Vectors: Still from Antonioni's *L'Avventura* (1960)

Figs. 19.5 and 19.6: Frames within frames: Stills from *L'Avventura* and Tarkovsky's *Nostalghia* (1983)

Fig.19.7: Artful grouping of figures within a frame (*Nostalghia*)

Fig. 19.8: Using classical painting as a visual reference: Still from *The Draughtsman's Contract* (1982), suggesting seventeenth-century Dutch painting.

Fig. 19.9: In the style of the painter Edward Hopper: Still from *Road to Perdition* (2003)

Lenses

Composition, in photographic mediums like film and television, is enhanced by the creative use of lenses. You can arrange actors on a set without any knowledge of lenses—but such ignorance will severely limit your control of your project. It would mean surrendering control of a large portion of the "look" of your project to the director of photography and the camera operator.

Different lenses have different effects on the picture

Lens selection can help to express your vision. A director should at least be able to discuss lens choice with her director of photography. DPs appreciate some kind of indication about lenses. Stipulating the exact lens-size for each shot is not necessary—though plenty of directors who can afford the few hundred dollars for a portable director's viewfinder do just that.

I'll discuss the properties of lenses in detail below, but here is a brief overview of the three main categories of lenses.

A director's viewfinder is a small (between three and five inches long), lightweight, exquisitely crafted, multi-lens viewfinder. Directors can view a shot by selecting the format in which they are shooting (35mm film, 1/2-inch video, etc.) and one of a range of lenses.

Director's viewfinders are used mainly in film, because variable zoom lenses are less common and a decision about using a specific lens is often made for each shot. Some directors have strong views about lenses and mandate their choices. Others prefer to discuss the choice of lens with their DPs.

Wide-angle lenses are more convex (fish-eyed) than other lenses, and gather images from a wider field. A wide-angle lens tends to separate characters from each other in a frame. It also tends to keep everything in focus.

A *narrow-angle* or *telephoto* lens does the opposite. Characters tend to get squeezed closer together (especially when one is positioned in front of the other) and part of the picture can go out of focus (OOF).

A *normal* lens (see note below) tends to reproduce objects as the human eye sees them, somewhere between the two extremes of wide and telephoto. If you were to measure this lens's angle of vision with a protractor, it would be about twenty-five degrees.

Lenses are defined by a number called "focal length," which is measured in millimeters.

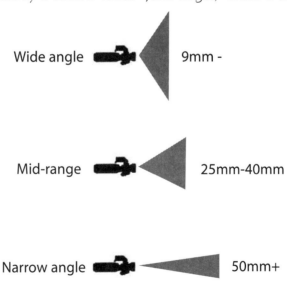

Wide angle — 9mm -

Mid-range — 25mm-40mm

Narrow angle — 50mm+

Fig. 19.10: Focal lengths for 16mm film

Note: What is considered a "normal" lens differs according to the format in which you are shooting. A 25mm lens is normal for 16mm cameras and a 50mm lens is normal for 35mm cameras. A video camera's normal lens is closer to a 16mm film camera's—though most video cameras operate with zoom lenses.

How do we get these numbers? The number tells us how far it is between the center of the lens and the film or (in the case of video) between the center of the lens and the imaging device (charge-coupled devices or CCDs). (See Fig. 19.11.)

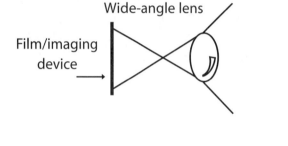

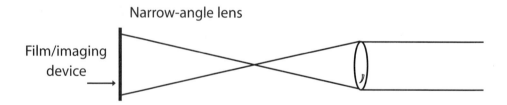

Fig. 19.11: Distance from lens to film or imaging device

In the old days (pre-1970), all film cameras used single lenses that looked rather like one of the thick lenses from grandma's spectacles and required intense lighting. Lens technology has come a long way since then and, today, individual lenses ("prime lenses") are enormously sensitive to light. Nowadays, a zoom lens (an encased array of different lenses that shift in relation to each other to give a continuous range of focal lengths) is increasingly used with film cameras. However, the principle of wide-angle, normal, and telephoto still applies.

Depth and planes

Consider the depth of a two-dimensional picture—such as a photograph of your family on holiday in the countryside, with a fence in front of them and a farmhouse behind them. Imagine that it has three layers or planes. The first layer nearest to you is the foreground (the fence). The middle layer is the middleground (the family). And the farthest layer is the background (the farmhouse). Lenses affect how we perceive all three of these planes.

Given bright lighting conditions, a wide-angle lens enables a camera operator to keep all three planes in focus at the same time. It allows maximum *depth of field* (the ability to keep objects in focus in all three planes). Thus, broadcast journalists arriving on the scene of an accident or covering a government reception will automatically use a wide-angle lens to keep everything (which often includes the unexpected) in focus. A clear, deep image was very popular in the late 1930s and early '40s, exemplified by *Citizen Kane* (1941), in which cameraman Gregg Toland achieved remarkable depth of field.

A narrow-angle lens does not keep things in focus so well. A really narrow-angle lens can confine you to one plane. This may be a disadvantage if you want the newsreel look of *Citizen Kane*, but it can be an advantage too. Francis Ford Coppola and his DP, Vittorio Storaro, used dark interiors and narrow lenses to evoke a claustrophobic atmosphere in the last act of *Apocalypse Now* (1979). A telephoto lens allows the camera to emphasize a specific object by throwing the rest of the shot out of focus. In this way, it can isolate a character in a crowd, or lose a distracting background. This selective focus aspect of the lens not only allows a director to concentrate on just one object, but to switch attention from one object to another by changing the lens's focus (also known as *throwing focus* or *racking focus*). We have probably all seen two-character scenes (American soap operas are full of them) in which first one person is in focus and the other fuzzy, but then the other is brought into focus as he starts to speak. (At a recent showing of a film in my local cinema, the projectionist asked the audience not to hold him responsible for the out-of-focus backgrounds in the movie we were about to watch. It was the director's fault, he explained, for using so many rack focuses.)

Perhaps most importantly, different lenses bring different moods to a scene. The clear-focused look of a wide-angle lens is different from the softer, selective-focus feeling that (under the right lighting conditions) a narrow-angle lens delivers. A normal lens that approximates human sight may give a more objective impression.

Mood will also be affected by the properties of separation and distortion.

Separation and distortion

In a confined space, such as a room, a wide-angle lens tends to emphasize the distance between people and make the space seem deeper and wider. Sydney Lumet, who uses lenses to great effect, applied this principle in his film *Twelve Angry Men* (1957). The whole drama is set in a jury room and, during the course of the movie, the atmosphere is intensified through the use of progressively narrower lenses, which bring the characters seemingly closer together.[1]

Narrower lenses make a space seem more confined, and they also compress space. Distances between people and objects become minimized so that things separated by yards seem to be stacked right up against each other. Kurosawa uses this property in *Seven Samurai* (1954). Here, the villagers, who have come to town to find a samurai to defend them, watch the townspeople pass by. Due to the narrow angle, the passersby seem to be walking only inches from the peasants. Another application of compression makes a character who is running toward camera seem not to get any closer—a device used effectively in *The Parallax View* (1974) and *Marathon Man* (1976), among other films.

Just as a narrow-angle lens can make objects appear closer than they are, so a wide-angle lens can push them artificially farther away. This capacity to really separate the planes can result in interesting effects. A traffic policeman who holds up his arm in front of a wide-angle lens will have an imposing hand. The cab of a truck parked in front of the camera will seem to dwarf the rest of the vehicle. A face close to the lens will begin to distort—the eyes becoming very far apart. In the 1970s, deep focus photography was adopted by Steven Spielberg and Brian De Palma, who were intrigued by its potential. On the other hand, filmmakers as culturally different as Hitchcock and Ozu have used normal lenses to convey the impression of everyday reality.

Perhaps the most dramatic lens effect was conceived by Hitchcock to graphically represent his hero's fear of heights in the film *Vertigo* (1958). Hitchcock rigged his camera high up in a bell tower overlooking the stairway, and then simultaneously dropped the camera downward and zoomed in from a wide angle to a narrow angle. Martin Scorsese used "the *Vertigo*-effect" to suggest isolation and separation in *Casino* (1995), and it was also widely used by British filmmakers during the 1990s.

---

[1] See *Making Movies* by Sidney Lumet for an extensive discussion of the use of lenses in his films.

20. Audio

You can direct actors without any knowledge of audio—but you would be severely limited. It would mean surrendering control of a large portion of the "sound" of your project to the sound recordist or the sound designer. Audio is a key production value, as essential as good framing. Effective audio tends to go unnoticed, while bad audio can ruin an entire shot.

Priority is usually given to the visual elements on most shoots, and the sound crew is expected to make do. This is a shame. Audio should be considered at least as early as the storyboard stage. Every shot has its corresponding audio that, at its most basic, conveys information in the form of either dialogue or ambient sounds. But audio can do much more than simply support the picture. It can comment ironically on its visual elements; it can appeal directly to the emotions through music; and (as we shall see when discussing audio postproduction) it can provide subtle and complex meaning through the layering of dialogue, sound effects, and music. Directors, especially in drama, do not have to be audio specialists, but they should appreciate its contribution and understand enough about it to include it in their planning.

Good audio is produced by the choice of an appropriate microphone, by placing the microphone correctly, and by the skilled services of at least two crew members.

Microphone types

On a small documentary production, the producer/director often takes responsibility for audio recording, and might employ various microphone types. However, narrative drama employs one kind of microphone ninety-nine percent of the time for film-style shooting—the shotgun microphone—and the director should understand how to help the sound department operate it most effectively.

The shotgun is a very sensitive microphone suspended just out of the shot (usually just above the top of the frame). It captures sound from the direction in which it is pointed. The ability to collect audio from just one direction makes it, in audio-speak, *unidirectional* or *cardioid*. Mics that are even more specific about the direction in which they pick up sound are the "super-cardioid" and the "hyper-cardioid." Cardioid means heart-shaped and reflects the pattern in which a shotgun mic picks up sound. (See Fig. 20.1.) A shotgun mic is a long, tube-shaped instrument, which—for film work—is attached to a pole (the *boom*) and held in position by a sound assistant (or boom operator). To reduce the low rumble caused by the wind, a shotgun microphone is usually encased inside a foam rubber tube, called a *windscreen*. Outdoors on a windy day, an additional fluffy layer called a *windjammer* might be applied. This makes the mic look not unlike a shiatsu dog. (Irreverent sound engineers have a variety of terms for the windjammer, including "the ferret.")

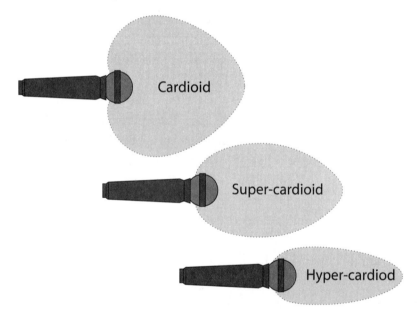

Fig. 20.1: Shotgun microphone pick-up patterns

The advantage of collecting sound from just one direction is that you can be fairly precise about what you are recording and minimize noises occurring to the side of the mic or behind it, such as the sound of the camera itself and movement by the crew. (This does not mean that the crew can be noisy during a take.) The converse is that every sound in the direction in which the mic is pointed will be recorded very faithfully, which may include not only your actors but also the noisy refrigerator or heating unit in the back of shot. The solution to this particularly common audio problem is simply to switch the machines off.

The technique of on-location sound recording is less than perfect. It depends to a great degree on the skill of the boom operator to hold the mic steadily in position and then maneuver it in the direction of whoever is speaking. On an exterior location in a noisy environment such as a city street, perfect sound is almost unattainable. Even in the countryside, overhead aircraft, farm equipment, and animals ruin takes. (Why audio technology is so primitive, I have no idea. You would have thought that by now we would have found a way to isolate a shooting area with invisible, sound-proofed, plastic.)

I should mention in passing some of the other types of microphone available. Journalists and documentary-makers, interviewing subjects, often use a hand-held (as opposed to a boom-mounted) microphone specifically designed to pick up sound from two people standing opposite each other, which is called a bi-directional mic. Audio engineers on a drama production might use this kind of mic if they were simulating an interview, though they might equally well give the actors a prop (or dummy) to hold and record with a shotgun microphone instead. (It would depend on the particular effect required in the film.)

A pop singer croons into another type of sturdy, hand-held microphone that favors sound reaching it from the top. (We've probably all seen rock stars with their lips very close to the top of a mic.) In a situation where live music is being recorded for a scene, the audio from the singer's mic may be carefully mixed with the other music tracks by the sound recordist. Complicated mixes, such as music recording, are generally done in a studio with sophisticated equipment rather than on location. It is more likely, therefore, that the song will have been recorded prior to the shoot and the singer will be miming to playback—in which case the sound department will bring a separate playback deck and speaker system to the location.

An in-studio interviewer and his guest will sometimes wear small clip-on microphones called *lavaliere* mics (so named because they resembled the pendant worn by Madame de Lavaliere, a mistress of the French king Louis XIV). The sound quality of a *lav* can be very good. It works best when the wearer is not moving, because clothing or anything else rubbing up against it produces a nasty rustling sound. Nevertheless, lavalieres are occasionally employed in drama when the larger shotgun mic would appear in the frame. For instance, a lavaliere can be taped to a car dashboard or visor if a boom operator has no place to hide a shotgun microphone in the vehicle. In shots that are so wide that the boom op cannot get close enough to the action to record good audio without being on camera, wireless lavalieres may be discreetly pinned to the actors. However, wireless microphones have to be of a very good quality to work well, and they are prone to radio-wave interference. I wish I could reclaim all the hours I've spent on locations waiting for sound engineers to get wireless mics to work. Luckily, wireless technology is improving all the time, and the latest models offer a large choice of alternative transmission frequencies and advanced tuning that minimize interference.

Sound perspective

Comparing lavaliere microphones with shotguns leads naturally to a consideration of sound perspective. In the shotgun/boom method of sound recording, where the microphone almost always has to be placed outside the frame, the wider the shot the greater the distance the mic is from the speaker. This means that sound perspective is automatically achieved, so a mid-shot, for instance, will have a slightly different audio quality than a closeup. The lavaliere microphone, on the other hand, is clipped onto the costume itself and is always at a constant distance from the speaker's mouth, which means that the sound perspective is consistently close. This effect can be slightly inconvenient and time-consuming during postproduction, when the audio mixer is attempting to achieve the impression of perspective. Still, mixers, who have a wide selection of audio effects at their fingertips, would prefer to work with good close sound than with sound that has been poorly recorded at a distance. And a wide shot with the very clear, close sound of a lavaliere can occasionally be a refreshing effect.

As far as drama is concerned, the process of audio recording is reasonably straightforward, so a good sound recordist should be able to explain any difficulty she is encountering to the director. However, there are a few recurring problems, which a director should anticipate or be prepared to deal with as soon as they arise.

Microphone placement

Occasionally, the script does call for a microphone to be in vision. Perhaps the hero of your TV series is the President of the United States (as in *West Wing*), who has to address the nation on television. The sound department might clip a lavaliere discreetly to his tie or use the actual microphone on his desk. In another scene, you may have to hide (or "stash") a microphone somewhere within the frame because the boom operator cannot reach an actor. Mics can be hidden behind flowerpots and pillars. In extremity, they may even be placed in the hands of a technician dressed as an extra standing with her back to the camera, next to the actor speaking the lines.

By far, the most frequent microphone placement is outside the frame. Camera placement and shot size—two important issues for camera operators—affect audio recording as well. The boom operator must be aware of any variations in framing so that the microphone does not appear in the shot. Before camera rehearsal (and often before the take itself), the boom op places the mic inside the shot and works with the camera operator to find the position that is just out of the shot. "In … In … In …" says the cameraperson till the mic disappears out of shot, at which point he says, "Out. That's good." The boom operator is then responsible for finding that exact position, take after take, and holding the mic there, which is not an easy task.

Due to human error (not always on the part of the boom op) the mic sometimes appears in the shot, necessitating a retake. If this happens, the director should ask the boom operator if she needs a few seconds to double-check her mic's position before continuing. A moment spent addressing the problem at this stage may save more time later on.

Of all the shots, the wide-shot is the one that causes the most difficulty for sound departments. For example, you have chosen to have two actors walk leisurely up a path starting in a wide shot revealing the trees on either side as well as the hills in the background. As they approach the camera the shot tightens till, at the end, it becomes a straightforward mid-2-shot. But at the start of the shot, where will the boom operator place her mic so she can get crystal-clear audio and at the same time be out of the frame? If she is lucky, she might be able to hide it behind an intervening tree (trees are helpful because the boom pole is sometimes mistaken for a branch), but more often than not the set or location offers no hiding place. A wireless mic might be an option, but in this case, the shot ends in a mid-2-shot and the lavalieres would almost certainly be noticeable. Perhaps the best solution is the following: Record the whole shot with the boom in place for the very end when the actors are in mid-shot and the mic can be safely out of shot. Then, for the opening of the shot, when it is so wide we cannot really see the actors' mouths clearly (i.e., cannot read lips), go back immediately after the shot ends and record their dialogue while they still remember exactly how they said it. During this second (audio only) take, the boom op will simply walk alongside the actors with the microphone in an optimal position. (In cases such as this, it sometimes helps to record the dialogue two or three times with the actors slightly varying the pacing of their lines each time, just to make sure you have material that will synch up with their moving mouths.) I shot a scene with actors on horseback once, and so much of their concentration was devoted to controlling the animals that they never remembered how they'd said their lines. We were glad, when we came to editing, that we had several different audio versions to choose from.

When an audio track is recorded separately from the picture, it is called a *wild track*.

Occasionally, a director arranges a number of actors in a wide shot and, because they are so spread, the boom op cannot reach them all in time for their lines. (See Fig. 20.2 and Fig. 20.3.) Imagine a high-angle wide shot in which two couples converge on a church gate. The boom op cannot possibly cover both the couple approaching from foreground left as well as the pair coming from background right. A director who is aware of this "split sound" problem should discuss it with the sound department in advance so they can think of ways around it. Perhaps the sound crew can stash a mic, or draft a second boom op, or even record one group's dialogue separately for it to be added in postproduction. Robert Altman is a director who stages complicated, multi-character shots that require several microphones and very precise audio recording. I imagine there was more than one mic stashed behind a soup tureen in the complicated tracking shots around the dinner table in *Gosford Park* (2002), when so many actors were speaking at once.

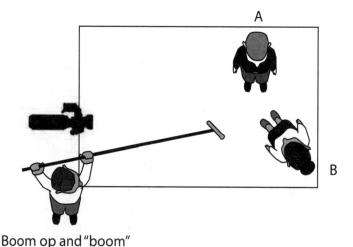

Boom op and "boom"

Fig. 20.2: "Boomable" position

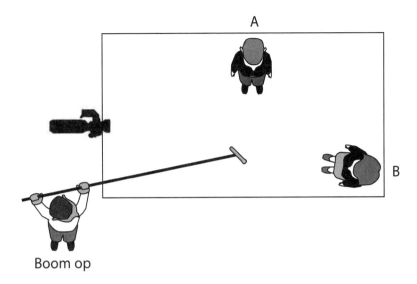

Boom op

Fig. 20.3: "Split sound"

Recording the best quality audio

While the boom op tries to get the microphone as near to the sound source as possible without it appearing in the shot, the recordist sits somewhere on the set with either a small mixing board or a recording device that allows for some *equalization* (adjusting of the quality of the sound by raising or attenuating various frequency ranges—the treble and bass controls on your home stereos are simple equalization controls). Audio must not only be clear and "clean" (i.e., free of competing sounds), it must be of substantially the same volume level and quality from take to take.

Recording audio in a protected environment, such as on a set or a soundstage, presents relatively few problems (though creaking floorboards, noisy workmen, and squeaky beds seem to be facts of life), but recording audio on location can be more complicated. The director shooting an exterior scene in a city has to decide whether to shoot synch sound (record the dialogue as it happens) or shoot the picture and add the dialogue later in a recording studio. Of course, if the scene has no dialogue then the street noises may not be a problem.

Shooting synch sound has the great advantage of realism. The actors can say their lines in the actual place where they are acting: There is no artificial separation between their physical performances and their vocal performances. The results are usually more satisfactory from an acting perspective. However, getting reasonable audio will require a certain amount of control over the environment—stopping passersby from talking, holding up traffic, halting street repairs, and so on. This can be very expensive, and it is a production manager's nightmare.

The alternative is to shoot the scene with imperfect audio and have the actors replace their dialogue at a later date. The technique for doing this is called *automatic dialogue replacement* (ADR). (See Part 6, Chapter 35.)

In theory, given a good environment, a good microphone, good mic placement, and good mixing, it should be possible to record even the quietest sounds. In practice, however, it is often difficult to understand whispers. If you have to record whispers, I'd suggest shooting the speaker in as tight a shot as you feel is appropriate. The tighter the shot, the closer the mic can get to the subject. Tight shots also allow viewers to read an actor's lips very clearly, which helps if individual words are indistinct.

Some famous actors have been recorded with all the technology available to Hollywood, yet their whispered lines cannot be understood. This is especially a problem if the movie theater has poor audio (as so many still do) or you are viewing on VHS, which lacks the superior digital audio of DVD.

Supporting the sound department

Crews accustomed to waiting long periods while lighting is completed and the camera is set up are sometimes less patient when it comes to audio. The director can help the sound department by insisting it gets the time it needs, and by anticipating problems before they occur. Here are some circumstances, fairly specific to drama, which the director should be aware of.

Gaps and overlaps

One of the golden rules of on-set audio recording is *make sure the actors leave a gap of at least one second after the director has called "Action!"* The gap allows the editor to apply the "scissors" before an actor starts speaking. It is surprising how often actors come straight in with their opening lines, almost overlapping the word "action," thereby necessitating a retake.

By the same token, *at the end of a take the director must leave a gap of a few seconds before calling "Cut!"*

Here is another situation, peculiar to drama, in which leaving a sound gap is important. *When you are shooting one person speaking to another person who is off-screen, their dialogue should not overlap.* Most of the time this is not a problem because actors wait for their cues before saying their lines. But occasionally (when you are shooting a heated argument, for example), an actor may anticipate a cue and an overlap occurs. Here is why this can be a problem: When one person is in frame, the microphone favors that person, not the person off-shot. If both actors speak at once, the off-shot person's voice will be recorded unclearly (she will be "off-mic"). Since she now appears on top of the well-recorded voice, the two cannot be separated, and the result is poor audio that may require re-recording at a later date. Plus, the editor will find it very difficult to cut back cleanly to the off-shot person for the rest of her line—because the first half is off-mic (poor audio) and the second on-mic (good audio).[1] (The editing implications of this scenario are discussed in Chapter 34.) If you happen to have rehearsed the scene and know in advance that an overlap will occur, discuss the problem with the sound department and see if they can suggest a solution. For instance, allocating a separate mic to the off-screen actor might be a possibility.

Atmosphere and wildtracks

As we will see in the next chapter, we can do things during shooting to facilitate editing. One of the problems of editing audio is that, despite the best efforts of the recordist, different shots have slightly different background sounds. Say you have been shooting all day in the living room with the central heating on. Some shots will register the buzz of the radiator more than others—depending on the mic's proximity to the radiator, and also due to the fact that the level of the buzz itself varies throughout the day. When the editor tries to cut together two shots, she may find that the background *atmosphere* (the ambient sound of the location) is distractingly different in both.

The simplest way to remedy this is to record the *atmos* in the living-room (without any voices or other distracting sounds), and then lay that clean atmos track under both shots during editing. This second layer provides both shots with a common audio element, and the change in tone between audio takes is less marked. (See Fig. 20.4.) At the end of shooting at every location, the sound crew should record two minutes of clean atmos.

---

[1] Not all directors agree with this advice. Both Sydney Lumet and Barry Levinson, for example, prefer not to compromise the performance, even though it creates problems during editing and occasionally necessitates actors being called back to rerecord their lines.

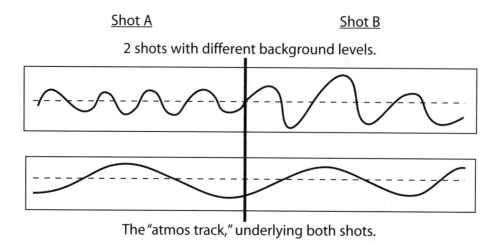

Fig.20.4: The atmos track

Other members of the crew who are hurrying to stow their equipment may object to being asked to stop work and be perfectly quiet, so it is important that directors lend the sound crew their support.

Recording wild tracks is not just restricted to more-or-less continuous sounds, like a background heater or an air-circulation system. Suppose you are shooting in a village where the inhabitants are cooperating by not creating noise around the set. However, from three houses away comes the periodic barking of someone's dachsund. Rather than stop every time the barking occurs (or slip the puppy a sleeping pill), the sound crew can record the noise there and then. If, during editing, the barking suddenly starts halfway through the scene, the editor has other instances of it that she can insert so it does not draw quite so much attention to itself. And if (heaven forbid!) the editor needs to cut to a shot that has only the tail end of a bark on it, then at least there is a chance of supplying a head. This practice is not confined to animals. It can work with police, ambulance and fire engine sirens, doorbells, and the like.

Aircraft noise is the bane of every film crew's existence. (It was at least partly responsible for the demise of Terry Gilliam's film *The Man Who Killed Don Quixote*, in 2002.) If an airplane drones overhead in the middle of a shot, you will almost certainly have to cut and start again. Jet aircrafts may make a loud noise but at least they pass by quickly. Smaller, slower, private aircraft, on the other hand, holds up shooting for a much longer time. If you are on location near a local airport, do not let the pilots know you are there or you will become an object of interest for every amateur aviator in the vicinity.

In the mid-1970s, as audio production and reproduction became more sophisticated, the role of the *sound designer* emerged. On certain major productions, the sound designer took overall responsibility for the whole *sound picture* (a film's complete sonic landscape), working with the recordist on the set and then combining and supplementing these tracks with sophisticated postproduction effects and music. In the absence of a sound designer, the director can encourage the sound recordist to provide sound effects indigenous to the location where they are shooting. Although there are mountains of sound effects available on disc that can be inserted later, few can improve on the real thing recorded on location. You can probably find a sound effects library that will give you something that sounds like a Scandinavian lake at dusk, but if you happen to be there you might as well record it. A resourceful sound crew is a blessing.

Because it is slightly removed from the center of attention, and also because its gear is easier to gather up at the end of the day, the audio crew often has more time on its hands than anyone else. This leaves it free for research. (It has been said that if it weren't for the sound crew no one would know the best restaurants on location.)

I was once in Florence, Italy, as the production manager on a documentary about the history of drama. (If you want to go to glamorous locations, become a documentary maker.) We spent half a day in the tremendous, high-ceilinged library of San Marco, achieving a single shot. The shot opened with a track along a row of illustrated medieval manuscripts, then the cameraperson threw focus to the other end of the library, where the distinguished presenter entered and spoke the words, "This library was designed by Michelangelo." After the shot was in the can, we gathered up our equipment and got ready to travel to Vicenza. The next morning, shortly before we were due to leave, the sound recordist joined me for a pre-work espresso. "I was wondering if I should mention this," he said, "but my guide book says that the library was designed by Michelozzo, not Michelangelo." Of course, he was right and the presenter was wrong. Who else would have had time to buy a guidebook and actually read it? The monks of San Marco were somewhat surprised to find us hammering at their elegant Renaissance portal later that morning, pleading for time to rerecord the speech.

21. An Introduction to Continuity

The object of the Hollywood Continuity Style (HCS) is to tell a story in a way that maximizes the momentum of the drama. The story must hook audiences, and nothing is to stand in its way. Individual shots that call attention to themselves are only very occasionally permitted, and then only if they serve the action by emphasizing a location or a character. The story is "foregrounded," along with those most-visible agents of the story—the actors. (One effect of this is to fetish actors, puffing them into "stars.") An economic logic underlies all this: Stories and stars *sell* properties. Individual shots, lighting, camerawork, and production design enhance the "properties" (as films are sometimes called) but are not as economically central in the Hollywood system.

The HCS contrasts with the Soviet-developed "montage" style that operated in very different economic circumstances, but also cast its influence on sequences in many classic Hollywood films. Soviet montage, as practiced in the 1920s by a group of filmmakers that included Sergei Eisenstein and the documentary-maker Dziga Vertov, highlighted the cut and thereby emphasized individual shots. (See chapter on "The Russian Connection" in Part 7, Chapter 37.) Central to this style of Soviet cinema was the idea of "juxtaposition"—placing shots with very different content next to each other. In Eisenstein's *October* (1927), shots of cannon are intercut with shots of civilians standing in a breadline in the snow, making a very specific comment about the effects of war.

Over time, elements of Soviet montage have been adapted to Western cinema. For instance, even Hollywood movies commonly use a form of montage with a music background. Some dramatic examples of montage appear in Stanley Kubrick's *Clockwork Orange* (1971). Brian de Palma paid homage to the Odessa Steps sequence from *Battleship Potemkin* in *The Untouchables* (1987). More recently, Barry Levinson used montage in *Liberty Heights* (1999) to interrelate different strands of the plot.

One of the goals of the HCS is to create a rhythm of shots that an audience unconsciously accepts because, having accepted a predictable shot sequence, it buys the content as well. As long as the story flows, spectators will suspend disbelief (at least until they get out of the cinema). Horror movies, with their isolated, sudden, scary juxtapositions that break the narrative flow, are effective precisely because they adhere to the HCS ninety-nine percent of the time. Hitchcock, a father of the modern horror genre, was a master of the HCS and knew how to manipulate its rules for effect. The murder of Janet Leigh in *Psycho* (1960) not only introduced montage into the movie's shot flow, it also broke the unspoken HCS rule against killing off your major character in the first act. Part of the reason for the impact of *The Blair Witch Project* (1999) on audiences was the way it broke the HCS rules with its entirely subjective, hand-held shots, and still managed to give the impression of traditional narrative flow. It made a fascinating contrast with the other successful horror movie of the year, *The Sixth Sense*, which used solid HCS storytelling and good performances to minimize disruptions in continuity. The sustaining of continuity (as well as other elements of the HCS) in *The Sixth Sense* actually led audiences to ignore the traumatic, dislocating event at the heart of the movie.

My discussion of continuity is divided to fall into two parts in this book: In the present section (in Part 4), continuity is discussed in relation to planning. My intention here is to help the beginning director produce a shooting script. In Part 5, I'll return to the subject to look at the implications of continuity during shooting—how it is worked out with the help of the camera operator and the continuity assistant, among others.

The traditional shot sequence

The key to good shooting in the classic Hollywood style is to produce a smooth flow of shots. Each shot should invite the next in a seamless succession of edits that is by no means arbitrary. In this style, shots form themselves into sequences according to accepted cinematic patterns and the logic of cause and effect. Here is how it happens.

The most widely accepted pattern is the traditional shot sequence discussed in Chapter 18. There is a reassuring rhythm to the pattern of wide shot, mid-shot, closeup, with wide or mid-shots periodically reintroduced to accommodate movement. Film audiences around the world have come to expect this sequence of events, and a director departs from it with trepidation. Not only is this sequence unconsciously lodged in viewers' minds, but the shots themselves have also come to have recognizable connotations (and it is in this very sense that we speak of film as a "language"). The wide shot, coming after a sequence of closeups, signals a new scene. The mid-shot suggests movement: either within the frame (as with the gestures of a comedy actor) or camera movement (pans, tilts, dollies, trucks, etc.). The closeup signals the climax of a scene, and also heralds its end.

The point in the sequence that offers the greatest opportunity for the juxtaposition of disparate shots is the opening. As discussed in Chapter 10, we expect scenes to start with some form of establishing shot—but this wide shot is itself a noticeably large jump in size from the (traditional) final closeup of the preceding scene. One may vary the pattern by, for instance, ending on a wide shot of two people walking into a house and then start the next scene with a closeup. This is a more satisfying transition than going from a wide shot to another wide shot, which is a visually weak cut. Another interesting opening juxtaposition is a cut from a closeup of a character looking out of frame one way (e.g., screen left) to a shot of another character looking in the opposite direction (screen right). This is a visual jump, but at the same time, a connection is being inferred between the two characters. In a wide-screen format, space at the edge of the frame may allow the inclusion of landscape as well, so such an opening shot could be a closeup and a partial establishing shot at the same time.

The reverse shot

In scenes with more than one person, we expect to see whomever is speaking. This desire is automatically satisfied when all the characters are in the same wide shot. But, as soon as this unity is broken by cutting to singles, the audience has to trust the director to show it the character it wants to see (usually the speaker), when it wants to see him. Other more experimental styles, such as the French New Wave, play with audience expectation by occasionally withholding the desired shot. In the HCS, dialogue produces a natural pattern of shot and reverse shot: We start on the person speaking and then cut to another person as he or she replies. This rule is so ingrained that it is difficult to break. Once, in a popular British television series, I wanted to open a scene with a shot of a character who was *not* speaking. But every time I called action, nothing happened. After several frustrated attempts, I finally understood the problem—the actor who had the first line could not believe he wasn't in the shot, and he was waiting for the camera to point at him before he spoke.

Most single shots imply a subsequent reverse shot. If more than one person is in the scene, sooner or later the audience will expect to see more than just the speaker. Tight shots, such as the MCU and CU, exclude so much information that viewers become restless if these shots are held too long. Audiences want to see both the cause and effect of every action. During speeches of four lines or more, directors tend to cut away to reaction shots of other people to give viewers the additional visual information they desire.

The HCS tradition requires an MCU or CU of one person to be followed by a matching MCU or CU of the other primary person (or people) in the scene. The initial closeup brings us into an unusual, intense intimacy with the subject. The composition is now the landscape of the face, and the drama becomes primarily emotional or psychological. But the audience's desire to see what is happening to all parties means that a *complementary* closeup of the other primary person (or people) is almost mandatory.

Sooner or later, most two-person scenes involve a 2-shot favoring one of the characters. It might be a mid-2 shot (see Fig. 21.1) or a tight 2-shot (see Fig. 21.2) or even an over-the-shoulder shot (see Fig. 21.3). Over-the-shoulder 2-shots are the perfect embodiment of the Hollywood Continuity Style. By favoring one character at the expense of the other, such shots arouse curiosity about the reactions of the person whose back is to the camera. That person is seen but also unseen, a mystery to the viewer. The unconscious pressure to have that mystery resolved forces the director to shoot the reverse shot. Very often the reverse of a 2-shot is not another matching 2-shot but some form of closeup. The favoring shot raises so many questions about the reactions of the unfavored character that only a closeup is strong enough to resolve them.

Fig. 21.1: M2s   **Fig. 21.2:** T2s   **Fig. 21.3:** O/S shot

Indication

When a character looks in a certain direction, the audience wants to see what he's looking at. This look, an indication, is one of filmmaking's strongest and most basic linking devices. The character not in shot is always implied by the look of the character who is. But the link can be made much more overt by strengthening the glance.

A character sitting at her dressing table looks up. What has happened? Who has entered? The suspense movie might delay the answer to increase the audience's unease, but most other genres will answer the question with a shot of the intruder.

A manager sitting at her desk suddenly looks up … we cut to the nervous worker who enters. A husband walks down the street and stops abruptly… we cut to a shot of his wife meeting another man. Such sequences are the stuff of drama.

Perhaps the strongest cinematic glance is the point-of-view (POV) shot. Generally preceded by an MCU or CU that firmly establishes whose POV it is, this shot shows us what a character is looking at, from his perspective. A child's point-of-view, for example, would be a low-angle shot looking up at grownups. The point-of-view of an Indian scout in a Western might be a wide shot of the enemy's camp. I once worked on a television series set in the countryside. After I'd worked on the show for a while, I had used up all the obvious angles, so I resorted to POV shots from animals' perspectives. My most successful was a pheasant's POV. I put the camera six inches off the ground (at the bird's eye-level) and got an establishing MCU of it. Then I shot the rest of the scene from the bird's low-angle perspective.

Actions can also prompt subsequent shots. Someone opens a drawer, and we want to see what is inside it. A person enters a hallway and picks up a note, and we want to know what it says. A gangster draws a gun, and we want to know how the other person reacts.

Audio is a very good indicating device. We hear a scream and want to know who's responsible. We hear a gunshot and want to know where it comes from. But even in the less melodramatic situation of a simple conversation, audio can prompt a cut. When one character interrupts another, we first hear the interruption and then cut to the person responsible. Some editors, as we will see, assemble a dialogue scene by cutting to a person *after* we hear that person's first word or two. In other words, they lead with the sound and delay the picture. This has the effect of momentarily arousing an audience's curiosity (Who is speaking?) and then resolving it. This technique can result in cuts that are extremely imperceptible.

Avoiding jump cuts

Cinematic information should generally be relayed as clearly as possible. To do this, allocate one shot to one subject at a time, alternating subjects with each cut. The challenge for the director is to provide enough information in each shot so that two similar shots of the same subject are not required in succession.

1) MS Alice picks up a stick.

2) MCU Bernard looks afraid.

3) MS Alice throws the stick.

The above shot sequence makes sense. If we changed the sequence to (1), (3), (2), the two shots of Alice in a row might be disconcerting. They might produce a "jump cut"—similar-size shots of the same subject that, when edited together, make the subject look like it has physically jumped.

Such jump cuts will occur if a director has not planned her shots properly or her plan has not been successfully implemented. Jump cuts also occur when like shots of similar subjects are juxtaposed in such a way that the viewer mistakenly reads them as the same subject (for example, a cut from a mid-shot of one blond child dressed in a pink smock to a mid-shot of another blond child similarly dressed).

Sometimes directors shoot successive mid-2 shots of the same people from similar angles, with the result that both shots are insufficiently differentiated .

Classical continuity suggests that every camera position be at least thirty degrees away from the previous one. In Fig. 21.4, positions "A" and "B" (which are both mid-2-shots) are from similar "frontal" positions. When cut together, they would produce a jump cut. Positions "X" and "Y" are preferable.

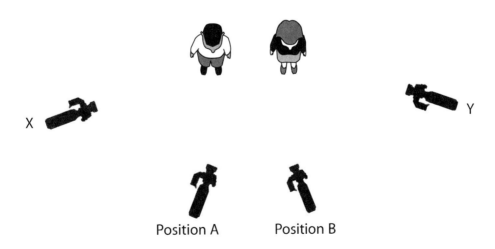

X   Y

Position A   Position B

Fig. 21.4: The 30-degree rule

Successive mid-2-shots of similar-looking couples often become jump cuts on a traditional television screen because the small screen does not always offer enough detail to tell them apart. For an instant, the brain reads the 2-shots as different angles of the same subjects.

To avoid a jump cut, noticeably vary both the shot size and the camera position. For example, if you are shooting a sequence in which John walks down the street, stops, and crosses to the other side, and you wanted to do it in 2-shots, here's how you could avoid the jump cut.

Shot 1: FL (full-length shot) John walking toward camera. The shot tightens as he approaches. He stops at the curb, in front of camera, in tight mid-shot. He exits left of frame.

Shot 2: FL John crossing street. Pan him left to Marjory. (See Fig. 21.5.)

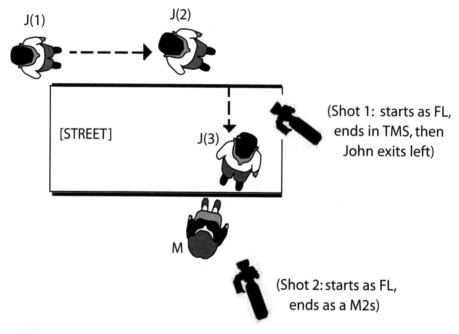

Fig. 21.5: Avoiding a jump cut—successive shots of different sizes

Another version of the jump cut is a "cut-along-the-line." This refers to two successive different-sized shots of the same subject from the same camera position. This is usually an awkward effect. Television people refer to it as a "film cut" (because it is not likely to happen in a multi-camera studio, I assume), but most film directors avoid it as well. However, it is sometimes used for effect. Hitchcock employed it in *Psycho* when Abrogast, the second victim, enters the Bates house. The unexpected cut-along-the-line throws the audience off balance. Francois Truffaut, who studied Hitchcock's technique, was less successful in *Fahrenheit 451* (1966), in which there is a singularly banal sequence of cuts-along-the-line to a ringing telephone. To avoid cutting along-the-line, remember to move the camera as well as to change the shot size.

Documentaries, which frequently deal with uncontrolled and unrehearsed material, tend to have more loosely constructed shot sequences than drama. (Real life has few "Take Twos.") So, jump cuts, line-crossings, and cuts-along-the-line are more commonly found in documentaries. Dramas that deliberately use the cut-along-the-line, such as *NYPD Blue*, may do so to convey a documentary feel. Good continuity is essential if you are using cuts-along-the-line. The subject's actions must match each other in succeeding shots if the sequence is to appear continuous.

Movement and screen direction

Movement within the screen always has a direction. It can be horizontal (left to right/right to left), vertical (top to bottom/bottom to top), or in depth (foreground to background/background to foreground). When a directional movement occurs, it creates a pattern, called a "vector," in the spectator's mind.

Screen direction (the left/right and up/down orientation of movement on the screen) is governed by some basic rules that should not be ignored. In Fig. 21.6 a character crosses the room to get a drink. In Shot 1, he leaves a 2-shot. In Shot 2, he enters a shot of the bar. Rules of screen direction insist that if he leaves Shot 1 moving toward the right of frame, he must enter Shot 2 left of frame. The reason for this? To keep the geography clear in the audience's mind, so he appears to be strolling across the room. Put another way, to preserve the continuous left-to-right vector that is created by exiting right and entering left.

Maintaining screen direction is important when a subject is moving from one place to another or is being pursued. Whenever your character is travelling, there is usually a predominant direction of travel. Maria gets in her car to drive home, pulls out into traffic, and travels across the screen, left-to-right. Her left-to-right vector has now been established. If you suddenly inserted a shot of her car going right-to-left (the opposite direction), it would, in the viewer's mind, imply that she was returning to work.

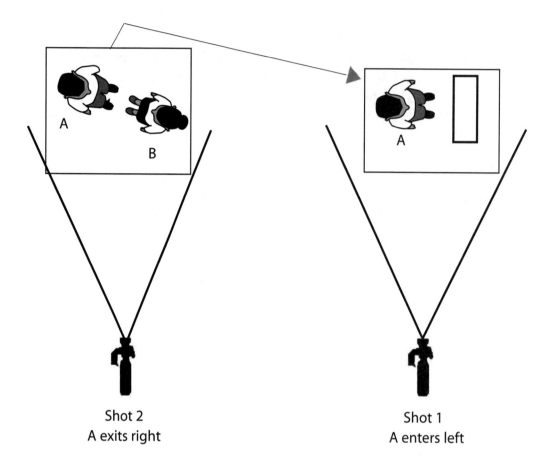

Shot 2
A exits right

Shot 1
A enters left

Fig. 21.6: Screen direction

These vectors (invisible lines of direction on the screen) can be established without movement too. A character looking to the left of camera and talking implies another character (or a mirror) listening and looking back.

I once had to direct a telephone conversation between a character in America and one in Europe. After pondering for some time, I realized that the character in America had to be placed left of frame looking out right, and vice-versa for the character in Europe. Why? Because when we look at a map or a globe, America is always placed to the left of Europe.

Screen direction, partly determined by vectors, is also partly determined by the "180-degree rule," which is discussed in the next chapter.

22. The 180-Degree Rule

"First there's the room you can see through the glass … that's just the same as our drawing room, only the things go the other way." — Lewis Carroll (*Alice Through the Looking Glass*)

If you want to make a cut that does not momentarily disorient the viewers, your characters have to appear to be facing in the direction the audience expects. The "180-degree rule," explained below, is the most effective way of ensuring that. If, for some reason, you don't want characters to appear predictably on screen, you can break the rule, as has been done before by Yasujiro Ozu, Stephen Sodeberg, the directors of *NYPD Blue*, and many others. But, in order to break the rule, you should understand it first.

The line

In Part 3, Chapter 12, we described an imaginary line between two people and showed how, when the camera was positioned close to the line, full-faced shots could be achieved. Now imagine that line extends a little beyond the two characters. (See Fig .22.1.)

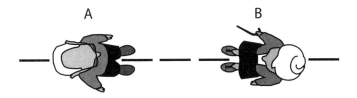

Fig. 22.1: The extended line

If we shoot a scene between Aaron and Betty in these positions, it is important to do it in a way that shows them facing each other. With that in mind, we place our camera in position "1" to shoot Aaron (see Fig. 22.2.) A *camera position* (or *setup*) is the physical spot in the set allocated to the camera by the director, from which it takes one or more different shots. When a camera is picked up and physically moved to another spot, a new camera position (or setup) is created.

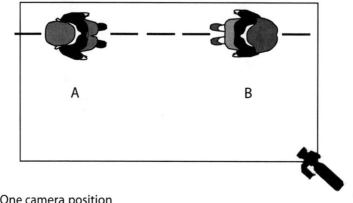

Fig. 22.2: One camera position   1

By placing the camera in position 1, we have Aaron looking right of camera, toward Betty. If we want the reverse shot of Betty (which means she should be looking camera left), where does the camera go?

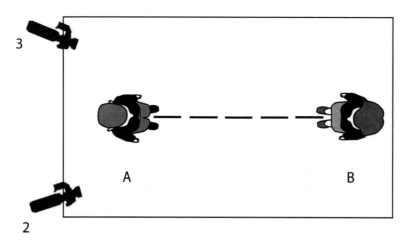

Fig. 22.3: Second camera position

Position 2 complements position 1, showing Betty looking left of camera. Position 3, on the other hand, has Betty looking right of camera, the same direction as Aaron, giving the impression they are both looking off-screen right instead of talking to each other. *To preserve screen direction* (i.e., have both characters looking toward each other, as they are in the scene), *both cameras have to be placed on the same side of the 180° line.* "Crossing the line" is the phrase used to describe breaking this rule. If you cross the line, you will draw attention to the shot and disorient the viewers. In Fig. 22.3, camera position 2 works, whereas position 3 is on the other side of the 180° line. Simple, isn't it? We will now spend the rest of the chapter looking at some of the ramifications.

One person and vehicles

If you are shooting just one person who is not talking to anyone else in the immediate vicinity, the line need not apply. Thus, in Fig. 22.4, if you have scene with a girl reading a book, you can shoot her from anywhere on the imaginary circle that surrounds her (I've arbitrarily chosen positions 1 and 2), though you would vary the shot size to avoid a jump cut.

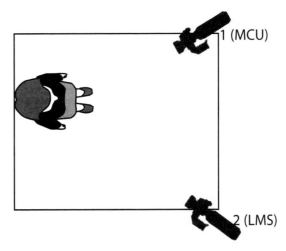

Fig. 22.4: Shooting one person

However, once the girl starts to move, she creates a line between herself and her destination (even if it's off-screen). To keep the impression of her moving in the same direction (in Fig. 22.5, left to right), the camera must take positions that are on one side of the line. The choice of side is up to the director, but once the decision is made, it should be adhered to.

Once you have chosen a side of the line, you can build whatever workable shot sequence you like. You can, for instance, have the girl exit right of frame and then shoot her back as she walks away. (Shooting people's backs is not always thee most informative angle, but perhaps this girl has a tear in the back of her sweater that we need to see or she is walking toward another person who is about to appear in shot.)

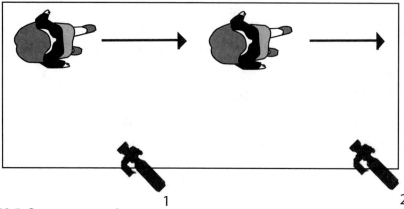

Fig. 22.5: One person moving

This principle of always positioning the camera on one side of the moving object applies to cars, cavalry charges, egg-and-spoon races, and all kinds of movement. It applies even when the character, animal, or object changes direction.

In Fig. 22.6, camera positions 3 and 4 are consecutive shots that preserve the left-to-right screen direction of the car. If we were to cut away from the shot of the car for a period of time and then cut back to it, a change of screen direction *might* be acceptable. In theory, once you cut away from an object, another convention comes into play—"out of sight, out mind." As long as the cutaway shot or sequence lasts for a reasonable amount of time (at least several seconds), an audience will accept that the car has changed direction. Thus, a shot from camera position 5 could follow a shot from position 3 (which is on the opposite side of the line), as long as a shot (or shots) of a different subject separated them. The exact length of the intervening footage would have to be determined during editing, but the longer it lasts, the more convincing the sequence would be.

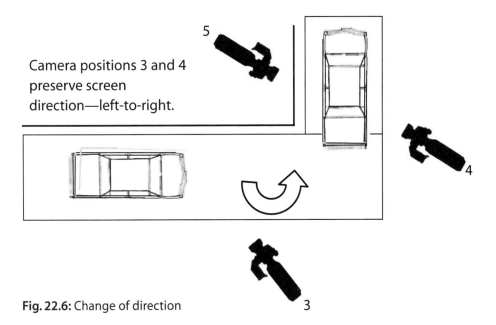

Fig. 22.6: Change of direction

Another possible way to get from camera position 3 to camera position 5 without disorienting the viewer is to interpose a "neutral shot" of the vehicle. A neutral shot avoids the whole question of left or right and shows the car travelling along the depth axis (see camera position 6 in Fig. 22.7). It could be a shot of the car either coming toward the camera or driving away from the camera. This position, which is exactly *on the line*, theoretically allows the shot that follows to be from either side of the line.

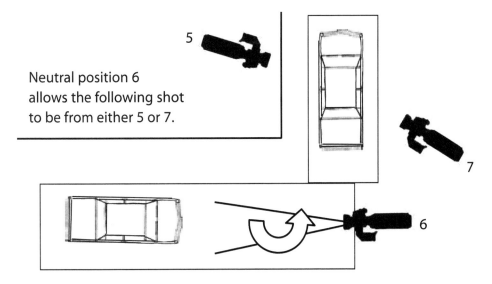

Fig. 22.7: Neutral position

Movement

When people move, the line moves with them. In Fig. 22.8, Charlie accuses Doris of taking the car keys. Doris crosses to the table, picks up her handbag, and shakes out the contents.

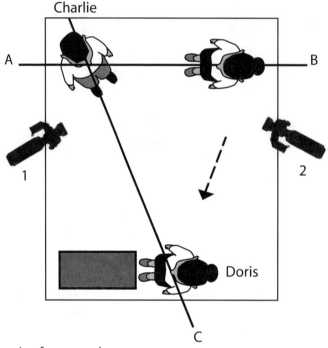

Fig. 22.8: Crossing foreground

The line shifts (A-B to A-C) as Doris moves to the desk. In doing so, it places camera positions 1 and 2 on opposite sides of the new line. Both camera positions should be on the same side of the line, so how do we solve this?

The director has to decide, in advance, which camera position will take the move. The most obvious position in this situation is number 1 (see Fig. 22.9). In most cases the attention will be on the person crossing and the camera will pan with her. In this case, the next shot must stay on the left of the line to ensure both positions are on the same side of the line. After the move, shots of Charlie will therefore be taken from position 3.

There may be a time, however, when you want to shoot from position 2 (in Fig. 22.8). You may be more interested in Charlie's reaction than Doris's move.

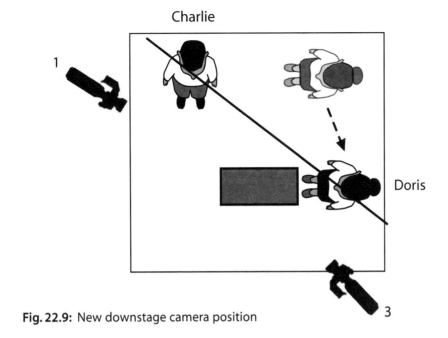

Fig. 22.9: New downstage camera position

So you hold Charlie while she crosses right-to-left *in front of the camera*. If the next shot is of Doris, then it has to come from the same side of the line as position 2—which is position 4. (See Fig. 22.10.)

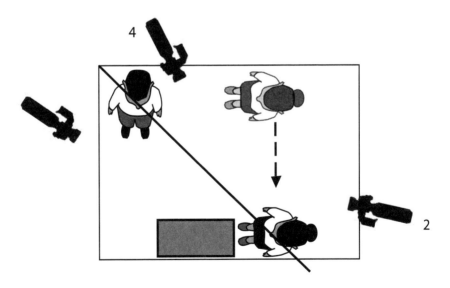

Fig. 22.10: Shooting the non-mover

Moves that bring a character forward on a new line (especially moves downstage), such as the one we are discussing, usually pose more 180° problems than moves from side to side.

Shooting three people and "the line"

Every time a character is added, the situation becomes more complicated. Fig. 22.11 shows all the possible 180° lines in a three-person scene.

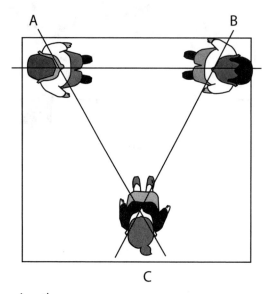

Fig. 22.11: Eyelines in a three-person scene

With three or more characters, actor placement is everything. Careful study of the script will reveal who the most important characters are, and therefore which of the eyelines is the most important.

In Fig. 22.12, two workmen, Bob and Don, ask Penny for a raise. Most of the dialogue is between Bob and Penny. Don has one line, but is largely a supportive presence. The director places Bob and Penny opposite each other and Don upstage. The bargaining between Bob and Penny can be shot from positions 1 and 2. Position 2 also gives a 2-shot of Bob and Don, plus a very nice single of Don for his line. Penny has very little significant dialogue with Don, so we can cover her entirely from position 1.

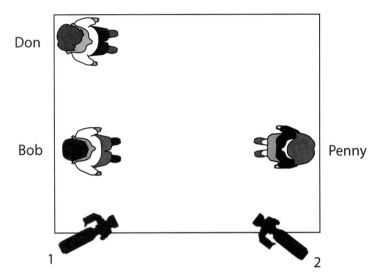

Fig. 22.12: Shooting three people in the "L" pattern

If Penny did have some important dialogue with Don, the director would have to create another camera position (3) to get a decent full-faced shot of her talking to him. (See Fig. 22.13.)

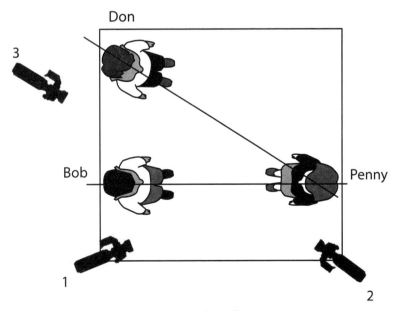

Fig. 22.13: Upstage camera position and eye-lines

Now, if the director shoots Penny's turn back to Bob from position 3, she will end up with positions 2 and 3 on opposite sides of the 180° line, which is now the line between Penny and Bob. This problem has two solutions. (See Figs. 22.14 and 22.15.) The director can either create a position 4 and continue to shoot Bob and Penny from the upstage side of the line (from 3 and 4) or take Penny's turn back to Bob from position 1.

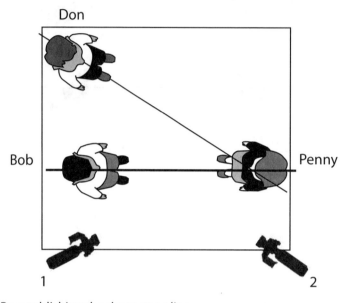

Fig. 22.14: Re-establishing the downstage line

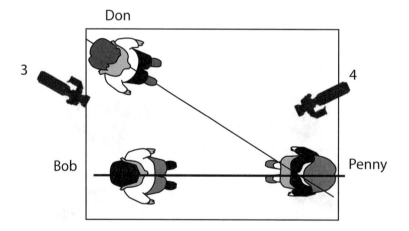

Fig. 22.15: Shooting from the opposite side of the original line

The scenario that follows is a common situation that is slightly more complicated. Surprisingly often, it causes directors to cross the line—especially in television drama. It is another three-person arrangement. Fred and George are Mafiosi who are demanding Max to repay a gambling debt.

```
SCENE 12        INT. POOLROOM   NIGHT

                      MAX
           What do you guys want from me?

                    GEORGE
           Everything you've got.

                     FRED
           And then some.
```

The Mafiosi are obviously intimidating characters, and the director opens the scene with a shot of Max framed between them. (See Fig. 22.16.)

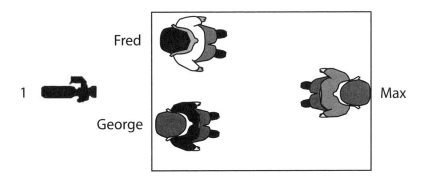

Fig. 22.16: Confrontational opening

Camera position 1 offers a fine opening shot of the Mafiosi dominating Max. But where does the director place the camera for the reverse shots of George and Fred?

The director has to decide exactly when he is going to cut back in order to establish the 180° line. This choice will determine the camera positions for the rest of the scene. If the director chooses to cut back for George's speech ("Everything you've got"), the camera position will be number 2, shown in Fig. 22.17.

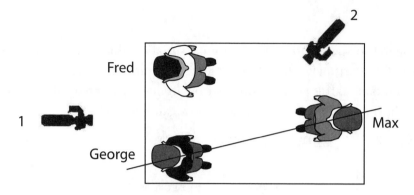

Fig. 22.17: Reverse shot favoring George

If the director cuts to Fred for his speech ("And then some"), the camera position will be number 3 in Fig. 22.18.

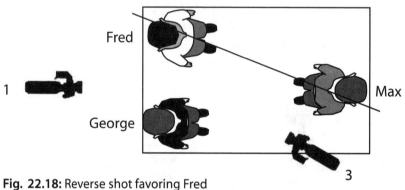

Fig. 22.18: Reverse shot favoring Fred

If Max proceeds to talk to George, then (to keep the shooting relatively simple), the director would shoot the Max-George dialogue from camera positions 3 and 4. (See Fig. 22.19.)

Fig. 22.19: Downstage camera positions

From position 4, the director can get a deep 2-shot of George and Max (favoring Max), an over-the-shoulder shot, and closeups of Max. From position 3 (with a little adjustment), he can get 2-shots and singles of George and Fred.

Shooting four people

Camera placement is also crucial when shooting four characters. And grouping comes even more into play. Everything depends on careful analysis of the script.

If the director keeps all four characters separated—at a dinner table, for example—shooting is potentially complicated. If each character speaks to all of the other three characters, then there will be a large number of camera positions. The number of camera positions in Fig. 22.20 (which only shows all the possible positions for *one* character—"A") would necessitate frequent adjustment of lighting and take a long time to shoot.

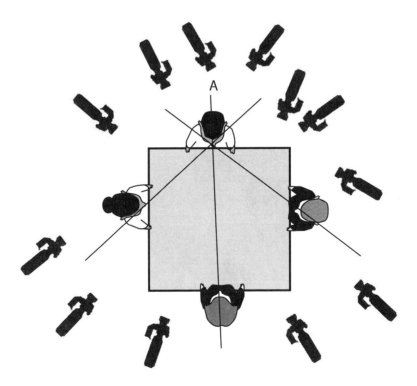

Fig. 22.20: Four people around a table

Unless the director has a large amount of time at his disposal, he would be advised to simplify his plan as much as possible. Simple blocking is preferable to needless complication. Not only does the director have to plan his shots, he has to indicate where and when they should be taken on location. A complicated plan can lead to problems with implementation.

Obviously, there are alternatives to the example (Fig. 22.20) above. First of all, it is unusual for *all* the characters to have substantial dialogue with each other. Usually, two or three characters dominate a scene and the director plans the shots around them. In Fig. 22.21, if A and B had the bulk of the dialogue in the scene, and C only had a short exchange with B, the following shooting plan would work.

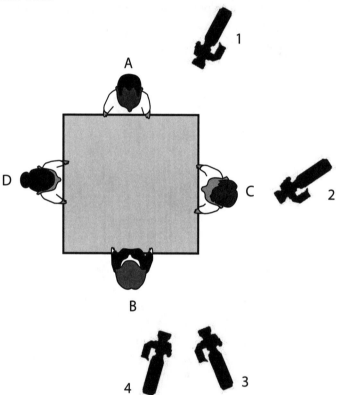

Fig. 22. 21: Simplified shooting

The positions are numbered in the order in which the director might shoot them. (The order in which shots should be taken is discussed in Chapter 25.) In Fig. 22.21, position 1 might offer an establishing shot of the table and shots of B. If additional cutaways are required of character D, they could be obtained by adjusting positions 1,2, or 3.

A second way of shooting our group of four would be to alter the shape of the table. A longer, thinner table, for instance, would suggest a two-versus-two arrangement. In the scene in Fig. 22.22, two couples meet over dinner to discuss their children's forthcoming marriage. The bride's parents (Angie and Bram) think that their daughter is too young to marry, so they're hostile.

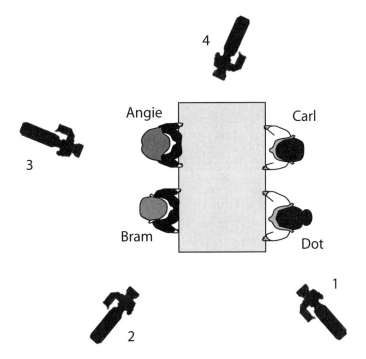

Fig. 22.22: Two-versus-two

- The director has decided to shoot the scene mainly in 2-shots from the downstage positions 1 and 2.
- These positions also work well for singles: Bram's dialogue with Dot; for Angie's remarks to Dot; and Carl's remarks to Bram.
- The director has analyzed the script and knows that Bram does not talk directly to Carl.
- Dot has a line to Angie that will be taken from position 3.
- Bram turns and talks directly to Angie. The director could shoot this in a 2-shot from position 1 but, if time allows, he will also cover Bram's lines to Angie from position 4.

The scene with five or more characters

The following example (Fig. 22.23) is taken from *All the President's Men* (1976), directed by Alan J. Pakula, a political thriller about the journalistic investigation that uncovered the Watergate Scandal. The scene is the editors' meeting at *The Washington Post*. It exemplifies two important shooting principles:

- Thoughtful placement and grouping.
- The busier the frame, the simpler the shooting.

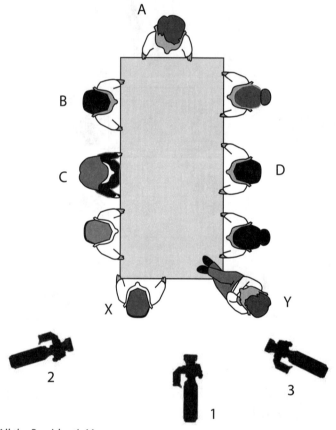

Fig. 22.23: *All the President's Men*

It is a long scene, but the debate is lively and three camera positions are sufficient. Position 1 gives an establishing shot of the table that excludes the editor-in-chief (Y) and his deputy (X), though Y's feet, which are in-shot on the tabletop, indicate where he is. An orienting establishing shot like this gives a necessary sense of the geography in a scene with lots of players. With a minimum of adjustment, position 1 can get good shots of A, B, C, and D, individually and in their groups, and works especially well because they refer so many of their remarks to the editor-in-chief (Y).

X and Y occasionally exchange looks and comments that are shot from positions 2 and 3.

The 180-degree cut

The 180 degree cut—cutting from a shot behind a group to a shot opposite and in front of it—often works surprisingly well. If you are shooting peoples' backs, the audience wants to see their faces and accepts the change of angle. And cutting to the opposite side of the line, directly in front of a group, is really a form of neutral cut (like cutting to the front of a car, as shown in Fig. 22.7).

A wedding scene is a common example of this situation. Viewers are so used to seeing weddings that they automatically intuit the geography of the church and are not easily disoriented. In Fig. 22.24, camera position 1 gives a high-angle wide shot of the church, looking toward the altar where the minister, groom, and best man are waiting. The bride and her father enter the lower right-hand side of the frame and proceed to walk up the aisle.

At this point the audience wants to see the bride's face. Position 2, which is a direct reverse shot—180 degrees opposite position 1—is perfectly acceptable.

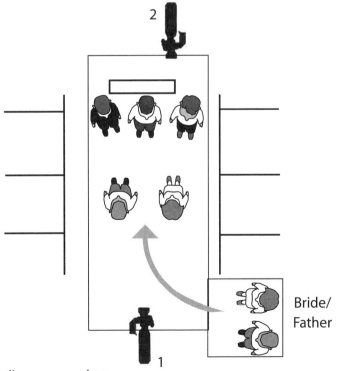

Fig. 22.24: The direct reverse shot

The wedding is just one example. This cut also works in simpler situations in which the geography is unambiguous. A wide shot of two people on a bench can be followed by a reverse shot from the other side of the bench. A line of policemen advancing down a street toward the camera can be followed by a reverse of the protestors.

Another cut along the 180-degree line is the subjective angle. Dramas do not normally have characters talking to each other in single shots while looking directly into the camera, but it can happen. If a director was to shoot a scene like this, the camera positions would be opposite each other (see Fig. 22.25).

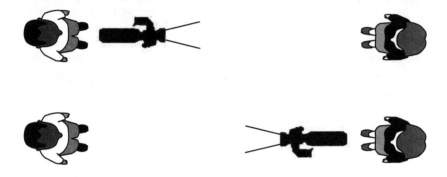

Fig. 22.25: Subjective shooting

Japanese filmmaker Yasujiro Ozu employed both the direct reverse shot and the subjective shot. His gentle masterpiece *Tokyo Story* (1953) deals with an elderly couple's visit to their children in the city. It is full of static scenes of familial interaction. The unorthodox 180-degree cuts from one side of a group to the other mirror the filmmaker's desire to show both sides of every conflict. And the subjective angles bring us close to some of the most sympathetic characters, making it appear as if they are talking to us directly, which draws us further into Ozu's narrative. At the other extreme, both Martin Scorsese, in the boxing ring sequences of *Raging Bull* (1980), and Samuel Fuller, in the opening sequence of *Naked Kiss* (1964), used subjective camerawork to draw us into acts of physical violence.

Do not get obsessed

Crossing the line can get very complicated. If you find yourself hopelessly mired while working out your camera positions, take a break. Then come back and look at the scene afresh and simplify it.

The world will not end if you cross the line. It has happened to famous directors. Orson Welles crossed the line in *Citizen Kane* for no apparent reason (except that the offending scene was shot late at night and he was presumably tired). There is also a growing tendency, particularly in television, to play fast and loose with the line. The documentary-influenced style of *NYPD Blue* frequently violates it, and there have been shots in *ER* that crossed the line as well. As the language of film continues to develop, apparently one of its changes will be a less strict application of the 180-degree rule.

23. Visualization & Formats

> "I get to make the movie at a really low cost—at the price of a few pencils and paper."—Peter Jackson on storyboards.

Isolated images flash into the director's mind as work begins on a script, and these visuals often have a power that written words lack. You may, for instance, be working on a scene featuring a child and have a strong image of a particular type of child for the part. Or you may be working on a fight scene and suddenly see certain parts of the struggle in detail. Play with these images for a while to see where they lead. At the same time, be prepared to jettison them if you realize they are not working. (The longer you hold on to ideas that don't work, the harder it is to clear your mind for new concepts.)

One of the disadvantages of working in television is that the director usually does not get enough time to indulge her visual imagination. Working to a tight schedule leaves few opportunities for originality, so directors are forced to follow the "house style"—thereby ceding creative power to the producer.

As preproduction continues, more opportunities for visualization occur. The production designer may produce set sketches and floorplans. Directors can begin to get a more concrete feel for what a set is going to look like from these. However, one of the drawbacks of a simple floorplan is that it lacks vertical perspective, so it does not give a director a sense of the height or the actual look of the contents of the set.

Thinking about shots and sets plans involves thinking about the *design props* (the basic design elements of a set—tables, chairs, cupboards, etc.) and their exact positions. It also involves thinking up specific actions for the actors in relation to these. Bearing this in mind, maintain close contact with the designer to keep track of the items being acquired. Sometimes a discussion about a particular prop will inspire new acting business. A scene in a kitchen, for example, calls for an actor to be baking bread. Is the bread to be kneaded and pounded manually or does the character have a food processor? Maybe the character actually has a bread-maker that provides both the breadmix and the oven as well? Clearly, in this case, the choice of prop will not only influence the action but comment on the character as well.

If the set is to be newly constructed, the designer may produce a scale model (see Fig. 23.1). Models are a designer's gift to a director: They can be picked up and scrutinized and, because they are three-dimensional, camera angles and action become easy to visualize. They are also particularly helpful when discussing shooting and set logistics with production personnel. You must consider these models critically. They offer a final opportunity to change the design of a set before construction gets underway.

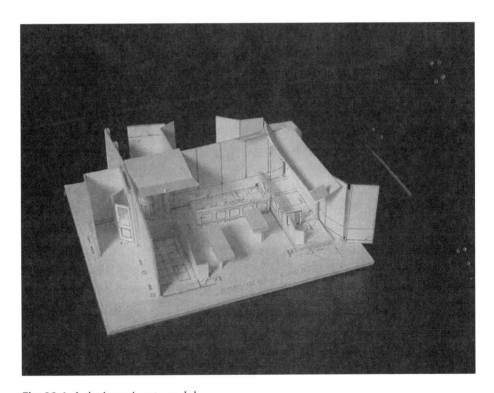

Fig. 23.1: A designer's set model

Storyboards

Storyboards are useful in several different ways. Primarily, they act as a kind of shot rehearsal, allowing directors to look at a series of shots before production gets underway. Storyboards are an important step in transferring images from the internal screen of the imagination to the external screen perceived by the eye (see Part 3, Chapter 9). They give directors a chance to work out a visual style as well as to think through individual sequences.

Some directors work very intently on their storyboards and stick to them closely when they shoot. Others use them as an initial guide and then improvise on them. The more visual the film, the more important storyboards become. Directors from Orson Welles to Steven Spielberg have used them. I have seen some of Ridley Scott's storyboards for *Gladiator* (2000) and learned from articles in *The American Cinematographer*[1] that John Woo and Manoj Night Shyamalan (among many, many others) use them. Storyboards challenge directors to engage the right (imaginative/associative) side of the brain as well as the logical left side. They remind us that directing actors for the screen involves aesthetics.

Storyboards are an extremely efficient way of presenting and explaining visual ideas. When I adapted a stageplay for TV, I produced detailed storyboards for the producers to show them how I would do it. (After the program was complete, a colleague told me he had given my storyboards to his children to use as coloring books—which goes to show how multi-purpose they are!) On other occasions, rather than explain a complicated shot verbally, I have drawn it out for the camera operator. When Alfred Hitchcock had to explain a visual effect (like the schoolchildren being attacked by crows in *The Birds*) or a complex montage (like the shower scene in *Psycho*), storyboards were the way he did it. A picture, as they say, is worth a thousand words.

The ability to quickly sketch a storyboard is also helpful when choosing individual shots. When I'm planning a scene, I often jot down little thumbnail storyboard frames on the blank sides of my script pages to help me choose different shot sizes and framings. When plans are changed on location, I quickly sketch out a storyboard to double-check continuity and other concerns. I believe directors should be able to do basic storyboard drawings, even if they are not naturally gifted draftsmen.

---

[1] "Summer Blockbuster Special," June 2000.

Basic drawing

Although increasingly sophisticated storyboard software has recently become available, most storyboards are still drawn by hand. I have not found a substitute for the direct connection between the hand and the brain that drawing requires. Certainly we are not all capable of drawing like Fellini or Kurasawa but, with a little effort, most of us can sketch well enough to convey our point. The initial effort is worth making, even if our attempts are turned over to a graphic artist for cleaning up at a later date.

Of all drawing styles, stick figures are the least satisfactory for storyboards. They bear no relationship to the human figure and sidestep the whole issue of trying to reproduce what's in your head. "Blobby people" (see Fig. 23.2) are an improvement on stick figures. Blobbies, though basically shapeless, are at least an attempt to come to terms with human form. One may argue that they take up the amount of space in the frame that would be occupied by an object in motion, and therefore are a truer guide to cinematic space.

Fig. 23.2: A blobby person.

Blobbies may suggest basic human shapes within a frame, but they won't help you draw realistic characters in an environment. However, a little knowledge of the basics of drawing can take you a long way toward this goal. Books designed to introduce would-be artists to the human figure are readily available in bookstores and libraries. Taking a few basic art classes will also prove useful. I found that purchasing an inexpensive wooden mannequin from an art-supply store was very helpful—it gave me an immediate sense of the shape of head and body, and their relative proportions. (Note: A number of books on the role of the storyboard artist and the process of drawing storyboards are now available.)

Warning: Sometimes, accomplished artists get so caught up in the process of drawing individual pictures that they lose sight of the dramatic thrust of a sequence as a whole. The novice director-drawer has an advantage in this respect—he is only trying to express what he hopes to see on film. Storyboards that look like Rembrandts may very well not make good films or television. Indeed, many professional storyboards are drawn in a simple, comic-book style (the roots of storyboarding lie partly in film animation) that *directly* communicates how the story will be told.

Types of storyboards

Basically, two types of storyboards are used in film and television. The first is a presentational style with six or eight or more frames arranged in rows *across* the page. These are most suitable for applications like advertising or industrial films and video work that requires the director to give the client a detailed overview of the project. The individual frames in this sort of storyboard tend to be small, with little space for additional information. Better, from the narrative drama point of view, are sheets with four or five frames arranged *vertically* down the center of the page, with space on either side of the frames for shot descriptions and audio notes. This slightly larger frame encourages more detail from the artist. The space for shot description allows the director to explain camera moves and movement inside the frame. The space for audio (generally on the right of the storyboard) focuses attention at an early stage not only on dialogue but also on music, atmosphere, and effects. (See Appendix for examples of storyboards— wide screen and 4x3.)

> Unless you happen to be an extremely fast and competent artist, use pencil for drawing. Erasing and redrawing is preferable to working with a mistake or crossing out a whole storyboard frame and starting again.

The shortcoming of all storyboards as a visualization tool is that they are static. A possible first step toward animating them is to produce *animatix*, which are storyboards shot in sequence (usually with a video camera) and then edited together with stand-ins reading the characters' lines. One area of recent computer development is the creation of motion storyboards. There are now 3-D-style motion programs that can accept blueprints and image maps, and then produce accurate pictures of sets and locations. Whole sequences can thus be previsualized, thereby assisting directors of large-budget action-type movies as they work out and refine their camera angles before shooting. This technique has been used on *The Lord of the Rings* and the *Star Wars* movies.

Formats

When we draw a shot, our composition is dictated by the proportions of the frame. These proportions are determined by the particular industrial film or television format you are using. The screen sizes of different formats are expressed as a numeric relationship of width to height (known as the *aspect ratio*). In these ratios, the height of a frame is always considered 1, and the width is a multiple of that. For example, traditional television systems and cinema's "Academy Format" (the standard frame size/shape for film before the advent of widescreen) are both approximately 1.33:1,[2] which means that the frame's width is $1^1/_3$ times its height (or $1^1/_3$ wider than it is tall). This particular format is also commonly expressed as the proportion 4x3, meaning that it is 3 units high and 4 units wide. Here are some of the most widely used film formats. (See Fig. 23.3.)

A. Academy Format

   1.33:1 (4x3)—Recognized as the standard 35mm movie format by the Academy of Motion Picture Arts and Sciences in 1932. Now more commonly used for 16mm film. It is also the traditional non-widescreen television format.

B. European Widescreen

   1.66:1—Common feature film format in Europe.

C. American Widescreen

   1.85:1—Common 35mm feature format in the USA.

Other available formats are the 2.2:1 screen of 70mm film and the very wide 2.35:1 "anamorphic" screen used for 35mm blockbuster movies. (An anamorphic lens squeezes the picture, usually horizontally, in the camera. When the image is projected onto a screen, another lens reverses the effect, allowing it to spread out.)

---

[2] The full 35mm Academy Aperture frame exposed by the camera is actually 1.37:1. However, when the film is projected, a mask in the projector's gate alters the aspect ratio to 1.85:1 (for U.S. films) or 1.66:1 (for European films). American projectionists who fail to adjust the gate for European films often reveal unwanted elements—such as dust, dirt, hairs, and even microphones—in the extremities of the frame.

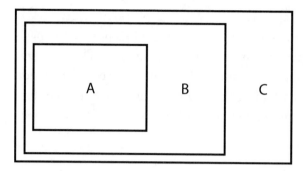

Fig. 23.3: Screen formats

Television has traditionally used the 4x3 aspect ratio. However, High-Definition Television (HDTV) has brought with it the 16x9 screen, which could be noted as 1.78:1. This means that it falls neatly between the two widescreen film formats shown in Fig. 23.3 above. Movies converted from the 1.85:1 format to widescreen HDTV lose only 2% of the picture area, as opposed to the 30% that is currently lost when converting to the standard 4x3 TV screen without the use of a "letterbox"[3] mask.

This loss of 30% of the picture (clipped from the left and right sides of the original frame) is what is implied by the statement at the start of most home videos: "This film has been formatted to fit your screen." The loss is somewhat mitigated by the technique of "pan and scan," whereby the camera in the video-transfer process "unobtrusively" pans from one side of the screen to the other when important action in the original widescreen version is framed in the extreme left- or right-hand corners (for example, when two characters are talking to each other from opposite ends of the screen in a wide shot). To avoid distortion by pan-and-scan when their films are shown on TV, some movie directors deliberately confine important action to the center portion of the frame.

The whole subject of framing for television is complicated by the fact that the parameters of the frame vary slightly from set to set. Television directors know that they have to allow for *cut off*—the (approximately half inch) area around the edges of the screen that may or may not appear on domestic sets, depending on how the screen has been adjusted by the manufacturer and the TV repairman.

---

[3] To preserve their widescreen effect on TV, films are sometimes simply reduced in overall size to fit the screen, leaving black spaces above and below the image—the so-called "letterbox effect."

Shooting considerations

Making the jump from planning a project for the "small screen" of 4x3 TV to planning one for the widescreen is more than a simple change of scale, it involves some visual reorientation. (We have already discussed how a television-style closeup may be the equivalent of an MCU or even a tight mid-shot on a fourteen-foot cinema screen, where every detail is magnified.) Other factors must be considered as well. For example, the traditional model for shot progression in a scene is from WS to MS to CU. However, a closeup in widescreen may only fill half the frame, leaving considerable space for additional background information. This makes the designer's task more challenging, but it also challenges the notion of separate WS and CU, because a closeup may contain a good deal of information about the environment. We may be able to cut directly from an establishing wide shot to a closeup (common practice these days in anamorphic format) because the closeup contains some of the wide shot's information in the corners of the screen.

Widescreen offers so much canvas that there is less need to move the camera from one area to another to capture individual parts of the picture. There is a tendency to use fewer pans, tilts, and trucks as well. Also, the current penchant in television drama for hand-held camerawork is less prevalent in widescreen because the resulting "wobble" is accentuated on the big screen. On the other hand, an audience that increasingly accepts hand-held shots on television will eventually accept them on widescreen film. J. T. Anderson's *Magnolia* (1999), for instance, contains many effective hand-held shots and "whip-pans" (extremely fast pans that tend to put everything out of focus except the objects the camera finally comes to rest on).

DVD and streaming

Narrative drama is currently available in two forms on the computer, as DVD and as streamed video. DVD can deliver full-screen resolution and impressive sound quality, as well as such additional features as commentary, biographies, and previews. Streaming, however, is plagued by issues of computer memory, bandwidth, and compression that currently limit both the size of the frame and the amount of information contained within it. For instance, streaming works best with small frame sizes, static subjects, and little or no camera movement. These limitations make it unsuitable for most drama, but as technology improves, the web will doubtless become a more effective transmission medium.

24. Styles of Shooting

"We deal with tempo-rhythm the same way a painter does with colors: We make combinations of all sorts of different speeds and measures."

—Konstantin Stanislavski

The term "rhythm" is derived from the Greek word meaning "to run" or "to flow." Dance, mime, and the classical theaters of Asia and the Far East give primacy to it. Many Western theaters in the later twentieth century (such as Grotowski's "poor theater" in Poland and Chaikin's Open Theater in the U.S.) constructed performances that were highly rhythmic.

Screen directors are closely concerned with rhythm, though the naturalistic mode in which most of them work usually precludes overt choreography (though blocking actors may be said to be a rudimentary choreography). Rhythm in TV and film drama primarily refers to the way shots of varying lengths are organized and sequenced within a scene. But individual shots have their own rhythms too, which contribute to a scene as a whole. (Consider the shot of the dancing plastic bag in *American Beauty*.) Rhythm is constantly fluctuating. Tempo refers to choices about speed, and it can be sustained over a number of shots or throughout a sequence or during an entire scene. The accelerations and decelerations of a narrative have a visceral effect on the viewer. From a director's perspective, rhythm and tempo are produced by a number of elements.

First of all, writing has rhythmic and pacing implications. Each writer has a distinct style. Their words, phrases, and descriptions are, in a sense, the notes that a director has to arrange in time. A David Mamet script has an entirely different feel from one by Atom Egoyan or the Coen brothers. Even in television, producers, directors, and actors are well aware of the differences between individual scriptwriters on the same series.[1]

The content of a shot brings with it important tempo and rhythm information. A shot of runaway horses will usually have a different tempo and/or a different rhythm from an establishing shot of a farmhouse. Early Russian filmmakers, such as Eisenstein and Pudovkin (those masters of juxtaposition), often exploited tempo and rhythm effects. For example, the shot of citizens running for their lives in Eisenstein's *Battleship Potemkin* (1925) contrasts in rhythm with the still line of troops firing at them. Rhythm may be effective when contrasting shots are juxtaposed, but some shots make a strong rhythmic statement on their own. The aforementioned shot of galloping horses has a visual rhythm of legs and flanks moving and an accompanying audio rhythm of panting and hoof beats. In fact, rhythm goes a long way toward explaining the fascination shots of this kind hold for viewers.

Camera movement can enhance or reduce tempo. For example, a whip-pan suddenly increases tempo, whereas a slow establishing pan across a field slows things down. Shot size has a significant effect as well. Closeups, for instance, generally increase tempo because movement is exaggerated—a tennis player's swing will appear faster in a tight shot, where the racket flashes prominently across the entire frame, than in a wide-shot of the court, where the racket is a much smaller detail. A close shot's attention to isolated detail often means that it occupies a shorter length of time on the screen than shots that show the whole scene. (It takes us longer to assimilate shots with a large amount of visual information.)

Thus far, I have been keeping tempo and rhythm distinct rather like a composer, who can separate the way her notes are arranged on paper (the rhythm) from her tempo markings. But such a clear-cut distinction is not always possible when blocking scenes and directing actors. Stanislavski believed that most actions, beats, scenes, acts, and plays had both tempo *and* rhythmic components, and that it was not always productive to separate these two ingredients. For those many instances when a dramatic event has both tempo and rhythmic implications, Stanislavski coined the composite term "tempo-rhythm."

Scenes with numerous cuts will have a different tempo-rhythm from scenes with few or no cuts. (Long and short takes are discussed in more detail below.) Directors may also distort time by using slow motion or fast motion effects.

---

[1] I am always struck by the difference in pacing between American and British soap operas. The driving tempo of the BBC's *EastEnders* is entirely different from the languid pace of ABC's *General Hospital* or CBS's *The Young and the Restless*. These differences, which reside primarily in scene length and the way the dialogue is constructed, are also a product of editing. (Rhythm and tempo in editing will be discussed in Part 6.)

The cessation of movement—the moment when a movement is resolved and before a new one commences—implies stillness and silence. A director may start to inject tempo-rhythm into a scene by looking for expressive pauses of this sort. If you have a uniformly fast-paced script, you might look to see if there are moments when activity can stop. Even enemies in the heat of argument stop to look for the next opening or to think of the next word. Scenes that are very verbal, such as exchanges between lawyers, politicians, or warring academic couples, sometimes benefit from a momentary suspension of dialogue, which breaks the previously established pattern of speech. This can have the effect of making intellectual aggression seem more physical and real or of momentarily taking us behind a professional's verbal façade. The effect, however, should not necessarily hold up the onward flow of the action (that would be very counter-productive) but add an extra layer of interest—a silent, psychological counterpoint to the verbal or physical activity. (A frustrated police officer, momentarily lost for words, slams his fist down on the table. An irate author wants to quote from an adverse review but has misplaced the publication.) Pauses can question characters' self-confidence and disrupt their predetermined patterns of behavior.

One of the ways musicians develop rhythm is by grouping and accenting certain notes. As we have seen, writers, actors, and directors also group speeches and actions within a scene into units called beats. By looking closely at the contents of each beat, directors can assign different qualities to them. The leisurely beat in which two relatives fondly peruse photographs of their family will contrast in tempo-rhyhm with the following beat when one of them suddenly remembers an appointment and springs to her feet. The first beat may be fond and leisurely, the second more urgent and fast.

The overall tempo of the beat is greatly influenced by the individual actions of the actors. In the above example, the repetitive action of slowly turning the pages of the photograph album contrasts with the stoccato actions of suddenly leaping up and reaching for an overcoat.

Scenes with two or more beats should probably contain contrasting tempo-rhythms that express the dramatic tensions within the scenes. After all, one would not read three-quarters of a page of prose or poetry without varying the tempo, and one should not direct a scene that way either. Directors dealing with short scenes that are part of a larger sequence may choose to treat each scene as a single beat, assigning it a different tempo-rhythm from those on either side of it. *Always check that you have consciously organized the temp-rhythms in a scene or sequence.*

Because the naturalistic school of performance pays more attention to psychology than movement, modern screen directors rarely consciously attend to the physical rhythms of individual actors in the ways that choreographers or mime artists do. Directors (often correctly) assume that a note to an actor about her character ("I think she is more excited when she sees him") will affect the tempo-rhythm as well. Nevertheless, there exists a small category of films in which tempo-rhythm has been assigned particular prominence. For instance, many of Fellini's films, including *La Strada* (1954), *Satyricon* (1969), and *Casanova* (1976), include choreographed elements. Overt rhythm is evident in the artful German Expressionist films of the 1930s. Chaplin and other silent-era comedians were strongly influenced by mime (and its populist relative "pantomime"), and mime also plays an important role in Marcel Carne's memorable *Les Enfants du Paradis* (1946, USA). Darren Aranofsky's *Requiem of a Dream* (2000) is almost a textbook of directorial tempo-rhythmic devices, and we will return to it when we discuss editing.

The long take

The general rule: *The more cuts, the faster the tempo of a scene; the fewer cuts, the slower.* British director Alan Clarke (see Part 9, Chapter 43) has said that, in his early days, if he thought a scene was too slow, he used to increase the number of cuts. Of course, he subsequently learned that a rapidly cut sequence had to be planned *before* shooting if it were to seem natural. If you are filming a dramatic two-person scene, you will probably have only a limited opportunity to radically increase the number of cuts during editing. There may be a reaction shot or two that can be inserted, but the dialogue and movement will basically dictate the cuts. The more people there are in a scene, however, the more opportunities there are for "cut-ins" (closer shots of persons or objects within the frame), "cutaways" (shots of persons or objects outside the frame), and reaction shots. These three categories of shot are referred to as "B-roll" in documentaries. *Directors shooting multi-character scenes—sports scenes and scenes set in classrooms, courtrooms, board meetings, etc.—should get as much B-roll as possible.* These shots will be invaluable if the narrative needs to be sped up in editing.

Long takes, especially ones with little or no camera movement, tend to slow the pace of a scene. A director cannot adjust the pacing of a single extended shot during editing. The effect is, therefore, theatrical—the camera captures a performance in its entirety. It is not unlike observing a stage play or watching an early, ten-minute silent film shot in a single long take. Many directors opting for the static long shot take an objective camera position—they make the choice not to cut or truck in to a more subjective viewpoint, such as a closeup. The emphasis here is on content and performance, not montage. Control of tempo is surrendered to the actors. (See the section on Steadicam below for an illustration of moving between objective and subjective camera positions.)

If I sound critical, I do not mean to be. Sometimes the long shot is very effective. Above all things, it is an "honest" shot, by which I mean that it represents events without much directorial mediation. Hungarian director Bela Tarr, for instance, has been criticized for his uncompromisingly long unbroken takes, which mimic the rhythms of daily life. The insertion of a long take into a sequence of shots or scenes that are much faster can provide a welcome change of pace. It can give viewers a breather before the tempo—and tension—is increased again.

Of course, there are long takes with both camera movement and shot-content movement that are anything but slow. The action movie, with its long helicopter shots of people fighting on the tops of trains or at the edges of precipices, are good examples of this. But, regardless of its effectiveness, Stephen Spielberg, Ridley Scott, and John Woo will usually alternate long takes with shots that are much shorter, in order to vary and control the pacing and rhythm. The adrenaline-filled battle scenes in *Black Hawk Down* (2001) are offset by moments of quiet while the troops wait for the next encounter.

Some directors, such as Edward Dmytryk, advocate taking cutaways after two or more satisfactory long takes of a scene. Cutting to a reaction shot of one of the characters, or even to an object like a glass or a poster, allows the editor to cut between different versions of the long take. Suddenly inserting one of these "protection shots," though, can often spoil the rhythm of the long shot.

One contemporary filmmaker who consistently uses the long take is Woody Allen. His movies generally deal with character and are therefore performance- and dialogue-centered. His long takes tend to show people in mid-shot or wider—the preferred framing for comedy because it reveals the expressive hands and body. Allen's long takes frequently include movement, especially on the part of the actors. Character relationship is revealed as protagonists circle or move toward and away from each other. The camera may move in order to follow the action or reframe, but its movement tends to be unobtrusive, functional, and minimal. These scenes, though intimate, are often highly animated and could easily transfer to the stage.

Hitchcock famously used the long take in *Rope* (1948), a film that consists of a series of ten-minute takes edited together to give the impression of continuous time. The origin of the screenplay was Patrick Hamilton's 1929 play of the same name, a play that observes the Aristotelian "unities" of time and space. This theatrical vehicle was the ultimate challenge for Hitchcock, who thrived on shifts of location, sudden cuts, and point-of-view shots. The result is an interesting technical experiment, but one cannot help feeling that he tied his own hands behind his back. The tempo is leisurely by his standards, and there is a lack of the important element of surprise (caused by effective changes of shot) that so characterizes his other pictures. The restless camerawork strains to offer us alternative viewpoints and does not replace the cut. You would think the effect would be to empower the actors, but the intricacy of the camerawork places great pressure on them to hit their marks and turns their performances into technical, rather than dramatic, tours de force.

One solution to the tempo problem of single-take shooting was offered by Mike Figgis in his remarkable *Time Code* (2000). Several storylines, all shot simultaneously, are projected on the screen at once and the viewer selects the one she wishes to view, though the action is organized so that no two scenes offer competing dramatic moments.[2]

Quick cutting

A cut represents a director intervening in the narrative. It is a conscious decision to change the viewer's perspective. In dramas that are shot with a single camera, it halts a particular performance and inserts another performance taken at a different time.

By presenting viewers with new information, cuts require them to readjust their perception. Increasing perceptual activity counteracts boredom and makes time seem to pass more quickly. Cuts are very often opportunities to speed up the action by trimming fractions of a second (or, sometimes, much more) off a shot.

Rapid editing between shots is evidence of a director retaining control. It is particularly associated with action movies, thrillers, horror movies—any genre that is highly manipulated by the director. Cuts can speed up a sequence and shorten time, but they can expand time as well: A man draws a gun. A woman's eyes open in fear. A second man reaches for his gun. The woman screams. The first man shoots. An incident that would have taken two or three seconds is

---

[2] Russian filmmakers, such as Andrei Tarkovsky in *Andrei Rublev* (1969) and Aleksandr Sokurov in *Russian Arc* (2002), have also explored the long take in interesting ways.

stretched into eight by the additional edits. The inserted shots are very short—barely two seconds each, which is almost at the threshold of cognition—so the sequence's overall impression is of great speed.

The result of strong directorial control is usually a reduction of actor integrity. In very fast-paced action scenes, the actor becomes an object the director manipulates. The actor surrenders the timing of her lines to the director, who reconstructs her performance in the editing room. The director, who is only interested in the moment of action or reaction, pares away whatever is on either side of it. In so doing, he discards the space in which the actor creates the mood for the reaction. The actress in the above example sees the gun being drawn and briefly registers the implication before becoming terrified. The director, however, cuts her transition and only uses her moment of terror. He steals just that one moment from the series of interrelated emotions she undergoes. Under these circumstances, an actor surrenders the visible through-line of her performance to the director, and she may have difficulty finding the confidence to sustain a layered emotional performance on the screen over time.

Moving the camera

When actors move, they can be captured by the camera in two general ways. The first is that the camera can remain still (or relatively still) and the actors can move in relationship to it. (Many long-take scenes are shot in this way.) When a character moves toward or away from a static camera, her size changes, becoming either larger (closer to the lens) or smaller (further away). Choreographing a scene within a still frame can be rewarding, but the actors have to be technically accomplished to pull it off.

The second way is to move the camera with, or in relation to, the characters.

Camera movement is generally understood to mean moving the camera from one position to another during a shot. Strictly speaking, however, the camera also moves when it pans, tilts, elevates, and depresses—even though these are all accomplished from a single position. A film or television program can be shot entirely from single camera positions and be perfectly effective, as many great directors (including Robert Bresson and Ken Loach) have proved. Learning how to accomplish camera moves starts with appreciating the immense expressiveness of the humble pan and tilt.

Two general criteria exist for camera movement, and a successful move observes both. First of all, *there has to be a good reason for moving the camera.*

Simply moving the camera to add visual interest to an otherwise dull scene is not a good enough reason. Roger Deakins—DP for Joel and Ethan Coen, Ron Howard, and others—observes, "Unfortunately, there are a lot of indulgent camera moves in films today. Sometimes I'll see a film and the photography is quite beautiful, but the moves are totally indulgent. They take me out of [the picture], and I think that's always a shame. Too often a camera move is in there to make up for other things that should be there, but aren't."[3]

Camera moves are most often suggested by character movement, so it is important to master blocking before resorting to elaborate tracking and crane shots. The camera has to be in the right relationship to the characters at the right time. Unmotivated camera moves—moves for which there is no apparent justification—draw attention to themselves and slow the pace of a film.

If you want to maintain a consistent shot size while a character is moving, the best way to do this is to move the camera in relation to her. Thus, if you want the camera to keep close to two people walking along a sidewalk (because what they are saying is important), you will probably have to track alongside them holding them in a mid-2-shot. Shooting from a static position with a zoom lens might be a possible alternative because a zoom lens can hold a relatively consistent shot size. But zooming does not allow the viewer to really experience the space through which characters move. Which brings us to the second criterion:

A camera movement transports the viewer through space and the viewer should experience this. *A crane or a tracking shot is always an opportunity to introduce visual interest.* Either the background should change or the move should take us from one environment to another. At the very least, we should experience moving past an object in the foreground. A tracking shot of two businessmen walking down the street may not be visually exciting. But it could be improved by taking us round a corner so that the perspective changes or by tracking past something interesting in the foreground (or both).

I have been referring to the track and the crane—the two most common camera moves—but many other movements and effects are available to a director. There are, in fact, almost as many types of moves as a director can conceive of. A director generally dreams up moves that will best express his vision and then discusses how to implement them with the director of photography or camera operator.

The most complicated camera move I ever witnessed was a shot somewhat similar to one that appears half way through the Coen brothers' *The Man Who Wasn't There* (2002). It started as a shot that tracked out in front of a character

---

[3] "Divorce American Style," *American Cinematographer*, October, 2003, p. 53.

walking down a corridor. Then, as he descended the stairs, the camera was smoothly lifted off its dolly by the DP and passed through the window to a camera operator seated in a crane. The shot then craned down the side of the building and met the man as he exited the front door. The camera did jerk a little when the DP handled it, but unless you knew what was happening, you probably would not have noticed it. Today that whole move could be done with a remote-controlled camera head mounted on a jib arm that is connected to a crane.

Carlos Saura's *Tango* (1999), for which Vittorio Storaro was the cinematographer, has many elegant camera moves. Many of them take us through the large studio where a fictional director is rehearsing a musical, moving from one gorgeously lit set to another. But there are some straightforward panning shots too, where precise framing and subtle lighting achieve remarkable effects.

Hand-held camera

Hand-held camera shots—especially ones that include movement—can be unsteady in the hands of unskilled camera operators. The film-school student learns early in her career that hand-held shots are not a satisfactory substitute for a tripod. The visual rhythms of hand-held camerawork can be unpredictable and they often impart a journalistic, "run-and-gun" sensibility that big-budget Hollywood productions have traditionally avoided. Directors who want their work to have a smooth, polished quality prefer to move the camera on tracks or wheels to avoid camera shake. Steven Soderbergh, who often operates the camera while directing, used hand-held shots extensively in the documentary-realist sequences of *Traffic* (2000), but was much more restrained in the use of hand-held shots in his more traditional *Ocean's Eleven* (2001).

I first worked on a dramatic film that used a hand-held camera in 1979. We shot on a remote, rocky location where tracks could not be laid, and the cameraman very reluctantly agreed to hoist the camera onto his shoulder. This one shot stood out like a sore thumb among all the other smooth, tracking shots in the finished film.

Hand-held shots seem to work best in realistic environments (often outdoors), lending the shot a sense of actuality. Hand-held shots have been associated with documentary films at least as far back as the start of the cinema verité movement in the early sixties. (Perhaps the almost daily hand-held news footage transmitted during the Vietnam War and subsequent conflicts has also encouraged its association with "reality.") No drama exploited this association more than the early episodes of *NYPD Blue*, with their very free and continuous camera movements that panned from character to character without cutting. But this style also placed technical restrictions upon actors who had to delay their lines until the camera reached them. In the end, the full-blown use of this approach was considered too challenging for the viewers and was subsequently toned down. But to this day, the camera on *NYPD Blue* deliberately crosses the line and jerks nervously, though predictably, in homage to documentary realism.

The hand-held camera is occasionally used for point-of-view shots. This is a convention. The somewhat jerky motion of the hand-held camera is meant to suggest the human head and eyes. If you think about it, this is not a true analogy—the eyes and head work together to provide an unusually smooth sense of motion. Assuming that if a cameraperson holds a camera unsupported in front of her eye, it is acting as an extension of her eye, is erroneous. The fluidity of tracks and other stabilization devices are actually closer to the mechanism of the head. Nevertheless, illogical as it is, hand-held POV shots can be effective, especially if their motions are controlled by steady operators.

The Steadicam and moving camera style

That 1979 film I worked on with the awkward hand-held shot also had a Steadicam sequence. The Steadicam in those days was a large, heavy harness worn by a special operator who had to be a part-time weightlifter. Modern stabilization equipment is more accessible, though a Panaflex Lightweight Steadicam still weighs seventy pounds.

The Steadicam itself is not a perfectly smooth platform—unlike tracks or wheels on a flat surface. The mechanism reduces the operator's jerky movements, converting them into smooth, flat waves of motion. If you take a moving panoramic shot with a Steadicam (with no human in the frame), the floating motion can make the viewer feel slightly seasick. However, this motion is masked when shooting action close to the lens. The great advantage of the Steadicam is that it frees the camera from the limitations of the pedestal and enables it to roam about the set almost as if it were another character in the drama, heightening our own voyeuristic association with the protagonists and events.

The Steadicam was regularly used in 1990s television series. One of its most common uses in the program *Homicide* was in the interrogation room, where, during intense interviews, the camera circled the two participants. The circling movement is particularly interesting because it takes the viewer through both objective and subjective viewpoints. (See Fig. 24.1.) The shot can start off as an objective 2-shot, showing both characters in relation to each other, and then move toward one character's point of view. The difficult moment in any circling shot occurs when the camera leaves the subjective position and transitions either to the 2-shot or pans across the table to a complementary subjective shot of the other character.

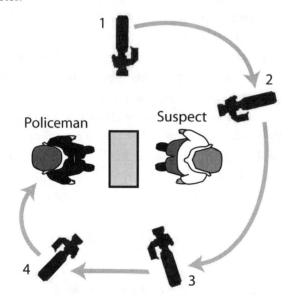

Camera position 1: "Objective" 2-shot of policeman and suspect
Camera position 2: "Subjective" shot of policeman
Camera position 3: Transition to objective 2-shot
Camera position 4: Transition to subjective shot of suspect.
(Requires the camera to pan across the table from the policeman to the suspect.)

Fig. 24.1: Circular camera movement

In the television series *E.R.*, the Steadicam roves around the large composite set with great freedom. In so doing, it ties together the separate areas—the waiting room, the administrative section, and the corridor—and encourages us to see them as parts of a working whole. (Cutting from one area to another, on the other hand, would have the effect of separating them—which might be useful if the director were trying to emphasize the distance between the areas.)

A great sense of bustle and depth is conveyed as the Steadicam maneuvers around people and objects. As with all types of camera movement, when a Steadicam moves with a character from one position to another, the movement appears to be natural and acceptable. On the few occasions when its move is not motivated by character movement, it draws attention to itself. The success of lengthy developing shots depends to a great extent on cooperation between the actors and the camera operators. For the latter, it is a kind of dance as they move in relation to one actor and then pass seamlessly on to another.

As our eyes have become more accustomed to hand-held and Steadicam shots, the number of projects using them has increased. Now one commonly sees whole scenes composed of these moving camera shots. If you are thinking of using this style, you should consider the following three points.

First, you need a good camera operator to make these shots work. An experienced operator senses the director's style and executes the Steadicam shot cleanly, without uncertainty about framing.

Second, certain projects and subjects lend themselves to a fluid style more than others. The style works well in the hurried world of hospital emergency wards and in the slightly melodramatic world of some thrillers (such as *Trapped*, 2002). It might not work so well in situations where the director wants a more distanced and composed effect.

Third, editing a series of moving shots together to form a scene can be time-consuming. If a director adopts this style and postpones decisions about precise edit points till the edit itself, he places greater responsibility on the editor.

Cutting moving shots together

It used to be axiomatic that two moving shots could not be juxtaposed. It was held that tracking or panning shots had to come to rest before they could be edited. In cases where directors wanted to cut away before the movement ended, they had to look at the shot very closely to find a point where the camera hesitated for a fraction of a section. (Oddly enough, this was frequently possible.) Due, in part, to the influence of music videos, cutting between moving shots is no longer taboo, though care should be taken when doing so. The problem is that it is very easy to make a cut that does not flow and is visually jarring. Therefore, everything that can be done should be done to minimize the impact of the cut. Some of the factors to be considered when cutting together moving shots:

- The speeds of the two moving shots should be the same. A cut that juxtaposes shots of noticeably different speeds will draw attention to itself. *The slower the movement, the easier it is to achieve the cut.*
- The direction of the two shots should be complementary. Shots moving in the same direction are the easiest to join. A moving shot followed by one moving in the reverse direction is the toughest to join without drawing attention.
- Audio plays an important part. Music videos, for instance, permit violent shifts between moving shots because the soundtrack distracts from the cut. Also, viewers tend to accept cuts that coincide with a strong beat—the synchronization point, in this case, providing an alternative "logic" for the cut.
- Although not actually involving two moving shots, a cut from a quickly moving shot to a static one can also be very dramatic.

Michael Mann, a director with a particularly fluid camera technique, is able to gauge the speed and direction of two connecting shots as they are filmed so that they cut together perfectly. Another expert on cutting on motion, John Woo, will often have a character moving on the incoming shot (the second shot), so the eye follows the character and is less aware of the camera movement.[4]

---

[4] Aficionados of the fluid camera style might also be interested in Geoffrey Sax's production of *Othello* (2001), which was originally produced for television.

25. Marking Up a Shooting Script

"… in order to arrive at a personal style, you have to have a technique to begin with ….. you have to have a place to make the choices from. If you don't have a basis on which to make the choice, then you don't have style at all, you have a series of accidents."
—Legendary music-composition teacher Nadia Boulanger to composer Philip Glass.[1]

In Part 2 of this book, I suggested a method of marking up a script for rehearsal. Now that marked-up script needs to be developed for shooting. The shooting script is the guide the director takes onto the set. It has her notes for placing the actors and her master plan for shooting the scene. It has to be very clearly laid out so she can anticipate what shots have to be set up and taken. Nothing is worse than fumbling around with a bunch of papers when twenty, forty, or a hundred people are waiting.

I must emphasize that there is no universal standard way of marking a shooting script. However, if you do adopt the following method, you will know you have considered all the important elements. I suggest you try it and then adapt it to your own way of working.

Here is the script as we earlier marked it for rehearsal.

---

[1] Quoted from an interview with Philip Glass on National Public Radio.

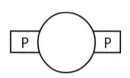

Props
Coffee cups + saucers
P M Teaspoons
Napkins
Sugar bowl
Maura's coat + handbag

INT. COFFEE SHOP   DAY

Maura and Paul are both in their mid-30s and
recovering alcoholics who are about to go to a
meeting. Paul, who is married, owns a small
construction company. Maura manages a branch of a
temp agency.

Paul has just told her they have to end their
affair.

                    PAUL
          You're not angry?

Beat 1
Maura's honest reaction
↓

                    MAURA
          It might make you feel better,
          but it wouldn't stop you going,
          would it?

Paul: to take the blame
Maura: to defend the
relationship

                    PAUL
          (He's suffering.)

          Look, I'm sorry. This shouldn't have
          started in the first place —

                    MAURA
          Yes it should.

                    PAUL
          (T) (He stops, looks at her.)

                    MAURA
          This is the best thing that's
          happened to me in a long time. I'm
          not going to wish it never started.

                    PAUL
(Beat)

Doesn't feel so great right now,
does it?

                    MAURA
No.

                    PAUL
It's not ….

(Paul trails off.)

                    MAURA
What? That you don't like me?

                    PAUL
(Shakes his head vigorously)

No. I like you a lot. That's the
problem.

                    MAURA
(Smiling)

That's not a problem. Look, I've only
known you for a few days, but I wish
it could go on a lot longer.

                    PAUL
I'm sorry.

                    MAURA
We could have really hit the big
time, Paul Jameson, believe me. If
you were footloose and fancy-free.*

(T) Maura stands, unable to hide her upset any
longer.

                    PAUL
Where are you going?

Beat 2
__What might have been__

Paul: to explain
Maura: to tell him
she loves him

Beat 3
__Maura's farewell__

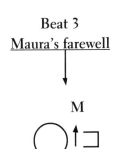

M

Paul: to release her
Maura: to leave

269

<u>MAURA</u> [Collects her coat and bag]
Home. Not really in the mood for the
meeting anymore.

PAUL

(Beat) No.

MAURA

(Hesitates)

Don't suppose I'll see you again.
You'll find another group to go to
from now on?

PAUL

(Another beat)

Yeah. Yeah, I guess so.*

She hesitates a moment, then leans over and kisses
him, softly, gently.

MAURA

So long.*

Beat 4
<u>Paul can't let go</u>

On Paul watching as Maura makes for the door.
He's completely torn apart by this. As Maura
actually gets to the door, he calls out.

Paul: to stop her
Maura: to cry

PAUL

(T) Maura—

Maura turns,* looks back at him, tears on her
cheeks.

(He gets up)*

Wait a minute...

Out on Paul.

The previous shot

The first shot of a scene does not exist by itself: It must relate to the last shot of the previous scene. There is only one scene in a script for which this does not apply, and that is Act 1. Scene 1. But even that can relate to what might precede it—the titles. Interestingly, the first thing a viewer often sees are the titles—the one visual that a director may have little or no control over.

The opening of a scene is a new beginning, but its freshness depends on how it is distinguished from the last shot of the previous scene. The rule of thumb is that a new shot should always be substantially different from the old one. Simple differentiation works for TV series, for which there is rarely enough time to plan really imaginative transitions, but in other genres more subtle effects can be achieved. Yasujiro Ozu would use design composition to link different scenes— for example, transitioning between two shots that both had a strong red color at the same place in the frame. Ozu would also imply a link between two characters in successive scenes, by placing them in the same position in the frame.

Audio may be used as a transition. A scream in the outgoing shot can turn into a shrill train whistle in the incoming one or a silent meadow can be juxtaposed with a noisy city street. Dialog or atmos from the outgoing scene can also be held on over the first shot of a new scene to comment on it (this is sometimes called a "sound bridge"). For instance, a neighbor tells a policeman "The last time I saw Ma Peterson she was alive and well," and the last three words are superimposed over a shot of Ma Peterson's corpse.

At a slightly more mundane level, film directors have long used the dissolve as a means of getting from one scene to another. As Cinderella leaves her kitchen for the palace, the camera tilts up to the ceiling. Next, it dissolves through to the ceiling of the ballroom and tilts down upon the gilded dancers. Similarly, a scene may start obliquely with a shot of an incidental detail, and then reveal the main subject. In *Havana* (1990), Sydney Pollack opened several scenes by starting on a feature at the side of the set and then trucking left or right onto the main portion of set.

Before starting to mark up a particular scene, a director needs to know what the last shot of the previous scene was. This information should also be displayed on the first page of the new scene, near the slug line, so that if the opening shot has to be changed during the shoot, the director can make an informed decision. The director needs to know the size of the previous scene's outgoing shot and the direction in which its character(s) was looking. The quickest way of presenting this information is in diagram form. Fig. 25.1 shows how this can be represented if the previous shot was an MCU of a character looking camera left.

271

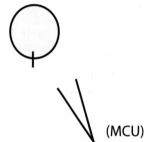

Fig. 25.1: MCU, looking camera left

The "V" is the camera angle. The character's nose is to the left of that, which shows he is looking "camera left." The angle of the "V" is small (less than forty-five degrees) indicating a tight angle, but just for complete clarity "MCU" is placed next to it. Clearly, if the shot were a group shot instead, we would increase the numbers of heads and widen the angle (see Fig. 25.2 below).

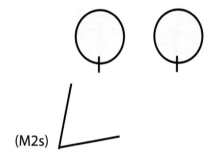

Fig. 25.2: M2s, looking camera right

This, as well as all the points that follow, are illustrated in the script at the end of the chapter (Fig. 25.8).

Naming and marking the shots

As a shot is taken, the continuity assistant notes where it starts and where it ends by drawing a horizontal line down the script page. She then enters the shot description next to the line. This way she can tell at a glance how a director has covered a scene and, during postproduction, the editor can see what shots are available. This style can be adapted by directors to note their own shots. (See Fig. 25.6.)

A director, in consultation with the DP, chooses the order in which the shots are taken. From any one setup (or camera position) the director can take a number of different shots. And, of course, each shot can be taken a number of times.

Once you have chosen the first setup it is designated 1. The next setup is 2, the next after that 3, and so on.

Each shot is given a letter. The first shot is shot 1A (setup or camera position 1, shot A). The next shot from that position is 1B, the next after that 1C, etc. Shot 1C will be a different-sized shot from 1B, even though it may cover the same lines as 1B, or may cover lines that occur several pages later—all that matters is that it is shot from the same camera position. Once the director has taken all the shots from position 1, the camera is moved to position 2.

The order in which you number your shots is important. *The first camera position is usually the establishing or widest shot.* Directors start with the widest so that the DP can set the overall lighting for the scene. Actors are also helped by working from the widest shot—in which they establish their positions—to the closer ones, in which their emotions are more evident.

To recap, the widest shot or the establishing shot is usually 1A. If you are taking a mid-2-shot from position 1, that shot becomes 1B; the subsequent mid-shot of a single character becomes 1C; and the following closeup becomes 1D. Then the director moves on to setup 2. Setup 2 will be the nearest adjacent position to setup 1 in a clockwise or counter-clockwise direction. Setup 3 will be the nearest position to setup 2 in the same direction. *By moving to adjacent positions around the set, lighting changes are minimized, saving time and effort.*

Here is an example:

In a dinner scene, the director has the following four camera positions (see Fig. 25.3).

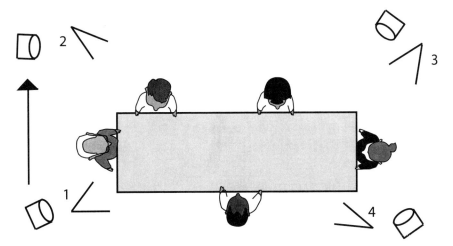

Fig. 25.3: Camera positions around dinner table

Setup 1 has the widest shot, so the director correctly starts with it. She shoots a wide shot (A), a mid-2-shot (B), and two singles (C and D). Then she moves on to adjacent camera position 2. (She might have gone counter-clockwise to position 4, but position 2 is slightly closer.) The move involves repositioning some lights, but if she had jumped to position 3, she would have had a much more extensive relight, since all the lighting instruments would have had to be moved to the opposite side of the room. *When plotting and numbering camera positions, always try to minimize the number of relights, which eats up valuable on-set time.*

One way to open the Maura and Paul scene would be with a symmetrical (or "square-on") 2-shot. This is pos.1, shot 1A. (See Fig. 25.4.)

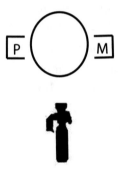

Fig. 25.4: Pos. 1, Shot 1A—symmetrical (or square-on) 2s

The next time we might use this camera setup is two pages later when Maura crosses to Paul and kisses him—"MS Maura. Pan left to Paul (M2s)." This is pos. 1, shot 1B. (See Fig. 25.5.)

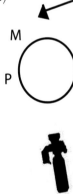

Fig. 25.5: Pos. 1, Shot 1B.—MS Maura, Pan l to 2s

The director decides where the shot starts and where it ends, and then picks up her pencil and ruler and draws a line in the margin (or if there isn't a margin, over the text of the script itself). The shot number is written at the top of the line, and the shot description is entered just below that. (See Fig. 25.6.)

INT. COFFEE SHOP   DAY

Maura and Paul are both in their mid-30s and
recovering alcoholics who are about to go to a
meeting. Paul, who is married, owns a small
construction company. Maura manages a branch of a
temp agency.

Paul has just told her they have to end their
affair.

Beat 1

Maura's honest reaction

1A

L/A symmet. 2s

PAUL
You're not angry?

Paul: to take
the blame

MAURA
It might make you feel better,
but it wouldn't stop you going,
would it?

Maura: to defend the
relationship

PAUL
[HE'S SUFFERING]

Look, I'm sorry. This shouldn't have
started in the first place —

MAURA
Yes it should.

(T) [HE STOPS, LOOKS AT HER]

MAURA
This is the best thing that's
happened to me in a long time. I'm
not going to wish it never started.

PAUL
[BEAT]

Beat 2

What might have been

Doesn't feel so great right now,
does it?

Fig. 25.6: Shot 1A marked on script

275

(Please note: "L/A" stands for low angle and "symmet" for symmetrical.)

The director may only intend to use this shot for the first two lines, but she keeps it going for several lines beyond that. This is important. Directors must give themselves as much latitude as possible when shooting. *It is necessary to have a firm idea of how the scene should look, but also shoot in such a way that you have options during editing.* Shooting more than is strictly necessary for this shot means that the director is not compelled to cut after the second line. If, during editing, she feels the establishing shot is holding, she has the option to extend it.

The director then turns over a couple of pages to shot 1B and marks it in the script. (See Fig. 25.7.)

The director may only need this shot from Maura's rise till her exit after "So long," but she starts the shot around the beginning of the previous beat in order to give the actors ample time to get back into the mood and pacing of the scene. She also extends the shot after Maura leaves just in case she might use that extra second or two on Paul. It is also simply good manners to wait till there is a natural lull in the action before calling "Cut."

Note that at the foot of the first page, the line has an arrow indicating that the shot continues onto the next. Where the shot ends, there is a short horizontal line. Where there is a major change in the shot (as Maura leaves) that is also reflected in the shot description, so the director remembers to pass the information on to the camera operator.

Having finished setup 1, the director proceeds to setup 2. The lines for setup 2 are placed to the right of setup one. (See Fig. 25.8.) The director continues noting down each shot until she reaches the end of the scene.

Coverage

When the script has been marked up, the director can clearly and graphically see how the scene is being covered. If some sections of the script have no lines opposite them, then she obviously needs to come up with a new shot or extend an existing one to cover the gap.

If some script sections have only a single line opposite them, these should be examined. One-shot coverage is minimal and slightly risky. On certain occasions, such as wide shots, moves, and tracking shots, single coverage is acceptable; but it can also indicate that the director has failed to plan a reverse shot or a reaction shot.

Lines should overlap other lines (i.e., shots should overlap each other)—this is a sign that the director has leeway to take a cut earlier or later than planned

1B

L/A MS M.
Pan 1 to M2s

PAUL
[BEAT]

Doesn't feel so great right now,
does it?

MAURA
No.

PAUL
It's not ….

[PAUL TRAILS OFF]

MAURA
What? That you don't like me?

PAUL
[SHAKES HIS HEAD VIGOROUSLY]

No. I like you a lot. That's the
problem.

MAURA
[SMILING]

That's not a problem. Look, I've only
known you for a few days, but I wish
it could go on a lot longer.

PAUL
I'm sorry.

MAURA
We could have really hit the big
time, Paul Jameson, believe me. If
you were footloose and fancy-free.*

(T)   [MAURA STANDS, UNABLE TO HIDE HER UPSET ANY
        LONGER.]

PAUL
Where are you going?

Beat 2
What might have been

Paul: to explain
Maura: to tell him
she loves him

Beat 3
Maura's farewell

M

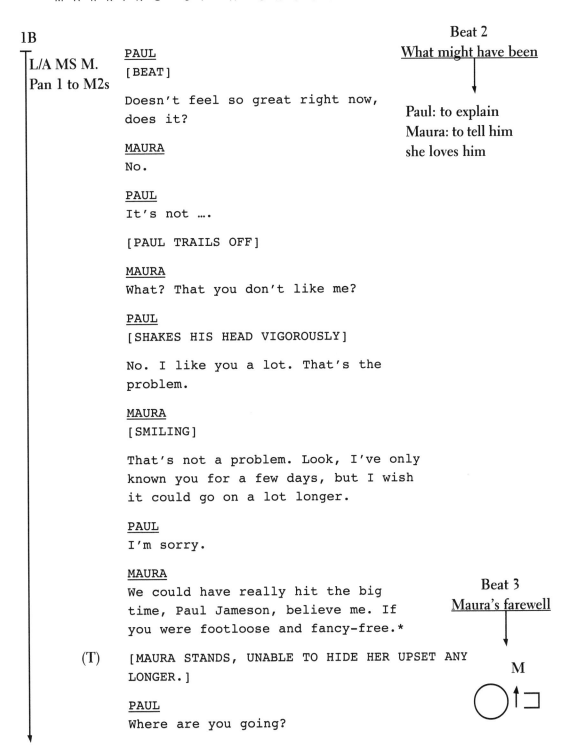

Fig. 25.7: Shot 1B (continues next page)

277

MAURA [Collects her coat + bag]

Home. Not really in the mood for the
meeting anymore.

Paul: to release her
Maura: to leave

PAUL

[BEAT]

No.

MAURA

[HESITATES]

Don't suppose I'll see you again.
You'll find another group to go to
from now on?

PAUL

[ANOTHER BEAT]

Yeah. Yeah, I guess so.*

[MAURA HESITATES A MOMENT, THEN LEANS OVER
AND KISSES HIM, SOFTLY, GENTLY.]

MAURA

So long.*

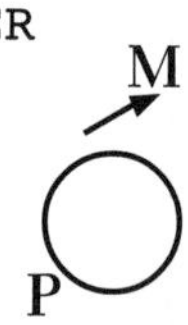

M leaves rt.
Hold P.

[ON PAUL WATCHING AS MAURA MAKES FOR
THE DOOR. HE'S COMPLETELY TORN APART
BY THIS.

Beat 4
Paul can't let go

Paul: to stop her
Maura: to cry

AS MAURA ACTUALLY GETS TO THE DOOR,
HE CALLS OUT]

PAUL

(T)   Maura—

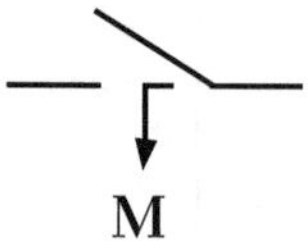

[MAURA TURNS,* LOOKS BACK AT HIM,
TEARS ON HER CHEEKS.]

[HE GETS UP]* Wait a minute...

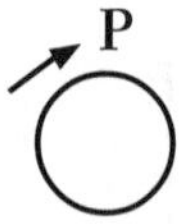

[OUT ON PAUL.]

Fig. 25.7: Shot 1B (continued)

if she needs to during editing. (Occasionally lines do not overlap—for instance, when both characters change their positions at the same time, or a scene is bisected by a new character entering the room.)

Employ the minimum number of camera positions

As I've mentioned earlier, moving the camera from setup to setup can be time-consuming. If you find you have a large number of setups for a contained scene, such as the Paul and Maura scene, your coverage may be excessive. In fact, I would *not* use the symmetrical opening position illustrated above. Two camera positions alongside the two characters should be enough. The opening shot (1A on Fig. 25.8) should favor Maura (even though Paul has the first line) because, in my opinion, seeing how she takes the news is more important than seeing how he delivers it. When Maura rises and crosses to Paul to kiss him, I would prefer to track the camera counter to her move, rather than cut to a wide shot. (See Fig. 25.8.)

Marking the camera positions

The director must be able to walk onto a set knowing where the camera positions will be. The lighting director and camera person will want to know the opening positions so that they can start to set up. The first assistant may ask for the number of setups in order to gauge how long the scene will take to shoot.

During the shooting, the director needs to continually think ahead to the next setup, especially if props or technical equipment are required. This information should be visible on the very first page. So add camera positions to the diagram on the left of the slug line. (See Fig. 25.8.)

Technical requirements

The director needs to note each scene's technical requirements so she can alert the camera crew well in advance. These technical requirements (or "tech reqs") might include dolly and track, a jib arm (a device that allows a camera to move up and down and, to some extent, in other directions as well), cranes, and special lenses.

In our scene, the director might decide to put down a length of track to allow the camera to adjust to the right when Maura stands up. (See diagram on marked-up script.) It is only one length of track, but it will have far-reaching implications for the shooting of the scene. The director and camera person may decide to put the track down first and shoot all the shots for position 1 from it.

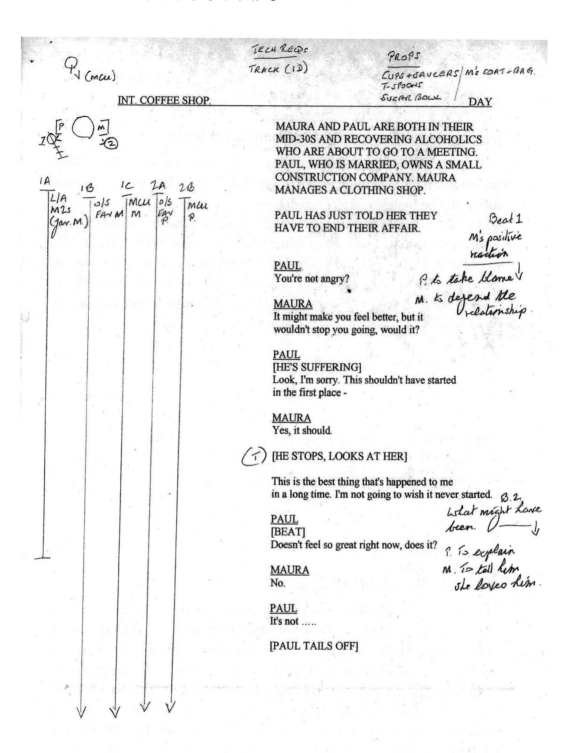

MAURA AND PAUL ARE BOTH IN THEIR
MID-30S AND RECOVERING ALCOHOLICS
WHO ARE ABOUT TO GO TO A MEETING.
PAUL, WHO IS MARRIED, OWNS A SMALL
CONSTRUCTION COMPANY. MAURA
MANAGES A CLOTHING SHOP.

PAUL HAS JUST TOLD HER THEY
HAVE TO END THEIR AFFAIR.

PAUL.
You're not angry?

MAURA
It might make you feel better, but it
wouldn't stop you going, would it?

PAUL
[HE'S SUFFERING]
Look, I'm sorry. This shouldn't have started
in the first place -

MAURA
Yes, it should.

[HE STOPS, LOOKS AT HER]

This is the best thing that's happened to me
in a long time. I'm not going to wish it never started.

PAUL
[BEAT]
Doesn't feel so great right now, does it?

MAURA
No.

PAUL
It's not .....

[PAUL TAILS OFF]

Fig. 25.8a: Marked-up scene

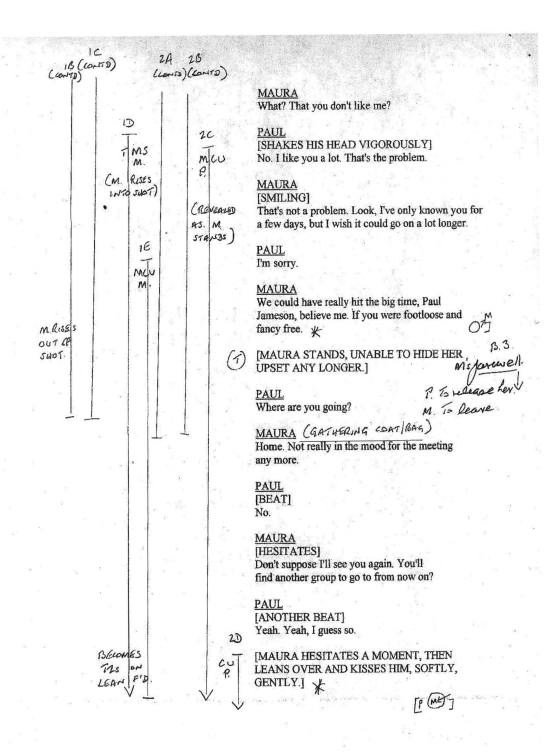

1B (CONT'D)
1C (CONT'D)
2A (CONT'D) **2B (CONT'D)**

1D
MS
M.
(M. RISES INTO SHOT)

2C
MCU
P.

(REVEALED AS. M STANDS)

1E
MCU
M.

M. RISES OUT OF SHOT.

MAURA
What? That you don't like me?

PAUL
[SHAKES HIS HEAD VIGOROUSLY]
No. I like you a lot. That's the problem.

MAURA
[SMILING]
That's not a problem. Look, I've only known you for
a few days, but I wish it could go on a lot longer.

PAUL
I'm sorry.

MAURA
We could have really hit the big time, Paul
Jameson, believe me. If you were footloose and
fancy free. ✳   O M

(T) [MAURA STANDS, UNABLE TO HIDE HER   B.3
UPSET ANY LONGER.]   M's farewell.

P. To release her ✓
M. To leave.

PAUL
Where are you going?

MAURA (GATHERING COAT/BAG)
Home. Not really in the mood for the meeting
any more.

PAUL
[BEAT]
No.

MAURA
[HESITATES]
Don't suppose I'll see you again. You'll
find another group to go to from now on?

PAUL
[ANOTHER BEAT]
Yeah. Yeah, I guess so.

BECOMES
MS ON
LEAN F'D.

2D
CU
P.

[MAURA HESITATES A MOMENT, THEN
LEANS OVER AND KISSES HIM, SOFTLY,
GENTLY.] ✳

[P (MS)]

Fig. 25.8b: Marked-up scene

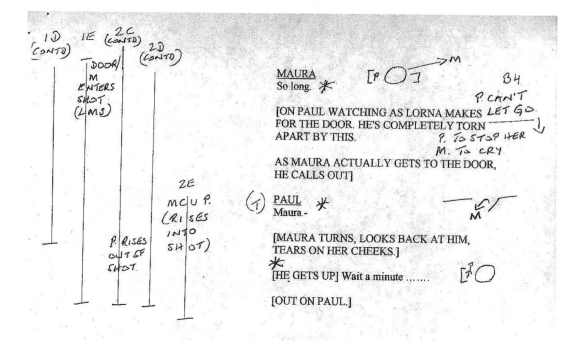

Fig. 25.8c: Marked-up scene

Having the note about the track right there above the slug line in the script ensures the director will discuss it with the DP or camera operator in good time. Forgetting to mention the track might cause the production to grind to a halt during the scene, causing a delay, in this case, of twenty minutes or more, while the tracks are collected and laid down.

Laying the track is the responsibility of the key grip, but he is supervised by the DP. All questions about significant lighting and camera issues should be referred to the DP, who is the head of the camera department.

Marked-up scene

Notes

The director intends to start with the L/A M2 (low-angle mid-2-shot) favoring Maura for the first two speeches—that means opening on Maura even though Paul is speaking.

The next few speeches are intended to be O/S shots (over-the-shoulder shots) followed at the bottom of the first page by MCUs. The MCUs are started from the very the top of the page because it is always wise to have a clean MCU (an

MCU without anyone else in the shot) as a safety shot when shooting an O/S. The back of the head of the unfavored person in an over-the-shoulder shot is so close to the lens that its slightest movement is noticeable. If a person moves his head in an O/S shot and is static in his MCU—or vice-versa—the shots will not match and the cut will not work. A clean single avoids this potential continuity problem. The top of the scene is also the most convenient place to start the MCUs, since it gives the actors a few lines to get into their rhythm.

At the end of the scene, Paul says "Maura" in CU or MCU and then rises out of shot. The director then intends to cut to Maura turning at the door, and then cut back to Paul standing in a MCU for "Wait a minute …"

26. Shooting Different Scenes

This chapter takes two scenes—a dramatic two-person and a four-person sitcom—and discusses the different approaches they require. Consider how you might prepare and block the scenes yourself, and then refer to my comments. There are no right or wrong ways of preparing the scenes.

The underlying assumption is that these scenes are *not* being produced for a big-budget picture. Simple tracking shots are possible, but helicopters, cranes, remote-control cameras, and even elaborate dollies and grip-work are not an option.

A dramatic two-person scene

<u>Int. Gus's Apartment</u>   Evening

Emily (early 20s) is a free spirit currently working as a waitress.

Gus (20s) is a policeman in the country town. They have been living together for several weeks.

Emily is almost finished packing when Gus comes in from work.

<u>GUS</u>
What are you doing?

<u>EMILY</u>
What does it look like?

                    GUS

I thought we were going to talk.

                   EMILY

Go on then.

                    GUS

I can't when you're doing that.

                   EMILY

Okay.

(Closes suitcase)

What do you want to say?

                    GUS

I don't want you to go. I know we've
had some disagreements lately...

                   EMILY

Disagreements!

                    GUS

Whatever. But they've been my fault. I
don't mind you being late ... Well I
guess I do, but I'm going to have to
live with it. I have to. I love you.

                   EMILY

I love you, Gus, but you can't expect
me to turn into a nice, loyal police
wife, keeping house for you, raising
your kids and helping you up the
ladder.

                    GUS

You don't have to.

                   EMILY

No? I remember all those police wives at
the presentation. They all wanted their
husbands to make a good impression so
they could climb up the next rung.

> GUS
>
> There's more to it than that, Em.

> EMILY
>
> Yes there is. Look, I don't want you turning into the typical cop, doing exactly what you have to to get promoted. I wouldn't care if you never got promoted.

> GUS
>
> You would if you saw the pension!

(Her face)

> That was a joke. Where are you going?

> EMILY
>
> Away on my own. I've cleared it with the restaurant.

> GUS
>
> Where?

> EMILY
>
> I don't know.

> GUS
>
> Can I come with you?

> EMILY
>
> No, Gus.

> GUS
>
> But I've booked my leave.

> EMILY
>
> You'll have to unbook it, then.

> GUS
>
> It's not as easy as you think. The Sarge'll give me hell....

(Stops as he realizes what he's saying.)

<u>EMILY</u>

(Almost pityingly)

I think that just sums it up, Gus.

(Kisses his cheek.)

I'll see you when I get back. Bye.

(She goes)

Here is a plan of the set (Fig. 26.1). I have included the main dressing props. (What action props do you need?)

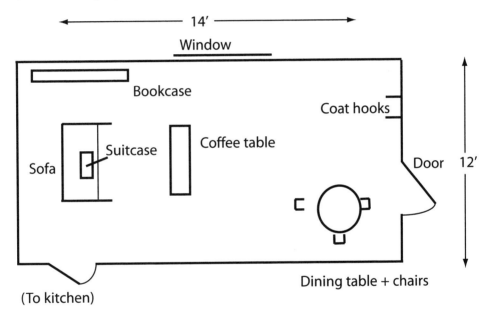

Fig. 26.1: Plan for Emily and Gus scene

My comments

1. Background

Think about the characters, their backgrounds, and their relationship. These affect the way they behave and move in the scene. What is the nature of the argument? When did they last argue? How upset is Emily at the top of the scene?

2. Beats, objectives, and transitions

The scene should be divided up into beats. (I think the scene has three.) Characters should have their super- (or scene-) objectives, as well as their objectives for each beat. Where are the main transitions?

After doing this work, the characters should begin to come to life, and their contrasting objectives should throw light on the scene as a whole

3. The opening

One of the challenges in preparing this scene is its opening. The actors will need to know the backstory, and may even want to improvise the row that precipitated this scene. But beyond that, one wonders how long Emily has been in the room. Is she trying to get her packing done quickly in order to avoid Gus, or is she trying to confront him? And has Gus come home early to find her or is this his normal evening routine?

How many bags/suitcases (or perhaps even boxes) has Emily got? Is Gus wearing a police uniform?

4. Movement

This is a scene with plenty of opportunity for movement. *Please consider how you would block and shoot it before reading my comments, which start in the next paragraph.*

Emily's actions are important, and they attract Gus's attention as soon as he walks through the door. So I would be tempted to start with a shot of Emily collecting her books from the bookcase, and then crossing the room and stuffing them in a bag.

When Gus enters, does he just stop in the doorway or does he come in and put his cap down on one of the chairs by the table?

I think he takes a step toward her when he starts his prepared speech, "I don't want you to go…"—but he does not get very far. Emily does not welcome his proximity and keeps the coffee table between them.

Much of the movement here is going to be to-and-away, as Gus tries to convince her not to go, and Emily tries to stay free. (I think their super-objectives are—Gus: to keep Emily; Emily: to stay free.)

Obviously, Emily is moving toward the door on Gus's line. "That was a joke. Where are you going?" Quite a lot of dialogue follows this line, so I would have her collecting stuff from the table or taking her coat from the coat hook, so that she is not stuck in the door with nothing to do.

Near the end, Emily steps toward Gus to kiss him, and then picks up her bags and breaks for the door (as the stage directions suggest).

As is common in these scenes, one character moves more than the other. Perhaps Emily, the freer spirit, should do most of the moving, while Gus remains trapped in one position?

5. Shooting style

No two directors will see this in exactly the same way. If we opt for a straightforward, cuts-only, static-camera style, then here is one way of approaching it.

Scenes traditionally open with the widest shot. We could start with a $^3/_4$-shot of Emily, taking her books from the bookcase to the couch (a short pan). Alternatively, we could start tight on a shelf of the bookcase and have her hand come in and remove some books. We could then establish their character traits through their choice of reading: *Last Exit to Brooklyn* (Emily's book) side by side with *Community Policing* (Gus's). Then we could cut to the wider shot for her cross to the sofa. (A delayed establishing shot.)

I think Emily's back is toward Gus until after she decides to give him her attention—after her "Okay." This is a transition, a change of objective for her since she is now going to listen to what he has to say. At this moment, we want to see her clearly—so the shot should be at least a mid-shot.

Gus's speech that ends with "I love you" is an important one for him, so I would take it in a medium closeup.

Emily then has three important speeches beginning with "I love you, Gus." I do not want to bounce back and forth between them in MCUs, so I would take her first speech in an over-the-shoulder shot. This serves to bring the two of them together in the same shot, and emphasizes their proximity. Her next two speeches could then be clean MCUs.

Emily has another transition after Gus says, "You would if you saw the pension." Again, it would be nice to be in some sort of closeup for that. I think I would also have her walk out of frame in this shot to collect her bags and coat.

The speeches in the last beat are much shorter. Gus's "Can I come with you?" is an important line. It is so pathetic, touching and maddening! I would like to be in close for that line. Gus has a transition near the end when he realizes his gaffe (after "The Sarge'll give me hell"). I would like to be close for that, as well as for Emily's reaction.

I think I'd keep the ending simple. Perhaps we pick Emily up in a mid-shot for "I think that just sums it up, Gus," and let the shot tighten to a tight mid-2-shot as she crosses toward Gus and the camera to kiss him. (See Fig. 26.2 below.) It's a short kiss and then the camera can pan with her as she moves past Gus to the door. (If we have tracks, we might track a few feet with her and exclude Gus from the frame, Fig. 26.3.) The final shot could be of the door closing *or* of Gus's reaction. I would definitely shoot both.

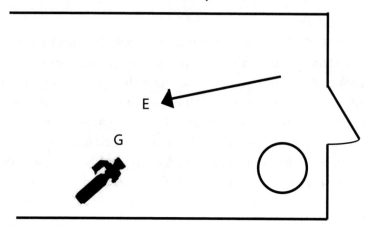

Emily crosses to Gus and the shot favors her (MS Emily / Pan l. and Contain move f'wd. into M2s fav Emily).

Fig. 26.2: Possible camera position for Emily's cross

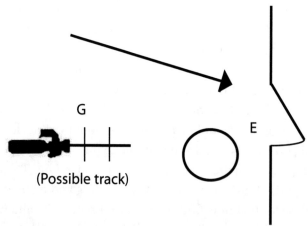

Emily crosses to door [TM2s (Em/Gus)/pan Em rt. to door (lose Gus)].

Fig. 26.3: Cross with tracks

A four-person sitcom scene

INT. FROTHY'S COFFEE SHOP   EARLY MORNING

Mrs. Booth (42) has recently opened a coffee shop
that she runs with the help of 3 staff: David,
Bobby, and Andrea. It is not a very successful
enterprise, but Mrs. Booth has aspirations.

As the scene opens, she is going through her mail.
David (32) is already there. David is a cultured
young man badly in need of a friend.

                    MRS. BOOTH
               (Reading a letter)

          Oh my gosh!

(Bobby, a 28-year-old fashion-conscious female,
enters.)

                    BOBBY
          Mrs. Booth, are you all right?

                    MRS. BOOTH
          The Coffee Consumers Association is
          coming to inspect us next week.

                    BOBBY
          And I have nothing to wear!

(Andrea, a 26-year-old medical-school graduate
student with an aggressive personality, enters.)

                    ANDREA
          A—choo!

                    MRS. BOOTH
          Good morning, Andrea.

                    BOBBY
          Bless you.

> ### MRS. BOOTH
> David, can you call the Association headquarters and find out exactly when they're coming?

> ### DAVID
> Affirmative.

> ### BOBBY
> Are you worried, Mrs. Booth?

> ### MRS. BOOTH
> Worried? No, no. Absolutely not. Everything's fine. Knock on wood!

(She does so and the counter collapses.)

> ### DAVID
> (On the phone)
>
> Coffee Consumers Association? Hi, my name's David. What's yours? Oh that's nice. Actually, I'm calling from Frothy's in Boston. We heard that you were going to inspect us next week and wanted to now exactly when you were coming. Why? So we could fix our counter for one thing.

> ### MRS. BOOTH
> David, don't tell them that!

> ### DAVID
> (Into the phone)
>
> Just joking!

> ### ANDREA
> A-a-choo!

> ### MRS. BOOTH
> Andrea, don't let them hear you sneeze!

DAVID

Oh, you don't say when you're coming because it's meant to be a surprise. That's very playful. How about if I guess and you say "hot" or "cold"? I know you don't play around. It was just a suggestion. All right, don't get uppity. Suit yourself then!
(Slams down the phone.)

MRS. BOOTH

Thanks, David. I'm sure that helped.

BOBBY

What's this with the Coffee Consumerswhatsit?

MRS. BOOTH

They're a very important body. And they issue beans.

BOBBY

Beans?

MRS. BOOTH

Yes, it's a ranking. Five beans means you're a really good coffee shop.

ANDREA

We haven't got any, have we?

MRS. BOOTH

No we don't, Andrea, but we deserve at least half a bean. And then they have regulations.

ANDREA

Like what?

MRS. BOOTH

About how long you roast. About cleanliness. About ventilation.

ANDREA
A-choo! What ventilation?

MRS. BOOTH
David, here's their list. See if you
can get through it before they come.

DAVID
Yessir.

MRS. BOOTH
Start with the fridge.

ANDREA
Why the fridge? How about the
cupboards?

MRS. BOOTH
The fridge is very important to them.

ANDREA
Well, it's important to me too.

DAVID
They say it's got to be kept at a
constant 42 degrees.

ANDREA
No way! I've got my research in
there. My flu viruses won't incubate
at less than 45.

MRS. BOOTH
Andrea! I've told you not to keep
your viruses in there. Grow them at
home.

ANDREA
I can't, they're too dangerous!

DAVID
(Scanning the list)

It's amazing. They have rules for
everything. The height of the bar,

the style of our aprons, even what
kind of music we play. How can music
affect the coffee?

                    BOBBY
Coffee beans like salsa. It makes
them feel at home.

                    DAVID
It says the music has to be tasteful,
preferably classical or jazz.

                    ANDREA
No punk rock? No Eminem?

                    BOBBY
It looks like you're going to have to
buy some new CDs, Mrs. Booth.

                    ANDREA
A-choo!

                    DAVID
And it says that nobody with a cold
should be working behind the counter!

                    ANDREA
(Hopefully)

I bet it doesn't say I can't keep flu
bacteria in the fridge, does it?

Here is the set.

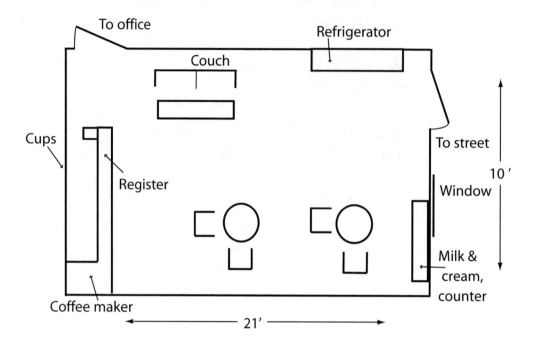

Fig. 26.4: Set

My comments continued

1. Background

The character descriptions provided in the text are very superficial. More work has to be done on background and relationships if the characters are not to appear as stereotypes. Although characters should almost always be well-rounded, usually one or two characteristics will predominate—especially in comedy.

Each actor's business will be very important in this scene. What the characters do and how they do it will depend on the character choices you make. A lot of humor is derived from how the characters interact, so consideration of their relationships will be particularly important.

2. Beats, objectives, and transitions

This scene is not difficult to break up into beats. How many are there?

Strong super-objectives are very important in comedy. What is important to each of the characters and what is each trying to achieve? Do they vary their tactics from beat to beat?

Comedy tends to have more transitions that normal drama. The scene actually opens with one—Mrs. Booth is surprised by the contents of her letter.

3. Opening

Openings are always particularly important. How long has Mrs. Booth been in the office? What is David doing? Where are Bobby and Andrea coming from?

4. Movement

This is another scene with plenty of opportunity for movement. However, bear in mind that four characters simultaneously moving about a set can become extremely complicated to shoot.

I think the first beat is about establishing the characters and ends with Bobby's "Bless you" after Andrea's entrance. The writer has given Bobby and Andrea different types of entrances, so the director should emphasize that. Andrea sneezes as she enters, which should be an amusing moment. Invoking the old theatrical saying, "Never move on a laugh line," Andrea's "A-choo!" might be more effective if she is standing still for it.

The key to blocking this scene is grouping. Do you see moments when a two-versus-two arrangement will work? Are there moments when a three-against-one grouping works better? Remember, you can have the characters go to whatever positions you want, as long as you have the appropriate business to take them there. Do you see moments when the scene is busy and all the characters are working? And are there also moments of stillness, when all stop what they are doing and listen to someone? Perhaps David's telephone conversation is a moment when everybody listens to what he's saying.

Props will be very important in this scene. It is in a work environment, so there should be plenty to do—from unwrapping and starting the morning's first brew to emptying the trash and putting out the milk and cream. Not all the business need be so active. Someone could be sipping their first cup of the morning or reading the newspaper.

5. Shooting style

Comedy tends to be shot slightly looser than drama, and this scene offers plenty of opportunities for group shots and mid-shots.

Would you use a medium closeup at any point? That would depend on your blocking, but I think there are a few MCU moments when the pressure is on one or other of the characters. You might shoot the telephone conversation in an MCU. It's also very important to Mrs. Booth that she qualify for at least "half a bean." And Andrea is definitely under some pressure to remove her bacteria from the fridge. There is also a possible MCU reaction shot of Mrs. Booth toward the end of the scene, after Bobby says, "It looks like you're going to have to buy some more CDs, Mrs. Booth."

PART 5
Production

27. Personnel Management and Rehearsing Actors on the Set

"A talented director lays out opportunities that can be seized on by other people—by other heads of departments and by the actors, who are in effect the heads of their own departments. This is the real function of a director, I believe. And then to protect that communal vision by accepting or rejecting certain contributions. The director is ultimately the immune system of the film." —Walter Murch[1]

When I discussed preproduction, my emphasis was on planning. But directors do not suddenly emerge from their studies to go shooting, like moles into the light. Plans that are constructed after consultation with designers, assistants, and others are subsequently modified by actors and crew. Directors are not like writers, who can—up to a point—work in a vacuum. Directors have to balance solitary work with human interaction. There was one, and only one, director I worked with as a production manager who did not turn up to the office during preproduction. To our amazement, he sent his production team a wallchart with all his requirements—including props, extras, and vehicles—color-coded and arranged scene by scene. There was no personal interaction and no discussion, merely the illusion of efficiency. The director was, in effect, saying, "I'm not interested in speaking to you." Predictably, the ensuing production was soulless, and the film itself was the most disappointing I ever worked on.

[1] Michael Ondaatje, *Conversations* (New York: Knopf, 2002).

The tech scout

Before starting the production phase, directors must consult closely with casting directors, designers, and their production team. They must also meet their lighting directors and discuss shooting issues in an extended on-site conference that the Americans call a *tech scout* (and the British call a camera "recce," short for "reconnoiter"). A good tech scout enables a director to discuss her vision in detail with the cinematographer (DP), production designer, and first assistant, so that, hopefully, no confusion arises when shooting commences. It also allows the DP, gaffer (chief electrician), and any other relevant member of the camera department to assess what lights and supplementary camera equipment (such as tracks and other grip-related items) it requires. Members of the production team may also use the tech scout to discuss and adapt the shooting schedule.

Directors usually prefer to shoot in "story order" (the order in which the scenes occur in the script) on each location, because it allows the actors to work in chronological sequence, developing their emotional continuity from scene to scene. Some directors, such as John Cassavetes, have placed a very high priority on this. However, shooting out of sequence is often necessary in order to accommodate certain technical issues. For instance, the DP may want to shoot a certain scene early in the day because of the position of the sun. A crowd scene may need to be postponed by a few hours in order to give costume and makeup enough time to get all the extras ready. Or a set may require a major "redressing" (rearrangement of props and furniture) in one particular scene, so it may be most efficient to schedule it at the start of the day in order to give the designer time to make the changes overnight. Or a scene with an elaborate tracking shot that requires an hour to set up may be scheduled after lunch to enable the key grip (the crew member primarily responsible for erecting the camera track) to work unhindered on the set while everyone else is eating.

The director must weigh the merits of shooting in story order against these conflicting demands. Generally, the tighter the production schedule (as on low-budget films and television series), the more the director is forced to compromise.

Depending on logistics and technical complexity, a ninety-minute movie with limited special effects can take between six weeks and three months to shoot. This can put considerable strain on the director and the crew.

The first movie I ever worked on as a production manager was shot during winter in The Fens—the bleakest and most windswept area of England. We shot in a run-down house from which we had to expel the occupants every morning. The star of the film was a handicapped boy with amazing energy, but who nevertheless had only one kidney and was vulnerable to infection. The wind blew up through the floorboards, and the location was so dispiriting that our leading actress cried every time she approached it. There was no room for the crew inside the location and the unit coach had to be parked 200 yards away at the end of the drive. This meant that the crew spent much of the day huddled around a brazier in the icy wind and snow. Then shooting was interrupted by a technicians' strike, which lasted a week. Things got so bad that our normally undemonstrative director of photography pushed the person responsible for finding the location down the stairs of the catering wagon. (I know, because that was me.) Through all this tension, our director, Anthony Simmons, showed admirable calm. He remained focused on the considerable problems presented by the script itself and did not seem phased by events. There is a lot to be said for directorial single-mindedness and persistence on a film. In the end, the movie was completed in two months—two weeks longer than planned.

Directors must have a range of characteristics—including creativity, single-mindedness and adaptability—but one of the most important is an ability to manage personnel. They deal with a group of equally strong-minded, creative individuals who must be coordinated and encouraged to give their best. Directors must be able to tolerate and reconcile differences, and they must have an effective working style. A weak director who cannot impose herself on a crew causes an authority vacuum that is filled by someone else—such as an assertive first assistant or experienced DP. This situation can not only cause dissension among the crew, it can make it more and more difficult for the director to get what she wants.

Good management involves good communication. Directors must not only have a vision, they must be able to articulate it so that everyone understands it and works "from the same hymn sheet." They will use whatever tools are available—documents, paintings, photographs, CDs, DVDs, etc.—to communicate with actors and crew.

For an account of the working methods of three different directors, see "Three Directors," Part 9, Chapter 43. That chapter, which offers concrete examples of many of the principles discussed here, may be read alongside the current one.

Crew psychology

Crew psychology varies from unit to unit, but certain factors usually apply. Crews generally want directors to succeed. Usually, they'll give directors a honeymoon period of about a week, especially in film, during which time they will reserve judgment. Sooner or later, however, directors have to prove themselves.

Directors can do certain basic things to create a healthy work environment. They can show consideration for the crew. Basic courtesies, such as knowing people's names and jobs, are a good start. Observing and appreciating their work is another. The director cannot always tell if the sound engineer is recording good audio on location, but the director can thank the boom operator for coping with a series of long takes. Directors traditionally communicate well with their immediate entourage, but do not always go out of their way to talk to scenery movers, costume and makeup assistants, carpenters, and painters. Acknowledging that these members are contributing to the overall success of the film is important for crew morale. Television and film crews are accustomed to working long hours, but a director should not take it for granted that they will. Many of the design departments are at work long before the sun rises, so directors should occasionally show their appreciation. Directors should thank "crew chiefs," such as the DP, sound recordist, and designer, for working overtime. They should also see to it that, as far as possible, the crew gets its meals on time. Crews resent directors who they feel are continuously chipping away at their breaks.

I have a theory that every member of a film or television crew gets tested at some point. Sometimes you wake up, have breakfast, walk onto the set, and realize that, for some reason, it is your turn that day. Generally, if you can continue to perform efficiently and withstand the pressure, the crew's collective gaze will move away from you and onto somebody else. It's a strange phenomenon. It is as though the group is trying to identify its weakest and least-efficient link. Life can be hard for the person so-identified.

The director, through her own example, is largely responsible for setting the working tone on a set. The very quiet and concentrated atmosphere on the set of a Clint Eastwood movie, for instance, reflects that director's own personal manner. I would suggest to directors at the start of their careers that a small amount of reserve and formality indicates respect for one's co-workers, and is not a bad thing. An intrusive and over-friendly directorial style can be as damaging as one that is removed and inaccessible.

Of course, the greatest courtesy a director shows the crew is efficiency. Directors who know what shots they want and keep to prior arrangements made with camera and design tend to keep the show on schedule (or even, occasionally, finish early). Directorial efficiency also sets a standard for everyone else. Good director-crew relationships are important both in television, where a series director may come back regularly over a number of years, and in film, where they will work together intensely over a period of months.

I once worked on a TV series for two years, always finishing the day's work early, sometimes by as much as two hours. The crews were very grateful and I reckoned I was storing up goodwill against the time when I would need to ask them a favor. Then one day the camera broke down and we lost several hours waiting for a replacement. To my surprise and dismay, the crew refused to work an extra half hour after the designated wrap time to complete the schedule. It was a union shoot and they would not set a precedent by breaking the contract. I must admit I placed less of a premium on finishing early thereafter.

Actors on the set

For most actors, there is a difference between rehearsing and shooting. Rehearsal tends to be informal and relaxed. Shooting occurs under pressure — especially time pressure. Actors, who are generally nocturnal creatures, have to get up early for filming and go through costume, makeup, and hairdressing before they appear on set. The set, unlike the stage, is not their space — it's occupied by technicians and equipment. You often hear theater actors lament that they cannot give their best in a studio or on a soundstage. As a director you have to convince them they can. You have to make them feel as at home under the lights and in front of the camera as they do on a raked stage in front of 500 spectators.

Actors who are nervous tend to do what we all do when we're nervous — talk too loudly and become distracted. Sometimes nervous actors will forget what they've practiced in rehearsal. The director can help them focus. Performers, like athletes, give their best when they can rid themselves of tension. Very often, you don't have to say, "You're talking too loud," all you have to do is put them at ease.

I once observed a distinguished, elderly director directing a play by Samuel Beckett for television. He controlled the performance from the studio floor instead of the control room. In those days, that was a very unusual practice, but it brought him closer to his actors. I was amazed by how little actual speaking he did. The whole shooting process was imbued by his manner—a calm, concentrated approach that infected the crew and performers alike.

The director can do certain common-sense things to put her actors at ease. She can introduce them to the technical staff who are physically closest to them: the DP, camera operator, and boom op. The less these people seem to be anonymous technicians, the less intrusive and threatening they'll appear. Many directors become so closely involved with the camera that they ignore those giving the performance. If snags and holdups arise, keep the actors informed so they are not left in limbo, wondering what is happening. Don't leave actors sweltering under hot lights when they are not in a shot. Adopt the usual courtesies of informing them what shot you are coming to ("We're going to do your closeup next"). Make them feel they have some minimal control over the conditions of their performance ("Are you ready?"). Makeup artists like to attend to actors before their closeups, and directors need to understand that this gives actors an artistic as well as psychological boost. Of course, you should always appreciate your actors' work and thank them at the end of a scene.

The on-set sequence

One of the calculations a director makes is how to give maximum time to the actors. Here is a common sequence for introducing actors to the set.

1. Line-run and blocking

The director asks for the actors, and extras if there are any in the scene, to come onto the set. If actors from the previous scene are also in the new one, they must be given at least a few minutes' break. (These actors may also have to spend some time changing their costumes.) Once they are assembled on the set, the director runs the lines with the actors in order to get them focussed on the scene. After that, she starts blocking. If there has been prior rehearsal, this blocking won't take long. If the director is blocking a scene for the first time, she will want as few people on the set as possible so she and the actors can concentrate.

2. Run-through

Having blocked the scene, the director will run it through at least once to cement the actors' positions. The lighting director, camera op, sound recordist, and boom op will also want to watch the run-through so they can start thinking about their contributions.

3. Using the time off the set

If the scene requires it, the actors can use the period while the lights are being set to run their lines and continue to rehearse. (The kind of rehearsing that can be done at this time is discussed below.)

4. Final run-through

When the overall lighting is complete, the lighting director may want to see one more run-through of the scene. It is always a good idea, at any rate, to run a scene at least once on the set before shooting begins so that actors can experience it as a whole before it is chopped up into takes. A film director might ask the actors to save their performances during the run-through—because they will have plenty of time during the next several hours to summon up their emotions. In a television shoot, however, where time is always short, the run-through can be a valuable final opportunity for actors to get into their roles.

Counting the director, production team, camera crew, audio crew, electricians, grips, members of wardrobe, and makeup artists, the smallest set will have at least fifteen people hovering around it. Depending on the type of film and the kind of scene being shot, this number could easily double or quadruple. All those people represent dollar signs to a producer or unit manager. As the clock winds down at the end of the day and some shots remain to be taken, everyone appreciates that time is money. The director is aware of this pressure but must shield the actors from it.

Problems of shooting without rehearsal

Film and especially television tends to be produced by people with screenwriting backgrounds who do not appreciate the value of rehearsal. Their emphasis is more on getting the script right than perfecting the performances. Their prevailing attitude seems to be, "If the script is right, then everything else will look after itself."

In most cases, if blocking is deferred till the shoot, it is bound to be somewhat superficial. The director will give moves to actors who will not have time to really absorb them. Furthermore, these moves cannot be too complicated because there is not enough time to practice them.

Rehearsal can give actors the opportunity to think more deeply about their characters and actions. This, in turn, endows them with the courage to be bolder and more interesting. Without rehearsal, they will tend to play the simplest choices, grabbing on to the first solution they find. They will "play safe" and not go for the more challenging and interesting emotional effects. Actors who are uncertain in front of the camera also tend to want to appear sympathetic. (After all, who wants to look nasty in front of millions of viewers?)

Occasionally, an actor will arrive on the set with a very clear idea of how the scene should be staged. If the director accepts this interpretation, she may be able to build on the actor's foundation and take the scene to another level of complexity. But, in a time-pressure situation, without rehearsal, the director will have to spend precious minutes running the scene a couple of times and rethinking her shooting plan.

What to do if no rehearsal time has been allocated

If no rehearsal period has been allocated, then the director should do her best to find rehearsal time during the shoot. Almost all actors are willing to devote an hour or two to improving their performances. If the project is being shot on location, rehearsal can take place on non-shooting days (weekends and at the end of travel days). Actors can be called before late-starts or in the evening immediately after the day's shoot. Sometimes, gaps in the day, such as those caused by a design change or a particularly elaborate lighting setup, can be utilized. Otherwise, the director has to maximize the twenty minutes or an hour while the lighting director sets the lamps for a new scene. When really desperate, you can suggest that the actors give up the last quarter of an hour of their lunch break.

If you are grabbing short chunks of time, rehearsal has to be very focussed. If you have only twenty minutes, you probably won't use improvisation or conduct a freewheeling conversation about character and background. Here are some suggestions for rehearsing under such time constraints:

1. Ask the actors to read the scene once, and listen very carefully for any uncertainty of tone. If you detect uncertainty, address those lines immediately, either explaining their importance, furnishing the subtext or, as a last resort, changing them.

2. Succinctly state the point of the scene. "This scene is about …" Such a statement may seem obvious, but it brings everybody onto the same page. Some actors may have missed the point entirely, and some may just have a more interesting take than you do.

3. Give very clear, pithy, grounded, *active* objectives. If the scene is a short one, it will probably involve only one objective. If the scene is a long one, with

two or more beats, start with its overall objective. If time allows and the actors are receptive, then add the beat objectives.

4. Working on character relationships is important. Make sure the script's given circumstances (those indicated in the text) are clear. If you can add a single interesting insight into character or background, do so. All direction at this point must be clear and specific. The comment, "You both met at a business conference two years ago and had an affair" is more helpful than, "You two have known each other for a while, off and on, and there has been some kind of attraction between you."

5. Watch carefully to see if the actors are achieving the main transitions. If they are, don't waste time discussing them. If they are not, point them out.

6. Keep the moves simple. An intricately choreographed scene may look nice, but too many moves will handcuff an actor. The more time available, the more moves you can introduce. If, during blocking, the actor moves at a slightly different moment or initiates a new move that works, consider accepting it and modifying your shooting plan. Actors will tend to play their own moves with more conviction than the ones you give them.

A few performance tips

If a scene starts at a high emotional level or in the middle of a discussion or an argument, you can reconstruct the previous beat (see Chapter 15). You can also help actors get into a scene quickly by giving them very specific actions before the scene starts. A doctor's waiting-room scene that opens with the receptionist saying, "The doctor will see you now," might be preceded by the patient putting down a magazine and glancing at the busy receptionist. The nurse might enter and speak to the receptionist about an emergency appointment, and the receptionist might dial a telephone number before delivering her first line to the patient. All this creates a mood from which the opening lines can emerge naturally.

You can help actors reach a high opening emotional level by taking them aside and motivating them. For example, a director can help an actress who has to enter in tears by graphically reviewing the given circumstances with her: "You've been left by your lover. He's found another woman. It's clear he's stopped loving you. It's your fault. You'll never find anyone else ever again." This is a powerful directorial weapon and should be used sparingly.

Immediately before doing emotional scenes that are predicated on a close relationship—such as husband and wife, father and son, or lovers—ask the two main actors to sit or stand opposite each other, look into each other's eyes, hold hands, and run the scene. You can also do this exercise before shooting closeups. It may be helpful in other situations as well, but don't over-use it lest it lose its efficacy.

Some directors, particularly those working with "method" actors, may use motivation that does not arise from within the drama itself. Both Marlon Brando and Anthony Quinn had played Stanley Kowalski in Tennessee Williams' *Streetcar Named Desire*. When Elia Kazan was directing them in a fight scene in *Viva Zapata* (1952), he told each one that the other thought he had played the role much better. Apparently this was just what was required to ignite their fury!

Sometimes props can instantly intensify the emotion in a scene. An ex-husband and wife argue about the future of their child. The director provides a framed photograph of the child on the set that serves to make the struggle more specific. The picture might also be referred to or even picked up by one of the parents.

An unseen prop can also be powerful. An actress has to play a tearful scene about the death of her husband, and the director gives her a ring or a St. Christopher medallion and tells her it belonged to her spouse. Just the presence of the prop in her pocket, or held in her hand, will serve as an impetus for her grief. (I'm sorry all these examples are so gloomy.)

Clear, simple business almost always helps an actor. Washing the dishes, reading the newspaper, preparing the dinner, folding laundry—all these activities provide a focus of attention, as well as something to do with the hands.

Extras

Extras are the group of anonymous characters who inhabit the background of a shot and occasionally the foreground and edges as well. They are the nameless shoppers in a scene set in a supermarket or the parents and children in the background of a playground scene or the cheering fans at a little-league baseball game. Unless specifically requested to vocalize some group activity such as cheering (for which they may receive additional payment), extras do not say a word. Pairs of extras in a restaurant scene, for instance, will carry on involved conversations with each other without uttering a sound. The effect, when you first encounter it, can be a little eerie.

The union agreement signed by most movies and television shows mandates the use of a certain number of Screen Actors Guild (SAG) members as extras. Once a production has filled that quota, it is free to hire other, less expensive, extras. The benefit of using SAG extras is that they are often more experienced than their non-union counterparts, which means that they are at ease in front of the camera, take direction easily, and are very familiar with the routine of shooting. Independent movies, especially those shot far from production centers like L.A. or New York, are less likely to employ SAG extras.

Directors consider the types of extras they need when they mark up the script. Some scenes require anonymous extras while other scenes call for more specific character types. The members of a crowd in a shopping mall will obviously be less individuated than a single couple sitting on a bench in an otherwise deserted park. As a first assistant, I once had to cast the athletes and crowd in a nineteenth-century Cornish wrestling match in southwest England. After consultation with the director, I cast the young men appearing in the actual contest from a local club that still practiced this arcane sport. Having been specific about the actual wrestlers, I could be less specific about the large crowd that observed the event, which I cast from a mixture of local farmers and other interested parties, including a couple of visiting American tourists. When I directed a television series with scenes set on a city street as well as inside a bar, I gave my first assistant a reasonably free hand casting the pedestrians in the street but was very specific about the extras inside the pub, who were more strongly featured by the camera.

Extras are usually positioned on the set by the first assistant or second assistant, but this does not mean that a director should not involve himself with them. A director will not only have specific ideas about the types of extras required, he will also have worked out where they will be positioned in the shot, and have strong ideas about where and when they will move. The director communicates this information to his first assistant and then double-checks that the first assistant has implemented it correctly.

Extras are one of the least appreciated groups on a shoot. They are often herded like cattle, forced to spend long periods waiting to be called onto the set, and denied most of the other courtesies accorded to speaking actors. There may not be time on a fast-moving shoot for the director to interact with the extras personally, but a few welcoming words addressed to them at the start of the day, and a few more words describing the scene that is about to be shot, can do wonders for their morale.

Directors (or their assistants) give general instructions to extras about their identities ("You are a group of football fans enraged by the tactics of the visiting team"), and about the timing of their actions ("I'd like you to get excited when this character scores a goal" or "Cross the street as soon as that character goes into the shop"). However, once an extra is singled out from the group and given specific direction or business ("You are a street entertainer. When this character passes, hold out your hat and silently demand some money"), that extra may be upgraded to a "silent bit player" with a consequent increase in salary. The young wrestlers in the above-mentioned Cornish wrestling scene were silent bit players who received additional payment for rehearsing and also for displaying special skills. When discussing extras with a first assistant during preproduction, make sure she has budgeted for a number of silent bit players in addition to the regular extras.

28. The Eyes

"A main problem was, could you look at a man with a hood over his face and could he engross you?"
Neil Jordan on shooting *The Crying Game* (1992)

"Since the audience is very aware of the actor's eyes, you should take care of them. For example, it is nice to wash your eyes in tepid water, blink your eye several times, look up, look down, right, left, and then move your eyes in a circle. After you have washed your eyes, you can give them a gentle massage. With the eyes closed, place the palms of the hands over the eyes, and push the eyeballs very softly inwards." —Yoshi Oida, actor[1]

When we need real insight into characters, we look into their eyes. The eyes are the surest guide to how a character is feeling in most situations. The reaction shot—the usually silent closeup that shows how a character is responding to the actions or speech of another—is one of the most telling shots.

Eyes not only tell us what a character is thinking, they reinforce actions. They flash with anger in a fight and melt with love in an embrace.

Eyes possess an innate expressiveness that cannot be matched by the movements of the mouth or the arms. Their pupils open with love and shrink with dislike. Their lids shield guilty stares and reveal curious ones. Their eyebrows rise with surprise and dip with scorn. Eyes have different colors that absorb and reflect light in different ways: the warmth of brown, the reserve of

---

[1] Yoshi Oida and Lorna Marshall, *The Invisible Actor* (London: Methuen Publishing Ltd., 1997), p. 4.

blue, and the fascination of green. And the eyeball, with its ability to roll or dart, is set off against the face by the sheer whiteness of its sclera. Unlike the mouth, the ear, or the nose, the eye is liquid. Its liquidity draws our attention when tears well up, but the water of the eye also serves to attract and reflect light. The membrane covering the eyes, providing it with its opacity, gives us the impression of seeing beyond the eye itself, into the mind and soul. Not surprisingly, many great actors, from Betterton in the seventeenth century to Olivier in the twentieth, have had large and expressive eyes.

If there are those who still need to be convinced about the expressiveness of the eyes, try the following acting exercise. A person sits silently in a chair, with the lower half of his face (below the eyes) covered with a scarf. At the other end of the room another person pretends to be his child and stares into his eyes for guidance. Between them are chairs or cones that represent mines in a minefield. Without moving his head or flicking his eyes, the first person must guide the second safely through the danger. The emotion that wells up in the parent's eyes as the child approaches danger is enough to ensure its safe passage. Alternatively, watch Robert Duvall's astonishing performance near the end of *To Kill a Mockingbird* (1962) or Sissy Spacek in *The Straight Story* (2000).

In real life, when we talk to other people, we don't often look into their eyes. Looking steadily into someone else's eyes is considered an invasion of privacy, and usually reserved only for lovers and optometrists. The screen, with its fondness for the closeup, offers us the thrill of breaking this taboo.

Mutual support

To be convincing, a performance must give the impression of being fresh. One of the greatest challenges of acting for the camera is that lines have to be repeated take after take. An actor who calls entirely upon his own resources to provide the freshness each time will only last two or three takes. Experienced directors are familiar with this type—often a leading actor in a television series who has had to turn in so many performances day after day that he no longer relates to other actors in the scene. The important thing for him is to do his job quickly and leave the set. If the shot isn't in the bag by the end of the third take, he blames the director (occasionally with some justification) for not having all the elements in place.

For an actor, an awareness of what the *other* actor is doing in a scene makes each take unpredictable, and therefore fresh. With the possible exception of monologues and one-man shows, the best actors do not act by themselves. Performances, especially on screen, are constructed by interplay among actors.

The acting teacher whose work most addresses the interplay between actors is the late Sanford Meisner. He encouraged his students to trust their senses rather than their intellect. He held that acting is about listening and observing and even smelling. Taking his cue from Stanislavski,[2] he asserted that actors must be aware of their surroundings and acutely aware of other actors. Indeed, they must be so focused on the other character—how she looks, how she moves, how she speaks—that they lose their inhibiting self-consciousness. This awareness also allows actors to become unusually responsive to their partner's slightest nuance. If the same scene must be played and replayed, good actors will find some subtle difference to keep it alive each time. The central aspect of the performance becomes the relationships among the characters rather than the mechanical repetition of an actor's personal, predetermined, choices. In this way, actors in a scene become each others' lifelines.

If this seems anti-intellectual, it is. Meisner, who had been a distinguished member of the Group Theatre (see Part 7, Chapter 39), gradually took up a position slightly apart from his fellow Stanislavskians. "You can talk about a part, but until it finds its living roots in you, it's in the head. And I'm against the head."[3]

Meisner developed a series of exercises for his beginner students that emphasized observation. In a group of exercises called "Taking the First Thing," students formed into pairs, stood back to back, and then practiced turning to face each other and articulating their first impressions. After training actors to come to each scene afresh, he went on to work with them on finding and deepening their emotions. He said, "Acting is doing. And meaningful acting is doing under emotional circumstances."[4]

The eyes are central in all this. The eye-line is a tightrope that keeps a pair of actors aloft. If you watch a drama and momentarily tune out the dialogue, you cannot help being aware of how often actors look into each others' eyes. In high-tension television shows that are taped under time constraints or in front of an audience, actors often cling to the eye-line for support. Turn down the volume in an old episode of *Seinfeld* and you will be struck by how much Kramer and Seinfeld maintain eye contact.

---

[2] Stanislavski himself had learned this lesson from the Russian actress Fedotova.

[3] Quoted from an interview in the documentary *Sanford Meisner: The Theatre's Best-Kept Secret*, 1985.

[4] Ibid.

The natural relationship between actors maintains the eye-line. When one actor speaks in the theater, the other actor usually stops what he's doing and looks at him. This focuses the audience's gaze on the speaker and does not draw attention to the listener. (An actor who draws attention to himself while another is speaking is guilty of "upstaging.") In television and film, where realistic physical activity is so important, the director may want his actor to continue fixing the car or stacking the plates, but actors will always instinctively stop what they're doing and look at each other for significant emotional moments. *Once eye contact is established between two actors, the moment when it is broken becomes very significant.* One of the things a director should do during rehearsals is to control the moments when actors drop their eye-line.

Example:

> ### MADGE
> You've let this family down once too often, my girl. This thing between you and Paul has got to stop. Right now! I mean it!

Madge is scolding her daughter, whom she looks squarely in the eyes as she delivers her rebuke. Her daughter may try and squirm away from the look at the end of the second sentence, but Madge grabs her by the shoulders and forces her daughter to look at her. Only at the end of Madge's speech, once she has made her point, does she let her daughter look away.

Breaking eye contact always makes a statement. If her daughter breaks eye contact after the second sentence, then Madge's last two exclamations become much weaker—she is threatening someone who has managed to get away from her. (This might be an alternative way of playing the scene.)

Eyes in lighting and camerawork

Directors and lighting directors have long paid special attention to the actor's eyes. In drama lighting, the *key light* (the principal light source) usually illuminates the face. Coming from the left or the right side of the camera, it tends to favor one half of the face more than the other. DPs compensate by adding a softer *fill light* to reduce the shadow on the unlit side. Both lights are set in the positions that are most effective for illuminating the subject's eyes. If the key light is placed too high, it can miss the eye altogether. If the fill is not set properly, it fails to catch the glint in the un-keyed eye. Occasionally, a lighting director will create an "eyelight" by aiming the beam from a small lamp directly at an actor's eyes.

In the 1930s and '40s, when black-and-white glamour photography was at its height, lighting directors aimed to combine the key and fill on their female subjects in such a way that a triangle of light was formed beneath the less brightly-lit eye. This patch of light, which is subtly present in many portraits by the Dutch master Rembrandt, was christened "the Rembrandt triangle." (See Fig. 28.1.)

Fig. 28.1: "Rembrandt lighting," *Portrait of a Man* by Rembrandt (M. H. de Young Memorial Museum San Francisco)

Shadows add a touch of mystery to an image. It is possible to veil both eyes in shadow (as Rembrandt himself did in some of his early self-portraits), but what is gained in mystery may be lost in expressiveness. Carol Reed used shadow artfully to obscure the mysterious Harry Lime (played by Orson Welles) in the British "film noir" *The Third Man* (1949). Lime, a black-marketer, dwells in the shadows from which he only occasionally and briefly emerges.

Another style of glamour-photography lighting was perfected by the German director Josef von Sternberg for his favorite star, Marlene Dietrich (see *Morocco*, 1930). Sternberg placed a very diffused key light above and slightly to one side of the camera. The light emphasized the forehead and eyes, but was often kept off the bottom half of the face, which went into shadow.[5] The hair was also strongly backlit. The proximity of the key light to the camera tended to flatten and smooth out the image, and the light's softness masked imperfections in the skin. Dietrich herself was so pleased with the effect that she insisted on being lit exactly the same way in almost every film she appeared in. The result, as with Rembrandt lighting, is often highly artificial. The screen actress becomes a goddess, her head perpetually swathed in ethereal light.

Although key and fill lights are still the basis of modern film lighting, their application has changed. Contemporary drama pays lip-service to

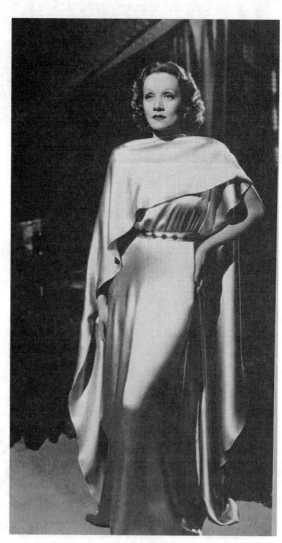

Fig. 28.2: Dietrich (from *The Garden of Allah*, 1936)

---

[5] An effect used by eighteenth-century portrait painters such as Gainsborough and Raeburn.

naturalism, so lights are usually set to appear as if emanating from a real source. Thus, when lighting an actor's closeup, a lighting director will be mindful of whatever primary light source there is in the vicinity (chandelier, table lamp, sunlight, etc.) and make the key light appear to emanate from that direction. Secondary light sources, such as background lamps or light filtering through a crack in a wall, are also used by lighting directors. They provide the excuse for *kickers*—shafts of light that glance off an actor's head or body.

Eyes are still the primary focus of modern lighting. John Woo says, "I feel the actor's eyes tell most of the story...."[6] In Fig. 28.3 below (a photograph from *Mission Impossible II*, 2000) Woo's lighting director, Jeffrey Kimball, has used light reflecting upward from a metal surface to isolate Tom Cruise's head, and has also found a background light source to motivate a soft kick-light on his hair.

Fig. 28.3: *Mission Impossible II*

Camera placement

Eyes play an important part in determining where the camera is placed. During dramatic scenes between characters in which emotions (rather than actions) are paramount, the camera has to be placed where it can get the best view of the individual performances. This means placing it where it can best see the eyes.

---

[6] "Secret Agent Man," *American Cinematographer*, June 2000, p. 53.

Capturing a performance involves seeing both eyes clearly—achieving what is known as a "two-eye shot." Singles (MCUs and CUs especially) should almost always include the eye farthest from the camera. Sometimes, directors shoot that upstage eye so that it is only just visible, intersected by the line of the cheek. Such shots make us subconsciously want to crane our heads around the side of the screen to see the eye more fully. A good two-eye shot does not threaten to cut off the upstage eye, and directors should insist that the camera be placed closer to the line to achieve this. (See Figs. 28.4 and 28.5.)

Illustration: Including the upstage eye

Fig. 28.4: Upstage eye partly visible   **Fig. 28.5:** Upstage eye visible

In his book *Acting in Film*, Michael Caine recommends that the actor always turn his head so that the upstage eye can be clearly seen by the camera. But not every actor is as technically aware as Caine. Wherever possible, the director should place the camera to suit the actor, rather than ask the actor to perform a technical trick.

Sometimes, however, there is just not the physical space in a set for the camera to get a good two-eyed shot. In this situation, the director has to "cheat" the actor's position, and have the on-camera actor slightly turn his head to reveal his upstage eye. (See the section below on cheating.)

Occasionally, a director will shoot an entire two-person scene in profile. Directors usually only do this after they have had a long run of scenes in which they have used two-eye shots. The profile single (or parallel single) is used to break the regularity of the shot pattern. (See Fig. 28.6.) Perhaps because it is used so infrequently, it tends to stand out, so young directors often notice it and try to copy it. Directors should be aware that audiences want to read a character's expression and may be frustrated only seeing half a face. Certainly, if you were an actor giving a strong performance, you would want both your eyes to be seen.

Fig. 28.6: Profile single

Some film writers call the profile shot an "objective shot." Objective shots (which I introduced in Part 3, Chapter 12) are taken from a camera position off the eye-line and generally show two or more people—wide shots and 2-shots are common examples. They orient us geographically; they tend to remove us from intense participation; they "cool down" the drama. The standard two-eyed single, on the other hand, is a "subjective shot." Subjective shots take us close to a character's eye-line. They enable us to read a character's feelings. They "heat up" a scene. A closeup profile shot is thus something of a contradiction—the closeup is designed to bring us closer to a character, yet the profile tends to distance us. It should be used with care.

Cheating with the eyes, body, and camera

The whole of television and filmmaking is, in a sense, an elaborate deception. We fool the eye into perceiving motion by projecting still images at 24, 25, or 30 frames per second. We cheat every time we make a cut, because we try to convince the viewer that what has taken hours to construct, shot by shot, actually occurred in real time.

In filmmaking parlance, however, "cheating" refers specifically to making shots work by changing the circumstances on the set. For instance, we are shooting on location in the room diagrammed in Fig. 28.7. Bentley (the butler) is at the sideboard, discreetly adding strychnine to Lady Drinkup's sherry.

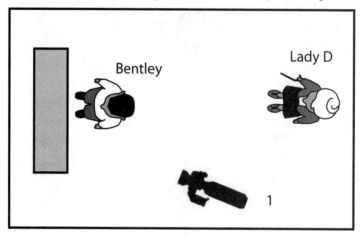

Fig. 28.7: The "un-cheated" position

Throughout this sequence, Bentley has been shot from position 1. But this position does not give us a good view of the poison going into the glass, and it certainly does not allow us to see Lady Drinkup in the background. To get that shot, the director has to bring the camera around in front of Bentley. But the wall is in the way. The answer is to "cheat" the sideboard forward from the wall far enough to get the shot—approximately five feet. Of course, the room has been shrunk as a consequence, but the viewer will probably not notice the difference. Cameras, unlike humans, do not have stereoscopic vision and can be tricked over matters of depth.

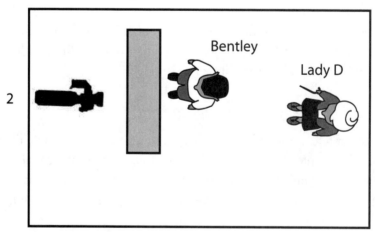

Fig. 28.8: The "cheated" position

There are many opportunities to cheat props and actors during a shoot. After all, shooting drama is about telling a story through the camera and microphone, not about adhering to geographical reality. Directors should feel free to manipulate circumstances to get exactly what they want in the frame, as long as they don't confuse their actors in the process. Here are two more examples of cheating.

The camera op has shot John in a mid-shot. There are only five minutes left to get John's MCU, but, in order to do that, he has to reposition the camera closer to the eye-line between John and the off-camera actor *and* move the lights. So, instead of moving the camera and equipment, the director simply positions the off-camera actor closer to the camera and asks John to cheat his look. In this case, John's look is closer to the side of the camera than it would be in reality. (See Fig. 28.9.) Cheats like this one are not something the director likes to do, but he is sometimes forced into them by the pressure of time. The chances are that the shot is so tight and excludes so much geographical detail that viewers won't notice the difference.

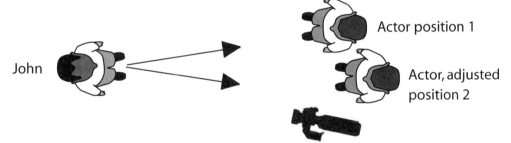

Fig. 28.9: Cheating the position of the off-camera actor

You are shooting in an open meadow. You have just completed a tracking shot that has ended in a 2-shot favoring Cleo (see Fig. 28.10). The next shot is the reverse shot of Greg. The obvious thing to do is to take the camera off the tracks and reposition it next to Cleo, on Greg's eye-line. However, the tracks, the dolly, and the jib may also be in the back of this shot, and, thus, may have to be removed. All this will take time. In this situation, working in a large open field, viewers will not notice if you keep the tracks down and reposition the actors in relation to the camera (see Fig. 28.11).

Greg's eye-line camera position

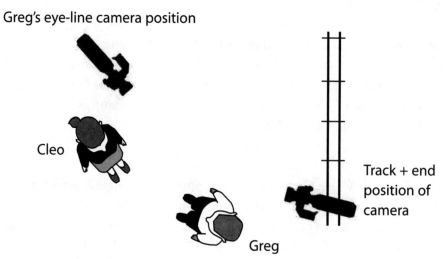

Cleo

Track + end
position of
camera

Greg

Fig. 28.10: Camera on Greg's eye-line

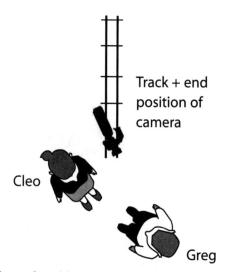

Track + end
position of
camera

Cleo

Greg

Fig. 28.11: Cheated position

Camera height

Camera height is largely determined by the eyes. Because seeing into the eyes is so important, the camera is usually placed on or about eye-level. It seems a simple principle, and yet it is ignored surprisingly often. One reason is that when only a few minutes remain to get shots "in the can," perfecting camera height sometimes goes by the board. Another reason is that shooting seated characters requires a low angle, and after several hours this becomes physically uncomfortable for the camera operator bending over the camera. This explains the natural tendency among camera ops to raise the camera height toward the end of the day. Directors have to stay aware of the camera level.

Shooting at eye level is the "natural" camera height—the default position. It is also a "neutral" placement, because it does not look up or down at the subject. However, some directors and camera ops prefer to shoot from a slightly modified height. Some, for example, like to shoot from slightly below eye level in order to pick up more *catch light*—(the reflective glint) from the eyes. If a character is lit from above eye level, the law of reflection ("the angle of incidence equals the angle of reflection") suggests that the light will be reflected below. (See Fig. 28.12.) Placing the camera slightly below the eyes also allows the actor to be more dominant in the frame.

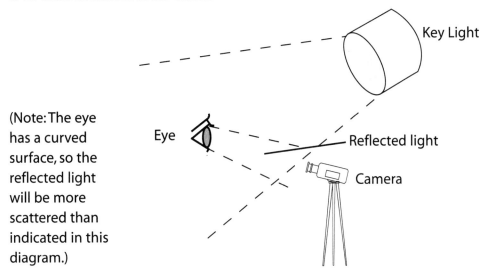

(Note: The eye has a curved surface, so the reflected light will be more scattered than indicated in this diagram.)

Fig. 28.12: Reflection

Placing the camera slightly below the eyes is different from choosing a genuine low-angle shot from below the head itself. Low-angle (L/A) shots tend to elongate the face. Eyes looking down toward the lens will appear dominant. The effect can be respectful if there is distance between the camera and the subject. If the camera is placed closer (requiring the use of a wide-angle lens), then the result can be distorting and scary. This low-angle shot has become a cliché in horror movies, but you can also see the technique at work in the way Orson Welles shoots the corrupt detective (played by himself) in *A Touch of Evil* (1958). If you choose to shoot from a low-angle on a soundstage, be aware that the designer might have to provide ceiling pieces to prevent the camera from shooting the missing top of the set. Ceiling pieces can take time to position and light.

High-angle (H/A) shots emphasize the actor's brow, masking the eyes and reducing their effectiveness. It also tends to shrink actors, placing them against the pattern of the floor. These shots are useful for showing geography but are also impersonal. (The painter Lucien Freud often adopts this perspective when painting nudes.) People seen from above tend to become objects. They can also appear slightly comical or subservient. For the extreme high-angle shot, the camera is placed vertically above the action and looks right down on the characters' heads. It tends to emphasize people's spatial relationships rather than their emotional ones. I have worked on shows with prison scenes in which this shot was effective. Shooting vertically down on a character in a cell somehow evokes a rat in a cage. Because this shot foreshortens its subjects (like the figures drawn from an overhead perspective in the diagrams of this book), it can be very effective in comedy. I once used the shot in a comic sequence in which a would-be seducer chased his victim around a table. Suddenly switching to the very high, objective, overhead shot made the whole chase look tactical and ridiculous. This shot is sometimes referred to as "God's POV." From God's point of view, we all look foolish and diminutive.

Point of view

Camera placement constantly plays with degrees of objectivity and subjectivity. *For each shot, the director makes a decision about how closely the camera (the audience's eyes) will associate with a character's viewpoint.* As we have seen, the choice ranges from the removed objectivity of a profile shot, to the intense subjectivity of the POV shot and the BCU, and all the degrees in between.

In Fig. 28.13, Martha talks to Nigel. If we want to see Martha exactly from Nigel's position, logically we should place the camera in position X. But to do so would make it appear she was talking directly to the camera and, by extension, to us instead of to Nigel. Generally, the camera takes an observer's position and overlooks the conversation between them. So the camera is placed at position Y.

As we've noticed, the closer Y is to the line (the line between Martha and Nigel) without actually being on it, the fuller the shot. The "rule" is that position Y should be close enough to the line to give a good two-eyed shot. But, as we've

Fig. 28.13: Proximity to the eye-line

seen, when you tighten a shot (say, from MS to MCU), the tighter shot should be slightly closer to the line. (See Fig. 28.14.) The reason for this move is that the more intimate the shot, the more we want to see the eyes. A camera position *very* close to the line creates ambiguity about whether its subject is speaking to the other character or to the camera. Some directors shooting closeups will squeeze the off-shot actor right up against the camera, so that the on-camera actor is almost looking into the lens.

Fig. 28.14: Almost looking into the lens

This technique is used in the movie *Philadelphia* (1993), in which the director, Jonathan Demme, plays with subjectivity. It's a film in which many of the characters (and, by extension, the audience) have to come to terms with homosexuality, and it is often ambiguous whether or not speeches are being delivered directly to the camera or to the audience. Demme occasionally breaks his subjective camera angles by offering a profile shot of his leading character (Tom Hanks), which distances us from the character and makes him momentarily inscrutable.

Although most shots are taken from on or about the subject's eye level, sometimes shooting from another character's actual perspective is rewarding. The most common use for this technique is when a director wishes to emphasize the difference in height between characters. In a children's drama, if a young boy talks to a giant, the director would be missing a trick not to shoot the giant from the boy's POV. The very low angle would underscore how intimidating the giant was. Children's programs, which like to use visually stimulating camera angles, lend themselves to such POV shots.

Here is an interesting camera-height situation. Terri is at the top of a flight of stairs, and Bart is at the bottom (see Fig. 28.15). Where would you place the camera—first for Terri and then for Bart?

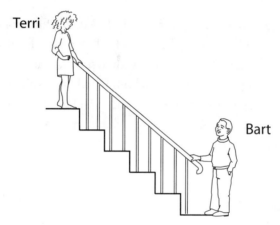

Fig. 28.15: Height differential

Clearly, there are advantages to shooting both Terri and Bart from the other's perspective. This offers a startling high angle and complementary low angle. If Terri were standing at the top of a cliff, the shot would be even more dramatic. The effect here is to diminish Bart and emphasize Terri's superior status. Many directors would seize this visual/psychological opportunity.

But if the scene is important emotionally, the director might choose to keep the camera at eye level and have the actors gaze up or down out of frame (see Fig. 28.16). This choice is also interesting visually. Although it reduces the verticality and depth of the shot, it does take us much closer to the performers.

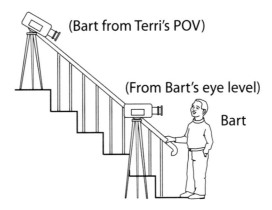

Fig. 28.16: Alternative camera positions for shooting Bart

The director who chooses to shoot Bart from the eye-level position can still shoot Terri from the bottom of the stairs.

Fig. 28.17: Bart shot from eye level

Fig. 28.18: Terri shot from Bart's POV

The strongest POV shot is the one in which we see things entirely from one person's perspective. This shot has already been discussed (see Part 4, Chapter 22) but should be mentioned in the current context. Imagine you are shooting the following scene. Jack and Nick are two twelve-year-olds being bullied by Alastair, who is fifteen. Alastair trips Jack, kicks him, and then turns toward Nick. The director may decide to show the event from Nick's point of view to experience his horror. The shot sequence may go as follows:

Shot 1: WS. Alastair approaches Jack and Nick. Alastair pushes Nick aside and then starts to trip Jack.

Shot 2: Tight MS or MCU. Nick watching (with horror).

Shot 3: Nick's POV. Hand-held. Alastair kicks Jack and turns toward Nick.

Shot 1 serves to establish the scene. Shot 2 is a dramatic cut to a reaction shot from a wide shot, and it establishes Nick's eye-line. (POV shots are often introduced by a tight shot to make it unambiguous whose point of view they represent.) Shot 3 is from Nick's POV. The hand-held camera suggests we are seeing things from a human perspective and not a mechanical one. In this sequence, we are once again dealing with the eyes: Shot 2 is there to establish Nick's eyes. And in Shot 3, the camera has actually become Nick's eyes.

29. Continuity Continued

In Part 4, Chapter 21, I discussed continuity in relation to camera placement. I'd now like to consider the continuity implications of shot size and performance.

Although certain continuity rules exist, every scene ultimately poses its own particular challenges. Continuity is one of those areas that tends to worry inexperienced directors. But the director who goes into a shoot with a well-thought-out shooting plan and gives clear instructions to actors and crew about moves and business will encounter few intractable problems. The ability to make continuity decisions becomes easier with practice.

Single and two-camera shooting

Unless the director is shooting each scene in a single extended shot (see Part 4, Chapter 24), scenes and sequences consist of multiple shots joined together to give the impression of continuous time. Each shot must therefore fit seamlessly with its neighbors. Most importantly, if there is movement (and most shots have some form of movement—be it a shake of the head or a helicopter crashing), it must appear to flow uninterrupted from shot to shot.

Continuity of movement may be achieved by shooting each scene with two or more cameras (as you might in a multi-camera television studio, see Part 8), which give you a real-time record of the event. This is not the general rule when making a film, because lighting directors and camera operators prefer to perfect one shot before going on to the next. However, on some occasions, using more than the one camera may be useful.

Multiple cameras are used on scenes that can only be taken once—a car falling over the edge of a cliff, for instance, or a house exploding. Directors who like to improvise scenes may use two cameras to capture the spontaneous interaction between two or more characters. Filmmaker John Sayles sometimes uses two cameras in scripted two-person dialog scenes to avoid multiple takes and, thus, maintain freshness of performance. Rob Marshall, directing the musical *Chicago* (2003), used two or more cameras for dance numbers so that the dancers did not have to break up their routines. Barry Levinson uses a freewheeling second camera to supply him with unplanned, expressive additional footage. Occasionally, a production that is on a tight schedule will bring in a second camera to speed up the shooting of certain reasonably static scenes—shooting an actor's mid-shot and closeup at the same time, for example.

Shooting with a single camera means that the actor (assisted by the director, camera operator, continuity assistant, and others) has to provide the illusion that things are happening sequentially. The only way this can be done is by repeating the action exactly the same way in shot after shot. This is tough on actors who are torn between the need to bring freshness to their performances and the need to perform each take exactly like the one before. *The ability to repeat outward, physical movements in precisely the same way, while at the same time thinking through the performance afresh each time, is a hallmark of good screen acting.*

Actor continuity

As I noted earlier, acting for the screen can require much more attention to the details of blocking than stage acting. Some actors feel restricted by screen acting's relative lack of spontaneity and by its restrictions on their physical movements. On the other hand, some actors relish its technical challenges. Film acting technique should not be underrated. In his book *Acting in Film*, Michael Caine discusses the craft of film acting from a technical standpoint. He demonstrates ways that actors can improve their performances by taking the camera into account, and proves that technical expertise does not reside exclusively with the director and the crew.

Let's look more closely at the technical aspects of acting for the screen.

1. *Repetition:* Actors not only have to repeat the same actions in take after take, they must perform them at the same points and in precisely the same way. The slightest difference might cause a jump cut.

Special attention must be paid to movement. If an actor raises her left hand or sets off walking with her right leg, then she must do precisely the same movement in subsequent takes.

Repeated movements must always be performed at the same speed. (As I'll discuss later, movement in a closeup can sometimes appear faster than it actually is, in which case, the director may ask the actor to compensate.)

Lines must be recited consistently. Sometimes, especially in long speeches, actors say their lines in the wrong order. If this happens near a cutting point, it can cause a continuity problem.

Actors must also say their lines with the same general intention. If an actor gives completely different readings in the closeup and the wide shot, the director may not be able to cut between the two. On the other hand, actors must not feel so constrained that they deliver every line mechanically in the same way take after take. And, as I'll explain later in this chapter, a director can guide an actor through the minefield of continuity, showing him where he can run freely and where he needs to pay strict attention.

2. *Marks*: Actors must be extremely accurate about their positions on the set, which affects their proximity to the camera. In a tight shot, for instance, a mere inch or less can make a tremendous difference to the focus and the framing. In terms of framing, it can cause an actor to be masked by another actor or placed too near the edge of frame.

Marks that tie the actor down to certain positions are often made on the ground with chalk or tape. A "starting mark" (or line on the ground) indicates where the feet are to be placed at the start of a shot. An intersecting line helps position the feet (see Fig. 29.1). A simple straight line may indicate where the actor moves to during the shot.

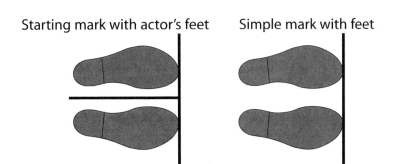

Starting mark with actor's feet   **Simple mark with feet**

Fig. 29.1: Actors' marks

The ability to "hit a mark" take after take requires practice. Even the experienced actor cannot always find them without a small, surreptitious glance down at the floor. (To keep from looking down, Michael Caine suggests counting the number of paces between the start and stop point. But, the longer the walk, the less accurate this method is.) The best marks are ones provided by the set itself. Actors find it much easier to move in to the corner of a desk or the back of a chair than to look for lines on the ground. Sometimes an assistant is asked to stand out of the frame and stop the actor either physically or with a hand signal—but this can be distracting for the actor.

3. *Camera-savvy*: Screen actors develop an awareness of the camera based on the principle that "if you can see the camera, the camera can see you." An experienced actor will automatically find a position that allows him to be seen. Many actors also go out of their way to form relationships with camera operators, which enables them to quickly learn the details of the shot—such as whether it is tight or wide, a single or a group shot. There is nothing wrong with this actor-camera operator rapport as long as the actor does not become over-dependent upon it. (Camera operators can be concerned with composition to the exclusion of other factors—notably performance.)

4. *Off-camera continuity*: When shooting a scene, a director traditionally starts with the widest shot and ends with the closeups. Experienced actors save their most intense performances for the tighter shots. These are almost always single shots with one actor in front of the camera and the other off-camera, "feeding" the lines. The off-camera actor can help the on-camera actor achieve continuity of performance by feeding the lines in a consistent and lively way, and not ceasing to perform because the camera is no longer pointed at him. Occasionally, an actor will leave the set after his closeup and ask someone else to read his off-camera lines. A director should resist this. *All actors, even the humblest day-players, are entitled to play their scenes with the same actor opposite them to ensure continuity of performance.*

5. *Lines*: Memorization is an important part of an actor's technique. A director is entitled to expect actors to know their lines. The inability to remember lines adversely affects an actor's ability to give a continuous performance.

Nothing is more frustrating for a director than dealing with actors who are insecure with their lines. Memorization problems slow down shooting, thus jeopardizing the film schedule, and also put other actors off their stride. Yet a director occasionally has no choice but to factor in time for memory lapses. I once worked with a distinguished elderly actor who had completely lost his facility to remember lines, so shooting had to proceed one line at a time. Another time, I worked with an extremely efficient actress on a show that was being shot on a very tight schedule. She was immaculate with her lines until the very last scene of the day, when the tension finally caught up with her and she could not recall a single word.

One has to have some sympathy with daytime serial actors who have to memorize forty or fifty pages a week. In Britain, where soaps have generally consisted of only two or three episodes a week, producers tend to insist on fairly accurate memorization. In America, where soaps are recorded daily, total accuracy is not always possible. I have been present during the taping of a well-known American soap opera where the leading actor read his lines off cue-cards (cards with an actor's speeches written on them that are held up alongside the camera). A credible performance is not possible when someone is gazing past his fellow actor to read his lines.

On-set continuity

Many people on a set—in addition to the director—are concerned about continuity. There is the script supervisor (or continuity person), whose role is discussed below. There is the camera operator, who keeps an eye out for such issues as character placement and crossings of the line. There is the costume designer, who is concerned that clothing details are consistent from scene to scene. (If a character's tie is loose at the end of a scene, it should also be loose at the start of the scene directly following it.) There are the makeup designer and hairdresser, who are similarly concerned about their areas. (If a character receives a wound in one scene, a scar must be evident the next time he appears.) There is also the designer or property master, who is concerned about the consistent placement of props during a scene, as well as an assistant in the property department who keeps an eye on prop-continuity issues, such as the level of liquid in glasses and the length of cigarettes.

When the first assistant calls the end of a scene, there is usually a blaze of flashing lights as many of the fore-mentioned crew-members descend on the set with instant or digital cameras to photograph the conditions of the actors and the positions of the props. These photographs are labeled and inserted into files, each department's forming a useful record of a given production.

The script supervisor or continuity person

A director cannot reasonably be held responsible for every continuity concern—if a button is undone or a pencil is in the wrong place, that is obviously not her fault. But she is responsible for all continuity relating to character placement and framing. This may come as a surprise to those who believe that the script supervisor is in charge of continuity. The script supervisor/continuity person *assists* with continuity, but ultimate responsibility lies with the director. I learned this fact the hard way: I shot a complicated scene out of sequence, and when it was cut together, one of the extras appeared to jump from one side of the room to the other. When the producer grilled me about this, I mentioned that the continuity assistant had missed the error as well. "Continuity is your responsibility," I was firmly told. "The continuity assistant is only there to help you."

The script supervisor generally does two jobs at once. Her first (and arguably most important) job is to be the link between the camera and the editor. She notes down the details of each shot, including, when shooting film, which shots the director wants printed. The editor uses this information to sort out the rushes (the first, rapidly developed, prints of the footage) and to build the first rough-cut (an initial arrangement of shots into scenes or sequences that follow script order).

Her second responsibility is to assist with continuity. She will keep track of "coverage," noting in her script all the shots the director has taken, clearly indicating where they begin and where they end. Marking the director's coverage not only serves as a valuable reference for the director, it subsequently allows the editor to see at a glance what shots are available at any point in a scene.

Then she will turn her attention to the scene, noting exactly where the actors' moves occur and watching for any changes in props or any special business. She will also keep an eye on the dialogue to ensure the actors' deliveries are error-free.

The script supervisor has a complex job, calling for unusual efficiency, powers of observation, and tact in dealing with the director and actors. In film, there is often a few minutes between takes and setups, so the script supervisor generally has the opportunity to make all her notes. In television (and especially video), shooting is more accelerated, so the continuity notes tend to be less detailed.

Shot-to-shot continuity

Achieving perfect continuity is almost impossible. Absolute repetitive accuracy is the realm of machines, not human beings, yet ninety-nine percent of cuts are invisible largely because the mind is predisposed to create order and overlook discontinuity.

An important distinction must be made between "direct" and "indirect" continuity. Direct continuity involves the appearance of the same image in *successive* shots, so it must appear to be exactly the same in both. (If John's jacket is buttoned in shot 1, it cannot suddenly be unbuttoned in shot 2 or 3.) Indirect continuity involves images that disappear from the screen and then reappear several shots or scenes later. The broad elements of continuity must be the same but absolutely identical replication (direct continuity) is not necessary (see Fig. 29.2).

Shot 1: MCU John

Shot 2: MCU Ruth

Shot 3: M2s Alex and Phil

Shot 4: MCU John in a different position

Fig. 29.2: A four-shot sequence

In Fig. 29.2, if John's hands are in a different position in shot 4, or his head is at a different angle, we automatically assume that the change has occurred during shots 2 and 3, when he was off-screen. In situations in which the same person appears in consecutive shots, or with only a brief shot in between, the actor must be in broadly the same position for us to accept the continuity. (See Fig. 29.3.)

| Shot 1 | Shot 2 (about 3 seconds) | Shot 3 |

Fig. 29.3: Direct Continuity

When judging continuity issues, a director's common sense comes into play. If an actress holds up a dagger in shot 1, and we cut away to her victims in shots 2 and 3, and we cut right back to her for shot 4—we expect her to still be holding the dagger (and not a rolling pin).

Film theorists call the direct continuity cut a "match cut," because both shots on either side of the cut match each other. But this match may not have to be 100 percent accurate. By cutting to a different angle or shot size, a director can often distract the eye, hiding a small discontinuity. Over a period of time, through experience, a director comes to know what will pass unnoticed on the screen and what will stand out. *What is crucial in continuity is that the salient objects—the objects that immediately present themselves to the eye—are consistent from shot to shot.* (I will look more closely at this subject when I discuss individual shot sizes below.)

A director who has done his homework and knows where the cuts will occur can help an actor relax during a performance by not insisting on perfect continuity where it is not needed. Consistency is only required at the point where the cut will be made. And, as I've just showed, if you cut away from the actor for a period of time, perfect consistency is less important. Here are some examples.

1. *Direct Continuity*
Shot 1: MCU. Jack reading newspaper. He closes it and rises out of shot.
Shot 2: MS. Jack rising from his seat. The camera pans him right.

In these consecutive shots the director must insist that the actor close his newspaper and stand at exactly the same points in both shots. The ideal place for the cut to occur is during the rise. If, as he rises, we can see the newspaper is folded in shot 1 but not quite folded in shot 2, the cut will not work.

2. *Two shots separated by a cutaway*

Shot 1: MS. Juggler practicing his art. He drops his batons when he sees the front door open.

Shot 2: FL. His wife enters the front door.

Shot 3: FL. The juggler stands amid the fallen batons, then slowly bends down to pick them up.

The batons start to fall in shot 1, but they fall out of the shot so we cannot tell where they land. It is important in shot 3 that the juggler stands in much the same position as in shot 1, but the director is at liberty to arrange the batons on the floor.

3. *Problem of an off-camera change of position*

Shot 1: June argues with her boyfriend. She strides around the room, picks up a cushion, and throws it at him.

Shot 2: The startled boyfriend receives the cushion in the face.

Shot 3: June sits down on the sofa and giggles.

Shot 1 contains a lot of movement but, because of the intervening shot, June's arm position does not have to be absolutely the same at the start of shot 3 as it was at the end of shot 1. However, seeing June sit down in shot 3 is very important in this sequence. The viewer who last saw her standing will expect to see her still upright at the start of shot 3. If we cut to her after she has sat down, that viewer will be disoriented by her new position.

One of the ways directors help actors with continuity, and also help them sustain a performance, is by giving them a generous run-in of several lines or even half a page before the starting point of each take. I try to take the actors back to the beginning of the beat, but sometimes you have to go even farther back than that.

Scene-to-scene continuity

The distinction between direct and indirect continuity applies to scenes as well. Adjacent scenes with action spilling over from one to the other require direct continuity. For instance, Sasha is in her bedroom, finishing her makeup for the senior prom. The doorbell rings and she steps out into the hallway to answer it.

The continuity between the bedroom and the hallway must be as good as possible. Her dress and makeup have to be the same in both shots. The speed at which she moves also has to be consistent. The bedroom scene might be shot at a location miles away from the hallway scene or the two scenes may be shot days or weeks apart, but the continuity is *direct*.

In situations in which the interval of time between shots is long enough for the actors and crew to have forgotten the precise details of the continuity, the editor can help out. If the film editor is working on location, he can play the take of Sasha leaving the bedroom so the actor playing Sasha can see how she was moving. In the case of video, the director or continuity assistant can ask the editor to send a copy of the previously recorded scene to be played on location. Also, if the camera operator still has the original tape, he may be willing to play it back there and then—though many camera ops are justifiably cautious about replaying master tapes lest they become damaged.

Direct scene-to-scene continuity is always tricky, and the director should note where it occurs in his script. A well-respected continuity assistant I knew once made the following mistake: A character was to have an argument and walk out of the house. The interior and the exterior shots were filmed on different days. In the interior scene, the character left the living room and headed, one presumed, for the front door. On the day of the exterior shot, it was raining and the actor's dresser put him in a raincoat. The result was that he exited the living room in his jacket and immediately appeared outside in a raincoat. At the script supervisor's insistence, the director took an intervening shot of the character grabbing his raincoat on his way down the hallway.

When scenes are not directly adjacent to one another, continuity is not so crucial. If the Dowager Countess Waistworthy climbs into her carriage in a dress in one scene and, two scenes later, enters the palace with a cape over it, the viewer may assume that her footman handed her the garment in the interval.

What to look for in different shots

Props tend to cause the most continuity problems. An actor picks up a pen from his desk, plays with it, and then passes it to his other hand. Once established in the first acceptable take, this activity has to be repeated in the same way in all subsequent takes—especially at those moments when the director might want to cut. We have all probably noticed continuity errors involving props. My favorite is still the breakfast scene in *Pretty Woman* (1990) when the croissant

Julia Roberts is eating curiously metamorphoses into a pancake. (This movie is particularly fruitful for continuity-error spotters.)

Shot size impacts continuity. Things that draw attention to themselves in the frame require continuity attention. Let's look at the main shot sizes individually.

The wide shot

In a wide shot, details of dress and props tend to go unnoticed by the audience, whereas the characters' positions are more clearly born in mind. In a wide shot of two people walking down a road, the length of their cigarettes or the number of shirt buttons they have undone is not important. But it is crucial that their physical relationship to one another remains constant in this and the ensuing shot. If you have props that really attract attention, they should be noted—e.g., if one of the characters carries a walking stick or wears a particularly eye-catching hat.

If you happen to be shooting something like the cavalry charge in Kurosawa's *Ran* (1985) and a group is galloping through the shot, the exact position of every horse is immaterial (see Fig. 29.4). However, the formation of the group must remain broadly consistent from shot to shot.

Fig. 29.4: *Ran.* Detailed continuity unnecessary

A far trickier situation is one in which only a handful of extras are in the background: a street scene, for example, in which half a dozen extras pass through the foreground and the background at prearranged intervals in take after take. In this case, with so few extras, each one of them stands out, yet tracking their exact positions at every moment is very complicated. The only solution here is to rehearse the scene in advance so that all the extras are well aware of their cues and marks. The director must then select two or three points in the scene from which to start takes and retakes—points at which everyone knows their positions. Thus, she might pick up shots from the very start of the scene, when all the extras are in their opening positions, and choose another point later on, when the leaders have all passed through the shot and there is a definite lull in the background action.

In a street scene, the more extras that are added to the background, the less precise the continuity has to be, because the viewer will tend not to perceive individuals but a crowd. However, if one individual stands out—is riding a horse, for example, or sporting a very colorful top or is walking with a pronounced limp—special attention must be paid to his position.

Full-length and three-quarters shots

The tighter the shot, the more small details stand out. On the other hand, the more people in the shot, the less individual continuity tends to matter. In a full-length group shot, peoples' positions in relation to each other matter. The continuity of the leading character, or the character in the most central position, should be especially closely noted.

Mid-shot

The MS is designed to show hand and arm movement and facial expression. Viewers will see props and costumes very clearly. Continuity is critical. The mid-shot requires the most attention to detail of all shots.

As with all shots, the less action there is, the more continuity matters. If the only action in the scene is an actor lifting a glass to her mouth, viewers will be very aware of it. On the other hand, if several people are beating drums, the exact continuity of each stick is probably not important. In a very complicated sequence, a director relies on the script supervisor to make detailed notes of all the important moves.

Medium closeup and closeup

The MCU is a tighter shot than the MS, so in-frame props appear larger and require careful attention. However, the shot is designed to emphasize the head, so much of what is happening with the hands is excluded.

In a scene, Mrs. McSnout is sitting in a chair doing her needlepoint. In the full-length and mid-shots we make sure that the points at which she draws the wool through the canvas are consistent, so we can cut from one to the other. In the MCU, we do not have to be quite so vigilant, because the needle and the hands are out of frame. However, if she holds up her tapestry to examine it and it enters the MCU, we must make sure she raises it at exactly the same moment as she did in the MS and FL (see Fig.29.5).

Fig.1: MS.
The prop is in shot.

Fig.2: MCU.
Prop is out of shot.

Fig.3: MCU. Prop is
brought into frame.

Fig. 29.5: A prop brought into a MCU

MCUs and CUs sometimes get directors out of continuity problems because they exclude so much of what may have been shown in wider shots. If you shoot kids playing with their toy soldiers, the continuity of toy placement can rapidly become very complex. By cutting to a tight shot, you can probably exclude all the toys on the table. This removes half the problem, although the actors still have to be consistent about when they lean in and out and move their shoulders to pick up the objects. The opening of Julie Taymor's *Titus Andronicus* (2000) features a boy playing with toy soldiers on a table. The continuity is good, but if it were not, the viewer would probably not notice the errors because: (a) The sequence is cut at a very fast tempo; (b) the camera angles are varied; and (c) the wide shots that show the toys are inter-cut with tight shots, so that the viewer forgets the exact positions of objects.

As I noted in Chapter 25, there is always the potential for continuity problems with an over-the-shoulder shot, because the smallest movement by the unfavored, foreground figure is exaggerated. When taking an O/S shot, it is advisable to take a clean single of the subject as well for safety reasons.

Props

As we've seen, the film and television industry distinguishes between two types of props: dressing props, which are provided by the designer as part of the set (tables and chairs, the grandfather clock in the corner, the pictures on the walls, and so on), and action props, which the actors actually handle. When an actor picks up a glass, it becomes an action prop. Guns, wallets, pens, hairbrushes, hip flasks, police notebooks, and the like are almost always action props.

As soon as an action prop enters a scene, continuity problems increase exponentially. An actor playing a soccer coach picks up a ball and bounces it in a locker room. How he picks the ball up (with which hand, from which direction, and at what speed) when he bounces it (during or between what lines), where he bounces it, and how he ends up holding it are all matters of continuity concern. The soccer ball is complicated enough, but at least it does not change its length, like a cigarette, or its level, like a glass of beer that is being drunk.

Objects that burn, such as candles and cigarettes, require careful attention. Matching shots of a person smoking a cigarette, which is bound to be a slightly different length each time it's photographed, is very difficult. All a director can hope for is that the inconsistencies are slight enough or surrounded by sufficient other activities as to render them unnoticeable.

However, there is a way of minimizing cigarette problems. The prop supervisor can cut up a packet of cigarettes into four different sizes—whole, three-quarters, half, and quarter-length. Assuming that the cigarette is full-length at the start of the scene, the three-quarters-length version can be substituted after a page or so of dialogue (approximately one minute). The half or quarter-length might be used near the end. Though they do not always burn uniformly, the principle is the same with candles.

In my experience, the two types of scene that cause the greatest headaches are card games and dinners. A card game scene requires an expert to keep track of the play. At the end of a take in which a round has been played, the cards have to be retrieved from both the pile on the table and the other players' hands so that the same action can be repeated in the next take. Even more complicated is when a shot is picked up from a *different* point in the game, without the benefit of the whole round being played, and the expert has to calculate who is holding what cards. Once, when we were shooting a game of bridge, we had an expert controlling the run of play and assistants watching each of the players, noting down what they picked up and discarded. (I dread to think what they must have gone through to get all the card games right on *House of Games*, 1987.)

Food is a continuity nightmare. Meal scenes have to be very carefully rehearsed to work well. Food is sloppy and difficult to control. At the end of each take, the prop department has to replenish the plates for the next take. Actors must also know what they are eating and at exactly what point in the dialogue they raise the food to their mouths, so that shots can be matched. But this requires a degree of rehearsal not commonly available in television and many films. In a scene with just one person eating, continuity may be tricky. With two or more characters cutting and lifting their food, the problems are multiplied.

There are ways of getting around the eating problem. You can ask your actor only to lift food to his mouth at one or two predetermined points. I was once shooting a date scene in a restaurant and asked the actress to struggle lifting some spaghetti to her mouth at a particular point. This one shot was enough to suggest to the audience that she had been eating continuously throughout the meal. Widely used alternatives either start the scene with the characters having one last bite and finishing their meal or end the scene with the arrival of a new course and the actors picking up their cutlery. Surprisingly, most viewers will believe that continuous eating has taken place.

As a prop man, I had several unfortunate incidents. One was the case of the nineteenth-century loaf. I was working on a children's film about a nineteenth-century family and their pig. The first scene of the day was set in their kitchen at breakfast. For this, the prop department provided me with four large square loaves. However, on my way to work, I happened to pass a bakery that was selling a much more elaborate and photogenic loaf and bought one. The director immediately agreed it had star quality. What I had not foreseen was that he would shoot the actress actually cutting a slice. We did one take of the cutting but the director was not satisfied. Of course, I had no back-up loaves for subsequent takes! I grabbed a nail from the carpenter, pinned the slice back into the bread, and rotated the circular loaf forty degrees. Take two was not satisfactory either and I had to nail back the second slice as well. Take three was no good, and neither were takes four and five. By the time take six started, the loaf was so full of nails I could hear it rattle as the actress cut it. At last I heard the director say, "That's fine. Print it." At that moment, my valiant loaf gave up the ghost and collapsed, scattering nails over the floor.

When a scene involves disposable props, such as food, the rule of thumb is that the prop supervisor provides three back-ups of each item to cover retakes. The director really should discuss this with the prop department, but in the absence of consultation, three is the accepted convention.

Some actors are better at continuity than others. Some, capable of great emotional performances, cannot lift a spoon at the same point in two consecutive takes. Most actors appreciate the technical demands of filming, but some just happen to be less coordinated than others. If you are working with the less-coordinated type, try to adjust your shooting so that a complicated sequence does not revolve around him.

Being on a set all day, surrounded by tasty morsels that you cannot eat, is tough. As prop man, I once ordered a very expensive plate of German cold-cuts from a specialty food store and managed to preserve it from the actors' forks by positioning myself alongside it. But as soon as the scene was finished, I made the mistake of turning my back to attend to other things. This was unfortunate because, ten seconds later, the director changed his mind and decided to do one more shot of the table, but the plate was empty.

30. Directing a Shot

The following account of how a director approaches individual shots within the shoot as a whole begins with a description of the procedure the director, assistant director, and crew use to start a take. Please note that film shoots and video shoots sometimes use different terms and that the terms may vary slightly among different directors.

Procedure for starting a take

When the director and actors are ready to start a new shot, the first assistant (or *first*) makes sure the set is quiet and everyone knows what is happening. "Quiet on the set. We're about to go for a take."

After checking again with the director, the first says, "Roll camera" or, "Turn over" or, in video, "Start recording."

The cameraperson and the sound recordist (in that order) reply "Rolling" or, "Turning over" or, "Speed" or, in video, "Recording" to indicate that their machines are running and ready to record.

The first then says, "Mark it," cuing the camera assistant to hold up the *slate* (a.k.a., *clapperboard*, *clapboard* or, simply, *the sticks*), snap it, and announce the shot and the take numbers ("Shot 55. Take 3."). Snapping the clapperboard provides a sharp sound impulse corresponding to a visual cue that allows the film editor to sync the picture and its related audio at the start of a take. In video, where sound and picture are usually recorded together on one tape, this is not strictly necessary. But the slate is still sometimes used as a reference and to ensure a gap of a few seconds between the start of recording and the director's call of "Action." This gap ensures that the camera mechanism has time to get up to speed. Some old-fashioned tape editing machines also require "pre-roll" (five or more seconds of blank footage before the take begins) to get themselves up to speed before an edit.

After the camera assistant claps the clapboard and runs back to the camera, the director says, "Action!"

The director will also usually end a take by calling, "Cut." It is important that a space of a few seconds is left between the end of the action and the director's "Cut." Over-enthusiastic directors who precipitously shout "Cut!" can find themselves on the film's soundtrack. The right moment for calling "Cut" at the end of a scene is when the energy, which has accumulated throughout the scene and lingers after the final word or action, has dissipated. This energy is similar to the forces that accumulate at the end of an orchestral piece, resulting in an energy-filled silence between when the final notes die and the moment when the audience begins to applaud. Accomplished conductors or soloists can usually hold back the applause, allowing the final notes to reverberate, by remaining motionless and not immediately lowering their instruments. Directors should use similar restraint before calling "Cut."

Sometimes the slate is not used at the start of a shot. If you are working with animals, the five or eight seconds it takes for the assistant cameraperson to enter and leave the set can be crucial. Untrained cats or birds do not have the good manners to hold their performances till the crew is ready. There are also occasions when the director just does not want to interrupt an actor's evolving performance by stopping for the slate. In these situations, the director calls for an "endboard," which requires that the camera assistant go in after the action has ended, yet while the camera and sound are still running, hold the slate board upside down, and announce the shot and take numbers.

What to look for during a take

The set is a busy place, and directors are at the center of it. What goes through a director's mind as he watches a shot unfold? Sydney Lumet describes his experience as follows: "Just before we roll I make a quick mental check of what preceded the moment we're about to film and what comes afterward. Then I focus my concentration on what the actors are doing. From the moment the actors start working, I play the scene along with them. I say the lines inside my head, I sense their movement and feel their emotions. I'm putting myself through the scene as if I *were* them. If the camera moves, out of the corner of my eye I'm watching the lens shade to see if the move has been mechanically smooth or jerky. If at any point in the take my concentration breaks, I know that something has gone wrong. Then I'll go for another take. Sometimes, on particularly good takes, I'm so moved that I stop "doing" the scene and just watch in awe at the miracle of good acting."[1]

Lumet's ability to split his mind between the performance and the camera is remarkable. All directors aspire to that. What follows is an expanded account that takes us step by step through the same territory.

The low buzz of several conversations permeates the set. The lighting director is getting his lamps into position with the help of the gaffer (chief electrician) and the sparks (electricians). The DP is waiting for the actors to take their positions. The audio mixer and the boom operator are conferring. Grips and the first assistant stand at the edge of the set. The actors and the director wait for the set to become theirs. Finally, the last light is ready. The first assistant informs the director of this and summons the actors onto the set. What is left of the background buzz ends when the first assistant calls for quiet.

The director steps into the silence and asks the actors to take up their positions. He reminds them what the first shot is and goes over any moves or business with them. Eventually, it is time to shoot. As the pre-take sequence just described unfolds, the director takes up a position either in front of a monitor or, if there is no *video assist* (see following section), close to the camera itself. The director always says, "Action," which sets the mood for what follows. It is important that "Action" is said in such a way as to help the actor with her first line. A loud, staccato "Action!" is fine for a chase sequence but inappropriate for a love scene. Similarly, a soft "Action" is ill-suited to introduce a heated argument.

The director must clear his mind of all concerns and focus on the shot. One trick that helps me is to blink before the first speech. The blink acts like the shutter on a camera—it presents a completely clean frame. If I know exactly when I'm going to cut to the take, I'll blink at that point. The blink then not only clears my mind, it serves as a pair of scissors, cutting me into the shot at the right moment. After the blink, my surroundings are excluded and I am focused on what is happening on camera.

The fundamental issue when judging a shot is, "Is it real?" I do not mean, does it look like the kind of everyday reality you might find on the street. I mean, are the performances truthful? Actually, I ask myself while I'm watching, "*Is there anything false?*" It's an aggressive way of posing the same question—it assumes there are going to be mistakes. A soft question produces soft results. If

---

[1] Sidney Lumet, *Making Movies* (New York: Vintage, 1995), p. 120.

there is any moment that is false, I work on it with the actors and try it again. If I am not sure about a moment—if it might be to the slightest degree false—I'll shoot it again. If I cannot find anything wrong but my instinct tells me we can do better, I'll shoot it again.

The test of "Is there anything false?" is important. In many circumstances, such as assessing shots in television soaps and series, it is the only one that counts. Sometimes, however, you can do even better than merely not being false. If you are shooting an important dramatic scene with good actors who have been well rehearsed, you can expect them to do better than merely reproduce reality. You can expect what Lumet calls "the miracle of good acting" when the actors fully live their characters and the performance creates a momentum that sweeps you up.

A director is always under pressure to accept a technically good take and move on. The camera op, sound mixer, and electricians are concerned with the technical challenges of the shot. If they think they have done their job well and the actors have managed not to fall on their faces, they want to move on. Sometimes, a director of photography will take hours to light a complicated setup, leaving only twenty minutes or so to shoot the actors. In these situations, the director is the only person who can speak up for the actors and insist that they be allowed to work without pressure. The performance carries the scene, so the director has to get that right. You (usually) get only one chance to shoot a scene. Very few directors have the luxury of a re-shoot during editing.

The video assist

In the old days, film directors never got to see a take directly from the camera's perspective. The director asked the camera operator's permission to view a rehearsal through the lens, but had to be content with watching the actual take from alongside the camera. This had certain advantages. Directors were free to leave framing and trucking concerns to the camera crew and concentrate on the performance. At the end of a take, if a director was satisfied with the performance, he would ask the camera op, "Did it work?"

These days, directors can utilize the *video assist* or *video tap*, viewing the take on a video monitor with an image that is fed from the camera's viewfinder. The quality of this image is not perfect and, although color assists are available, many directors prefer the more reliable black-and-white versions. Smaller, hand-held video assists have also recently become available.

Having a monitor makes the film director more like a television director, sharing with the crew the responsibility for spotting technical mistakes, such as faulty camera moves or mics in shot. It is yet another way in which film and television practices seem to be merging. When only one video assist is available on the set, it soon becomes the gathering point for everyone who has an interest in the scene, from the designer and continuity assistant to the second assistant and hairdresser. I know a director who insists that the area around the video assist is his "office," and members of the crew are only allowed there on sufferance.

How many takes to take and the pick-up shot

Always do a take two. Occasionally, everything comes together for the first take: The performance is superb, the camerawork immaculate, the lighting just right, and the sound clear as a bell. Even in these cases, shoot a second take.

A second take insures you against problems that might have gone unnoticed the first time. These problems might be purely technical, such as a *hair in the gate* (a strand or particle lodged in the front or the back of the lens of a film camera that gets reproduced on the celluloid) or a tape jam. The actors, who have been waiting a long time for the lights and camera to be set, usually like to have more than one opportunity to give their best. Sometimes actors hesitate or misspeak in ways that are very hard for a director to detect from her position several yards away. These tiny errors are called *fluffs*, and often the actors themselves are not even conscious of them.

When doing retakes, however, beware of the following syndrome: Directors doing retakes for safety can become so intent on perfecting the safety that they forget they already have a good shot in the can.

Here is an example: A director, Michelle, is shooting a three-page prison scene between two inmates playing a game of chess. The main 2-shot works well in the third take. Michelle rightly decides to go one more time because takes 1 and 2 fell apart before the end of the shot, and she would like "safety" coverage of the second half of the scene (see Fig. 30.1).

Take 4 falls apart early on. Take 5 does hardly any better. Take 6 is promising but an actor moves the wrong chess piece and they have to stop. At this point, there is no reason to retake the first page that has already been covered four times. Indeed, it's not really necessary to retake page two either, since it has been satisfactorily covered in takes 3 and 6. Michelle now just has to get a good

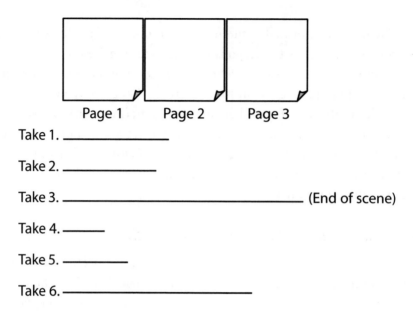

Fig. 30.1: Safety coverage

backup of page 3. So, she does a *pick-up shot*. She finds a place to start the actors halfway down page two, and runs the take to the end of the scene. The actors find this easier, because they only have to concentrate on half the scene, and everyone else is happy to get the shot in the can. (See Fig. 30.2.)

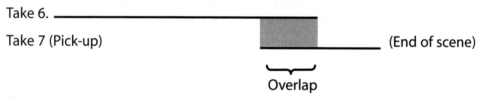

Fig. 30.2: Pick-up shot

The overlap between the shots serves to give the actors half a page to pick up the rhythm of the scene and be in their stride for page 3. If the director is lucky and the actors turn in a good performance of the bottom of page 2, then she can cut to take 7 even earlier.

Directors have different philosophies about retakes. Television directors, who are constantly under time pressure, try to get the scene done in the most efficient manner possible. They have a tendency not to reshoot a take if it is passable. In soap opera, where time pressure is particularly acute, directors have been known to accept performances in which actors have lost their lines and ad-libbed their way through the scene! Television directors frequently use the time-saving pick-up shot.

During some takes, directors sense that an actor is almost achieving what they want, so they go straight away for another take without interfering, allowing the momentum from the first take to carry on and build into the next.

The master of the retake was the great William Wyler. Wyler did not direct actors, he simply took a shot time and again until he was satisfied. Some actors hated this method, while others, Bette Davis and Lawrence Olivier among them, eventually came to appreciate it. Of course, his producers, who paid for the film stock, were probably less than enthusiastic. Olivia de Havilland was awarded an Oscar for her performance in Wyler's *The Heiress* (1949). In the scene in which she is deserted by her suitor and climbs the stairs to her room alone, Wyler retook the shot so many times that the exhausted actress threw her prop suitcase at him. Wyler promptly had the suitcase filled with books to make it heavier, asked her to ascend the stairs yet again, and achieved the effect he was looking for.

Sydney Lumet insists on extensive rehearsal before the shoot. The film for him is almost a theatrical entity with the shoot being its performance. Since he looks for his actors to implement the work they have done beforehand, numerous retakes are not usually necessary.

Although he did not insist on a rehearsal period before the shoot, Hitchcock also implemented a predetermined plan—his own carefully worked-out, intricate vision. Shooting, for him, was often a struggle to maintain this vision in the teeth of what he considered to be willful actors and technical compromise. His shooting style was slow and meticulous.

Working with actors on the set

During the shoot, the director must try to keep the set in a state of tension-free concentration. This is not the same as relaxation, which implies a lack of effort. The set should be a place of quiet application, where everybody is doing their job. People should feel free to contribute ideas at the appropriate time. Humor is welcome, but it should not be disruptive. The crew should be mindful of the actors' needs and not distract them before a take.

Maintaining concentration and intensity take after take is hard for actors, and some are better at it than others. Some actors give their best, most natural, performances in the first two or three takes. Others only start getting warmed up around take 4. Actors can easily get over-intense if they have to play an emotional scene repeatedly—for the wide shot, then the mid-shot, and finally for the closeup. As they go again and again, they often try to bring more and more meaning to their lines till they overdo it. If this happens, take a short break and talk to the actor about not pushing so hard. A five-minute coffee break after several hours of continuous recording can do wonders.

If you have to shoot numerous retakes, you might help the actor keep it fresh by suggesting different readings: "Why don't you play it this time as if she's thinking about her own relationship?" "He's saying goodbye to her, but he's confident they'll meet again."

Shooting is the application of machinery to a performance, and machinery has its own momentum. Once shooting starts, this momentum can be hard to interrupt. However, the director must be prepared to step in if he feels that the actors are unduly pressurized.

The most effective piece of direction is always an incisive adjustment. The best adjustments happen when the director works so closely with an actor that he knows exactly what she needs. Once you are on an actor's wavelength, completely understanding what she is trying to do, the adjustment is almost automatic. To an actor who is trying too hard, suggest, "It's important to him, but he's going to try *not* to show her." To an actor who is not friendly enough, "He realizes he can really trust this person." To an actor who is talking too fast, "You want to make this person understand—so take your time and really spell it out to her."

The actor should feel that the director is on her wavelength and working toward the same goal. Once a director has shot a scene that has been challenging or complicated, he should take his actors aside and thank them. Specific references are helpful. "I thought you did the closeup really well." " I liked take 2 but I'll also look at take 4." It is also important to allow the actor some control over her work, so always add the question, "What do you think?" and listen carefully to the reply. Ultimately, it's the actor's face up there on the screen and, if there's a bad performance, she will have to live with the consequences.

Sooner or later a situation will occur that a director regrets but cannot fix. For instance, a day-player who has been on the set all day finally gets to deliver her one sustained speech five minutes before the wrap, when you have no time to give her attention or the benefit of a second take. Or the star of your television episode has to record his closeup and then leave the set for reshoots with another unit, leaving the actress playing opposite him to deliver her closeup lines to the second assistant director. All you can do under these circumstances is commiserate and try to keep the performers from tensing up.

Beyond the shot

I have been examining the individual shot in this chapter because that is where a director focuses most of his concentration during a shoot. One shot succeeds another until there are no more shots to be taken.

Of course, a director sometimes must think about other things besides the shot in progress. As I hope I have indicated, the director is also concerned with time, money, and the management of personalities on the set. The shooting schedule, which is supervised by the production team, also concerns the director. When changes are made to the schedule (and changes almost always occur), the director has to adapt. Directors must be prepared, within reason, to bring scenes forward and even adapt to a new location if the old one suddenly becomes unavailable. In *Day for Night* (1973), a captivating film about moviemaking, François Truffaut comments that he starts a shoot hoping to achieve one hundred percent of his vision, and ends it grateful if he can achieve fifty percent.

The first assistant may assume responsibility for watching the clock minute by minute, but a director is still ultimately responsible for completing the production on time and within budget. Directors should not allow themselves to become obsessed with the progress of the second hand around the dial—that is a recipe for developing ulcers. Worrying about meal breaks and the scheduling of makeup calls and transport is what the production team is paid for. On the other hand, directors must take responsibility for finishing when they said they would and for not incurring too many penalty payments, such as unbudgeted overtime.

The director should also be aware of the personalities around him and do what he can to promote a harmonious working environment. This may involve accommodating (within reason) a demanding creative personality or dampening a simmering conflict.

I cannot remember the final shot of any production I've been associated with. This may be because the final shot is an ending, and I don't like endings. Being on a shoot is an intense experience that fosters loyalties and all sorts of emotional ties. Crews have mechanisms for dealing with the moment the first assistant calls the wrap on the final day. One of these is the wrap party, which defers fragmentation for a few days and allows members of the crew to say, "See you at the party" instead of, "Goodbye."

Another reason I don't recall final shots is that, by the time shooting ends, I have already begun to think about the next stage, which is editing.

31. Choosing Film Versus Video

At the opening of the twenty-first century, film is the medium of choice for prestigious productions. Most movies and primetime television dramas are shot on it. Film seems to have a unique aesthetic quality that has thus far eluded video. Its look is so identifiable that most people simply call it "the film look." This look is hard to define but has something to do with the following:

(a) The innate quality of film itself, which is a chemical substance incorporating silver. It has been suggested that the metal particles catch the light and make the result shiny and attractive.

(b) Film is a lighting director's medium. The range of tones between white and black that can be effectively reproduced on film is far greater than present-day video. This is expressed as the *contrast ratio*, which is, at very best, 1000:1 for film—an approximately ten-stop range of brightness. The contrast ratio of traditional video in comparison is still only approximately 30:1 or 40:1, a range of about five stops. Video in the USA is further degraded by the current fifty-year-old analog television transmission system, which is known by the acronym NTSC. (Engineers joke that the letters stand for "Never Twice the Same Color.") Fortunately, NTSC is gradually being superceded by digital television.

(c) Film, which is projected at 24 frames per second, has a pleasing effect upon the eye. This "flicker effect" is not so present on television screens where a complete picture is (traditionally) formed 30 times a second in the United States, and 25 times a second elsewhere.

I suspect that part of the attraction of commercially released films is that they are projected onto screens that occupy a large proportion of the audience's field of vision. A television viewer concentrates on a small box that is situated (ideally) eight or ten feet away. The process of watching TV is less involving, and a more passive activity.

However, the ground is shifting. A growing number of independent narratives are being recorded on videotape. *The Blair Witch Project,* one of the surprise successes of 1999, was largely shot on video, and the public accepted its hand-held documentary style. It may well be that narrative will eventually follow the genre of documentary, which embraced the digital formats of the mid-'90s.

The quality of the video image has been improving. The new digital formats such as D5 and Digital Betacam produce a very sharp image. The latest generation of video cameras can also shoot at 24 frames per second, which is the same frame rate as film. The Sony Digital Betacam and HDTV (high-definition TV) "digital cinematography" cameras were specifically designed to be used as alternatives to the movie camera, and companies have developed film-type accessories for them such as matte boxes, extension viewfinders, and special lenses. The digital image can be enhanced during shooting by adjusting the in-camera settings and also by the judicious use of filters—especially ones that soften the image, such as a (non-black) Pro Mist. The prosumer DV format is a good low-cost alternative to the professional digital formats and filmmakers, including Hal Hartley, with his *The Book of Life* (1998), and Lars Von Trier, with his *Dancing In the Dark* (2000), have experimented with it. However, attempts to apply a "film look" in postproduction with software applications are not always entirely convincing.

It seems inevitable that electronic technology will reach a level where it will compete with film. The much-heralded switch to digital television transmission, which may be delayed beyond the initial 2006 implementation deadline, will improve picture quality for viewers. If HDTV is adopted as well, then viewers may finally have a video picture with the equivalent of 35mm film quality and a screen format close to cinema widescreen (see Part 4, Chapter 23, on TV and film frame formats).

Most films are now edited on digital non-linear editing systems, such as Avid and Final Cut Pro. If viewers express a preference for viewing movies at home on HDTV, then production will be the only part of the production/postproduction/transmission sequence that will not be completely digital.

However, that too may be changing. In what many consider a landmark decision, George Lucas shot *Star Wars: Episode II—Attack Of The Clones* (2002), with its numerous digital effects, on HDTV. A few primetime drama DPs and independent filmmakers, including Robert Rodriguez, director of *Once Upon A Time in Mexico* (2003) and *Spy Kids* (2001), have also started shooting on HDTV and are satisfied with the results.

Perhaps the most significant difference between current film and video practices and shooting styles is time. Film, which is much more expensive, takes a lot longer to prepare, shoot, and edit. Film lighting can be a delicate and time-consuming operation. I once had to watch a lighting cameraman fiddle with a tiny 60-watt spotlight for an hour before he was satisfied with its effect. Although instances such as that are rare, perfectionism is often the rule in film. If the lighting is superior, then the camerawork must match. And if these technical standards are high, then the director will be inclined to do more retakes. The result is that an average feature film produces in the region of two minutes of cut film a day. A faster-working, lower-budget production (such as an independent movie or a made-for-TV production) may achieve four minutes a day. (Some Roger Corman-inspired filmmakers have achieved more than four minutes a day, but they are rare.) A primetime television series shot on film in the studio with the option of a second camera shoots between five and seven minutes of the script a day.

Most current video styles are all about speed. A multi-camera, studio shoot (say, a soap opera) can achieve over forty minutes a day. Working with just a single camera on location, video can produce at east eight minutes of cut footage a day. If a second camera is added, this total can be increased to twelve. The speed of production means that TV directors must always be thinking ahead to the next shot, the next setup, and the next scene. Schedules are always tight, so they are always working against the clock. Every possible error has to be anticipated because a five- or ten-minute holdup can prevent the shooting schedule from being completed that day. The TV director constantly applies the quick-fix—adapting the shot, cheating the angle, adjusting the actors' positions—in order to get through the sheer volume of work. A TV director shooting a street scene may find himself with twenty or thirty extras, but there is no chance of careful placement to achieve a particular effect. The crowd has to be given simple, repeatable moves that will not retard the forward momentum of the shoot.

The different tempos of film and TV production have their effects on directors who tailor their shots to the time and budget available. A fifteen-second helicopter sequence from a John Woo movie may take as long to shoot as several episodes of *General Hospital*. Tracking shots require technical rehearsal and set-up time. They may also require additional lighting. Television directors have to ration the number of tracking shots they use, reserving them for the most important moments. Hollywood movie directors, on the other hand, can often afford to be much freer with the camera.

If filmmakers were to adopt digital production, the relative cheapness of tape would encourage more shooting and thus a higher shooting ratio.[1] The ease of video playback would enable directors and actors to review takes and make instant improvements. The compact size of video recorders might encourage increased use of real locations and guerilla-style shooting (see, for example, Michael Rehfield's *Big Monday*, 1998, which was shot in a New York bus station and on the subway). Recording in the digital domain would also reduce the cost of digital optical effects (because there would be no film-to-video transfer) and make them easier to produce. These are exciting times.

---

[1] The shooting ratio is the ratio of total footage shot to final footage appearing in the film.

PART 6
Postproduction

32. The Structure of the Edit

> "I wish I could compose music; I wish I could play music. But I think I get as close as possible with the editing of a film." — Martin Scorsese. [1]

For some directors, editing is chiefly the pasting together of shots that were planned during preproduction and executed during the shoot. For many others, it is an opportunity to look at the project with an objective eye and to rework scenes and review the structure of the movie as a whole. During planning, directors are usually very aware of issues that will affect editing, such as how to link each shot with the next, how to transition from scene to scene, and how to maintain screen direction. In the 1930s and '40s, the heyday of the Hollywood studios, directors planned and shot their movies but left most postproduction chores to editors and the supervising producer. Most directors seemed happy with this arrangement. It left them free to do the broad creative work and move on to other projects. Who in their right mind would want to spend weeks in a dark cutting room when they could be out in the California sun?

For a few directors, such as Hitchcock, the project is, in a sense, finished before shooting has even begun. And yet, if shooting and editing are simply the mechanical working out of an inflexible directorial plan, wouldn't the end product tend to be lifeless? What keeps a drama alive are such things as the way actors respond to the text, the way directors respond to locations, and the way input from such creative professionals as the DP, the production designer, and the editor can cause a directorial master plan to be reconsidered. Even the best Hithcockian master plan sometimes needs to be tinkered with.

---

[1] *Movie Maker*, Vol. 9, No. 48.

Editing drama and documentary

Many first-time drama directors, especially students, come from a documentary background and may not have considered the differences between these two most basic forms of filmmaking, especially when it comes to postproduction. Likewise, directors who have worked exclusively in drama are often not aware that documentary editing practices are slightly different. I think it is instructive to consider the differences, if only to come to a clearer understanding of drama postproduction.

Editing drama traditionally differs from editing documentary in the following important respects.

Typically, documentary footage is shot in an unrehearsed and fairly unpredictable manner, whereas narrative drama is almost always based on a shooting script. During the early stages of editing drama, the text acts as scaffolding on which the individual shots are hung. A well-defined storyline is there all the time and should be apparent in the first rough-cut. In certain types of documentary (direct cinema/cinema verité especially), the story might only emerge after weeks of editing. The editor and director produce a series of rough-cuts, each a rearrangement of the material in a more coherent manner, until the final form is arrived at. Although the content of dramatic films may be re-ordered during post, the movies that really depend on editing to define the story tend to be those that are improvised. John Cassavetes, for example, spent long periods editing and re-editing his movies, and Mike Leigh has acknowledged the important contribution of his editor, John Gregory.

"B-roll" consists of extra shots (such as cut-ins and cutaways) of objects that a filmmaker uses to supplement the primary footage (or "A-roll"). In the unscripted world of documentary, B-roll is edited in to cover jump cuts and to shorten interviews. Although it is occasionally used in narrative drama, B-roll is more fundamental to non-fiction.

Broadly speaking, the same general Hollywood Continuity Style rules discussed in Part 4 of this book apply to shooting and editing both drama and documentary, but they are often applied less rigidly in documentary. Edits that a drama director would certainly think twice about—such as cuts along the line, cutting on a moving frame, jump cuts, and crossing-the-line—are more frequent in most documentary productions.

On the other hand, the distinctions between documentary and drama are not as great as they sometimes appear. Innovative drama directors and producers have often gone to documentaries for inspiration. "Cinema verité" had a strong impact on many filmmakers in the 1960s and early '70s (consider Godard's *Breathless*,1959, and Lumet's *The Pawnbroker*, 1964), and some of the most successful primetime dramas of the 1990s (*NYPD Blue*, *Homicide*, etc.) adapted documentary shooting and cutting styles.

As we will see, drama editing is not always predictable. Movie directors often alter their projects during editing because the excitement of actually seeing what has been shot provokes a rethinking of certain elements of the drama. Steven Spielberg actually works with his editor during production and adjusts his shooting according to how the film is being cut. This kind of improvisation with the editor is uncommon. However, given the two or three or more months available to edit most Hollywood movies, not surprisingly, some directors take that opportunity to alter elements within scenes and even reconsider the whole film. And in television in the United States, where both the primetime director and the producer are allowed their separate cuts of the finished episode, the two versions sometimes differ markedly in style. (The producer's cut has priority.)

Film "rushes" or "dailies"

As Spielberg's method of working suggests, a clear-cut separation between shooting and editing doesn't always exist. *Rushes* or *dailies*—the unedited print takes developed by the labs—give the film director an idea of how camera and performance are coming together. Most movie directors will view rushes at least once or twice a week during shooting (and every day on big-budget productions). Dailies are particularly important at the start of a shoot when visual style guidelines are being set. They are of interest not only to the director but to most of the other departments as well. The DP will attend dailies screenings to check the lighting, the audio technician will check sound quality, the dolly grip might attend to check the tracking shots, and the hairdresser to see to see if the wig was convincing. Even actors, when invited to do so, turn up to gauge their performances. If actors attend the screening of rushes, bear in mind that they can be disappointed or disturbed seeing their performance on screen for the first time and without the aid of sound effects and music. On the other hand, as the late Sir John Gielgud observed, when else does an actor get to see the back of his head?

Directors must be sanguine about dailies. After the inevitable rush of excitement of seeing your work on the screen for the first time, depression can easily settle in as the same action is repeated in take after take and you become obsessed with its shortcomings. For an interesting take on rushes, read Chapter 8 of Sidney Lumet's *Making Movies* in which he writes about the magic of seeing a movie gradually take on a life of its own. He also describes the experience of seeing one that does not come alive at all.[2]

The film editor takes charge of the rushes and sometimes sets up her editing equipment in the production office or at the location hotel. While the director is shooting, the editor will begin cutting the rushes to produce a rough assembly of completed scenes. Cutting while on location gives the director a chance to see if he needs additional shots. Unlike the rushes, which are usually projected, the rough assembly will be created on a Steenbeck (a film workbench) or (more commonly these days) a non-linear editing device, such as an Avid. Both machines have relatively small screens, so the director must constantly imagine the footage on a cinematic scale.

Assembly and rough cuts

Once the dailies have been screened, the editor commences a preliminary edit of individual scenes and sequences, called an *assembly*. Assemblies are usually constructed using the script as a guide, plus whatever information the editor has gleaned from the continuity assistant's notes and discussions with the director during the screening of the rushes.

Directors do not usually interfere with the editor's first assembly. For a start, they are either often still completing the shoot or taking a well-earned day off after the wrap. But many directors also appreciate having an objective compilation made by fresh and experienced eyes. The editor's assembly may not reflect the director's vision, but it often brings to light fresh possibilities and new juxtapositions that are worth considering.

The director sits down with the editor and reviews the assembly shot by shot and edit by edit. Shots are units of energy that the director and editor control. The energy of an individual shot must be harnessed to the energy of the project as a whole and contribute to its forward momentum. When making an edit, the director and editor focus on the edit point itself, trying to find the precise moment when the energy from the outgoing shot is best transferred to the incoming one. This entails choosing an edit point, making the edit, reviewing the edit, and, usually, fine-tuning it further until the optimum edit point is discovered.

---

[2] See Lumet, *Making Movies*, Chapter 8, "Rushes: The Agony and the Ecstasy."

Gradually, shot by shot and scene by scene, the director and editor reconstruct the whole project until they have produced the first *rough cut*. The rough cut affords the director, editor, and producer their first overview of the project and will prompt further alterations. It will likely be too long. The pacing will also probably need to be adjusted. Some scenes may need to be recut, repositioned, or deleted altogether. Each edit point will be scrutinized: A myriad of small adjustments will suggest themselves.

Directors strive to be objective throughout this process, but critical assessment can be hard after months of sustained creativity. It is tough to have to occasionally sacrifice shots to which you have become attached. It is also hard viewing a rough cut objectively immediately after it has been completed. Different directors have different strategies for achieving objectivity. I always try to give myself a break in order to clear my head before viewing a rough cut. I prefer to come in first thing in the morning after a night's rest, but if that is not possible, I'll take a long walk before the screening.

Subsequent rough cuts are produced, each one a refinement of the one before. The process is largely one of honing, though material that has been cut in a previous version may well be reinserted.

Eventually, a time arrives when the picture editing and the laying down of the basic dialogue tracks stop. Either a deadline has been reached, causing the project to move on to the next stage, or the producer or director (whoever has authority over the final cut) has declared himself satisfied. At this point, the picture is *locked* (i.e., work on the visuals stops) and work begins on the opticals and the sound elements. (Audio editing is discussed in Chapters 35 and 36.)

An overview of postproduction

Having discussed how most collaborations between a director and an editor start, I'd like to outline the different stages of postproduction in both film and television. I have broken this overview into the four most common film and television working models. Perhaps the greatest difference between film and TV editing (apart from the difference between celluloid and magnetic tape) is time. Movies allow more time for editing, so the director can reflect on his choices and tweak and improve the product. In the absence of time, editing tends to become the mechanical implementation of the director's editing plan.

Film

Step 1: At the end of each day's shooting, the camera footage is packaged and sent by a camera assistant to the laboratory for processing. Within, typically, one or two days, a print of this footage or, in 35mm formats and above, a print of the director's selected takes, is delivered to the editor and screened for the director and crew. (These are the dailies) This footage is then used as a workprint by the editor: that is, she edits from it in order not to disturb and possibly damage the original film negatives.

Audio is also transferred at this time from the magnetic tape or DAT or whatever format it was originally recorded on to magnetic film known as *mag stock* so it can be synchronized to the dailies. (Often, an identical numerical coding is applied to both the synchronized workprint and mag stock to ensure that synchronization can be easily maintained throughout the editing process.[3])

If, as is increasingly the case, the edit is done on a digital nonlinear editing system, then the dailies will be transferred to a digital video format (via a process known as *telecine*). A video copy may also be made at this time to be shown as dailies. (An advantage of viewing celluloid dailies is that they can be projected onto a large screen, allowing the director and crew to check for problems that might not be visible on a normal monitor.) With the proper equipment, the audio component may be digitized straight from the production audiotapes onto the nonlinear system or, if the audio has been synched to the rushes on a high-quality video format, such as Digital Betacam, it may be imported at the same time as the video.

Step 2: When working with celluloid footage, the editor (with the aid of an assistant) carefully organizes the material and then begins constructing the assembly. An editor working on a digital editing system will, in a like manner, order digitized footage into computer folders or *bins* (named after the physical bins used to store lengths of celluloid film) and start assembling the material. The assembly can begin while the film shoot is still underway, allowing the director to consider possible additions or substitutions while cast, crew, and locations are still secured.

Step 3: While they can collaborate in a variety of ways, the director and editor typically work together on individual scenes, which they then start grouping with other scenes. Eventually, they produce a rough cut of the whole movie, which is usually intentionally over-long, so they can consider the film in its entirety before making further cuts.

---

[3] When picture and sound coincide perfectly, they are said to be "in sync."

Step 4: Second and subsequent rough cuts are constructed until the picture is finally locked.

At their most accelerated (working on a TV movie, for example), Steps 1 to 4 may take only a few weeks. For the average medium-budget feature film, these steps may take two or three months.

Step 5: Working from a print or video of the project, its audio components are chosen, assembled, and edited. During the sound edit, sound effects are added, and the overdubbing of actors' voices occurs. Music will also be recorded separately and then integrated.

During the mix (which occurs between the completion of the sound edit and the creation of the answer print in Step 7), the sound elements are combined, given appropriate color and ambience, and their levels adjusted relative to each other. This intensive series of sessions may take between two and four weeks to complete. Movies with substantial musical underscoring always require more time (see Chapters 35 and 36).

Step 6: Sections of the film requiring visual effects work, such as freeze frames and wipes, are pulled from the workprint and constructed in the laboratory from the original film negative. These *opticals* might also include the opening titles and credits. If the edit has been done digitally, the video version will be used as a template from which to cut the original film and apply the opticals.

Step 7: If the project has been edited on film, the lab takes the camera original (the film negative actually exposed in the camera) out of storage and cuts it up to match the locked, marked workprint. This delicate and time-consuming process is known as *negative matching* or *conforming*. Prints of the movie are then made from either this new original or a second, *protection* copy of the original negative called the *intermediate*.

If the film is edited digitally, the conforming process is done from a numerical *cutlist* (a list of every shot and its start and stop times) generated by the computer, along with a video output of the film that the lab uses as a reference when cutting the original film negative.

Step 8: The director, who has not been involved in Step 6 (other than determining when and what types of opticals are used), and may or may not have been involved in creating the titles, now re-enters the process to check the color of each shot of the print. This is a process known as *color timing*. Feedback about the shot-to-shot trueness and density of the colors, the quality of the optical effects, and the smoothness of the negative matching from the director and the editor is used to produce the first *answer print*, so called because it is the film lab's response to their comments. A number of answer prints may be necessary. Film labs can prepare an answer print in two or three days, and the whole of Step 8 may only take a couple of weeks. Eventually, all parties agree on a *release print*, which is the finalized version of the film.

Step 9: A Hollywood movie intended for commercial release is usually previewed to selected audiences. The producers may request changes based on the test audiences' reactions. Most movies are altered in response to previews. The openings of *Blue Velvet* (1986) and *Savior* (1998), for example, were not added till after the impact of the edited movies had been evaluated.

The process outlined above (Steps 1 through 9) is lengthy and differs widely from film to film. Postproduction on an average studio film takes between four and five months. Post on an independent film might take less time. A movie with complex visual effects might easily take twice as long.

Having described the film process in detail above, the following three sections outline alternative models in a more abbreviated manner.

Primetime U.S. television shot on film

Step 1: As soon as shooting is completed, the editor, working on a digital nonlinear system, produces an assembly over a period of two or three days. The director may or may not be present for this work.

Step 2: The director works with the editor for between one and two weeks to produce the director's cut. The director's contractual obligation usually ends at this point.

Step 3: The producer reviews the director's cut. Television producers almost always have the right to a final cut, which means that they can substantially alter the director's cut if they wish. At the end of this process, the series' generic titles are added and the show is brought "to time" (i.e., made to fit an exact time window), including commercial breaks.

Step 4: Additional audio editing is done and the sound is mixed.

Step 5: The producer supervises credit sequences and any opticals.

Total postproduction time may be as short as three or four weeks.

Single-camera video for television

Step 1: The director reviews the footage on videotape and notes the *time code*, a specific number ascribed to each frame of video (expressed in hours, minutes, seconds, and frames), of preferred takes. These notes are sometimes called a *paper edit*.

Step 2: The director and the editor work together, using the paper edit, to produce a rough cut, which they then bring to time.

Step 3: The producer, who almost certainly has control of the final cut, asks for changes, which the director implements.

Step 4: The director or the producer attends the sound edit (a.k.a. *sweetening*).

Multi-camera video for television

Step 1: The director makes a paper edit from a video copy of the recorded takes. In a multi-camera production, whole scenes or extended shot sequences are recorded at once, so the paper edit is not necessarily as detailed as that of a single-camera production (for which the details of each individual shot have to be noted).

Step 2: The director and the editor assemble the program based on the paper edit, and then tighten up some of the cuts made during the recording by the *technical director*, who assembled the scene or sequence during the recording from the shots offered by all the cameras. In the U.S., these small edits between shots are called *pull-ups* (see Part 8 for multi-camera production).

Step 3: The producer's notes are incorporated into the final cut.

Step 4: Music and sound effects are added and mixed. As industry deadlines get shorter, as they have in the last decade, the director has less and less control over editing. Sometimes a producer in charge of postproduction supervises sound work and the final mix. If the director is lucky, he can give the supervising producer a list of suggested music and effects.

33. Working with the Editor

"The editor and I were in need of some therapy, I
think, by the end."—Scott Hicks on editing *Shine*.[1]

Editing is a craft that combines technical expertise, artistic judgment, and the ability to work with others. Editors have to be adaptable, even-tempered, and highly technically proficient. Being able to gauge the amount of work to be done and to pace yourself accordingly is important. Video editors work against pressing deadlines, so speed is of the essence. Film editors working on longer-term projects often develop a slightly less frenetic yet still efficient approach.

The editor's first task is to find out what the director wants. Every director has a distinct style and way of working. The editor must attune himself to the director and understand her sensibility. One of the advantages of reviewing an assembly with the director is that the editor becomes aware of the differences in their approaches. Directors appreciate editors who can anticipate their comments and suggest changes in line with their vision.

Directors who have worked for an extended time on a drama often become locked into one way of approaching it. Editors can bring a welcome pair of fresh eyes to a project, suggesting new cutting points, changes in the speed of a scene (by making a cut or slipping in an extra shot), and better ways of achieving a particular effect. They may also see opportunities for re-ordering the scenes that improve the whole project.

Once an editor understands a director's approach, he can bring his own creativity to bear. In some genres, such as children's television and music TV, the editor's contribution is highly visible. The editor's contribution to drama tends to be less radical. It usually consists of hundreds of adjustments to sound

---

[1] Jeremy Kagan, ed., *Directors Close Up* (Boston: Focal Press, 2000), p. 177.

and picture that have an enormous cumulative effect. Once in a while, though, he offers moments of sheer inspiration that transform an entire project. In the classic western *High Noon* (1952), the inspired suggestion to inter-cut the close shots of the town clock with the scenes of Gary Cooper waiting for the outlaws, which helped define the look and palpable tension of the movie, originated with the editor. In Michael Ondaatje's book *The Conversations*, Walter Murch describes the editor's role in re-organizing the script of *The English Patient* (1996) in the editing room—swapping an early scene with a later one and changing the overall character of the film.[2]

A director wants his editor to be able to handle all the technical aspects of postproduction. The editor must understand the grammar of the cut and how to cut on motion—which means making an edit seem invisible to the audience by cutting during an actor's physical movement. He and his assistants must be compulsive housekeepers, keeping order in the cutting room, keeping track of each frame of film. Those editing on nonlinear systems must be extremely careful about keeping backups and saving different versions (different edits) of their work. Editors on video projects that will be mastered to film must also understand the intricacies of transferring from video.

Many of the difficulties that occur during editing do not have obvious solutions, so editors must be prepared to think around problems. Audio problems, for example, often require an editor to hunt for replacement audio clips and then spend time synching them to the picture. Faced with a cut that is not working, an editor must massage the picture and sound till the right cutting point is found or suggest an alternative shot.

The editing room

Editing rooms, especially video ones, tend to be small and cramped. Editors need to be able to control the light so that they can best view the images on monitors or film workbenches called Steenbecks, which means that editing suites also tend to be dark.

Editing requires great concentration. The very deliberate process of looking for a cutting point, executing a cut, reviewing it separately and then in context, adjusting it, and re-reviewing it remains the same in both film and video.

Long hours come with the territory. On short projects, editors may work concentrated ten- or twelve-hour days and receive additional days off as

---

[2] This book and Murch's *In the Blink of an Eye* offer rich insights into the art of film editing.

compensation. On longer projects, the hours are often agreed upon between the director and the editor. This can mean some very long shifts, especially if the team is on a roll. An editor friend of mine once worked till two o'clock in the morning with a famous director. When the editor asked to go home to get some sleep, the director pinned him up against the wall and threatened him. Disagreement on this scale between a director and an editor is rare, but their relationship can be highly pressurized (as we will see in the next section).

Editors require breaks to remain sharp. One of the objections editors used to traditional film editing have against digital editing is that it is too sedentary and does not allow for the pauses and physical movement that splicing celluloid naturally provides. Thinking time for both editor and director is reduced by computer editing. Sometimes the momentum becomes so furious that it is difficult to slow it down and take stock. Editors working on computers are forced to put in a considerable number of hours in front of the screen. This is obviously not healthy, and the resulting fatigue can lead to a loss of acuity. Directors should not be afraid to get up and clear their heads, and they should be sympathetic when an editor calls for a short time-out to clear his.

The director/editor relationship

Certain members of the production team and crew become close to the director. The cameraperson is involved in the creation of every shot, the continuity assistant and first assistant are constantly by her side, but the editor, with whom she shares a room for weeks on end, usually becomes the closest of all. If shots, sequences, or (heaven forbid) the whole drama is not working, then the director has only one person to turn to—the editor. You cannot hide any deficiency from the person who is reviewing your footage and meticulously assembling your shots.

When a director finds an editor who is personally sympathetic and closely allied in both working methods and aesthetics, she will try to work with him again and again. Among many examples of long-standing editor/director partnerships are Steven Spielberg's association with Michael Kahn, Martin Scorsese's with Thelma Schoonmaker, and Barry Levinson's with Stu Linder. No one in a production is the director's servant—the editor least of all. The director/editor relationship works best as one of equals, in which both parties have freedom to comment and experiment.

Editing requires a director's patience. It is a marked change of pace from shooting. The director is less active during editing and yet she must remain absolutely alert to respond to the editor's work and make creative decisions. The director is not always driving this particular car. And when you are not at the wheel, the ride sometimes feels longer than it actually is.

Essentially, directors come in two types: those who give editing notes and then leave and those who work intimately with their editors. When working for television, time pressure usually ensures that the director works intensely with the editor at some point. In a feature-length movie, the process can be less clear-cut. Some directors prefer to supervise rather than get intimately involved, and some editors prefer to work for periods by themselves (at least while they are assembling the material). Each director/editor partnership must work out its own rules. An important factor in determining these rules is the director's shooting style. Those who shoot with maximum coverage will generally require more editing time to try out different shot permutations than those with a definite visual concept.

Choosing takes

Selecting the best takes is the director's unique contribution to editing. It begins during the shoot. Film directors (especially those shooting in the more expensive formats of 35mm and 70mm) decide whether or not to print a take immediately after they have shot it. When shooting 16mm film or video, a director will usually ask his assistant to mark the good takes so that the editor can go straight to them.

While the editor is largely (though not exclusively) concerned with constructing a technically seamless project, the director must constantly ensure that the best takes and best performances are being used. As mentioned above, movie directors will begin talking to their editors when rushes start coming in and then go over the rough assembly with them. Even during the subsequent preparation of the rough cut and the final edit, the director must keep an eye on the footage the editor is incorporating to make sure that it is the best available.

Every take has a technical element and a performance element. Ideally, both should fuse perfectly but, occasionally, one must preside over the other. If one important element is clearly unacceptable, you cannot use the take. A wonderful performance that is out of focus is clearly unusable. A perfectly executed camera movement in which an actor stumbles over his lines is also unacceptable. Sometimes, however, there are close calls. You may have two takes of a tracking shot in which one track stops at precisely the right moment and the other is a fraction of a second late. If the performance is superior in the technically inferior take, what do you do? The rule of thumb is, if in doubt, go with the performance. A good performance will affect an audience, and a small technical imperfection may go unnoticed.

Time and timecode

NASA cannot have foreseen that the electronic numbering system it invented to synchronize the components of its spacecraft would be its most enduring gift to the film and television industry. Timecode is an imprinted electronic signal that allocates a specific number to every *frame*[3] of video, so material can be identified and accessed with precision. Unlike edge numbers on film, timecode is not visible and requires decoding via a device such as a VCR or computer program.

Timecode is represented as hours, minutes, seconds, and frames, so that, for example, the eight digits 01:12:27:09 would designate one hour, 12 minutes, 27 seconds, and 9 frames.[4]

In video, and increasingly in film, the director receives a videotape of what has been shot. The tape has *burned-in time code* (BITC) that allows her to identify the start of every take and any subsequent fraction of a second. Directors view these tapes to compare takes. A conscientious director will watch each take critically and note which moments are working. She will then select the best moments from all the different takes to be edited together.

Using timecode is particularly crucial in television, where the networks determine a program's running time and, usually, allow the director only a few seconds' latitude. By noting the timecoded in-time and out-time of every shot, the director can calculate not only the length of each shot but, by adding the selected shots together, also the length of each scene, each act, and the program as a whole. The director enters the edit room with pieces of paper on which she has noted her selected timecodes (the in-points and out-points for each shot)—this is her paper edit.

If the in-point of a selected take is 00:08:16:22 and the out-point is 00:08:20:28, the length of the take (calculated by deducting the in-point from the out-point) is four seconds and six frames. A director doing an estimated timing for a paper edit will generally round the figure off to the nearest second

---

[3] Video is constructed of frames in much the same way film is constructed of single photographic frames. There are thirty frames per second in standard American (known as "NTSC") video, though other frame rates are also available.

[4] Standard timecode in the U.S. is SMPTE (pronounced "simpty") Timecode, which is the version approved by the Society of Motion Picture and Television Engineers.

and not be overly concerned with individual frames. So, in the above example where the take lasts four seconds and six frames (a fifth of a second), she would round the take out at four seconds. If the calculation had showed the number of frames to be sixteen or above, she would round the number up to five seconds. When calculating timecode, be sure to remember that, although there are sixty minutes in an hour and sixty seconds in a minute, there are only *thirty frames* in a second (in the American NTSC system).

During editing for television, the director and her assistant keep a very close watch on the length of each scene, which, due to trimming, may differ from the paper edit timings. If each scene in a show with thirty scenes loses one second as it is edited, the program as a whole will lose half a minute and may come in under time. Directors of half-hour TV shows generally create paper edits that are twenty or thirty seconds too long in order to allow for editing-room tightening.

The paper edit that a director of episodic TV brings to the cutting room is only one step in a series of time checks. The process begins in preproduction with a producer's page count (standard formula: 1 page = 1 minute) and the director's own, more exact, stopwatch timing. The director's assistant will keep track of individual shots and scenes during shooting to check whether the overall running time of the show has "spread" or "shrunk." If scenes are running noticeably longer than expected, the director and the producer may agree to cut material before it is actually shot. On the other hand, finding oneself editing a show that is under-running (i.e., shy of material to fill the program's allotted time) is a directorial nightmare, forcing you to keep unwanted pauses and poorly delivered lines.

The power of juxtaposition

In most contemporary, naturalistic, Hollywood-style productions, the story and the performances are primary. Great care is taken not to disrupt the flow of events and not to distract from the illusion of intimacy with the star. With relatively few exceptions, editors working in this style strive to make each cut invisible. Good editors, so the saying goes, cut their own throats—which is to say, they strive to make their work invisible in the finished product.

However, editors may still make their presence felt. One way is juxtaposition. The craft of editing has been significantly influenced by Russian montage that juxtaposed contrasting shots in order to make a point (see Part 7, Chapter 37). While most editing attempts to maximize the connection between shots in order to convey the impression of continuity, Soviet montage-style juxtaposition emphasizes discontinuity. Editing two contrasting images together makes the viewer forge a connection between them. A woman sits at her dressing table brushing her hair. A man with a weapon inches his way down the corridor. The spectator makes a connection and realizes that the woman is in danger.

Juxtaposition between scenes is more common than juxtaposition between images and is often implied by the screenplay. One scene ends in a small, dark office and the next one starts in an open landscape. Martin Scorsese is a master of juxtaposition. His films frequently deal with the slightly melodramatic world of crime, which always lends itself to stark juxtaposition. A man leaves his office and strolls down the street. In the next shot we see him on a slab in the morgue. The cut has snuffed out his life as surely as a gangster's bullet.

Generally, the more obvious the editing, the less naturalistic the drama. Strong juxtapositions tend to interrupt narrative flow and discourage viewer association with a story's characters. Television series, which are very script- and character-based, do not usually employ the kind of cuts associated with a Scorsese film. Any dramatic juxtapositions that occur are likely to be the result of parallel story-lines devised by the writer. We often see this parallel story juxtaposition in *E.R.* and *NYPD Blue*, which utilize powerful cuts as they move from one strand of the story to another, cutting from one character in agony to another in love or from one person about to be operated on to another happily exiting the hospital.

Perhaps the most common cut between scenes shows one character leaving a room and another character entering a different one. This is potentially a strong directorial statement—perhaps a basic existential statement of "as one door closes another one opens"—but it is so often used that it has lost much of its metaphorical power.

Sudden juxtapositions draw attention to themselves and thus tend to momentarily pull the viewer out of a story. But this is not to imply that they cannot be used successfully. Certain visceral movie genres deliberately set out to provoke shock or a sudden infusion of adrenaline. Think of the excesses of *Batman* (1989), *The Mask* (1994), *Mission Impossible* (1996), and *Men in Black* (1997), to mention just a few where editing and digital effects engage the viewer emotionally. I cannot remember the plots of any of the above movies, but I can recall the excitement of watching them.

The lineage of both the modern thriller and the modern horror film can be traced back to Alfred Hitchcock, who used film like an experimental psychiatrist to induce vivid mental and emotional states. In *Psycho* (1960) he deliberately created a naturalistic, HCS narrative that he suddenly and powerfully subverted. This clever use of naturalism to defy audience expectation is also a characteristic of the work of Hal Hartley (*Henry Fool*, 1997), Ethan Coen (*Fargo*, 1996), and M. Night Shyamalan (*The Sixth Sense*, 1999), in which a naturalistic style of presentation encourages us to accept events that are far from naturalistic.

In this post-MTV era, the wild, fast-paced editing of music videos has had a great impact on feature films. Oliver Stone's *JFK* (1991), for which the editor Robert Richardson won an Oscar, the Wachowski brothers' *The Matrix* (1999), and Darren Aronofsky's *Pi* (1998) maintain hectic cutting paces. This fast editing, with its frequent flashbacks and subjective viewpoints, takes us into fractured worlds with more than a hint of paranoia. Such pacing makes demands on the viewer. We may feel a tension between our natural wish to get involved in the story and the characters and the disorienting effect of the editing. Perhaps this experience of being immersed and then suddenly removed from the narrative encourages audiences to become aware of the issues being tackled in these movies.

Directors should bear in mind that a non-naturalistic production and editing style is a tightrope act that has to be carefully planned during preproduction. It cannot be imposed on unsuitable footage during editing.

Tempo and rhythm

Tempo is the speed at which cuts occur. It is, of course, a product of the length of time shots are held (their duration). In most circumstances, short shots will produce a fast tempo, long shots a slow one. At its most basic, the editing tempo can increase or decrease the excitement level of a story. Bearing this in mind, a director will generally increase the number of cuts as she approaches a climax and decrease them afterward (and increase them again toward the next climax). A fight, a murder, or a chase sequence's tempo will accelerate until it is complete, after which usually comes a longer, more restful shot as a new scene is established. Here is an example: Our hero struggles against time to defuse an atomic bomb. A shot of him sweating in front of the mechanism is intercut with shots of enemy soldiers searching for him and the villain barking orders into his cell phone. The shots of our hero are held slightly longer than those of the soldiers and the villain, so that a fast tempo is maintained while allowing a little extra time to be spent on the hero, establishing him and his activity as the center of the sequence. If he manages to defuse the bomb, we will inevitably be treated to a moment in which time seems to stand still while we savor his success—perhaps via a close shot in which his relief is palpable—before the chase resumes. Such arrangements of shots of differing length produce rhythms, which I'll discuss shortly.

Content affects a scene's perceived speed as well. A single shot of two cars dueling on a road, or two characters fighting, may be held for a number of seconds and still be perceived as fast-paced and exciting. Content can also slow the pace down: Long takes without much action or camera movement will impose a slow pace on a sequence. In the final fight sequence in *Gladiator*, the contest is intercut with slower and more static and subjective images of the hero's rural home. These rural images restrain the narrative flow and foreshadow his death.

Tempo can be used to describe character. Stanislavski pointed out that individual characters in a scene have their own tempos. Generally, the farmer has a naturally slower tempo than the journalist, older characters have slower tempos than young ones, and the angry executive has a faster tempo than a ministering priest. Inside each of us is a metronome ticking at a speed that is different from one individual to the next. Ed the barber, the central character in the Coen brothers' film *The Man Who Wasn't There* (2002), has what his creators called "a slow metabolism" because he lives at a slower pace than everyone else around him. Here is Sidney Lumet describing how tempo-rhythm affected his shooting and editing of *A Long Day's Journey Into Night* (1962): "I always shot Katherine Hepburn in long, sustained takes, so that in the editing, the legato feel of her scenes would help us drift into her narcotized world. We would move *with* her, into her past and into her own journey into night. Jason Robard's character was edited in exactly the opposite way. As the picture went on, I tried to cut his scenes in a staccato rhythm. I wanted him to feel erratic, disjointed, uncoordinated."[5]

The script provides the filmmaker with character-tempo clues. I used to direct a show that had a mixture of very old and very young characters. The scenes with the elderly were always slower than the ones with the kids. The older actors spoke in a more measured way and had longer speeches. The young ones used slang and tended to rush their sentences. A director like Lumet deliberately builds on these differences and incorporates them into his directorial vision. In *Pi*, a film that predominantly reflects one character's point of view, the hectic cutting tells us about the person's disturbed and obsessive state of mind. The whole film, in this case, is constructed around one character's erratic tempos.

---

[5] *Making Movies*, p. 162.

Rhythm[6] is the pattern formed by the juxtaposition of shots of various lengths, sizes, and contents. A wide shot has more detail than a close shot (unless the close shot is of a very intricate pattern) and, therefore, takes longer to "read." A landscape, for example, with hills, valley, river, and a group of small characters crossing it, requires more screen time for the viewer to take in all its information than a closeup of a face or an object. The time that is needed for an audience to fully register a shot's content may be considered an aspect of rhythm. And in this respect, one may satisfy or short-change an audience's expectations.

As we have noted, dialogue tends to impose its own pace on a scene. Scenes without dialogue offer directors much greater opportunities to manipulate both tempo and rhythm. How these elements unfold in chase sequences is largely determined by the director, who can extend or contract shots as she chooses. Adventure movies with their vivid action sequences offer directors many opportunities to create stylized and interesting editing effects without being too tied down by the script. For particularly striking examples of rhythmic editing, see Darren Aronofsky's *Pi* and *Requiem for a Dream*, which have groups of images recurring thematically throughout. (Aranovsky calls these groups "hip-hop montages." In music, a specific recurring theme that represents a specific dramatic character or subject is called a leitmotif.[7]) For instance, when the main character in *Pi* returns to his New York apartment, he ritually fastens a number of chains across the door. This chain-fastening sequence represents his isolation and fear. Accelerated and pared down to its minimum, it recurs several times in the movie.

Music acts as a powerful rhythmic organizer. Musical rhythms may be strong and hard to resist. Be careful when choosing music because it can color and impose its own organization on everything on the screen. Look at the beginning of *Mission Impossible II* (2000), in which flamenco dancing is intercut with shots of an attempted robbery. The director and editor allow the dance to drive the whole sequence. The cuts are timed to the beat of the music, and shots of the dancers' heels stomping the floor are juxtaposed with shots of the robber's heels running up the stairs. The sexuality of the dance itself provides a charged background to the first meeting between the hero and the leading actress.

---

[6] To help understand the difference between rhythm and tempo, think of the opening of a piece of music (perhaps Beethoven's Fifth Symphony or The Beatles' *All You Need Is Love*). The individual notes form themselves into rhythm, which you can probably clap (short-short-short-long for the Beethoven and long-short-short-short-long for the Beatles). But there is also the underlying tempo, to which you can steadily tap your feet. The rhythm will inevitably change, but the tempo will probably stay the same.

[7] See the section on "Working with a composer" in Chapter 36.

The film musical is an animal unto itself. Most musicals juxtapose two broad rhythms—the rhythm of naturalistic drama (mainly speech rhythms), which is occasionally interrupted by the more artificial rhythm of song and dance. (This parallels the distinction in classic opera between the "recitative," which conveys the plot, and the arias, the songs themselves.) With the exception of the Indian film industry, movie musicals have somewhat fallen out of fashion. But the tradition still exists in films like *Pennies From Heaven* (1981), *Billy Elliot* (2000), *Dancer in the Dark* (2000), and *Moulin Rouge* (2001), in which music is closely integrated into the drama. In *Billy Elliot*, which has the most straightforward narrative of the four examples, the contrast between the gritty realism of Billy's background and the artistry of his dancing is expressed in their very different rhythms and tempos. Interestingly, the fast-paced musical *Chicago* (2003) has fewer pretensions to naturalism, and blurs the distinction between narrative and musical elements. But its story—that of a disadvantaged, lower-class character drawn to the alternative world of dance—is strangely similar to *Billy Elliot*. And *Chicago* maintains a residual difference in tempo between the scenes that serve the forward momentum of the plot and those that represent fantasy. I will discuss music editing in more detail in Chapter 36.

34. Making Edits

Directors think about edits almost from the moment they pick up a script. Edits are considered during planning, storyboarding, blocking, and marking up the shooting script. If you have rehearsals, one of the surest ways to find out when and where to cut in a dialogue sequence is to notice when and where your eyes are drawn during rehearsal. More often than not, they are drawn to the person speaking—but not always. Trust your instinct: It will probably be the same as your audience's. Walter Murch, Academy Award-winning editor, suggests that a cut is the equivalent of a blink. Just as we blink when we look at something new or get excited, so we cut when our attention moves to another subject or we need to express excitement.[1]

Editing dialogue

Between the first rehearsal and the edit, you will have seen and heard the same lines dozens of times. A good editor can view a project with fresh eyes and suggest where the cuts should occur. Even though I may have planned all the edits and marked them in my script, I always let the editor suggest the cutting point just in case she sees something new. Some editors will see scenes completely differently from you, some will see them exactly as you do. Some are so absorbed in the technical details of the task that they miss cutting points altogether.

In dialogue scenes, the director will take his initial cue about rhythm from the script—though there may still be opportunities to vary the tempo by inserting pauses or moments of action. Different writers have different patterns. Two writers writing the same character in a long-running series will not only put different words in her mouth, they will compose speeches of differing lengths and rhythms. A director can play against this to a certain degree. Reaction shots

---

[1] Walter Murch, *In the Blink of an Eye* (Beverly Hills: Silman-James Press, 1995).

of other characters in a scene usually help break up speeches that are over-long. Sometimes, under the right circumstances, the director can choose not to dwell on the speaker at all. Some directors introduce extra cuts in dialogue scenes in order to increase the pace and visual interest. Be careful if you do this, though — speeding up a sequence by increasing the cutting tempo can feel very artificial unless it is done well.

A dialogue scene may be cut in two ways. The first is "cutting on the nose," which means cutting exactly at the start of each character's speech. If Gerty tells Earle not to eat the children's dinner, and Earle protests he's hungry, then the editor will cut away from Gerty as soon as she finishes her speech, and cut to Earle just before he starts his.

One advantage of cutting on the nose is clarity. We are cutting to the speaker for the start of every speech, and do not miss a phrase or even a part of a word. Another advantage to this method is that it precisely captures the writer's rhythm since it is cut exactly as implied by the text. In *Secrets and Lies* (1995), Mike Leigh has the photographer (Timothy Spall) and his wife (Alison Steadman) engage in a tightly cut, back-and-forth, "on the nose" dialogue sequence, which defines the emotional tenor of their relationship.

Cutting like this is fine if the dialogue is rhythmically varied, but it can become boring if the speeches are long or rhythmically predictable. Consider the following example:

```
Gerry and Blaize are two young college friends who
have not met in a while.

                    GERRY
          Baz! What are you doing in town?

                   BLAIZE
          Gerry! How are you?

                    GERRY
          Fine. Well, better than fine,
          actually.

                   BLAIZE
          Yes, you look very pleased with
          yourself.
```

> GERRY
> Do you remember Diane Gregory - the
> girl in the dorm across the road?
>
> BLAIZE
> Yes, I do. She was a stunner.
>
> GERRY
> Well, I've come to town to propose to
> her.
>
> BLAIZE
> That's funny. So have I!

The writing may be cute but it is also predictable. To cut at the start of every line would reinforce the slightly formal, one-line-per-speech construction, and the scene would soon become monotonous.

An alternative is to "slip the cut." This means not cutting at the start of each line but letting the audio lead the picture—so that the cut to the speaker is slightly delayed. In line 3, for example, we might cut to Gerry *after* the word "Fine." And then cut back to Blaize after "Yes."

Slipping the cut helps break up the predictable rhythmic pattern, and it is also very much how we perceive a conversation. We hear people start to speak and then we turn to look at them. Our eyes tend to follow our ears. In media terms, this "softens" the cut (makes it less obvious) because the audio prepares us for the new, incoming shot. In classic Hollywood fashion, the audio has motivated the cut. Editors may also refer to this as a "split cut," because the sound is split from the picture at the start of the shot, or an "L-cut," because this can be represented graphically as an "L." (See Fig. 34.1.)

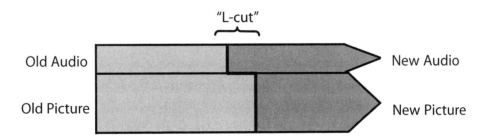

Fig. 34.1: Audio leading picture in a "split cut" or "L-cut"

When planning a scene and again when editing it, take a moment to consider its rhythm and tempo. Does it have a conscious rhythmic feel? Or does it play out somewhat monotonously in an unchanging way? Does it have a varied and progressing tempo? Can you pick up the tempo toward its climax? Does each separate beat have a distinct feel?

Now, think about the *scene-to-scene* rhythm of the *whole* drama and consider if it has a variety of rhythms and tempos. One of the problems with many daytime serials is that the pace varies very little from one scene to the next. Remember, variation in tempo is important. A slow tempo is perfectly acceptable as long as it serves as a contrast to faster tempos, thereby lending a film variety and a sense of motion.

Finally, we must consider a couple of technical issues that are particularly relevant to drama.

Checkerboarding

When editing dialogue, assigning each character a separate audio track can be very helpful. If two people—let's say Dwight and Yolanda—speak in a scene, Dwight's dialogue will go on Track 1 and Yolanda's dialogue on Track 2. (On a digital nonlinear system new tracks may easily be introduced for many additional characters.) Keeping each character's speeches separate helps the audio supervisor monitor and mix the dialogue.

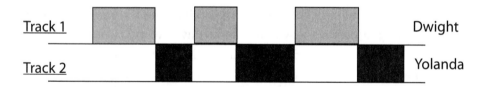

Fig. 34.2: Checkerboarding

Overlapping audio

As I have noted in Part 4, Chapter 20, recording overlapping dialogue can cause a problem. Consider a shot of Alex with Martha's voice over his, perhaps recorded when Martha fed Alex lines from outside the shot. These two voices cannot be extricated. This is especially problematic if Martha's line is "off-mic" (inadequately recorded by the microphone because it was beyond the mic's optimal pick-up range).

What does an editor do when faced with this problem? She asks the director to take a long lunch break and then devotes meticulous, time-consuming attention to the cut. She identifies the precise syllable where the problem starts to occur. She then examines the footage of Martha when the microphone was pointed at her to see if she can find a version that exactly matches her off-mic delivery. With luck, the matching shot will be the one the director has selected as Martha's next shot (the incoming shot). If not, she will try to find another clean (without the overlapping lines) matching take and lay that over the off-mic lines (so that the clean take becomes more audible than the off-mic line). A resourceful editor can usually fix the problem, but in irremediable situations the words either remain indistinct or the actors have to be brought in to re-record their lines.

The joy of making cuts

Directors generally fall into two categories: those who tolerate their work being pared down and reshaped and those who resist all alterations to the bitter end. If you are a fully conscious "auteur," for whom every shot is an essential piece in a grand pattern, then you will frown on the assault to your work's integrity by producers trying to get your movie in under two hours so it can play in the maximum number of theaters. Of course, all directors are sorry to see shots or scenes on which they have spent long hours left on the cutting-room floor. This almost inevitable aspect of the job is sometimes referred to as "killing your darlings" or "murdering your babies."

Most directors (those without unusual amounts of clout) cannot afford to be too sensitive about cutting. If you are a TV director trying to get your show in under twenty-four minutes and fifteen seconds to fulfill your contract with the network, you will have to slash and burn till you get there. If you are directing a comedy or a thriller in which "dead time" (slow sequences) cannot be tolerated, you will pare your show down till it becomes as lean and efficient as possible. No one exemplifies the joy of cutting more than Woody Allen. "When you take something out," he has said, "it gives the film such an exhilarating pace. Once you see it out, the joy of the speed is so exhilarating that I can never bring myself to put the material back."[2]

Theater directors often use the latter half of their rehearsal period to progressively simplify performances in order to make them more direct and compelling. Well-known British director Peter Brook calls this process "sifting,"

---

[2] *New York Times Magazine*, November 16, 1997, p. 93.

and it also occurs in film during editing. Cuts of all kinds are made during editing—they may be as draconian as the deletion of whole scenes or they may be as small as just a few frames (known as *trims*). Film theorists call the process of converting real time into condensed, dramatic time "ellipsis." *Opportunities exist in almost every scene to shave frames off between cuts.* For example, dialogue can be sharpened by cutting out the "air" (sometimes just a few frames) between speeches. Performances that appeared hesitant and sluggish can suddenly be given new energy and pace. Scorsese has remarked, "When you get down to trimming a half-foot here and there from a film—when you trim milliseconds—that's when you get to know the true nature of cinema."[3]

Actors' moves can also almost always be tightened either by a few frames or even a few seconds. Max gets up and crosses to the door, which is eight feet away. He rises in one shot and enters the next shot by the door. The editor can cut out at least half of his cross (four feet) by letting him leave the first shot and almost immediately enter the second. As long as there is sufficient movement and the time being cut out is not too huge, the audience will accept the cheat. A surprisingly great amount of tightening in this way can be done without the viewer noticing.

An editor can "condense" real time by inserting a shot. Joan watches Frank walk across the square toward her house. We see Frank fifty meters away. We cut to Joan's reaction for two seconds. We cut back to Frank, who is now ten meters distant. In real time, he would take eight or ten seconds to cover those forty meters, but in screen time, he took only two. Here and elsewhere, emulating the non-fiction director's B-roll can be very useful. If a character mentions a specific prop—a weapon, a photograph, a letter—always take a shot of it. Slipping in a cutaway to this object will increase the cutting tempo, and may allow you to condense time as well.

Cutting away to a character can suggest a hidden intention. For example, in a high-level discussion about war plans, the director momentarily cuts to a character with the hint of a smile on his face, suggesting the character's subversive intention. Editors often find these telltale reaction shots (actors smiling or blinking) in outtakes or at the head of shots before "action" is called. Although a director should always be careful about slowing the onward flow of a scene, sometimes such cutaways can add to, rather than subtract from, the effect of a dialogue scene. However, bear in mind that appropriating a shot out of context is, in a sense, breaking an unspoken agreement with an actor, by using

---

[3] *Movie Maker*, Issue 48, Vol. 9, Fall 2002, p. 66. Scorsese is paraphrasing Thorold Dickinson.

her image in a way she did not originally intend. If you do steal a shot—and most directors, including myself, have done so—make sure it achieves the desired effect and enhances the actor's performance.

Scripts are logical constructions: They take you from point A to point E, via B, C, and D. Sometimes, if you cut out one of the steps—say, step C—the audience has to make the connection by itself. One of the rules of visual storytelling is that very often all you need to do is *show* that something has happened for the audience to accept it. If one shot shows a child fretting about an exam and the next shot shows her receiving a diploma, the viewer will surmise she has passed. This can also make for an exciting juxtaposition of images and rhythms.

Another technique for making cuts is the "late in"—trimming the beginnings of individual speeches. As Woody Allen says, the effect can be exhilarating. Here is a speech by an irate father.

GEORGE

```
        Henry, don't mention her name to me.
        It's repugnant! I never want to see
        her again! I never want to hear her
        name again! I don't want anything to
        do with her!!
```

It is a strong speech, but it can be made even stronger by a late in. The director could cut the first two sentences and start the speech with, "I never want to see her again!" Directors, especially those in episodic TV, are constantly making cuts like this in order to deliver a show that precisely meets its length requirement.

Cutting may eradicate dead wood and pick up the overall speed of a drama, but it is good only up to a point. Remorseless speed is not always effective, especially in longer dramas, where it is important to vary the tempo. Maintaining a slow pace can require courage on the part of a director. Dwelling on a beautiful landscape allows the viewer to appreciate it and, in a sense, enter it. Consider David Lean's famous, long, shimmering desert shot in *Lawrence of Arabia* (1962) or the length of time Polanski takes to establish the ruined Warsaw Ghetto in *The Pianist* (2003). Simply observing characters often allows a viewer to identify with them. Think of the lovers in *Elvira Madigan* (1967), or Scorsese's scrutiny of DeNiro in *Taxi Driver* (1976).

Sometimes, a director may simply need to call time-out from a hectic pace of action, as in the bicycle scene from *Butch Cassidy and the Sundance Kid*

(1969). I have always admired Jean-Luc Godard for, among other things, including moments of boredom in his pictures, as if to say that a complete portrait of human existence must include *ennui*. And certain dramas simply cannot be rushed. Martin Scorsese said of his "biopic" of the Dalai Lama, *Kundun* (1997), "It's a little difficult on a picture like this because their world is a world where they had no roads, and they walked from place to place. That's the pace. It's not New York. So you have to say, 'How do you show that pace without boring an audience to death?'"[4]

Digital nonlinear editing has brought a new facility to cutting. Cuts can be tried out and replaced with ease and scenes can be almost instantly rearranged. The limitless plasticity of modern nonlinear editing, therefore, has considerable advantages. One drawback, however, is that with all the instantly viewable choices it offers, making concrete decisions becomes more difficult, and projects tend to get extended so that the eventual product is not a definitive version but the last version that happened to be on the hard drive when the deadline arrived.

---

[4] Loc. cit.

35. The Sound Edit

"The most exciting moment is the moment I add
sound. At this moment, I tremble." —Akira Kurosawa

Once the picture is locked, the project has an air of finality. No more
structural changes are to be made. At this point on a project without a
dialogue editor, the picture editor may have already separated and
synched the audio tracks and, if you have been working digitally, done some
elementary mixing.

Although committing project-destroying errors during audio editing is
somewhat difficult to do, you can fail to choose the best sound effects or music
or misjudge appropriate track levels during the mixing session, but, most likely,
anything you do is bound to be an improvement on the dry sound of the
unadorned picture edit.

In fact, sound effects and music will add a great deal to a film and can even
be more powerful and more immediate than the visuals. Sound adds presence
and reality to pictures. And it strengthens the mood of scenes and individual
moments within scenes by appealing directly to the ear and the heart.

Sound smoothes over uneven edits and polishes sticky moments. It can help
unify the flow of a film's images by bridging visual discontinuity between shots
(continuity errors or awkward juxtapositions). A loud sound effect or a distracting
musical score encourages us to ignore visual discontinuity—as happens in music
videos all the time. Not only does the sound seemingly distract the eye but, if it is
well-synchronized with the offending cut, it also tends to give the cut credibility.

Sound effects, music, and dialogue can be used to link different scenes
together. The sound of a train passing at the end of one scene is continued (with
a different perspective) into the next. This tells the viewer that the two scenes

are taking place in the same neighborhood, with the second immediately following the first without a break in time. A variation of this is the "cut on sound," which juxtaposes different effects that share a common element—such as the shrill keening of a high trumpet note and an ambulance's siren—forging a link between them. Think of the Hitchcockian edit where a train whistle is cross-faded with a human scream, linking the two sounds and also energizing the edit point itself.

Before going farther, here is a review of the audio postproduction sequence.

The audio postproduction sequence

The process of sound editing in film and video usually follows picture lock (or *pixlock*).[1]

Step 1: The sound editor screens the drama, scene by scene, and notes what effects are required. The director may also be present at this screening, which is known as the *effects spotting session,* in which case she will use the opportunity to present her vision of the project's sound world. On a large project, also present may be a sound designer, who may supervise or refine the project's whole audio landscape; a dialogue editor, who will prepare the dialogue tracks so they are "clean" and ready for mixing; a sound effects editor; and a music supervisor.

As soon as is practicably possible, the director will sit down with the project's composer and discuss where certain types of music should appear in the picture. A music supervisor and music editor are also often in attendance at this session.

Step 2: A sound editor prepares the film or video.

When working with film, the dialogue tracks and the ambience tracks from the picture edit are recorded onto separate *mag tracks* (reels of magnetic tape) and placed on *dubbers* (separate recording machines) that are synchronized to the picture. Additional mag tracks are created for the music and the sound effects. (The process of allocating different types of sound to different tracks is called *track-splitting.*)

In video, the tracks are *lifted off* (or *stripped*) from the edited master tape and *laid over* (copied) onto a digital audio workstation (DAW) or a computer equipped with one of a number of editing systems. As in film, extra tracks are created to receive the sound effects and music.

---

[1] Sound effects and music may occasionally be required before pixlock. Possible reasons for this are described in Chapter 36.

Step 3: *Sweetening*—Effects are selected from sound effects libraries and, if need be, created by a sound effects editor, sound designer, or by a *Foley artist* in a process described later in this chapter. These effects are placed at precise positions in the project (e.g., when a car starts on the screen it also does so on the sound effects track). In film, having the dialogue, sound effects, and music on separate mag tracks gives the editor control of the placement of each element, which he will later record onto a *master dubbe*r in Step 4.

In video, effects and music are placed in their appropriate tracks on a digital editing system's *timeline* (a computer file that organizes the material and displays it in chronological order).

Music is recorded or selected and integrated at this stage.

Step 4: *The sound mix* or *final dub*—In film, the *sound mixer* (or *rerecording engineer*), aided by sound editors (if available) and working off *cue sheets*, which are prepared by the sound editor, mixes all the audio elements together in the presence of the director or whoever is supervising the edit. In video, the sound editor himself may execute the mix on a digital editing system.

On a feature film with a great many sound effects, the sound mixer may select several edited effects tracks and premix them onto a single track called a *stem*. These stems are then used in the final mix, thereby reducing the total number of tracks.

In both film and video/DVD, the audio is mixed so that it may be used by a number of different sound systems, such as various surround-sound formats as well as simple stereo, and also so that dialogue tracks may be stripped out for foreign dubbing.[2]

Step 5: The mixed audio channels are combined with the pictures. In film, the sound tracks are taken to the lab, where they are placed on the celluloid alongside the pictures to form a composite print. In video, the mixed sound tracks are *laid back* onto the master tape by the sound editor at the end of the mixing session.

The "soundscape"

Sound may emanate from the shot in the form of dialogue or background sounds from the location itself. Or it may be specially constructed to comment upon or organize or complement what is seen on screen—e.g., voice-over commentary or narration or music and sound effects.

---

[2] Foreign distributors often request an "M&E" track—a track with just the film's music and effects on it, excluding dialogue—so they can rerecord the dialogue in their own languages.

In our industrial world, we are almost always surrounded by ambient sound. The absence of sound can be unsettling. The only time in my life I have experienced absolute quiet was twelve thousand feet up in the Himalayas. The effect was liberating at first and then a little disorienting. We rely on sound to inform us about our environment, and without those clues we can become lost.

On the other hand, as Robert Bresson remarked, the advent of sound allowed the cinema to discover silence. Silence on the screen is not conveyed by the absence of sound, but by the diminution of sound. A completely silent scene is lifeless and disengages our hearing so that we become conscious of our environment—the theater and other viewers.

A girl stands in her room and looks at herself in the mirror. The sounds we hear are distant traffic or a birdsong or the footsteps of her parents downstairs or her brother's stereo across the hall. If she is a Tibetan girl, all alone in a house in the Himalayas, we will still hear the rustle of her skirt as she moves and the gentle sound of her respiration. Or we may hear the eerie sound called *white noise* (the sound of all available frequencies combined at equal levels), reminiscent of a steady, Arctic wind.[3] Another effective way of representing silence, tellingly used by Ingmar Bergman in *Face to Face* (1975), and much imitated by others, is a soundtrack stripped bare of all but a ticking clock.

Audio engineers talk about the *sound picture* or *soundscape* because the arrangement of sounds suggests pictures. This link between our ears and our visual imagination is potentially powerful, and greatly extends a director's choices. If we walk in the countryside and hear a drone in the sky, we subliminally picture an airplane. If we are on a road and hear a siren, we picture a police car or an ambulance. Sometimes, sound can be even more vivid than pictures. In the opening of *On the Run* (2002), the first film in a trilogy by Lucas Belvaux, a prison escape is dramatized entirely by sound effects.

Since sound has the ability to evoke pictures, it is a pictorial element as well as an audio one. When sounds are combined with pictures, they add an extra visual layer, which can support what is on the screen or add additional information to it or occasionally even overwhelm it. It is its audio-visual quality that makes sound such a powerful element.

If sound is used to supplement the visuals, it helps the audience perceive a scene as "real." A woman walks down a path and we hear the clear, crisp tap of her footsteps. A silent radio on the kitchen shelf suddenly emits music. A crow

---

[3] White sound is also described as sounding like a household fan or the air being let out of a tire.

lands in a tree in the background and we hear its call. All these are sounds that are likely to be added in postproduction.

Audio is very effective at evoking states of mind. Hitchcock used music to suggest mental disassociation in *Spellbound* (1945). Coppola, aided by his sound designer Walter Murch, used a sound effects montage at the start of *Apocalypse Now* (1979), which contrasted jungle sounds with the urban sonic atmosphere of Saigon to convey the hero's displacement. In many horror movies, sounds are unnaturally heightened so that they become threatening. To a heroine hiding in a cupboard, every creak and footfall is as loud as an explosion.

Audio may comment ironically on the visuals as well. For example, a lilting ballad may be laid over a battle, casting an elegiac mood over the scene. The nineteenth-century waltz that accompanies the shot of the spaceship in Kubrick's *2001: A Space Odyssey* (1968) creates a lovely but unsettling effect. In Jaques Tatti's *Mon Oncle* (1958), various members of the family have different sounding footsteps that reflect their personalities.

Types of sound effects

Sound is particularly good at giving us clues about time and place. A well-chosen sound element can suddenly take us back or forward in time or transport us across the globe. Radio dramatists have known this for generations—radio drama stimulates imaginary pictures in a way that no other form can because sounds often bypass the rational mind and leap directly from the ear to the imagination.

The sound of a needle dropping on a scratchy record tells us that we are probably somewhere between 1920 and 1950. Hooves on cobblestones is a pre-automobile, nineteenth-century sound. The chirp of a robin is a summer morning sound. The sound of distant carolers tells us it is Christmastime. Sound effects are an elegant way of informing us about the time of day or year or the historical period.

Sound effects are also good at suggesting place. The sound of bombshells takes us to the battlefront. The sound of the alpine horn takes us to Switzerland. The sound of the bagpipe …

Natural sounds have an almost subliminal effect in placing us. Readily available sound-effects libraries are rich in generic *atmosphere* tracks of the natural sounds we might encounter in the countryside or an urban park. Library atmospheres with titles like "Countryside in winter" or "Prairie sounds" or "Northern lake in summer" provide initial background layers. Individual sounds may be added to these tracks or new atmos tracks can be constructed out of such individual elements as birdsongs, winds, insect sounds, etc.

There's nothing like a good "moo" from a cow to accompany a shot of a dairy. I once did a series that had a character who kept dogs. Not only did we lay the sound of barking over the shots of his house, but also, whenever and wherever the poor man appeared, we added the sound of distant terriers. It became his leitmotif.

When using library effects, be aware that just because a sound effect is labeled "Barn interior" in an index does not guarantee it is the precise barn interior you want. Listen critically to each suggested sound effect and be prepared to reject those that do not work. At the same time, discuss your reasons for rejecting it with your sound supervisor because, if you are lucky, he might be able to adjust the tonal quality of the effect during the mix so that it becomes satisfactory. He may, for instance, be able to turn a small barn into a larger one by adding reverberation.

Machine-generated sounds subliminally place us in a specific environment and are the urban equivalent of natural sounds. Sound effects libraries will offer such generic tracks as "City at night" or "Busy urban street." Ambient sounds such as computer buzz, refrigerator hum, and the whoosh of air-conditioning units permeate the urban landscape. There is invariably an airplane passing overhead or a car driving down a street.

Sound theorist Michel Chion further distinguishes two additional categories of sound effects, which he calls "On-the-Air" sounds and "Internal Sounds." On-the-Air sounds are a big part of our environment. They are the sounds of radio, television, telephone, and all recorded music.[4] Internal Sounds, on the other hand, emanate from within us. In a film they might include a character's heartbeats, breathing, and those voice-over moments when a character describes what he is thinking.

While most effects are added during sweetening, some elements have to be planned as far back as preproduction. If you know you are going to hear an orchestra tuning up in the background, you should record that sound before sweetening. (If you had hired an orchestra to play on screen, you would probably contract to record it tuning up as well.) If your drama is about a musician and your leading actor is miming to music (as in most musicals or shows about musicians), then the music tracks have to be recorded before the shoot begins.

---

[4] On-the-air music is often categorized as "source music," which is discussed in Chapter 36.

Most directors have favorite stories about creative sound-effects editors. Mine concerns the end titles of a production that were so long they exceeded the music we had recorded for them. I could have speeded up the titles, but then no one would have been able to read them. I could have re-started the music—a tune that had been electronically treated to sound like it was coming from a nineteenth-century organ-grinder—but just going back to its beginning without some kind of sound bridge was boring. We worked on the problem inconclusively for an hour and then broke for lunch. When we came back, we found that the effects editor had solved the problem. He had recorded the sound of his thumb running across the top of his comb, which sounded uncannily like a street organ clicking its way through its perforated metallic sheet before hitting the first note of a tune.

After several seconds of this effect we reintroduced the music and this time it worked!

Creating effects

Walla and wildtracks

Atmosphere tracks often require *human-vocal sounds*. Sound effect libraries offer basic tracks of laughter or conversation in such locations as theater lobbies or restaurants. Background hubbub in which individual words do not stand out is often called "walla." (Film and theater extras have traditionally murmured the non-plosive and non-sibilant phrase "walla-walla," which does not interfere with the main characters' dialogue.) If you have a crowd scene in your shoot, your sound recordist will almost certainly record "walla" on location. If, for some reason, walla is not recorded on location, it may be picked off an effects disc or produced by a group of players—a so-called "walla group"—supervised by the automatic dialogue-replacement editor. On the other hand, if you need a distinct human voice to provide a scream or to impersonate a radio announcer, you may have to hire a professional voice-over actor or come to an agreement with a radio station. (If you are tempted to record the voice-over yourself, check the union regulations for the area you are working in. You might need to be a member of an actors' union.)

Some audio elements, such as the crowd scene described above, are collected *during* the shoot. Your sound recordist should record wild atmos at every location. These wildtracks will be sounds that are specific to a scene or location. If you are shooting at a farm, the recordist may go into the barn and tape certain animal sounds. It is almost always preferable to use the specific sounds recorded on location than the rather generic, overused ones available on sound effects discs. Not many of us can tell the difference between various species of pig, but you might as well record the right one while it's at hand. (Someone in the audience can always tell the difference.) If you have been shooting near a school and the school bell and the chorus of children exiting the gates appear on your sound track, your sound recordist will want to get separate recordings of those to facilitate editing. If you are shooting a scene on a soccer field, a wildtrack of the referee's whistle is a must.

Foley

Individuals and/or companies that specialize in providing sound effects associated with human movement (footsteps, rustling of fabric, etc.) are called *Foley artists*. By walking on sand or concrete or gravel or other surfaces, while synching their movements to the moves of on-screen characters, these artists replicate footsteps. Do you want the sound of someone being punched to add reality to your fight sequence? The Foley artist might bring a large cabbage (or whatever her preferred object is) to the recording room and pummel it till the required effect is achieved. Do you want the sound of a smoldering cigarette? The Foley artist will press her thumb into a trough of dirt. Given enough time and money, there is no limit to the effects that can be created. The soft sounds of fabric and every chink of china can be layered in till your audio texture is rich and deep. The right Foley effect applied at precisely the right time is not only satisfying to the ear, it helps weld the viewer to the story. Moments when sound and picture come together with unusual force can be achieved by both a gifted film composer and a gifted sound crew, including a Foley artist. (Punching and stabbing sounds in Scorsese's films are often memorable. The very realistic stabbing sounds in *Goodfellas* (1990) were produced by Foley artists digging knives into raw meat.) Sound effects (particularly Foley sounds) also tend to punctuate a scene and thereby help to establish rhythm. Clear, crisp footsteps along a path or the rapid kicking of a karate fight add distinct rhythms to a scene and propel it forward.

The sound designer

The presence on some films of a sound designer can take audio to different level. Ground-breaking examples of sound design were Ben Burtt's work on *Star*

Wars (1977) and Walter Murch's work on *Apocalypse Now* (1979). Both were present at the planning stages and then worked with production recordists, picture and sound editors, composers, Foley artists, and mixers to create a unified and unique soundscape in harmony with their directors' visions.

The contemporary sound designer, however, has a more limited role than his 1970s predecessors. Rather than overseeing the whole soundscape, he is more concerned with the creation, manipulation, and organization of certain nonmusical sound effects during postproduction. When a film can't rely on effects libraries or needs to create "new" sounds beyond the scope of the sound effects editor or the traditional Foley stage—such as the sounds of new technologies or the speech of monsters in a science-fiction movie or the sounds inside John Malkovich's head in *Being John Malkovich* (1999)—a sound designer is hired to create these sounds. A sound designer may be employed to beef up common sounds—such as gunshots or fight sounds—in such a way that they become hyper-dramatic and larger-than-life. Sound designers may also be called in to "open up the frame" by designing unusual atmospheres or effects that emanate from outside the shot (e.g., a neighboring apartment in Los Angeles might have Mexican music playing in it and leaking through the wall into the in-shot apartment).

Strategies for placing sound effects

Directors go into the audio sweetening process with a general idea of what they want: "I want this scene to be busy." "I want to give the impression that there is a lot of activity in other parts of the building." "Let's keep this quiet with just the sound of the fireplace in the background."

A soundscape can be lean, containing little extraneous noise, thus heightening the audiences's concentration on few but important sound elements. Or a soundscape can be richly embellished with detailed and complex foreground, midground, and background sounds.

Because sound effects and music are usually selected or created after the shoot, they are slightly artificial elements whose choice and placement require good judgment from the director. Working on sound postproduction is a negotiation with perceived "reality." The director has to gauge how far to modify the reality of the location soundtrack. He may decide to heighten reality, as is often done in horror films. Or he may decide to create an artificial, alternative reality, as is often the case in science-fiction films. Or he may simply utilize the sounds that already exist on the location soundtrack or are suggested by the story or location's geography.

Having decided on a general approach—detailed or lean, heightened or natural—the director and the sound editor work to add relevant effects. The whole process can be slightly improvisational. If a soundscape feels too empty, someone will suggest a sound to fill it. If the tapestry of effects is somewhat dense, someone will suggest subtracting sounds from it. Gradually the scene becomes adequately covered and then, if time allows, it can be polished.

The only alternative I know to this procedure is one that was described to me by an audio supervisor. He said he once worked with a director who created a separate story *around* the one that had been shot. This separate scenario then generated its own effects and the director did not have to look beyond it. Here's an example:

Let us assume that the scripted scene, the one you have shot, is an interrogation that takes place in a small, windowless room attached to a detectives' office. It lasts about two minutes.

The scenario you make up to generate the sound effects is as follows. In the outer (off-screen) detectives' office, two policemen march a suspect to a desk. (Sounds of door opening and closing, footsteps, a chair dragged across the floor, and voices.) The suspect is questioned and a form is quickly filled out. (Sound of voices, a drawer opening and closing.) An emergency call comes in. Another detective takes it and races downstairs. (Telephone ring. Low conversation. The receiver is slammed down. Quick footsteps and a door slam.) Then two more detectives arrive. (Door opens and closes. Footsteps. A raised voice.) As soon as they get to their desk, there is a call. (Chairs. Telephone ring. Conversation.) The original two detectives take their suspect out the door to a cell. (Chair scraping. Footsteps. A scuffle as the suspect resists. Someone kicks a table. Handcuffs are taken out and applied. Raised voices. Door slamming shut.)

Of course, the audience will not be able to picture this scenario exactly or completely by listening to the sound effects. But, with luck, they will sense that something is happening—something more purposeful than just a general background wash of office sounds.

You should consider two principles when choosing and placing sound effects and music. First, sounds with irregular tempos tend to add tension to a scene. Andrei Tarkovski, who exerted unusual control over all aspects of the filmmaking process, used the sound of irregularly dripping water to increase unease. (It has become a much-imitated effect.) Continuous or sustaining sounds (the slow approach of a train, for example) tend to animate a scene less.

Second, high-frequency sounds tend to command our attention more than low-frequency ones. This appears to be a genetic trait that humans share with animals. High-frequency sounds tend to trigger our "fight and flight" mechanism. Those who doubt this principle should review Bernard Hermann's scoring of the shower scene in *Psycho*. In the scene in *The Godfather* when the young Pacino has to prove himself by killing a gangster in a restaurant, Coppola searched for something to give the moment extra "oomph" and also to illustrate Pacino's state of mind. His sound designer, Walter Murch, solved the problem with the screech of an elevated train making a turn.

Regularity versus unpredictability is very apparent in the film scores of Philip Glass (for example, *The Hours*, 2003), which combine repetitive themes with sudden changes in key or tempo.

When applying sound effects, bear in mind that the ability to hear high frequencies decreases naturally as we age. A really subtle, very high-frequency effect may be lost on the seniors in your audience. Good hearing is as important a sense as good sight, and directors should take care not to damage their hearing by exposing themselves to loud sounds, such as explosions or over-amplified music. The great William Wyler, who severely damaged his hearing while filming aboard bombers during the Second World War, became totally reliant on others in this area. "You are my ears," he told Leon Becker, his sound recordist.

Automatic Dialogue Replacement (ADR)

Dialogue can be recorded on location, as filming takes place, or it can be recorded in a studio after the visuals have been edited. Automatic dialogue replacement (ADR) is the process by which actors attempt to recreate in a controlled recording environment the delivery of their lines during production— often a less than optimal recording situation. They do this by watching their on-screen performances as they rerecord their lines. ADR involves trying to time a phrase or sentence being played back through headphones so that it perfectly syncs with on-screen lip movements and other gestures—a process that is not only technical, but requires actors to imitate the original production track (the *guide track*) recorded at the location. An imitation of the original is almost always second best to the original. Performances recorded at the time, on location, have a credibility and spontaneity that is hard to recapture. Dubbing the dialogue weeks or months after the event is just not the same. This is why directors should attend ADR sessions to help the actors keep their lines alive.

Achieving good ADR also requires time to perfect the performances and more time during the mix to construct a convincing background atmosphere.

The argument in favor of ADR is that an enormous amount of time is wasted on location either waiting for quiet or having to reshoot because of audio problems. This argument resonates with some of us who have spent very many hours of our lives in suspended animation waiting for a break in traffic or planes to pass by overhead so we can resume shooting. Furthermore, the number of assistants required to stop traffic and other peripheral noise inflates the size of the production unit. The noise problem is especially intolerable in cities, where dialogue has to compete with police sirens, drills, and similar raucous urban sounds.

Shooting a dialogue scene in the middle of a major city without resorting to ADR is almost impossible. Television series ostensibly set in New York or Chicago (*Hill Street Blues, NYPD Blue, ER*) or London and Manchester (*EastEnders, Coronation Street*) may have some establishing shots taken in the proper city, but the actual exterior scenes are filmed on studio lots where the sound environment is more controllable.

Unfortunately, many productions have strict deadlines and only superficial sweetening is possible. On lower-budget productions, the audio editing crew often consists of simply the director and a sound supervisor (and, occasionally, an effects editor). However, it is amazing the results a creative sound supervisor can produce with a good effects library and a well-programmed synthesizer.

36. Music

Music, that most powerful of organizers, can appear in two different ways in a dramatic project.

1) It can arise from within the scene as part of the location or action as, for instance, a radio or jukebox or violinist practicing in the next apartment. This is known as *source music*.

2) It can appear as a composer's underscoring of the picture, an enhancement of or comment on what is going on on-screen.

In both cases, it will probably be added during postproduction, because playing music while shooting a scene may well cause audio-level and continuity problems.

Source music

Music of any description will inevitably cast its influence over a scene. If your scene takes place in a bar or a restaurant, you can use source music to set the mood. You can select romantic music for a love scene or punk rock for a fight (or vice versa if you want to be ironic). If you are working with a composer, then include her in the process of choosing source music because she will be interested in all the music featured in the project.

Music can change halfway through a scene, mirroring a change of mood and tempo in the scene itself. Finding the correct volume level is important with source music, and sometimes you must push it deeply into the background with the superimposition of other sounds, such as people talking.

If you plan to add source music or any loud sound to a scene, you should remind the actors to speak up. Whispering won't work if the blare of a military band is going to be added in post. If you have a recording of the music that will be added (or a track that is similar), playing it during the final rehearsal can help the actors can find the level at which they have to pitch their voices. Raising one's voice to compensate for a sound that will be added later is a technical adjustment that most actors find tricky, so you may have to remind them to sustain the appropriate volume in multiple takes.

Jukeboxes and military bands tend to be background sounds, but source music can also appear in the foreground of a scene. It can be the nightclub piano or orchestra to which your main couple is dancing. It can be the saxophone that the Charlie Parker character plays in *Bird* (1988).

Let's look at the specific example of a disco scene. First of all, the music you use will dominate the scene as surely as if your composer scored it (which he might have, if it is an original musical), so care must be taken when choosing it. The background music is going to be very loud, but, if the scene has dialogue, you cannot play the music during the take. So you play it briefly before the shot starts to remind the dancers of the tempo and rhythm, and the speaking actors of the level at which they have to project. Playing back music on location before each shot is a time-consuming process, and you are very reliant on the efficiency of the sound department. Occasionally, if the director thinks it's necessary, source music can be played at a very low level in the background during a take, in the hope that the final track will drown it out. However, to do this requires faultless judgment on the part of the sound recordist, because, if the location track is not drowned out by the overdubbed track, you will not be able to cut between different takes.

If you have your source music at hand during the picture edit, it can be assigned a track and synched to the picture. If not, it will be added during the sweetening stage of post. The level of the music in relation to all the other sounds in the scene will be set during the mix.

Copyright

Music almost always has copyright implications. Copyright may not concern you if you are only making your project for yourself and your friends or fellow students. But as soon as it leaves the classroom or your intimate circle for public viewing, copyright has to be considered. Note that there are people whose job it is to police the airwaves and other distribution systems to ensure that music rights are enforced.

If you hire a composer to create original music for your drama (as discussed in the following section), then copyright issues will be addressed in the contract. This is usually the most straightforward and convenient arrangement from a copyright standpoint. However, if you want to use music that has already been recorded (such as that found on commercially released CDs, tapes, and records), the copyright situation can be complicated and surprisingly expensive.

In theory, copyright in the United States expires seventy-five years after the composer's death (and fifty years in Europe). This means that if you want to use a march by John Phillip Sousa, you should be free to do so in 2007. However, copyright extensions and other issues complicate the matter. I once heard a prominent Hollywood copyright lawyer declare that he considers a piece of music is potentially problem-free if the composer has been dead for over two hundred years. This means that Beethoven's music is not yet in that category.

Consider this scenario: A filmmaker wants to make a short film with an anti-war message and decides to include forty seconds of music by her favorite rock stars, including her main character singing along to The Beatles' "Let It Be" on the car radio. She intends to submit the film to various festivals and, hopefully armed with prizes, seek wider distribution. Her first step proves successful: She garners awards at two significant festivals. (Festivals are considered private showings and do not *usually* require copyright clearance.) She subsequently receives an offer to have the film screened on television, and there is talk of including her piece in a video collection of anti-war "shorts." However, the cable network and the video producer both require copyright clearances, which she does not possess.

After the Herculean task of producing the movie, she assumes that obtaining copyright clearance for forty seconds of music will not be too difficult. However, certain complications arise. First, she discovers that she has to obtain permission from the record company, which not only wants its own fee but also charges her on behalf of the musicians who played in the original recording. (Both fees are part of the "master use license.") Then she finds she has to negotiate with the publisher of the song as well. (This is the "synchronization license.") The negotiations are detailed and protracted and, in the end, the fee is one hundred times greater than the expense of making the original film. She tries to find alternative sources of music, but none sound as good as her first choices. And then there is that shot of her hero specifically singing "Let It Be."

Pop music is very appealing because it instantly conveys a broadly understood mood and a period. There is no better way to establish the 1940s than to play appropriate big band music or the 1960s than by playing appropriate rock. The young director cited above might have been imitating Martin Scorsese, who has used pop music very effectively in many films, including *Goodfellas* (1990) and

Casino (1995). He states that he starts the process by looking for "holes" (moments when the soundtrack needs musical embellishment) during editing. "So I start to fill those gaps in a very simple way. I go to the period of time that that scene is taking place — 1962 or '63, let's say. I'll check all the popular music from '63 back to '55 and figure if anything like that can be heard. Then I narrow it down to a few songs I like. And within that I make further choices, particularly based on the lyrics … I don't want the lyrics to hit too literally on the nature of the picture."[1]

If you have a limited budget and want to include existing music, research its rights costs before you use it. In rare instances, certain music companies will waive their fees because they consider they are getting excellent publicity for new or up-and-coming artists, but most commercial tracks are not cheap. And a track by The Beatles (such as "Let It Be") will obviously be very much more expensive than a track by a less-well-known band. The context in which the music appears in your movie is also significant. For instance, if your chosen music track is associated with a character committing murder or suicide, the owner of the copyright might be reluctant to grant you permission, regardless of your bankroll. It is helpful to have a music supervisor who can negotiate copyright on your behalf. Otherwise, if you have the resources, you can hire someone who specializes in music clearance.

Working with a composer

All music, and especially music specifically composed for a project, can do three things:

1. *It can directly reinforce the action on the screen.* The speed, danger, and exhilaration of a chase sequence can be underlined. A passionate love scene can be intensified. A climax can be emphasized. John Williams' scores for many Steven Spielberg and George Lucas movies work on a number of levels, but they all unfailingly succeed in capturing and reinforcing the spirit of what is happening on the screen. However, as composer David Bell has observed, "If deep, multi-dimensional dramatic content doesn't exist somewhere within the film, the music can't fabricate it."[2]

2. *It can bring out themes inherent in the scene and/or play a scene's subtext.* Many of the great musical scores, including those of John Williams, have

---

[1] "Martin Scorsese's Comfortable State of Anxiety," *Movie Maker*, Fall 2002, Issue 49, Vol. 9, p. 66.

[2] David Bell, *Getting the Best Score for Your Film* (Beverly Hills: Silman-James Press, 1994), p. 2. I am grateful to Mr. Bell for his clear elucidation of these three functions of underscoring.

themes or "leitmotifs" that represent certain characters or places. These themes tend to appear whenever the associated character or location does, but may also appear in their absence and thereby evoke them. A good example is Howard Shore's score for *The Lord of the Rings* (2001). Among the themes he develops are those associated with place (the "Lothlorien" and "Isengard" themes), and those associated with people and relationships (the "Arwen and Strider" theme, as well as the haunting "Fellowship" theme). He also has themes associated with the ring itself. (It is interesting that the leitmotif approach was first developed by opera composer Richard Wagner for his nineteenth-century mythic epic *The Ring Cycle*.)

Subtextual scoring comments obliquely on the events being portrayed and places them in a different light. Thomas Newman's score for *Road to Perdition* (2002) deliberately emphasizes the American-Irish, folkloric aspect of the story. Elmer Bernstein's score for *Far From Heaven* (2003) helps create that film's retrospective, 1950s atmosphere. Another example (taken from Danny Elfman's score for *A Simple Plan*, 1999) is of three men counting the millions of dollars they have just discovered in a crashed airplane. The men joke about the discovery, but the underscoring is somewhat somber, suggesting that the matter is more serious than they think. This unsettling, or "foreshadowing," effect is quite common.

3. *It can play against the action in the scene*. This is an exhilarating effect, but also one that is not easy to achieve. It seems to work best at extreme or climactic moments when opposing impulses seem to attract each other. Stanley Kubrick used one of the sweetest movie musical songs — "Singin' in the Rain" — to underscore a brutal moment in *A Clockwork Orange*. Martin Scorsese used a plangent operatic intermezzo to accompany a boxing bout in *Raging Bull*. And soaring strings and choral music were the audio background for many of the realistic battle scenes in Terrence Malick's *The Thin Red Line* (1998), suggesting epic and universal significance. Musical "playing against" defies expectation and surprises an audience. In many respects, it is the equivalent of the acting strategy of "playing against" described in Part 3, Chapter 16.

Finding a composer with whom you see eye to eye is important. To contact a suitable (and affordable) composer, professional directors can contact agents, listen to demo reels, and then meet their top choices. Student directors may be able to contact student composers from a music school. Once you have aesthetically connected with a composer, and assuming you enjoy music, the rest is sheer pleasure.

Sergei Eisienstein, whose collaboration with Prokofiev on *Alexander Nevsky* (1942) and *Ivan the Terrible* (1942–6) is one of the most celebrated in cinema, was not limited to one approach. There were scenes where he arranged the shots around the music, and sequences where the music was composed to the pictures. When trying to describe certain effects he wanted, Eisenstein resorted to metaphor: "At this point the music must sound like a mother tearing her own child to pieces." "Do it so it sounds like a cork rubbed down a pane of glass." When words failed, he provided still images from the film itself. If music is central to the film—as with a musical or a music video—it should probably be composed first. When Sergio Leone planned his innovative spaghetti westerns in the 1960s, he took the unusual step of asking Ennio Morricone to compose the music before he started shooting. The music, in turn, inspired the sequences.

The most common procedure is for a director to approach a composer and explain what he wants. The composer then starts thinking about styles and themes and begins to construct the bare bones of a score. Before going much farther, she will need to see some visual material. The director may invite her to the set during shooting or show her selections from the rushes or ask her to view a rough cut, which will not reflect the final, edited timing of these scenes. Obviously, the composer has to know the exact duration of the sequences she is composing, so she generally waits for picture lock before getting down to actually completing the score. The director tries to arrange his collaboration with the composer so that she is not kept waiting for picture lock.

However, on rare occasions, the score, or parts of it, may be required before pixlock. A sound house working on a project with a tight deadline may want the music in place for the rough cut, in order to anticipate later trackwork. Directors also like to know the approximate mood and tempo of the music they will be using so that they can edit to them. The composer may help by providing either a preliminary piano or synthesized recording of her initial theme ideas (a *scratch track*). A common alternative is for the director, working with the composer, the picture editor, and probably the music editor and sound supervisor, to construct a *temp score*, which may utilize music by the chosen composer as well as other composers. One way of doing this is to edit together tracks from extant CDs. Thus, if you want Russian-style music for a scene in your movie, you might choose a track from a balalaika CD. You could then edit to this track, which would eventually be replaced by the composer's original track during the final mix.

It is very easy to be seduced by a temp score you have heard many dozens of times during editing. Music by Phillip Glass was used as the temp score for *The Hours* (2003), and was subsequently retained as the actual underscoring (for which it received an Oscar nomination). Once, when working on a scene with a particularly evocative temp track, I became so attached to the music that I had to be convinced by the editor and the producer to accept the composer's excellent replacement.

At some point before the final audio mix, the music score is recorded. Whether the music director (who is often the composer on a low-budget venture) is working with a small group of professional musicians or a full symphony orchestra, try to attend the score's recording session. This is a late stage for a director to have much substantial input, but if the recording session time is not too limited, the director may ask the composer to make small changes on the spot. Usually, the director comments on the mood and texture of the sound. ("It's too dark at that point. Can we lighten the mood a little?") And specific cues may need to be changed. ("That trumpet call comes too late. Can it come in at the moment he raises his arm?") When time is not so pressing, the director and composer may have the opportunity to step into the sound booth and critique a rough mix of the orchestration, sound effects, and dialogue. If session time is available, you may also want to work with the composer on recording extra material, such as alternative versions, isolated themes, and "stings" (short musical phrases that can be used for dramatic effect) derived from the full score. Watching a group of professional studio musicians strive to provide the very best music for your project is an experience you will not want to miss.

Alas, few of us get to work with John Williams or the London Philharmonic. Most of the time, directors work with small groups of musicians or just one composer and his synthesizer. Low-budget producers prefer the independent-contractor arrangement with the composer whereby he composes, arranges, and plays all the music in his attic on his synthesizer or hires musician friends and pays their fees from his own all-in composing fee.

Original music is most directors' preferred option, but it can be expensive. (Though, in major production centers, such as Los Angeles, many young, untried composers are eager to work for low wages.) At its most inflated, an original score requires payments to the composer, the arranger, the copyist, the musical director (if different from the composer), the music supervisor, union musicians, the recording studio, and the engineers. There are alternatives.

Discs

One way to avoid the problem posed by copyright (for both professionals and students) is to license music from a collection of generally inexpensive, pre-cleared tracks called a music library. (Music libraries obtain music from composers who agree to sell off ownership of their music to the library.) There are a variety of music libraries publishing their collections on discs or via the web. Although convenient, in my experience, these libraries fail to provide the right track more often than they succeed. They are certainly no substitute for a good composer when it comes to wit, charm, and specificity.

In addition to music libraries, a number of individual compilation CDs are available. Want a track that sounds like The Beatles, but are unwilling to pay the huge amount for an original? Go to a CD with ersatz Beatle tunes. Generally, payment is by "needle drop" (the particular track you choose) and duration (how much of the selected track you use).

If you are using one of these off-the-shelf tracks for background music, it can be laid down in three ways.

1. You could front-time the track—that is to say, you start the track at the same time the scene opens. This works if the track has a particularly striking opening that you feel energizes your scene. Otherwise, this strategy can appear too obvious—after all, only queens and presidents enter a room exactly when the band strikes up.

2. You could choose a section from within the track. If the scene is one-minute long and the track itself lasts two minutes fifteen seconds, the director and editor may choose a one-minute segment that starts, for instance, twenty, thirty, or forty seconds into the track.

3. One of the most satisfying ways to use background music is to back-time it. In this arrangement both music and scene conclude at the same time. It is less obvious to the viewer than front-timing, and adds a sense of finality to the end of the scene.

Mixing

The mix is the culmination of the audio postproduction process. It is the time when all the various sound components are balanced and then recorded onto the master tracks. On a big-budget movie, three or more mixers/editors may work together—the dialogue editor, the effects editor, and the music editor—with a specialist sound mixer actually controlling the overall mix. On small-scale productions, such as an episode of a television series, there may only be the sound supervisor or the supervisor plus an effects editor. I've always appreciated the ease of communication and personal rapport that working with a single supervisor allows. On shows that have not had a strong union presence, I've also been able to go into the sound booth and record Foley effects as well as provide background voices. This is one of the pleasures of low-budget production.

Sound mixers are usually experienced professionals who are both technically proficient (operating the mixing board, adjusting levels, equalizing sounds, applying audio compression to increase a sound's perceived overall intensity, and other audio tasks) and unusually objective about analyzing the results of their work. On a lengthy project, such as a movie or a multi-episodic serial, the mixer must also be able to maintain a consistent quality of sound over a period of days or weeks.

Regardless of a mixer's expertise, the director is ultimately responsible for the project's audio. The director must monitor the sound quality as the editors and mixers meticulously prepare, rehearse, record, and (inevitably) re-record each audio segment. This requires a good deal of sustained concentration, since ten or fifteen minutes can pass without anything to do before an important decision is suddenly required. This way of working does not suit everyone and people have been known to get frustrated. I know of one edit suite in Los Angeles that supplies its clients with a dartboard to allow them to vent their frustration. In London, BBC sound supervisors used to present directors with a baby's activity board (complete with bells, mirrors, and lots of things to push and pull) to keep them occupied between decisions.

The director must be prepared to ask the mixer to make many adjustments to the levels or the sound quality till he is fully satisfied with the effect. Bear in mind as you do so that a rich sound is not effective if it obscures a primary sound element, such as dialogue. If your magnificent montage of swamp sounds (frogs, cicadas, surfacing catfish, etc.) overwhelms the foreground dialogue, then the montage probably needs to be pruned or attenuated. Sound effects and music are usually at their most evocative when supporting action or dialogue. Music and sound effects may also sometimes fight with one another, causing the director to choose one over the other.

At one time, a huge distinction was made between mixing for film theaters, which benefited from large speakers, and television sets, which had inferior mono ones. When mixing for TV, we used to switch off the main speakers in the suite and listen to the mix through a pair of tiny ones (with a "tinny" sound). Very often, so much detail was lost by the small speakers that we had to remix an entire scene to allow essential sound elements to maintain the foreground on the TV speakers. Television audio has improved significantly over the years to the point where hi-fi is now common and surround-sound readily available. But poor speakers still exist, and the director and the mixer must often produce a compromise soundtrack suitable for different formats.

A note on post-partem depression

The end of the mixing session can be a time of dislocation for the director. The project on which you have been working for months or years is rapidly drawing to a close. The audio crew may be talking about their next gig and you may not have a project immediately on the horizon. Under these circumstances directors can feel a little low. If you feel depressed, you can comfort yourself with the fact that almost everyone who has been dedicated to a creative project over a long period of time experiences the same feeling. It does not last beyond the start of the next project.

PART 7

A Brief History of American Screen Acting

37. The Russian Connection

Knowledge about the development of screen acting will make you more aware of acting trends. It will improve your interaction with actors and place your own style of working with them in a context.

The history of film acting is a huge and fascinating subject. In a book of this size we can only attempt an overview—an introduction to the story of twentieth-century acting in the United States and the discovery of ways to apply the techniques of stage acting to film.

Stanislavski

The history of modern acting begins at the turn of the twentieth century, when the Russian actor-director-teacher Konstantin Stanislavski (1863–1938) brought a new standard of psychological realism to the stage. A tendency toward realistic stage interpretations of human experience was discernible throughout Europe in the late nineteenth century—at the Theatre Libre in Paris, the Independent Theatre in London, and the Freie Buehne theater in Germany. Stanislavski himself had been greatly influenced by the attention to historical detail displayed by the Meiningen Court Theater when it played in Moscow. But he applied a new realism standard so rigorously to design, production, and, especially, acting, that he created a revolution. Almost all Western acting in the twentieth century was influenced by Stanislavski, by individuals either accepting and extending his theories or rebelling against them.

Of the famous Moscow Arts Theater (MAT), which he co-founded with the playwright-director Nemerovitch-Dantchenko between 1897 and 1898, Stanislavski wrote:

> We protested against the customary manner of acting, against theatricality, against bathos, against declamation, against overacting, against the bad manner of production, against the habitual scenery, against the star system which spoiled the ensemble, against the light and farcical repertoire which was being cultivated on the Russian stage at that time.[1]

The list of playwrights produced by the Moscow Arts Theater included Henrik Ibsen, Gerhart Hauptmann, Maxim Gorky, and, above all, Anton Chekhov. These productions went to unusual lengths to create a sense of reality on the stage. Cast and crew carried out extensive research, borrowed authentic props from museums, and rehearsed at original locations. For their production of *Othello*, for instance, the whole cast actually traveled to Cyprus to gain a sense of the island on which the play was set. This emphasis on realism is important because the scrupulous concern with props, settings, costume, make-up and all aspects of production is shared by modern film. A century later, Oliver Parker's *Othello* (1995) was actually shot in Cyprus.

The nineteenth century, which had begun with the towering classical performances of John Philip Kemble, Edmund Kean, and William Charles Macready, ended with a melodramatic style that was declamatory and "external." Stanislavski described the traditional manner of playing the stock figure of the romantic Russian knight:

> For these there exists a specific manner of walking, wide gestures that are established once and for all, traditional posing with hands on the hips, a mighty heave of the head to free it from the falling waves of their hair, a special manner of holding the hat, which is mercilessly crumpled for the mechanical strengthening of passion, brave vocal attempts at the high notes of the register, and a chanting diction in the lyric places of the part.[2]

Stanislavski admired the great contemporary actors of his period who brought depth of characterization and extraordinary technique to their work (Mikhail S. Shtchepkin, Glikeria Fedotova, Eleonora Duse and, above all, Thomaso Salvini, whose performance of *Othello* is vividly described in Stanislavski's autobiography *My Life in Art*). However, he lamented the lack of formal actor

---

[1] Konstantin Stanislavski, *My Life in Art*, trans. Elizabeth Reynolds Hapgood (London, New York: Eyre Methuen, 1991), p. 330

[2] Ibid. pp. 192-3.

training available in Russia. He set out to remedy this by making the Moscow Arts Theater a conservatory as well as a playhouse, and by writing down his theories of acting. What became known as the "Stanislavski system" is encapsulated in three books—*An Actor Prepares*, *Building a Character*, and *Creating a Role* [3]— which deal with actors' emotional and psychological training, physical training, and the application of this training to specific roles. The books are conceived in the form of an imaginary dialogue between a teacher and his students. His writing is detailed, down-to-earth, and very readable.[4]

Although Stanislavski's principles were particularly suited to the "naturalistic" plays of the period, they were intended to help actors in all theatrical genres. He was concerned with showing actors how to bring their own experiences and personalities to a role, so that a performance was not merely superficial posturing. A performance, which is, after all, *pretense* (an actor pretending to be a writer's portrayal of someone else), could nevertheless be *truthful* if the actor were so convincing that she persuaded the audience to believe she was real. Stanislavski realized that in order to do this, the actor had to first convince herself of the reality of the character. Many of his techniques, especially in *An Actor Prepares*, are concerned with forging a strong link between actor and character.

"The mistake most actors make," he wrote, "is that they think about the result instead of about the action that must prepare it."[5] When they were on stage, his Moscow Arts Theater actors concentrated on what their characters were trying to achieve in a scene, and how they were physically accomplishing it. In a remarkable section, in *Building a Character*, he offers his technical thoughts as he delivers a speech from *Othello*:

> "*Like to the Pontic sea* (whose icy current and compulsive course keeps due on to the Propontic and the Hellespont …)
>
> "I must take care not to hurry. After "sea" I shall make a tone rest.
>
> "It will last for two, at most three, notes.

---

[3] Stanislavski actually conceived the first two books as one, entitled *The Actor's Work on the Self*. However, they were originally published as separate volumes. Recent editions have corrected this error.

[4] English translations (especially those by Elizabeth Hapgood) may have made Stanislavski more readable than he actually is. Jean Benedetti asserts, "When he sat down to write about his methods, in his effort to be absolutely clear, he relentlessly crossed all the 't's' and dotted all the 'i's,' thus achieving the very opposite of what he wanted." (Jean Benedetti and Alice L. Crowley, *Stanislavski and the Actor* (Routledge, NY: Theatre Arts Books, 1998), p. viii.)

[5] *An Actor Prepares*, p. 117.

"When I come to the next rests (there will be many of them) I shall begin to raise my voice more.

"I shan't take the highest note yet."[6]

The passage continues in this vein for five pages. Stanislavski did not want his actors to strive for empty, abstract effects. They were not to try to be "noble" or even to be "angry." Nobility and anger were to emerge as a result of characters interacting with the circumstances in which they found themselves. His system introduced a logic to the training of actors, based on the principal that "Whatever happens on stage must be for a *purpose*."[7]

One of the first things an actor had to do was fully imagine her character. "Never allow yourself externally to portray anything that you have not inwardly experienced and which is not even interesting to you."[8] He advised his students to begin with the "given circumstances" of a play, and then to bring their imaginations to bear on them. The given circumstances of *Othello*, for instance, include the military occupation of the island of Cyprus, the chain of command that places Iago below Othello, Roderigo's hopeless infatuation with Desdemona, and the color of Othello's skin. Actors must find ways of personally identifying with their characters by imagining episodes from their characters' lives, by trying to understand their characters' thought processes, and by recalling episodes from their own lives when they have felt or acted similarly (Stanislavski's "emotional memories"). An actor thus creates her role in an act of disciplined creativity, which is as important as the work of the director, and even that of the writer. To produce a performance, a play's "given circumstances" must interact with an "inner chain of circumstances" that an actor has created.

Stanislavski, a contemporary of Freud, was interested in the psychological aspects of acting technique. For instance, the idea of utilizing "emotional memories" was derived from the work of the French psychologist Theodule Ribot.[9] But beyond this, Stanislavski believed that all the conscious, disciplined, technical work carried out by his actors served to access their wells of unconscious creativity. He said he strove for "unconscious creativeness through conscious technique."[10]

---

[6] *Building a Character*, p. 167.

[7] *An Actor Prepares*, p. 35.

[8] Ibid. p. 50.

[9] Emotional memory intrigued other artists and thinkers of the period, including Marcel Proust.

[10] Ibid. p. 29.

Stanislavski was not preoccupied with mental preparation to the exclusion of the physical. He was well aware that actors required extensive training in areas such as voice, posture, and articulation. Although his works primarily deal with the classes he himself taught on acting technique, they constantly refer to the physical training that was going on concurrently at the school. (Long passages in *Building a Character* deal specifically with movement, diction, and intonation.) And, as his notes about the speech from *Othello* quoted above indicate, he was very much concerned with providing a technical approach to underpin the mental and emotional exercises. As a matter of fact, his interest in pure technique increased as he grew older, and his later writings lay considerable emphasis on it.

In *Creating a Role*, which takes us through preparation for three roles and serves as a recapitulation of his principles, he suggests that creating "the inner circumstances" might follow upon creating the outer, physical ones. In other words, experiencing how a character carries out certain tasks and interacts with other people might precede recreating his inner life. This change in emphasis—dubbed "the method of physical actions"—led Stanislavski to begin a rehearsal with improvisations instead of with the usual discussion of character and text. Finding the physical action (or "business") that best expressed the author's intention became the first object of rehearsal, and character developed from that. An important corollary of this shift in emphasis was that, while still stressing the importance of imagining oneself in the circumstances of the play, he no longer placed such a strong emphasis on emotional memory.

Stanislavski's training methods evolved during the course of his lifetime, but the core insights, especially those elucidated in *An Actor Prepares*, came to be known as "the Stanislavski system," and form the foundation of most modern actor (and director) training. (They have also formed the basis for the discussion of rehearsal in Part 2 of this book.) The term "The Method" is sometimes used synonymously with "the system," but, as we will see in Chapter 39, "The Method" more precisely describes a particular interpretation of Stanislavski developed by the American teacher Lee Strasberg.

Stanislavski's successors

The work of Stanislavski and his Moscow Arts Theater (MAT) stimulated a torrent of theatrical activity in Russia. The years prior to, during, and immediately following the Russian Revolution (between 1906 and 1928), when the first generation of his pupils began extending his principles, was a period of unparalleled energy and experimentation. Describing the work of some of these individuals is important because the theories and styles they developed are influential to this day.

Michael Chekhov, the actor and teacher (and nephew of playwright Anton Chekhov), identified three influential Russian directors who followed Stanislavski. The first, Eugene Vakhtangov, who was born in 1883 and died thirty-nine years later, was a protégé of Stanislavski. "You, Eugene, teach my Method better than I," the master told him.[11] Vakhtangov used the system but, like many of Stanislavski's best pupils, he also adapted it to reflect his own concerns.

Vakhtangov felt restricted by the MAT's naturalism that subjected everything to the test, "Is it truthful?" He looked for a style that was more "theatrical," which combined inner truthfulness with a more exaggerated external quality. "In the theater, there must be theater," he proclaimed, and dubbed his new style "fantasy realism" or "fantastical realism." This style was at its most distinct in his production of Strindberg's *Erik XIV*, in which he abandoned historical realism in favor of an approach where every gesture was carefully composed for maximum theatrical expressiveness.

Vakhtangov's students vouched for his perfectionism, and his audiences appreciated his humor and lightness of touch. "There is always a little laugh or two in his sad plays," wrote Michael Chekhov, who had played the title role in *Erik XIV*, "and always a little tear or two in his comedies."[12]

Vakhtangov left no recordings for posterity, so being specific about his style is difficult. He did, however, direct *The Dybbuk* in the last year of his life, for the Jewish "Habimah Company" in Moscow. It is possible that a grain of his spirit lingers in the wonderful 1938 Yiddish-language Polish film of the same play, also made by a Jewish company. I believe his vision lingers in movies that bravely introduce elements of the theatrical to cinematic naturalism without sacrificing character depth—movies like *Citizen Kane* (1941) and *Mephisto* (1981) and many works by such filmmakers as Bergman, Altman, Fellini, Kurosawa, the Coen brothers, and Mike Leigh. It is an impressive heritage.

Second on Chekhov's list is Vsevolod Meyerhold (1874–1940). Though trained in the MAT, Meyerhold was in many respects the antithesis of Stanislavski and Vakhtangov. He was an uneven genius, but his work had a considerable influence on twentieth-century theater and film. Like Vakhtangov, he reacted against Stanislavski's pure naturalism. But his reaction was so extreme

[11] Ruben Simonov, *Stanislavski's Protege: Eugene Vakhtangov* (New York: 1969), p. vii.
[12] Michael Chekhov, *To the Director and Playwright* (Westport, CT: Greenwood Publishing Group, 1977), p. 54.

that it led to an entirely opposite style. Meyerhold staged performances in sets that were pared down to a symbolic minimum. He rejected Stanislavski's naturalistic, psychological acting style, replacing it with a purely physical style he called "biomechanics." His actors underwent severe physical training to become clowns, acrobats, and jugglers all rolled into one. The text itself was no longer of primary importance. What mattered to Meyerhold was that a revolutionary message be communicated through dramatic motion.

Meyerhold's emulators included some of the early Russian filmmakers, and his inspiration is also apparent in the work of Bertold Brecht and such modern filmmakers as Godard and, perhaps, Fellini. This is not a style that caught on in Hollywood, though I think it may have surfaced in the Expressionistic worlds of *Modern Times* (1936) and *Edward Scissorhands* (1990). Sadly, during the Stalinist era, when socialist realism became the officially accepted style, Meyerhold's productions attracted criticism and he was sent into exile and executed.

The third post-Stanislavskian director on Chekhov's list is Alexander Tairov (1885–1950), of whom he wrote, "For him the focal point of a performance, the criterion, was whether the spectator would accept it and be immensely impressed."[13] Tairov was not a disciple of Stanislavski, though he briefly studied with Meyerhold. He emphasized scenic design rather than actor interpretation. Once he had a conception for a production, everything including the acting was subordinated to it. If the resulting style was somewhat like a pantomime, he carried it off with a mixture of flair and great attention to detail. Tairov is the prototype of the commanding director who is primarily concerned with spectacle and effect. His film lineage would include Cecil B. De Mille epics and the special-effect-laden productions of James Cameron.

Eisenstein

Naturalistic film acting has become so well established in the West that it is easy to think of it as the only available style, but this is not so. In Russia, for instance, a group of theorists and filmmakers developed a very different approach. It is important to consider their work in order to be aware of at least one alternative to naturalism, and also because their influence is still occasionally felt.

During the period immediately after the revolution, when experimentation in all the arts was encouraged in Russia and theater admission was free, a movement arose that combined both spectacle and the principles of Meyerhold. "Proletcult" offered audiences circus-like performances and the stylized, physical

---

[13] Ibid.

movements of biomechanics. Prominent among Proletcult directors was the young Sergei Eisenstein (1898–1948). His plays were performed in a style similar to what has become known as "agitprop" (literally, "agitation" and "propaganda," it is a form of art and theater that promotes a particular political or social position), with actors portraying capitalist figures succumbing to proletarian forces. As a student of Meyerhold, he insisted his actors undergo physical training. The plays themselves consisted of loosely structured scenes in a variety of styles (music hall, circus, Grand Guignol,[14] projected film) intended to achieve their points via a cumulative effect. The director himself was not so much concerned with the details of performance as with controlling and shaping the sequence of actions. Eisenstein took enormous liberties with his texts, staged scenes on and off the stage, and did away with the curtain in order to keep the flow of action uninterrupted. It was, quite consciously, a form of theatrical montage.

Eisenstein was also influenced by Japanese *kabuki* theater (he was studying Japanese at the time) and the nascent art of film. The film industry in Russia, immediately after the revolution, suffered from a shortage of film stock. To make the best use of this precious material, the government established a State School of Cinematography, among whose teachers was the influential Lev Kuleshov (1899–1970). Kuleshov's approach to acting was largely external and mechanical. Actors, occasionally aided by the director, would identify a feeling or emotion and then find a mechanical sequence of movements to express it. According to the film director Pudovkin, Kuleshov gave commands like "jut out your chin, open the eyes wide, bend or raise the head …"[15] Kuleshov believed that the effect created by an actor's performance was not as important as the order in which the director placed the shots. He argued this point with a matinee idol called Polonsky, and the two of them agreed to carry out an experiment.

Kuleshov and Polonsky improvised two short scenes. In the first, Polonsky portrayed a long-term prisoner who is suddenly offered the opportunity to escape. In the second, he was a starving beggar who was shown a bowl of soup. When Kuleshov edited the two scenes, he swapped the crucial closeups showing Polonsky's reactions. The shot of the beggar reacting to the soup was inserted into the prison scene at the point when the prisoner first sees the open cell door, and vice versa. According to Kuleshov, the audience could not tell the difference between the two reactions.

---

[14] Grand Guignol was a melodramatic, excessive style popular at the turn of the twentieth century. It dealt with sanguine and frightening subject matter. Its cinematic equivalent was the "Hammer Horror" movies of the 1960s.

[15] Vsevolod Pudovkin, *Film Technique and Acting* (London: Grove Press, 1970), p. 144.

This was a significant experiment for a number of reasons. It strongly suggested that the position of actors in film was very different from theater. As long as actors gave a director a variety of expressions, the director could assemble them into a meaningful whole—so the director was not reliant upon a sustained performance. Actor training for film could therefore be a physical process not unlike the training advocated by Meyerhold. It also confirmed the primary importance of the director in film, because it was the director who constructed the story through the juxtaposition of shots.

Eisenstein believed montage was a universal principal that was exemplified in film. His reasoning was along the following lines: When we think, don't we piece together separate thoughts and memories that have a cumulative meaning? When actors work on their roles, doesn't "inner technique" consist of evoking and then piecing together separate imaginary episodes from their characters' pasts to produce the required emotion (emotional memory)? And isn't film itself exactly this kind of accumulation of individual moments and scenes? He wanted his actors to produce the most dramatic physical expression of the agreed-upon emotion. Actors, for Eisenstein, were like figures in a painting. They evoked feelings, while the director actually brought them to life by assembling and juxtaposing them.

This is an entirely different process from traditional theatrical performance. As an example, let's look at the way "transitions" are accomplished. Transitions, of course, are those moments during a performance when an actor changes in front of our eyes: changes purpose or emotion or demeanor. They have been called the jewels of a performance because they are, to some extent, tests of an actor's ability. However, transitions in montage tend not to be accomplished by actors changing in front of our eyes, but by the cut. We show a happy crowd of smiling individuals. Then we cut to a line of soldiers lifting their rifles. Then we cut back to the crowd, which is now startled and afraid. The transition has occurred via the second cut. In fact, the director does not even need to cut back to the actors themselves—he can show fear and disarray through details like a hand nervously opening and closing, a head turning, or a pram rolling out of control down some steps.

Eisenstein was not interested in traditional "bourgeois" acting styles. In *Battleship Potemkin* (1925) he employed untrained actors who gave him natural, non-theatrical performances. As long as they provided him with the expressions he required, montage would take care of the rest. Also, since he was not interested in sustained performances, he was free to cast according to looks rather than ability. Remember, this was the era of the silent film—movies were exclusively visual. Directors often made their points by cutting to expressive faces, so non-actors who simply had the right physiognomy could be used. Thus, if Eisenstein were casting the part of a wealthy merchant, he could choose someone who appeared self-confident and well-fed; if he was looking for a revolutionary, he could cast someone young and bright-eyed. The idea was that the characters became distillations of character types. This technique, used by many Russian directors, came to be known as "typage."

Nicolai Cherkassov starred in *Alexander Nevsky* (1938) and *Ivan the Terrible* (1944) and had the dubious privilege of accompanying Eisenstein to a meeting

Fig. 37.1: Cherkassov acting in Eisenstein's *Ivan the Terrible*

with Stalin to assure him of the ideological purity of their work. (Stalin, however, may have over-estimated Cherkassov's influence on Eisenstein.)

Cherkassov had begun his career in the theater in St. Petersburg, where he had been trained in the naturalistic MAT style. Eisenstein must have appreciated both his striking demeanor and his willingness to adapt his performance style. By the time they worked together on *Ivan*, Eisenstein had sufficient confidence in him to delegate direction of his scenes to an assistant. Cherkassov's performance is primarily external and physical, conforming to a dominant directorial vision. Each shot requires a specific stance and/or look. The eyes are used to considerable effect, staring straight ahead or darting to the left or right. The voice is always deep, resonant, and formal. Every element is premeditated, and there is none of the spontaneity and freshness we expect from contemporary Hollywood performances. Eisenstein's direction often consisted of sketches the actor was supposed to study and embody, and Cherkassov was diligent in doing this. In the famous final sequence of *Ivan the Terrible* Part 1, where he waits for the citizens to call him back to Moscow (see Fig. 37.1), he was forced to find and hold a particularly difficult position. In his *Notes of a Soviet Actor*, he complained about having to "practice long and tiringly to produce the tragic bend of Tsar Ivan's figure" and of Eisenstein treating his actors "like wax dummies." Cherkassov dominates the other characters in the film, but without Eisenstein instilling what he called "living feeling" through montage, the film would be a series of stunning but lifeless set pieces.

The significance of Eisenstein's work

The beauty of Eisenstein's images and the effectiveness of his sequences influence directors to this day. One immediately thinks of the pram tumbling down the stairs of Grand Central Station in Brian Da Palma's *The Untouchables* (1987), which is a reference to the Odessa Steps sequence from *Battleship Potemkin*. Indeed, whenever montage is artfully used to achieve a particular effect, such as the opening dream sequence of Ingmar Bergman's *Persona* (1966) and Malcom McDowell's fantasy in Stanley Kubrick's *A Clockwork Orange* (1971), among many others, that director is, to some extent, invoking Eisenstein's work, even if she is not using precisely the same technique.

With his background in Meyerholdian "proletkult" theater, and his emphasis on physical movement and posture, Eisenstein represents the opposite end of the spectrum from Hollywood naturalism. The tension between naturalism (realism in drama) and stylization has always existed in the theater. Eisenstein is one of a small group of filmmakers (including the German Expressionists, Fellini, and others) who remind us that this tension is potentially present in film as well. It may be that some filmmakers in the future will seek to introduce a more physical and stylized form of performance to the screen. If they do, they will draw inspiration from Sergei Eisenstein.

38. Silent Film Acting

In 1912, when she was nineteen years old, American silent screen star Mary Pickford made a short movie called *The New York Hat*. The story is simple. Mollie (Miss Pickford) is a young woman whose mother dies, leaving her an inheritance to be administered by Minister Bolton, the town's handsome clergyman (played by Lionel Barrymore). When Mollie needs a new hat in order to attend the Sunday service, her stepfather refuses to indulge what he perceives as her vanity. Minister Bolton, however, views this as an opportunity to discharge his responsibility and purchases the New York Hat for her. Unfortunately, this starts tongues wagging in the town, and Mollie is snubbed by the townsfolk and scolded by her stepfather. In desperation, she visits the minister to find out what she has done wrong and is followed inside by a group of indignant parishioners. Minister Bolton produces the letter from Mollie's mother and the crowd is appeased. When the furious stepfather enters, he too is shown the letter and is mollified. Then, once the townsfolk have departed, Minister Bolton proposes to Mollie, who at first tries to run away but then changes her mind and asks her stepfather's permission to accept. This time her request is granted.

Although the movie features actors who were to give notable performances in other films, the acting of Mr. Barrymore and Miss Pickford stand out. Hers, in particular, is a performance without a trace of the exaggeration one associates with silent movies. She remains perfectly natural in all her scenes, responding genuinely and spontaneously to every turn of events. If we look at the final scene in the minister's house, we can see that she acts credibly "in the moment," in a way that would do credit to a contemporary actor.

In Fig. 38.1, the minister shows the letter to the crowd assembled in his study. Mary Pickford, on the left-hand side, absorbs the revelation. She does not react "dramatically" by throwing up her arms, she does not even turn to the camera— she remains perfectly in character.

Fig. 38.1

Fig. 38.2

Fig. 38.3

Fig. 38.4

Fig. 38.5

In Fig. 38.2, her stepfather confronts the minister. Mollie is weeping, but she has transitioned so subtly that we only gradually become aware of it through the perfectly natural gesture of her wiping her cheek with her hand.

In Fig. 38.3, the minister restrains her as she tries to run out of the house. This is the only time in the scene that she is turned fully to the camera. Again, her emotion is not overplayed.

In Fig. 38.4, Mollie asks her father if she can marry the Minister. The framing, with the Minister standing so artificially close to them, stretches our credibility. Credibility is also stretched by the stepfather's exaggerated reaction. But Barrymore and Pickford themselves remain perfectly natural and at ease.

In Fig. 38.5, Mollie accepts the minister. This is her fourth emotional transition within two minutes in the same scene (and probably in the same continuous take), and it is perfectly credible.

This is not the style of acting we commonly associate with the silent cinema. It suggests that good screen acting is timeless, and that silent screen acting deserves our serious consideration.

Performance trends in America at the turn of the twentieth century

The theatrical revolution in Russia, which started in the late 1890s, was not to impact America for another twenty years. Acting west of the Atlantic was still rooted in nineteenth-century traditions, and early film acting, with its histrionics and vocabulary of gestures, was no exception. Mary Pickford described the style of acting she encountered in the industry as "the French school of pantomime"—by which she means it was influenced by the example of Francois Delsarte and his followers.

Francois Delsarte (circa 1812–1871) was a brilliant young Frenchman who had studied the relationship between physical posture and meaning. His premature death meant that his acting system was taught in a narrowly formalized way by his followers. In New York, two schools claimed to teach his technique, but the training at both consisted of simplified and external gestures. Agony, for instance, was portrayed by putting the weight on the back of the left foot, placing the fingertips of both hands on the back of the neck, and letting the head roll on the left shoulder. Unsatisfactory as they were, the Delsartian schools at least represented a step toward formal actor education.

For most of the nineteenth century, actor training in the United States had been haphazard. Many people came to the stage via such musical arts as opera, ballet, and music hall. This was perfectly logical because theater in those days, like silent film, was always accompanied by music. The need to make oneself clearly understood in a large hall and above a live orchestra encouraged a style of acting that was not intimate. Some actors underwent an apprenticeship with theatrical companies that consisted of learning, by imitation, how to play certain roles. There was no sense of a living American tradition of acting. Many of the most visible performers were foreigners touring the country, and among these the vast majority were English. As Stanislavski had lamented, performance was centered on gesture, and gesture had become formal and meaningless for the actor.

Realism as a literary movement, exemplified in the novels of Dickens, Balzac, and Zola, manifested itself in the theater as naturalism. As noted in the previous chapter, acting companies in some European cities specialized in naturalistic performances. Certain individual actors also embraced a style that was considered realistic by the standards of the day. One has only to look at surviving footage of performances by the two theatrical legends Eleanore Duse and Sarah Bernhardt to appreciate the remarkable restraint of the former. At the turn of the twentieth century, there arose a group of American actors who were influenced by the new realism. Among them were Richard Mansfield, Louis Calvert, William Gillette and, most notably, Minnie Madden Fiske (who came to be known simply as Mrs. Fiske), who worked to create controlled and truthful performances drawn from personal experience.

The early years of the new century were also marked by a new style of theatrical production, at once both grandiose and realistic, epitomized by the Broadway producer David Belasco. Belasco's productions were noted for their spectacular theatrical effects, such as the on-stage blizzard in *The Way of the West* (1905). But his productions also showed a remarkable attention to detail. In *The Easiest Way* (1909), a boarding-house room was reproduced in minutest detail and, when staging plays set in Japan and ancient Rome, his actors were encouraged to rehearse in kimonos and togas to become accustomed to them. A similar mixture of spectacle and realism is characteristic of many silent films (and modern ones too), and the great silent movie director D.W.Griffith was referred to as "the Belasco of motion pictures."

Belasco and many theater actors of the time were contemptuous of the cinema. How could one act under circumstances that allowed for very little rehearsal and involvement in two or more movies a week? How could one possibly give a performance under the stop-go conditions of film shooting? These are, of course, fundamental questions about cinema acting that are relevant to this day. (Some students in theater schools across America and Europe are still convinced of the inferiority of film.) Fortunately, a good number of actors were willing to take a risk with the new medium. A significant initiative was the formation in Hollywood in 1912 of The Famous Players Film Company, which included well-known artists from both stage and screen. Mary Pickford and John Barrymore were founding members, and they were joined by a succession of theatrical luminaries that included James O'Neill (Eugene O'Neill's father) and Mrs. Fiske herself. Alla Nazimova, an acclaimed actress from St. Petersburg and an early product of the Stanislavski system, also appeared in a number of Hollywood films between the late 'teens and the early 1940s.

D.W. Griffith and the rise of Hollywood

Sometime between 1909 and the completion of Griffith's epic *Intolerance* in 1916, film acting changed. This fact was apparent to contemporary filmgoers. As early as 1912, critic Frank Woods, writing about the cinema of three or four years earlier, observed, "In those days the actors were told to 'step high' in walking or running. Each player called by gesture on high heaven to witness each assertion. Talking, gesticulating, and grimacing at the camera was the constant habit."[1]

The demise of American film acting's version of "the French school of pantomime" may well have been due to the influx of fresh talent, as Mary Pickford would have us believe, but there may also have been other reasons. The predominant style of acting gradually shifted toward naturalism nationwide and the movies may have experienced the effects of that.

By 1909, fictional narrative had asserted itself as the dominant film genre and began to be the object of innovation and screen stories became more character-driven—a trend that demanded a higher level of acting. Also, a large portion of the production section of the film industry relocated to the West Coast in 1910, prompting a shift in relationship with the parent-company executives who remained in the East. Up until then, most film work was done in and around New York City. This made sense—Broadway provided a stream of talent, and the movie pioneer the Edison Company was located in New Jersey. For a while, the logistics of filming made Fort Lee, New Jersey, just across the Hudson from New York, the center of the industry. The move to Los Angeles distanced the film companies from the inspiration of Broadway, but it also distanced the directors from the day-to-day interference of the owners. On its own in a new land, the industry was free to develop in its own way.

One person above all others was prepared to take advantage of this freedom— D.W. Griffith. Griffith was an itinerant actor who drifted into movies. By all accounts he had not been the most effective of thespians. When he asked Billy Bitzer (who was to become his trusted cameraman) whether he should cross over to the other side of the camera, Bitzer resolutely advised him against it because "I couldn't see how a man who was not a passable actor could direct a flock of geese."[2] By the time the bulk of the U.S. film industry moved westward, Griffith had directed hundreds of one-reel, twelve-minute films for the Biograph Company and was secure in his craft.

Griffith initially responded to Southern California by widening his shots to include more of the open landscape of this then-sparsely-populated region. However, he soon became increasingly interested in the fundamentals of storytelling and performance. He followed the example of pioneer editor Edwin

---

[1] Quoted from Janet Staiger, "The Eyes Are Really the Focus," *Wide Angle*, Vol. 6, No. 4, p. 19.
[2] Eileen Whitfield, *Pickford: The Woman Who Made Hollywood* (University of Kentucky, 1997), p. 83.

S. Porter, who had broken the convention of shooting everything in one long master shot by editing in shorter sequences. Griffith was one of the first directors to introduce single shots of individuals. And, from singles, he progressed to the facial closeup—an innovation that drew howls of protest from the executives, who insisted they were paying to see the whole of an actress, not just part of her. The closeup is the shot that really distinguishes film acting from the theatrical because it requires great subtlety in the interaction between performer and camera. Griffith said: "We're striving for real acting. When you saw only the small, full-length figures, it was necessary to exaggerate acting, what might be called 'physical' acting, the waving of the hands and so on. The closeup enabled us to reach real acting, restraint, acting that is a duplicate of real life."[3]

With a company of actors that included Pickford, Lilian Gish, Mae Marsh, Henry Walthall, and Robert Harron, Griffith could provide the simplicity and truthfulness his new shots demanded. It is still thrilling to experience the intense intimacy of an early closeup with someone like Gish.

Griffith saw the advantages of a more natural acting style, and his films gradually reflect this. There are remarkable passages of effective understated acting in his two great movies of this period, *The Birth of a Nation* (1915) and *Intolerance* (1916), but he is not consistently naturalistic. His work is characterized by a plurality of acting styles—from the melodramatic to the naturalistic. Mary Pickford complained about his lack of realism, and both she and Lillian Gish objected to the energetic way he wanted them to portray children, which Gish described as "a St. Vitus dance." Nevertheless, when working with long-term associates, he was able to draw out remarkable performances. Mae Marsh's acting as an ex-gangster's wife in the contemporary storyline of *Intolerance* is moving to this day. In the scene in which she finds her father dead, Griffith had criticized her initial performance: "I don't know what you were thinking about when you did that, but it was evident that it was not about the death of your father."[4] In a process remarkably similar to Stanislavski, he urged her to bring her own feelings to the part in order to make it real.

Many of the styles and practices of present-day moviemaking were created in the silent era, but the silent films were a law unto themselves as well. The speed of turnaround made preproduction in the modern sense unachievable.

---

[3] Robert E. Walsh, "David W. Griffith Speaks," *NYDM*, Vol. 71, No. 1830 (January 14, 1914). Reproduced in *The Classical Hollywood Cinema* by David Bordwell, Janet Staiger, and Kristin Thompson (New York: Columbia University Press, 1985), pp. 190-91.

[4] Mae Marsh, *Screen Acting* (Phot-Star Co., 1921), p. 79.

Griffith walked around with his pockets stuffed full of notes to which he rarely referred. He ran, in a sense, an extended directorial improvisation. Rehearsals occurred, but they were usually rapid and primarily concerned with finding the right positions on the set, rather than with acting. The noise from carpenters and crew was constant, even during a take. Throughout, the director stood beside the camera calling out instructions to his actors. The effects could be dazzling as far as transitions were concerned. Silent screen actors and actresses had the ability to change from tears to laughter and back again in the blink of an eye—all in response to the director's instructions: "Now laugh … Now cry!" Claire McDowell, recalling Griffith standing by the camera, said, "He'd cry, laugh—he'd simply draw it out of you." But Griffith, in particular, could also be sensitive and insightful. In one scene, he gave her the impressive directorial adjustment: "You're standing amid the ruins of everything you've tried to do. Ashes all about you."[5]

Looking at these early efforts, probably projected now at speeds faster than intended, we often have difficulty appreciating their true quality. Applying the standards of modern naturalism to films that had no sound and consequently required expressive gesture to assist the storytelling is unfair. Griffith was a source of inspiration for filmmakers worldwide, including Eisenstein.

Nemirovitch-Dantchenko, the co-founder of the Moscow Arts Theater, wrote a letter of appreciation to Lillian Gish that included the sentence, "A combination of the greatest sincerity, brilliance, and unvarying charm places you in the small circle of the great tragediennes of the world."[6] And Stanislavski himself was said to have approved of the acting of the noted theatrical and silent-screen actress Laurette Taylor.

---

[5] *Pickford*. Ibid. p.91.
[6] *Lillian Gish: the Movies, Mr. Griffith and Me*, Gish, N.J. (1969) p.293.

39. The Legacy of the Russians

Change cannot often be traced back to a single event, but the tour of the Moscow Arts Theatre to America in 1923 is a case in point. By the time Stanislavski and the MAT had completed their first visit, the seeds had been sown for a profound change in the style of American acting. Reviewers marveled at the vividness and realism of the company's performances and regretted that such a system of actor training was not available in their own country. The troupe was immediately called upon to provide teachers, and over time many of the foremost members of the MAT emigrated to the United States. This group included Richard Boleslavski, Maria Ouspenskaya, Leo and Barbara Bulgakov, and Michael Chekhov, all of whom began teaching and performing not only on the stage but in films as well. A young actor called Lee Strasberg saw every MAT production. He was so inspired that he sold his share in the family business and auditioned for Boleslavski and Ouspenskaya when they opened their school in New York.

Boleslavski's influential book *Acting: The First Six Lessons* is a distillation of his teaching. It takes the form of a dialogue over a number of years between Boleslavski and a young actress he calls "The Creature." It is not as detailed as Stanislavski's works, and it lays particular emphasis on certain techniques. For example, Boleslavski encourages The Creature to recall powerful memories and, when she wonders if she has memories that are strong enough, replies, "Plenty of them—just waiting to be awakened, just waiting for a call. And what is more, when you do awaken them, you can control them, you can make use of them, you can apply them in your craft."[1] This was a version of Stanislavski's emotional

---

[1] Richard Boleslavski, *Acting: the First Six Lessons* (New York: Routledge, 1949), p. 42.

memory, a technique Stanislavski started to de-emphasize some time after the American tour. For Boleslavski, it was number two of his six lessons and, therefore, taught early on. Strasberg, who was also to make emotional memory central to his own system, quit Boleslavski's American Laboratory Theatre before completing the second half of the course, where the emphasis turned from memory to physical action.[2] However, the excitement Strasberg experienced at the American Laboratory Theatre was palpable thirty years later, when he wrote, "Boleslavski said in his first talk, 'We posit a theatre of real experience. The essential thing in such experience is that the actor learns how to do, not through mental knowledge, but through sensory knowledge.' Suddenly I knew, 'That's it! That's it!' That was the answer I had been searching for."[3]

Boleslavski eventually left New York for Los Angeles, where he was joined by a growing number of influential MAT teachers including Ouspenskaya and Michael Chekhov. In Hollywood, he directed a number of films, including the Oscar-nominated *Les Miserables* (1935), starring Frederick March and Charles Laughton. His directing technique consisted of close script analysis and working with his actors to find their overall objective or "spine," though he subsequently also experimented with improvisation to evoke greater spontaneity.

The Group Theater

In 1931, Lee Strasberg joined producer Cheryl Crawford and theater historian (and later distinguished director) Harold Clurman to found The Group Theatre. The work of this company is chronicled in a number of books, notably Clurman's *The Fervent Years* and Robert Lewis' *Slings and Arrows*. The Group Theatre applied the Stanislavski system to new works, and its production style was emulated by other companies throughout the country. Clurman lectured and discussed theory with the actors while Strasberg led them in exercises concerned with visualization, improvisation, and, of course, emotional (or, as he termed it, "affective") memory.[4] But, gradually, dissatisfaction with Strasberg's methods set in. Stella Adler, one of the most prominent actors in the company,

---

[2] Richard A. Blum, *American Film Acting* (Ann Arbor: University of Michigan Research Press, 1984), p. 24.

[3] Robert Hethmon, ed., *Strasberg at the Actors Studio* (London: Theatre Communications Group, 1966), p. 145.

[4] Ibid. p.109. Strasberg said, "Affective memory is not mere memory. It is memory that involves the actor personally, so that deeply rooted emotional experiences begin to respond."

visited Stanislavski in Europe and brought back copious notes and a chart that explained the latest incarnation of his continuously evolving system. Her version of Stanislavski, which emphasized physical action and downplayed emotional memory, was in direct conflict with Strasberg's, and a rift ensued that led to his departure from the company.

In Strasberg's absence, The Group found new creative personalities. Adler herself subsequently became an important teacher, Clurman began his distinguished directing career, and such prominent actors as Luther Adler, Morris Carnovsky, Robert Lewis, and Sanford Meisner received enhanced status in the organization. It found in Clifford Odets (*Waiting for Lefty*, *Awake and Sing*, *Golden Boy*) and other young playwrights works that were to ensure its continued success into the early 1940s. Much of actor training in the United States today has evolved from the teaching of individuals involved with The Group Theatre. One of its alumni, Elia Kazan, went on to Hollywood and achieved considerable success with such films as *A Streetcar Named Desire* (1951), *On the Waterfront* (1954), and *East of Eden* (1955). In Hollywood, Kazan drew upon a new generation of young actors who were associated with his and Lee Strasberg's next enterprise—The Actors Studio.

Kazan arrived in a Hollywood that was receptive to his ideas. The major studios had early realized that talkies required a different kind of acting from silent films. Suddenly, actors had to perform without a director guiding them through the scene: They had to memorize lines, and they had to work on sets that became eerily quiet when it was time to shoot. From 1933 onward, the major studios began to hire dialogue coaches to work with specific actors on specific roles and drama coaches to train their young contract players. The coaches themselves required a technique to underpin their work, and they naturally gravitated toward the Stanislavski system. Independent acting teachers, such as Boleslavski and Ouspenskaya, also began to arrive in Hollywood, and in 1941 several former prominent actors from the Group Theatre founded the influential Actors' Laboratory.

Acting in the early talkies

In the thirties and forties, casting directors often looked for actors with theatrical experience. At this time, performance style was somewhat broader than it is now, so the transition from stage to screen was considered an adjustment that could be learned in a short time.

Bette Davis, who had briefly attended drama school and taken classes with Martha Graham (one of the founders of American modern dance), had a uniquely expressive, unsentimental style. She believed, "It may take a little time and some guidance for the stage actor to become accustomed to the degree of projection which will be most effective on screen," and added, "the camera will often reflect what a man thinks, without the degree of demonstration required in the theatre."[5]

Spencer Tracy, another great movie actor, also came to Hollywood via the stage. Tracy did not discover his vocation until he attended college after serving in the navy during the First World War. He went on to study at the American Academy of Dramatic Art, then worked extensively in stock companies and occasionally appeared on Broadway. It was seven years before he made his first movie, and he was thirty-seven before he achieved star status. Tracy gave perhaps the pithiest and most quoted advice on film acting: "Turn up on time, know your lines, and don't bump into the furniture."

On the other hand, Lawrence Olivier, who gave a memorable performance in his first film, *Wuthering Heights* (1939), found the transition agonizing. "How do you want it?" he pleaded with his director, William Wyler. "I've done it calm, I've shouted, I've done it angry, I've done it sad, standing up, sitting down, fast, slow—how do you want me to do it?" "Better," replied the taciturn Wyler.

In the end, Olivier adjusted his successful theatrical style to the cinema, and received an Academy Award nomination. This first brush with Hollywood also taught him another lesson: "I haven't yet the authority to boss the director, [and] he is the chap who has all the fun … The sum total of an actor's work in a picture depends entirely upon the arbitrary manner in which the director puts together his mosaic."

As in our own day, actors have always gravitated to the cinema from a variety of sources. The Stanislavski system was highly influential in the field of drama, but it probably meant little to W.C. Fields, who came from vaudeville, or Jeannette MacDonald, who had apprenticed in stage musicals. Many of the great film actors of this period (1930–1954) had limited formal training, but created an impression through a mixture of ease, charm, and good looks. Gary Cooper (would-be political cartoonist), Jimmy Stewart (ex-architecture student), and Cary Grant (ex-stilt-walker), made minimal concessions to character in their movies and gave, essentially, variations on a single performance. This is not to

---

[5] Alan Lovell & Peter Kramer, eds., *Screenacting* (London: Routledge, 1999), p. 37.

disparage their work. Many value this quality very highly. Lee Strasberg commented, "The simplest examples of Stanislavski's ideas are actors such as Gary Cooper, John Wayne, and Spencer Tracy. They try not to act but to be themselves, to respond or react. They refuse to do or say anything they feel not to be consonant with their own characters."[6]

Lee Strasberg and The Actors Studio

Elia Kazan, Cheryl Crawford, and Robert Lewis established The Actors Studio in New York in 1947 in an attempt to perpetuate the traditions of The Group Theatre. In 1949, after Lewis's departure, Strasberg was invited to teach there, and two years later he became its artistic director. Strasberg's thirty-one years at The Studio, teaching his version of Stanislavski that became known as "The Method," is one of the most fascinating and controversial episodes in acting history. Supporters of The Studio point to the very long list of successful and talented actors who passed through its doors, first in New York and subsequently in the Actors Studio West. (The names of some of the most prominent are mentioned below.) They note the unusual intensity, power, and freshness of its best practitioners. And they also note its success in both theater and film. Opponents of The Method have criticized Strasberg's reliance upon emotional memory. They claim that many method actors are more concerned with their emotions than the clarity of their speech. As Lewis observed, "If crying were the sole object of acting, my Aunt Rivka would have been Duse."[7] And they accuse Strasberg of inappropriately addressing acting problems with possibly dangerous psychological solutions, thereby exceeding what is permissible in a teacher.

No one can deny The Actors Studio's influence on American acting, especially in film. To this day, to be "a method actor" is considered a slightly controversial identity, evoking the early, daring, naturalistic performances of Marlon Brando, Montgomery Clift, and James Dean. What are the characteristics of Method performances? Strasberg laid great emphasis on relaxation, believing that spontaneity and creativity flow most easily from a body that is at ease. Concentration is also important because it strengthens the powers of observation and enables actors to create the illusion of reality. Strasberg said, "Everything is concentration! Everything involves concentration!"[8] And building on this is a

---

[6] Quoted from Jeffrey Meyers, *Gary Cooper: American Hero* (New York: Cooper Square Press, 1998), p. 156.

[7] Robert Lewis, *Slings and Arrows* (New York: Applause Books, 1984), p. 281.

[8] *Strasberg at the Actors Studio*, p. 159.

highly developed ability to recall specific sensory impressions and emotional memories: An actor who can recall the specific circumstances surrounding a past emotional event will be able to produce that emotion. When doing this, the actor should not try to concentrate on the emotion itself (that will lead to superficiality), but on the sense memories and circumstances that caused it in the first place.

Although Kazan had directed in Hollywood in the 1940s, it was his work in the '50s with Actors Studio graduates that introduced a new, intense level of realism to the screen. His films of this period, starring Brando, Karl Malden, Eva Marie Saint, James Dean, Rod Steiger, Julie Harris, and others, retain their magic to this day. Later generations of method actors, or actors strongly influenced by Strasberg's work, include Dustin Hoffman, Jane Fonda, Al Pacino, Jack Nicholson, Robert DeNiro, Robert Duvall, Sally Field, and many others. While overestimating the impact of The Method on Hollywood acting may be difficult, I must note that many of these famous actors were initially trained by other teachers. An early teacher of both Dean and Nicholson, for example, was Jeff Corey, a blacklisted actor who had worked with Michael Chekhov. Corey stressed the ability of actors to find most of the personality traits of their characters within themselves, whether they are playing Hitler or Peter Pan—an approach that has clearly helped Nicholson adapt himself to a number of outlandish roles.

Many of the twentieth century's great acting teachers appeared in movies. Toward the end of his life, Strasberg appeared in *The Godfather Part II* (1974), *The Cassandra Crossing* (1977), *And Justice for All* (1979), and *Going in Style* (1979). In *The Godfather Part II*, he illustrates many of his own principles. He gives a supremely relaxed performance, yet at the same time it is intensely concentrated. In one scene in the film, he is found on his bed with his shirt off, watching the TV, and we feel we've been given a privileged insight into his private existence. (In his classes, Strasberg worked on getting his students to achieve the effect of a "private moment.") There are clear "actions"—he is always doing something for a purpose. And, although he is playing a Mafia boss, therefore, a very powerful person, his performance is consistently understated. Is Strasberg using emotional memory? The scenes do not call for strong emotions, and yet the whole performance is suffused with a kind of paternal attitude. One wonders if, especially in scenes with the young Al Pacino, he isn't recalling his own memories of fatherhood.

Michael Chekhov

Michael Chekhov was chosen by Namirovitch-Dantchenko and Stanislavski to head the Second Moscow Arts Theater. Though they had theoretical disagreements, Stanislavski admired and encouraged his work. According to Chekhov, the disputes centered on the degree of identification the actor was supposed to have with the character. Chekhov took the attitude that too close an identification with a role could be limiting for an actor. To counter this, Chekhov laid great emphasis on visualization. "My technique then, as now, was to imagine the character as being *outside* of me and to ask myself what I would do, and how, if I were in his circumstances."[9]

Chekhov's acting was a *tour de force*. Robert Lewis, observing his performances in New York in 1935, felt that he was watching "total acting" for the first time:

> By that I mean each part Chekhov assumed was minutely executed from the point of view of physical characterization—the walk, the gestures, the voice, the makeup—all were meticulously designed to illuminate the character he was playing. Even more remarkable was that, at the same time, his emotions were full, all equally chosen, and experienced according to the minds and hearts of the personages he acted. Here was the supreme example of the complete "inside" coupled with the complete "outside," each deriving from the other. Never again could one willingly accept the proposition that emotion was all-important, and that if one felt truthfully, characterization would take care of itself.[10]

When Chekhov left Russia, he went first to England, where he taught at the experimental Dartington Hall school, and then to the United States. He appeared in movies, notably Hitchcock's *Spellbound* (1945), in which he gives a performance of extraordinary variety, humor, and control, executed with a choice of vivid physical actions (for which he was nominated for an Academy Award). When he started teaching in Hollywood, he gathered around him a group distinguished by its lively, open, and physical response to roles. Among its members were Akim Tamiroff, Anthony Quinn, Yul Brynner, and Jack Palance. Chekhov's example provided, and still provides, one of the few proven alternatives to strictly naturalistic work in Hollywood-style films.

---

[9] Michael Chekhov, *To the Director and Playwright* (New York: Proscenium Publications, 1963), p. 49.
[10] *Slings and Arrows*, p. 81.

John Cassavetes and Mike Leigh

Between 1959–1984, maverick filmmaker John Cassavetes made a series of low-budget movies with remarkably intense performances. Cassavetes had attended drama school in New York City in the early 1950s, where he had become aware of the ferment being created in acting circles by The Actors Studio. His early work as an actor was largely in television drama, where he joined a group of young directors and actors that included Sidney Lumet, John Frankenheimer, Arthur Penn, James Dean, Paul Newman, Rod Steiger, and Sidney Poitier. Television was a rigorous training ground in which performances were created with minimal rehearsal and then recorded live. In his own films Cassavetes avoided such practices. He tended to favor character over plot and allowed his actors a high degree of creative freedom. Honesty and realism were important to him, and he collected around him a group of actors, including Peter Falk, Ben Gazzara, and his wife, Gena Rowlands, who responded to his demanding standards.

Cassavetes believed in extending the circumstances of the film into real life. In *Husbands* (1970), for instance, he worked to create an off-camera comradeship between his male characters that could be transposed to the screen. He also demanded an unusual dedication to the project in hand. Here is how he describes the making of the emotional *A Woman Under the Influence* (1974): "At night we'd collapse, make coffee, then start talking about the work.... We'd wake up in the night and talk some more. It was that kind of total commitment."[11]

Cassavetes, with his aversion to traditional Hollywood filmmaking—its separation between cast and crew and its inflexible shooting schedule—is the quintessential independent filmmaker. Although he died prematurely in the mid-1980s, his work is relevant today as the low cost and adaptability of small-crew digital filmmaking make his vision of performance-centered production a real possibility.

Cassavetes' use of improvisation and his creation of an off-camera environment to support on-screen relationships has been developed by British filmmaker Mike Leigh. Cassavetes usually wrote his screenplays prior to production, but Mike Leigh uses character-based improvisations to create his scripts. The script for a Leigh film is created over an extended rehearsal period that often lasts many months, during which time the actors are given every opportunity to research their characters. Thus, an actor agreeing to participate in a Mike Leigh film cannot judge in advance how central his character will be. Although improvisation is fundamental to the early stages of rehearsal, Leigh

---

[11] Tom Charity, *John Cassavetes: Lifeworks* (London: Omnibus Press, 2001), p. 131.

443

has pointed out that the cast progresses beyond it. "All art is a synthesis of improvisation and order.... You arrive at it by improvising and distilling that down. Putting order on it and working and working until you have something which is refined and precise."[12] The result, as in the Oscar-nominated *Secrets and Lies* (1995), is performances of remarkable commitment, freshness, honesty, and depth.

Screen acting 1990-2000

A look at the Academy Award winners for Best Actor and Best Actress between 1990 and 2000 suggests a shift away from the dominance of Method acting. While Method-trained actors Pacino and Nicholson appear on the list, they are far outnumbered by performers with a variety of backgrounds. Anthony Hopkins, Emma Thompson, Jeremy Irons, Jeff Rush, and Judi Dench are classically trained actors who have successfully adapted themselves to movies. Many (Kathy Bates, Holly Hunter, Frances McDormand) have had an eclectic university training. Some, like two-time winner Tom Hanks, as well as Susan Sarandon, Helen Hunt, and Nicholas Cage, have had very little formal training. Jessica Lange had an interesting apprenticeship: She briefly attended college but then pursued mime and dance in Paris, as well as training at The Actors Studio.

Method actors may be relinquishing their almost total domination of American film acting, but Method-based techniques are still part of an eclectic actor's repertory. For instance, Anthony Hopkins has spoken of the influences of Strasberg and Chekhov on his work. Kevin Spacey is an actor whose style exemplifies Strasberg's (and Stanislavski's) teaching on relaxation and concentration. And another distinguished actor, Tommy Lee Jones (who, like Jodie Foster, studied literature at an Ivy League university), when asked if he used emotional memory, categorically replied, "That's what the job is."[13]

Throughout this chapter I have been concerned with tracing the influence of Stanislavski in Hollywood. It is, therefore, not a survey of all the acting traditions available, especially in Europe and other parts of the world. A case can be made for the persistence of Delsartian gesture—particularly in the films of the forties and fifties.[14] Although Bertolt Brecht's collaborators Kurt Weill and Hans Eisler wrote music for Hollywood and a recognizably Brechtian element

---

[12] *Screen Acting*
[13] Carole Zucker, ed., *Figures of Light* (New York: Plenum Press, 1995), p. 47.

is recognizable in movies like *The Truman Show* (1998) and *Pleasantville* (1998), I have not discussed Brecht's theories. A case can also be made for the influence of Jerzy Grotowski (the experimental Polish theater director, whose development of Stanislavski's theories in the 1960s and '70s has greatly influenced modern theater) on independent American and European films, especially the Dogme group of filmmakers. A future survey might have to include the rigorous physical and vocal training of the Japanese teacher Tadashi Suzuki. However, it is remarkable how one man's system, evolved a century ago, still remains so central to Western acting. Perhaps another Stanislavski will appear and change all that, but, at the moment, there is no sign of that happening.

---

[14] James Naremore, *Acting in the Cinema* (Berkeley, CA: University of California Press, 1988), pp. 61-67. Naremore argues that Cary Grant, James Stewart, and others unconsciously adopted Delsartean gestures. I would also add to the list characters in Disney animated movies and certain performances in soaps and melodramas.

PART 8
Multi-Camera Production

40. The Studio

"Everything depends upon our manipulating
technology in a proper manner as a means."
—Martin Heidegger

A studio's only limitation is your imagination. A studio or soundstage is
a magic box that can be converted into almost any location you desire.
It can be a Victorian parlor or, through the use of a "green wall," an
orbiting space station. However, the studio presents a paradox: Its complete
malleability can also be its shortcoming, because many producers and directors
prefer starting with a more-or-less defined space and then embellishing it.

Soundstages and studios have come to be seen as cost-saving options to location
work. A producer with a long-running show will erect his sets on a soundstage,
where they are accessible week after week. The production offices will be close
by. The actors' dressing rooms will be part of a building complex that also houses
costume and makeup, storage areas for the regulars' wardrobe, and a canteen.

Studios built specifically for television work have many technical assets. They
are often sound-proofed and have smooth floors that enable *pedestal cameras*
(cameras mounted on heavy, maneuverable dollies operated by the cameraperson)
to glide without shaking. They have a lighting grid with a large number of lamps
that usually can be raised and lowered. They have storage areas for sets that are
not in use (such sets are called *swing sets*). They have parking lots, restrooms,
and telephones. They are also configured to enable multi-camera video
recording (which can allow up to twenty times more material to be shot in a
day than on most single-camera film productions.)

The privacy and self-sufficiency of a television studio, combined with the
speed of production it fosters, has meant that, with regard to drama, it is primarily

used for television series production—especially soaps and sitcoms. This is fine, but in the '50s, '60s, and '70s, cutting-edge long-form programs were also produced in such studios, where the relative inexpensiveness of production also meant that new writers and directors could cut their teeth on important projects. That now seems like a long time ago, but I still believe that remarkable results can be achieved by a team of creative individuals working together in a TV studio's flexible environment.

Multi-camera television studio performance

Single-camera production tends to chop a performance up into a series of isolated takes. The actor, working in the moment, becomes very concentrated, with a self-involved intensity that is rare even on the stage. At the same time, the off-camera actor with whom he is performing may not be as intensely focused.

A television studio offers a middle point between theatrical and movie acting. It is filmic in the sense that it is recorded in chunks (albeit longer chunks than are commonly shot for movies), and the sensitivity of the recording equipment makes vocal projection (in a theatrical sense) unnecessary. On the other hand, like the theater, a real-time performance is given by a group of actors. The natural time constraints of TV work mean that the latitude for retakes that exists on a film set does not exist for a TV show. Performances, therefore, often possess the element of adrenaline.

To work well, studio performances generally have to be well rehearsed. As in the theater, actors must know their lines, be confident about their moves, and trust each other totally during the performance. Of course, there are lucky actors who are so relaxed that they can create credible performances without much rehearsal, but they are in the minority. Unfortunately, time constraints (especially on long-running series) mean that rehearsal for studio drama is often perfunctory at best.

Preproduction and the shooting schedule

The speed at which most material is recorded in the multi-camera television studio means that directors have to arrive at the very start of the day knowing exactly how they want their episode to be blocked and shot.

Continuing series (soaps) in Britain are stylistically very different from American ones, and this is reflected in their schedules, which, with a few exceptions, allow a little more time for preproduction and shooting. In Britain, where soaps tend to be a half-hour long, directors are generally allocated three shows, a week's worth of programming, at a time. Some series give directors two or more weeks to prepare scripts, cast non-principal actors, and meet with production personnel; others provide less. Since these series often have both a non-studio component (material shot on location or on a studio lot) as well as a studio component, two sets of planning meetings with the lighting designer, camera supervisor, set designer, and other crew members are scheduled. Prior to shooting, the director produces a camera plan that is typed up by his assistant and circulated to the various departments.

In the United States, where soaps are often longer, the system is less formal. Directors working on an hour-long program (actually only about forty-four minutes after time is allowed for commercials) receive the script between four and seven days prior to recording. The whole episode is usually shot in the studio in one day, so almost all of the preproduction period is devoted to working out how to shoot and block the scenes. A brief conversation with the lighting designer may occur the day before the recording, but the first glimpses the lighting, camera, and sound crews get of the director's plan is when he blocks the actors on the morning of the shoot. This is last-minute production, but the crew is so used to the sets, the characters, and the overall style of the show that the director is easily accommodated. Recording starts in one set and proceeds till all the scenes in that set are completed before moving on to the next. Each new scene is usually run once, adjusted, and then recorded as many times as necessary or as time allows.

In America, the director arrives on the day of recording with his marked-up script. (An example of a studio script appears at the end of Chapter 42.) On some shows, the *technical director* (or *TD*)—the person who actually presses the buttons, which lay the shots selected by the director from the various cameras down on tape—receives the director's marked script in advance in order to produce *camera cards* (or *shot sheets*)—cards with an individual camera's shots listed on them. If the technical director has not seen a copy of the script, she will be given the cutting points before each scene, and the director will also indicate where the cuts occur by snapping his fingers, calling "cut," or some similar method during the rehearsal and takes.

The American system allows no time for rehearsal. The British system used to permit some rehearsal (about twenty minutes a scene) prior to the recording but no longer does. This is a shame because even minimal rehearsal saves time on the set. It allows actors to absorb and discuss blocking with the director. It can avoid misunderstandings between directors, who might be new to a series, and established actors. It breaks in new actors and also allows the cast to try out their moves and improve on them. Above all, it gives actors the chance to run their lines together and give something more than a last-minute improvisation.

Limitations of multi-camera studio production

Traditional, dramatic, multi-camera-video studio production has several technical limitations, foremost of which is that most multi-camera scenes shot on video have to be "camera scripted" (i.e., have all their shots and blocking worked out in advance of recording). This means that the director has to commit to an almost inflexible sequence of shots well before he starts working with the actors. Moreover, once the shots have been laid down on tape during the recording session by the technical director, it is very difficult to adjust the order in which they have been arranged. The director is thus very reliant on the technical director to make the cuts between cameras at exactly the right points during the recording. If a scene is repeated, the TD must cut at exactly the same points in all takes, so that the director can edit cleanly between them during postproduction.

In a situation where numerous retakes are impossible—such as recording a sitcom in front of an audience—directors may use *iso cameras*. An iso camera has its own separate recorder so its entire output is available during editing. Designating one or two cameras as isos is probably a good insurance policy.

Many of the most popular American sitcoms are shot in a studio on film. Shooting with four film cameras is, in effect, the same as shooting with four iso cameras. In such a situation the director is less reliant on a camera script. While shooting, he carefully scans the individual camera monitors to make sure that the action is being covered in the most effective way. A feed from all the cameras is available to the technical director, who produces a version of the program solely for the benefit of the studio audience. As in traditional film postrpoduction, the output from all the cameras is then made available to the editor, who constructs an initial assembly, which is subsequently viewed and critiqued by the director.

The fourth wall

In the theater, the set's "fourth wall" is the proscenium arch. The fourth wall of a studio set is the side that is open to allow for the placement and movement of cameras and sound booms. This means that there is a point beyond which a director cannot position a camera upstage and have it shoot a character downstage without the camera shooting off the set (see Fig. 40.1).

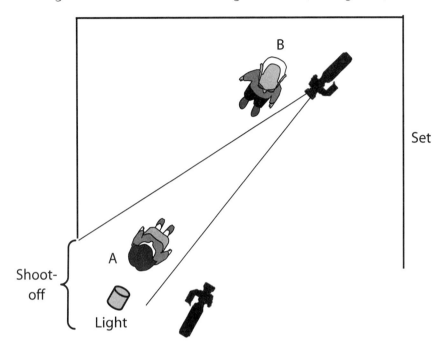

Fig. 40.1: "Shooting off"— The problem of an upstage shooting position in a studio

Flats (or *flattage*) are the decorated boards the design department places side by side to form a set's walls. In a situation such as depicted in Fig. 40.1, where the shoot-off is minimal, the designer might be able to provide an extra flat to extend the set and avoid the shoot-off. But the situation is complicated by the fact that the farther the camera goes upstage, the more it is shooting back into the lights that illuminate the upstage character ("B").

Audio

Audio in a professional studio is captured by technicians sitting on *perambulator booms*—platforms with large boom poles that telescope out over the cameras. The further the boom extends into the set, the more likely it is to pass in front of a light and cast an intrusive shadow. Studio lighting directors often place the key light (a character's main light) upstage of the actor so that the boom shadow is cast downstage (in the area of the imaginary fourth wall), out of shot and away from the back wall. If the position of an actor and the angle of the boom produce a visible shadow, all a director can do is encourage the lighting director and the sound supervisor to work out a compromise that will allow shooting to continue.

Directors watching a take must be vigilant that the boom does not dip into the shot and does not cast a boom shadow. Sometimes the microphone accidentally sneaks into the very top of the frame. In this case, the director has to decide whether to shoot again or judge that the mic was in the area at the edge of the frame called *cutoff*, which is not viewable on home receivers. If he has any doubt, he will go again. The director may have to make a similar judgment call about boom shadows. The average viewer may not be notice a static shadow, or may read it as the shadow of something else, such as a tree branch or some sort of light fitting. However, once a shadow moves, it draws attention to itself and is revealed for what it is.

41. Multi-Camera Studio Technique

Superficially, the director of a multi-camera television drama has a considerable amount of authority. Unlike a sitcom director, she has no time for rehearsals and precious little consultation with the other production departments, so what she says goes. And on the "studio day" (shooting day), time is at a premium, so there is little opportunity to question her choices about shots and blocking. On the other hand, this power is illusory. Given its time constraints, the shooting is likely to be unambitious, and her objective will simply be to get through the day with as few problems as possible. Furthermore, should the director depart from the house style, the producer, who is usually seated behind her or at a monitor close by, will object. In television, producers always have the last word.

The pressure of television production means that a high degree of professionalism is required from all departments. Actors have to know their lines, the lighting designer has to be able to make quick adjustments, the boom operators and sound supervisor have to be alert and adaptable, and everyone else associated with the production has to be able to act speedily to forestall problems. The director is therefore very reliant on the crew.

Technical director, director's assistant, and floor manager

Three people work particularly closely with the director: the technical director (TD), the director's assistant, and the floor manager. The technical director acts as instant editor, so communication with him must be very open. A good TD will intuit a director's style and even improve on it. His efficiency will also make the camera and sound crews confident that their work is being competently assembled.

The technical director sits on one side of the director and on the other is the director's assistant. (Most control rooms I know in the Unites States and Britain position the TD on the director's left.) The assistant calls the shots during rehearsal and taping: "Shot 1, camera 3 next … Shot 2, camera 1 next …" etc. On shows where camera cards/shot sheets have not been prepared, the assistant may also describe the upcoming shot: "Camera 3 next. MCU Zandra." She times the takes with a stopwatch so that the producer and director have an approximate idea of the total running time. She also logs the takes and notes the director's reactions to them. Some directors dictate an instant edit immediately after finishing a scene—"We'll start on take 2, go to take 3 for Gladys's line, and then end on take 1." This first reaction is helpful, but it is important to review the takes again before editing.

The floor manager runs the studio. Like a first assistant on a film shoot, he will organize the actors and all the supporting departments so that everything is available when the director needs it. He verbally identifies each take: "Scene 20. Take 2." (A clapboard is not used in a TV studio.) If the director is working from the control room, the floor manager becomes the director's presence on the studio floor, which involves passing on directorial comments to actors. (Directors who are removed from their actors can get very irritable when under pressure. Floor managers try not to transmit a director's anxiety. "Tell that — — actor to move to his right as he was told!" is translated by the floor manager as, "Jack, please don't forget to move to your right.") It also involves watching the monitor in order to step in during a break to adjust an actor's position or have a studio grip (stagehand) move a piece of furniture.

Studio days are long and tiring, and the director must do everything within reason to maintain a good working relationship with the crew. On the middle day of a particularly long studio shoot, a colleague once broke into an Asian Indian accent to amuse the camera operators. The ploy worked for a while until he looked over his shoulder and saw an Indian electrician staring at him incredulously from the doorway. There are levels to which you do not have to stoop to entertain your crew!

Where does the director direct?

No ideal place exists for a drama director during a studio recording. If she sits in the control room she is divorced from the actors. If she stays on the studio floor, she is removed from the technical director, her assistant, and other technicians.

Traditionally, the director sits in the control room flanked by the TD and the assistant. Nearby, in separate rooms, are the sound supervisor and lighting director. The line producer sits either behind the director or in an office the push of an intercom switch away. American directors prefer to work from the control room, which makes sense since they relay the cutting points to the technical director. Being in front of a bank of monitors also helps directors talk the cameras through their shots and add extra shots during a take if a scene is going slowly.

Working in the control room makes even more sense if the director has discussed the actors' performances with them, thus freeing her to concentrate on technical concerns. Over the years, however, I have come to prefer working from the studio floor. First of all, British series are faster-paced than American ones and the need to suddenly insert a reaction shot to increase the tempo does not often arise. Secondly, the British practice of having the technical director (known as "vision mixer" over there) cut from the director's typed camera script means that the director does not have to be in the control room in person. On the studio floor, the British director can position herself near a monitor and wear a microphone and headset to keep in contact with the TD and director's assistant.

Working from the studio floor allows directors to interact with actors. Being able to discuss a point with a member of the cast in person is so much more effective than having the whole conversation relayed through the floor manager or bawling an instruction to the studio over the loudspeaker system. Opportunities for informal, creative discussion are multiplied by having the director alongside the cast and camera operators, where she can support the actors during challenging scenes and give them feedback immediately after a rehearsal or a take. It also sends a message to everyone involved with the production that performance is a priority.

Three-Camera technique (or *I Love Lucy*)

Broadly speaking, most studio scenes are shot in one of three ways: with three or more cameras, with two cameras, and with one camera. Let's start by looking at the most basic of the three.

Three-camera technique was pioneered by the early American sitcoms, notably *I Love Lucy*. The show's producers noticed that, in most scenes, there were two groups of actors, with one person (usually Lucille Ball) occasionally doing a turn in the center. By arranging three cameras in a semi-circle around the set, all the action could be covered (see Fig. 41.1).

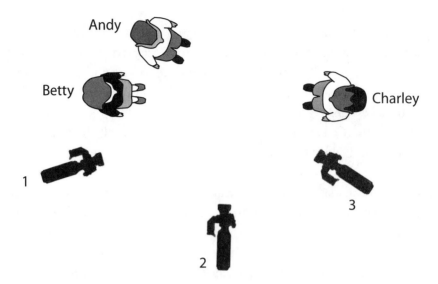

Fig. 41.1: Basic positions for three-camera shooting

When the characters are positioned in two groups, they can be easily covered by cameras 1 and 3. As soon as one character, Betty, moves, her move can be taken on camera 2. In the early days of sitcom and even to this day, directors simply cut to a wide shot for this sort of move. The basic three-camera setup offers a simple solution to practically every eventuality on a program with relatively few characters. It works particularly well if the character doing the movement plays his business "out front" (to the camera rather than to his fellow players), appealing directly to the studio audience. It is very efficient for sitcoms with characters using physical comedy like Lucille Ball, Dick Van Dyke, or *Seinfeld*'s Michael Richards.

A variation on the three-camera setup is used in some contemporary sitcoms, such as *Friends* and *Frazier* (both shot on film), which tend to use four cameras—two positioned at the edges of the set (with telephoto lenses) and two working closer to the center. By grouping characters on either side of the set (or opposite each other), one camera is usually available to give a wide shot and another a tighter single. The cameras with the wide shots can also follow characters when they move across the set.

One of the potential problem with three-camera technique is that cutting to the wide shot for movement is not always satisfactory. The camera 2 position is very square-on and often produces a profile shot. This is particularly problematic in drama, where characters are less likely to perform "out front" to an audience.

Drama depends more on subjective shots in which we see both eyes and are drawn into events through a sense of intimacy with the characters.

Do not let the three-camera technique compromise your shooting. Avoid grouping your characters baldly on the left and right of the set. Always begin by blocking characters in their optimum positions, as if you were going to shoot them single-camera style. If your blocking breaks down because another camera is in-shot or you cannot get a decent eye-line or you are shooting back against the open fourth wall, then massage character and camera blocking to get the best alternative.

Single-camera technique

As noted when discussing the long take (Part 4, Chapter 24), a whole scene can be shot with one camera. One of the differences between shooting a film-style long take on location and doing it in a TV studio is the maneuverability of the pedestal camera. The ped, with its horizontal steering ring and three wheels, is designed to move fluidly and easily. The simplest moves are ones in which the distance between the character and the camera remains constant, because the operator does not have to refocus during the move. Such moves include *dollying* in or out with a moving character and *trucking* (or *crabbing*) left and right alongside a character, and *arcing*, which is moving the camera in a semi-circle around a subject.

As soon as the distance between the subject and the camera varies, camera maneuvers become potentially more complex. The operator has to do three things: (1) physically move the camera by setting the direction ring and pushing or pulling, (2) adjust the zoom to control the size of the frame, (3) ride the focus. All of this requires one more hand than most humans possess. Directors should note that, when this kind of maneuver is necessary, even professionals require time to practice it.

The trick with single-camera shooting is to keep the frame alive. At some point, there has to be motion, either from the actor or the camera or both. If the camera moves, the movement should be motivated by either a movement within the frame or the desire to see who is speaking or being spoken to. The film camera has become increasingly fluid in its movement over the years and, consequently, we now expect all camera angles, even studio ones, to be interesting. Simply holding an objective wide shot is no good—the camera and the actors must form interesting, oblique, evolving relationships.

Two-camera technique

Most scenes, especially the two- or three-person scenes that are the staple of soap operas, can be shot with two cameras. Placing cameras on either side of the set (see Fig. 41.2) entails sacrificing the flat, square-on, objective shot, but offers interesting alternatives too.

Abe   Blanche

1   2

Fig. 41.2: Two-camera placement

In two-camera shooting, shots are almost always close to the eye-line, so the viewer is brought into a subjective relationship with the characters. Moves tend not to be from left to right or right to left across the frame—as they generally are in objective shots. Instead, they are more toward or away from the camera. This allows for considerable depth of composition. It also helps illustrate relationships because characters are constantly moving into and out of the frame. In Fig. 41.2, if Abe moves toward Blanche, then the shot on camera 2 will start as a single of Abe and end as a 2-shot favoring him. Abe has been brought into relationship with Blanche and we can read his expression clearly. If Abe moves away from her, we can read her reaction on camera 1 as he exits and she is left alone in the frame. *Cross-shooting* can be more visually interesting and expressive than simply cutting to the wide shot.

All screen actors have to be technically aware, but television studio actors have to be especially so. Time pressure means that they have very little latitude for mistakes. Moves have to occur at exactly the right time and marks have to be hit. A few actors seem to have an instinctive understanding of these techniques, but most need time to learn them. Actors who come from the theater have to acclimatize to a performance environment where a responsive audience is replaced by a room full of metallic equipment and a handful of silent technicians. Directors have to be patient with actors who are new to a particular series or new to television studio procedures and encourage them to feel at home in the studio.

If you are shooting a two-person scene or a scene in which the actors can be divided neatly into two groups, then the two-camera style usually works well. But if a third person enters the room, you'll probably need an extra camera. You might also want a third camera for an initial establishing shot or a cutaway. A third camera is handy, too, for "speciality shots"—such as those from a special dolly or a hand-held camera or a Steadicam. Technicians can prepare a third camera for such shots in advance.

Directing the scene

Directing a multi-camera production in a studio requires the director's deep concentration to each take and the same critical approach ("Is there anything false?") described in Part 5, Chapter 30. But, whereas in single-camera shooting the director applies herself to one shot at a time, in the studio she shoots all of a scene's shots at once. On a film-style one-camera shoot, the director often works intensively with one actor at a time, whereas in multi-camera shooting she works concurrently with all the characters in the scene. In film-style production, the takes are frequently quite short, so the director can concentrate on each moment and be aware of an actor's slightest nuance (the lifting of an eyebrow or the incline of a head). This degree of attention is impossible in the studio.

Unless the actors are very good or the show has been rehearsed beforehand, studio performances can be disappointing. On a single-camera shoot, rapport develops between the cameraperson and the director, and they come to share responsibility for each shot. In the studio, the director works with several operators at once and, therefore, never gets as close to any one of them. As the person overseeing the whole process, the director is also a little more exposed in the studio than on film. She must be both technically aware—looking to see if the boom is in the shot and gauging if the shots are working individually and in sequence—as well as aware of performance and composition. All directors feel a tension between technical and artistic demands, but it is particularly intense in multi-camera work.

One way to diminish this tension is to work hard on the technical aspects during studio rehearsal in order to concentrate more on the artistic during the takes. I think this is easier to accomplish in the British system, where the director delegates cutting to the technical director, than in America, where she continues to indicate cutting points even while the scene is being recorded.

Here is the procedure I like to follow, but if I'm running short of time I will adapt it to fit the immediate situation. (Note that blocking, as well as the number of run-throughs, may vary according to whether I've rehearsed the actors in advance.)

Blocking studio drama

Read the scene with the actors. This is important because it focuses their attention and allows them to brush up their lines. If an actor raises a question or queries a line, address it at the outset. This is also a good time for suggesting the super-objectives for each character (e.g., "She wants to get him to leave" or, "He's trying to save her life.").

Next, give the actors their opening positions and start working through the scene. (If time is short, ask the actors to write down their moves in their scripts before you start working in the set.) Then methodically work through the scene, making sure everyone knows exactly when, where, and why they should move.

Rehearsing

So much of studio directing is about communication. You have to be able to communicate a great deal of information in a short period to the actors, camera operators, sound crew, and technical director. Start discussing the shots with cameras in the minute or two you are waiting for the actors to appear for blocking. You need not talk about every shot in the scene, but the three or four trickiest ones should be addressed. (E.g., "Jack, in shot 8, you have to truck left with Jan as she crosses to the desk. She'll be walking quite fast, so I'll cue you when she's about to move.") Remember, good manners demand that you call your operators by name instead of by their camera numbers.

When blocking is finished and the camera rehearsal is about to start, the director's attention returns to the cameras. I try to remind the actors that the first rehearsal (or "stagger-through") will be a slow crawl for the benefit of the technicians, and, sure enough, it is usually full of stops and starts as problems surface. Inexperienced directors are sometimes reluctant to interrupt a rehearsal's flow and bring it to a halt, but solving problems at this stage makes things go much more smoothly later on.

Most of the time, a drama director watches a large color *program* or *transmission* monitor, which shows the shots mixed by the TD. However, if you work from the control room, I highly recommend occasionally scanning the monitor wall (with its displays of the output from all the cameras) to see if a camera operator is offering a stunning angle you had not considered. Talking the camerapersons through tricky moments in a scene is also a good idea. If, for example, I know a camera movement is coming up, I warn the operator and give him a running commentary. "Okay Nat, your move is coming up. Truck right with him…. That's good …. And now steady as he reaches the desk."

When you are instructing cameras, be as clear as possible. Try not to use indefinite phrases like "a little" (as in, "Zoom out a little"). Include a specific reference point: "Zoom out to include the table top" or "Tighten to his breast pocket."

If a scene is short and the shots simple, you might try going for a take after only one rehearsal. More often, though, the stagger-through is followed by a second run-through that cements the camera moves and gives the actors an uninterrupted run. If a scene is very long or complicated or the second rehearsal has been stop-and-go, you might want to have a final run-through (or "dress run"). Given the time pressure, recording the final run-through is always tempting. There is no harm in this, except that actors sometimes perform better when they sense a clear demarcation between rehearsal and recording.

Recording

Try to sit back and be objective during the recording. A director who is worrying about shots will not notice performance, and vice versa. If you decide to go for a second or third take, give feedback to the cameras and the actors and try to explain why you want to go again. This will help them understand your concerns and, if possible, improve their performance.

Some directors prefer to record a whole scene in one take. This is often helpful for the actors who can give a complete performance each time, and it often simplifies editing by providing the director with a complete master take to work from. However, if there is a point where the scene repeatedly breaks down (perhaps because an actor is having trouble with lines or there is a technical problem such as a boom shadow), it can be simpler to restart the scene shortly before the breakdown. Soaps commonly have good recordings of the whole first half of a scene and then have to cover the remainder in two or three "pickup shots."

When you have finished a scene, remember to thank the actors and the crew before going on to the next one. Studio work is not easy but the work occasionally takes wing. A scene with good performances captured in one or two takes is a little miracle requiring talent and trust on the part of the actors, skill and precision from the crew, and good judgment from the director. Such moments should certainly be acknowledged.

42. The Studio Script

Directors of multi-camera video productions have to communicate a good deal of information as clearly and succinctly as possible, so their scripts are offset to the left-hand side of the page (to the right in Britain) to allow space on the right for notes and important markings. What follows is a suggested way of marking up a multi-camera shooting script. Even if you do not plan to adopt this exact method, please read the section because it contains information with which you should become familiar.

All the points discussed below are illustrated on a specimen script page at the end of the chapter (Fig. 42.12).

Remember to use pencil when marking up a script because it allows you to erase.

The last shot

As we have seen with single-camera shooting, directors have to know the last shot of the preceding scene in order to create the first shot of the current one.

The last shot can be described in graphic shorthand on the top left of the first page.

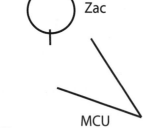

Fig. 42.1: Last shot diagram

Fig. 42.1 indicates that the last shot was an MCU of Zac looking camera left.

Floor plan

Directors have to be able to block actors very quickly. They also have to make sure the furniture and props are in the right positions for each scene. Some directors attach an annotated copy of the designer's floor plan to the front of each scene in their scripts, but I find that doing this makes an already thick file even thicker, so I quickly draw a thumbnail plan at the top of every new scene. Be sure to mark the actors' opening positions on the plan (even if they are starting outside the door), and the positions of the main tables, chairs, and other important props.

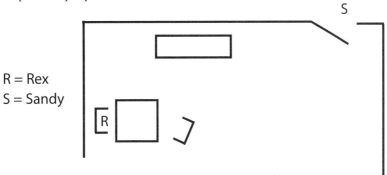

Fig. 42.2: Opening positions floor plan

Furniture moves

Props don't always stay in the same position from scene to scene. For instance, you may be shooting a series of scenes in the office of Hubert, the manager of a small dry-goods company. In the first scene, he enters, looks out his window, crosses to his desk, and sits down to check the accounts. This is shot in one trucking shot with the camera starting in the set, then pulling back. As the director, you note that the carpet has to be rolled back for this scene so that the camera can move unhindered.

In the next scene he is at his desk when an employee enters and sits opposite him. Before you rehearse the new scene, the carpet has to be rolled back into place. You also bring the desk downstage (toward camera) one foot to facilitate cross-shooting (see Fig. 42.3). The table has now been moved to "position 2."

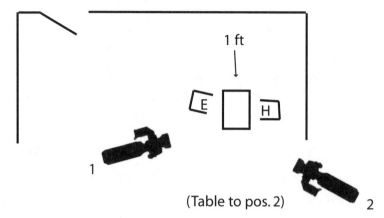

Fig. 42.3: Table to position 2

In the next scene, two people sit opposite Hubert, so his desk is moved back to position1 and angled slightly clockwise ("clocked") so camera 2 can get a full-faced shot of the upstage character.

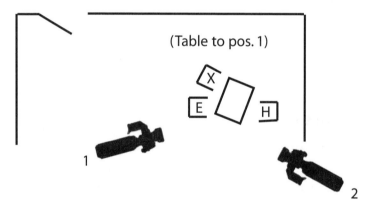

Fig. 42.4: Table position 1 and clocked

Small cheats like this almost always go unnoticed by the viewers. If you know you have to alter the position of the design props, note the change at the top of the scene's first script page, over the slug line, as well as on the diagram itself. This may sound unnecessarily cautious but, as the day hurtles on, overlooking details becomes easy.

Camera positions

Directors also have to make sure the cameras are in the correct opening positions, so you should include cameras on your thumbnail plan as well (see Fig. 42.5).

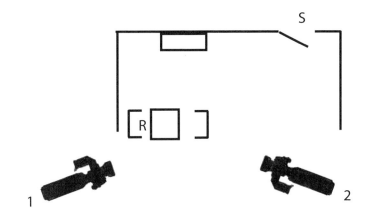

Fig. 42.5: Camera positions

Cabling

Each camera in a studio has its own number, which it prominently displays. Cameras do not change numbers.

Ideally, cameras should be arranged left to right across the set, with camera 1 on the left, 2 in the middle, and 3 on the right. But a camera's position is determined by the cable that connects it to the wall outlet, and which carries the signal to the control room. Directors have to be aware of where the cable points are, so that as cameras move from set to set around the studio their cables do not become entangled.

The problem of tangled cables used to be more serious than it now is. Switching off the cameras, unplugging the old, thick, coaxial cables and then restarting them used to take a long time. Modern, lightweight cameras unplug more easily, but it is still advisable to arrange them so that the cables are not entwined like spaghetti.

The studio shown in Fig. 42.6 has two sets: A and B. The numbers of the cameras are indicated on the diagram, as well as their corresponding cabling points in the walls. In set A, the director can place cameras 1, 2, and 3 from left to right across the set, without entangling the cables. When he moves to set B, however, cabling considerations force him to arrange them 2 ,3, 1 across the set from left to right. (Set B faces the other way, so he has turned the plan upside down, and camera 2 is now on the left.) If he were to go in the order 3, 2, 1 across the set, then the cables of cameras 2 and 3 would cross (see Fig. 42.7).

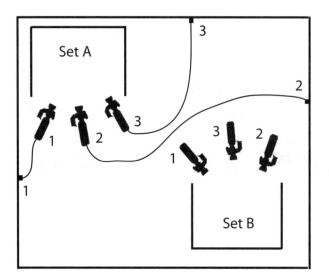

Fig. 42.6: Cabling in two sets

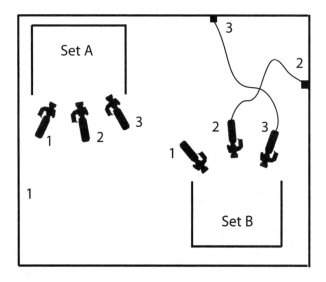

Fig. 42.7: Crossed cables

Sometimes, when directors find themselves in this situation, they ask camera 3 to lay its cable in front of camera 2 instead of crossing it (Fig. 42.8). In this situation, camera 2 is said to be working "in camera 3's loop." The problem is that camera 2's forward movement is impeded by camera 3's cable, so it is not an ideal solution.

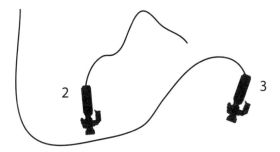

Fig. 42.8: Working in the cable loop

Changing shot

Camera operators either note down their shots before a scene starts or are given camera cards (or shot sheets) with their shots written on them.

Sooner or later a camera will have to change shot—go from, say, a mid-shot to a medium closeup. A change of shot requires the operator to zoom in or out and to reframe. Cameras cannot change shot and reframe in an instant. Directors have to make sure that the camera is off-shot (not being selected by the TD) long enough for the camera op to make the change, and even professional operators require between two and three seconds to do this. A second is approximately equivalent to three spoken words, so, in order to give operators a good chance to change a shot, directors should allow them to be off-shot for at least eight or nine words.

If you plan to ask an operator to do an extra-quick shot change, you should warn her before starting work on the scene. To remind yourself, make a note of the camera and the number of the shot on the top of your script, just below the camera plan. Note the shot numbers of all shots that are tricky or complicated, so that you can discuss them with the operator.

Marking the moves

If you are lucky, you may have five minutes to block an entire scene with the actors. Actors' moves must therefore be clearly marked on the director's script. As with the single-camera script, mark each move in the margin opposite where it occurs, and indicate the exact point where the move happens in the text with an asterisk (see Fig. 42.9).

JACK (J.xs)

It's uncanny. */ She is never in the same place twice.

J ▯

Fig. 42.9: Marking movement in the margin

Cameras and cutting points

You have spent many hours considering your floor plans in conjunction with the script in order to arrive at a shooting plan. Now you need to indicate four things that will enable you to communicate with the technical director about the shots.

Assign a camera to the shot

Once you have divided the scene into shots, enter the appropriate camera number on the right of the page (see Fig. 42.10).

Describe the shot

Shots in multi-camera-video studio production have to be described even more fully than in single-camera-style production, because multi-camera directors do not have time to discuss them in detail with the camera operators. Here are some guidelines.

1. Describe how the shot starts: e.g., "MS Buck"
2. If the shot changes, describe how: "Maud enters l" or "Pan Buck rt to Maud."
3. Describe how the shot is resolved: "M2s M+B." Putting "M" (Maud) first indicates that she is farther to the left of frame than Buck.

4. If the characters move at the end of the shot, describe how that affects the framing: "Pat rises OOS" ("OOS" stands for "out of shot") or "M leaves l/ hold B" (Maud leaves frame left, stay on Buck). When you do not want operators to pan or tilt with the characters as they leave a shot, you might add the phrase "still frame": for example, "B leaves l/ still frame."

5. Enter the shot description in the script at the end of the line or, preferably, under the camera number (see Fig. 42.10).

Indicate exactly where you want the cut to occur

To indicate where the cutting point occurs, draw a line (with a ruler) under the camera and extend it across to the text. You can also add a tail to indicate the exact position of the cut (see Fig. 42.10).

```
Search the fish tank, Wally. Jaws, you look          Cam. 2
downstairs.
                                                     MS Jaws
```

Fig. 42.10: Camera number and shot description with tail

Where you place the tail—the spot where the cut occurs—is entirely up to you. You could cut after the end of the speech (placing the tail after "downstairs"), or you might cut halfway through the word "downstairs" in order to catch the character Jaws just before he turns to go.

Number the shots

The director or his assistant or, on some shows, the TD numbers each shot, either continuously from the first shot of the day to the last (i.e., from shot 1 to shot 300) or scene by scene (i.e., starting afresh with shot 1 in each scene). (See Fig. 42.11.)

```
Search the fish tank, Wally. Jaws, you look    22    Cam. 2
downstairs.
                                                     MS Jaws
```

Fig. 42.11: Shot number

Information on characters

In soaps, recording is usually done one set at a time, which means that the show is not shot in strictly chronological, story order. (However, the scenes in each individual set are shot as far as possible in story order, starting with the earliest and ending with the last.)

A major character may be in eight consecutive scenes in one set, and by the time the last two scenes are recorded, all she can do is just remember her lines. Directors can help actors deal with this situation by reminding them where they are in the story, and where their character last appeared. Note each character's last appearance on your script.

Timing

The floor manager's job is to keep the studio running efficiently, and he will have his own estimate of how long each scene will take to shoot. Directors should not be obsessed with time—they have enough concerns without glancing at their watches every couple of minutes. Directors work as quickly and efficiently as possible, knowing that some scenes will eat up time while others will pass like greased lightning. Constant clock-watching creates tension that is not conducive to efficiency. It fosters irritability and makes the day seem much longer than it actually is.

Nevertheless, before starting the studio day, make you own calculation of where you think you should be when you're halfway through the morning session, at lunchtime, and halfway through the afternoon. Note these three points in the script. If, when you reach these signposts, you think you have fallen significantly behind, increase the pace or simplify the way you shoot the next couple of scenes.

Note: Film director Rob Reiner has said, "The toughest thing about directing is the physical part of it,"[1] and many other directors would agree. The remorseless pressure of multi-camera studio directing makes it one of the most taxing forms of directing, so you can really help yourself by making sure you are well-prepared and well-rested before you start.

---

[1] Jeremy Kagan, ed., *Directors Close Up* (Boston: Focal Press, 2000), p. 137.

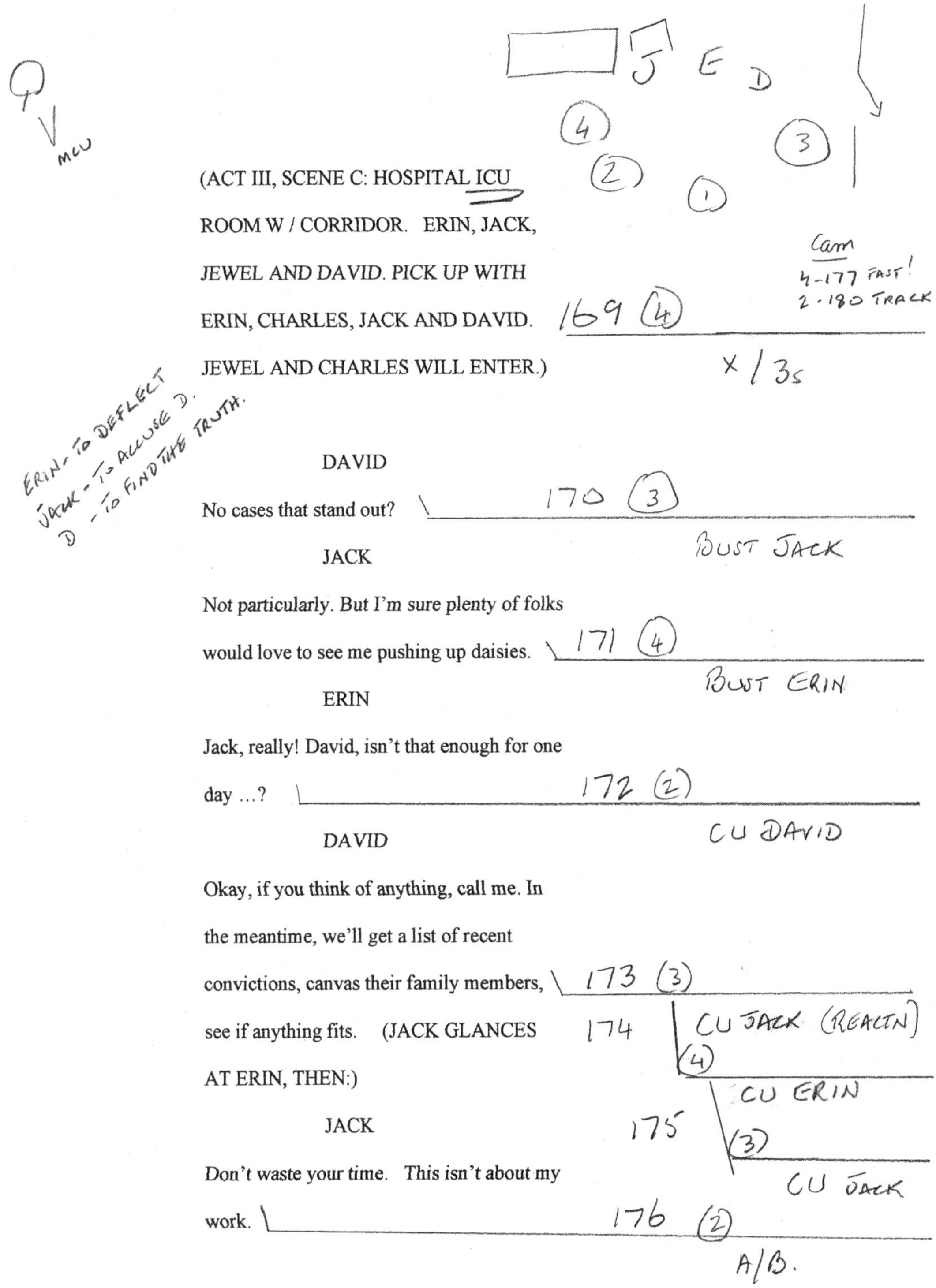

Q
MCU

⎡   ⎤ J   E   D
⎣   ⎦
④   ③
②
①

(ACT III, SCENE C: HOSPITAL ICU

ROOM W / CORRIDOR. ERIN, JACK,

JEWEL AND DAVID. PICK UP WITH   Cam
                                       4-177 FAST!
ERIN, CHARLES, JACK AND DAVID. 169 ④ 2·180 TRACK

JEWEL AND CHARLES WILL ENTER.)   X / 3s

ERIN - TO DEFLECT
JACK - → ACCUSE D.
D - TO FIND THE TRUTH.

        DAVID
No cases that stand out? \   170 ③

        JACK
                                   BUST JACK
Not particularly. But I'm sure plenty of folks

would love to see me pushing up daisies. \ 171 ④

        ERIN   BUST ERIN

Jack, really! David, isn't that enough for one

day ...? \   172 ②

        DAVID   CU DAVID

Okay, if you think of anything, call me. In

the meantime, we'll get a list of recent

convictions, canvas their family members, \ 173 ③

see if anything fits.   (JACK GLANCES   174 CU JACK (REACTN)
                                        ④
AT ERIN, THEN:)
                                        CU ERIN
        JACK   175 ③

Don't waste your time.   This isn't about my   CU JACK

work. \   176 ②

                                   A/B.

Fig. 42.12: Marked studio script

473

PART 9
The Director's Life

43. Three Directors

"The problem with America is that we take everything for granted and, therefore, nothing surprises us.... I only embark on material that I feel is wide open at the end, when I don't know where the journey will end, don't know what the final production will look or feel like."—Peter Sellars, theater director[1]

Ideally, creativity on a set flows from the director to the actors, director of photography, and designers, and then spreads to the rest of the crew. Such collaborations are a joy to work on. The fundamental condition for a good shoot is that everyone concerned is really committed. This spirit occurs more on movies and made-for-television films than on episodes of TV series, which tend to be units of industrial production (though not always). However, collaboration is easily sabotaged by a director's megalomania or a star's ego.

Directors' working styles reflect their personalities, their training, and their experience. One of the benefits of working in the industry as an assistant director is the opportunity to observe directors at work. Every director is different. From some directors one learns how not to do the job, and then there are those whose manner and style are a revelation. What follows is a description of three directors with whom I worked as either a first assistant or production manager in the late 1970s and early 1980s, before I started directing myself.

I present a short account of working with each one in order to convey their different directorial styles and strategies. Each in his own way can serve as a role model for aspiring directors. These accounts are deliberately anecdotal because, short of working on a set, I know of no other way to convey the actual flavor of production.

---

[1] Arthur Bartow, *The Director's Voice* (New York: Theater Communications Group, 1988), pp. 275-277.

John Schlesinger: the demands of professionalism

John Schlesinger (1926-2003) started making films when he was eleven years old. His early commercial movies—*Billy Liar* (1963) and *Darling* (1965)—propelled him to the forefront of the British New Wave. His subsequent move to Hollywood produced the original and highly successful *Midnight Cowboy* (1969). He produced over twenty features and became one of the most enduring directors in Hollywood.

Schlesinger's career began in documentary. But even as a documentary-maker his interest in narrative drama was apparent. Unlike the American "direct cinema" producers who were active during the early '60s, he (like many other British documentary-makers) had no qualms about staging certain shots and hiring extras to make them work. Working with actors was to become one of Schlesinger's greatest talents. When he stepped into dramatic filmmaking in the mid-'60s, he achieved instant success with a string of movies that featured outstanding performances. I first became aware of his work when he did a television film on the actor-director Harold Lang, then teaching at The Central School in London.

I worked with Schlesinger in 1980 and '81 on his first production for the BBC in twenty years. The management, the producer, and all of us who worked on the project were nervously excited by the return of this "auteur." The excitement turned out to be justified. The film, *An Englishman Abroad*, scooped every British Academy Award except one.

It was said of Hitchcock by the writer John Lehman, "Hitchcock had a certain authority that went beyond the record of his proven achievements; his body shape, his manner, his way of speaking somehow gave him an extra measure of power over those within his orbit. The fact that he *was* judgmental, that he did tend to look down on other filmmakers, that his elaborate diction did hint at superiority of attitude, ironically gave those who worked for him an advantage they may not have been aware of. I, like the writers who had gone before me, worked doubly hard in order *not* to be looked down on by Hitchcock, in order not to be deemed inferior."[2]

John Schlesinger did not have Hitchcock's intimidating manner, but we were all aware that we were working with a highly successful professional. Like Lehman, we tried doubly hard not to be outclassed by those Hollywood professionals who had preceded us. The first meeting between the director's team and the director took place not in our office but in his spacious London home.

---

[2] Donald Spoto, *The Dark Side of Genius: The Life of Alfred Hitchcock* (Cambridge: Da Capo Press, 1983, p. 388.

The significance of meeting on his territory was not lost on us. It was as if he was saying, "I'm independent of the BBC. You are going to work on my terms." It was a lesson in directorial independence.

Despite his reputation, he did not stand on ceremony. He was informal and generous with his team. He was always personally available or at the end of a telephone, during preproduction. If problems arose during shooting he was prepared to do what he could. I remember that we had scheduling difficulties about halfway through, and were grateful that he stayed up till the early hours helping us solve them.

Schlesinger's courteous working manner masked a very demanding temperament. He made no allowances for the fact that our crew was half the size of an American one. In his view, the job had to be done to the highest standards regardless of the crewing. Of course, he was right to take this attitude, even though it meant some of us got very little sleep. He was pleasant when things were going as he wanted. When not, he could employ a lacerating wit. When short of time and under pressure, he had a short fuse. But this occasional irascibility was acceptable in a director who was well organized and accessible to the crew. (I caution readers that indulging one's temper is probably the oldest and least effective directorial strategy.)

An Englishman Abroad was set predominantly in Moscow, and finding locations in Britain that would pass for Russia was not easy. We—the two production managers and the designer—scoured Great Britain singly and in pairs till we discovered that certain parts of Scotland possessed stone buildings of a comparable scale to Moscow. Schlesinger, who spent much of the project's limited preproduction period immersed in casting, traveled north to approve the results of our labor. Having discovered architecture in Glasgow and Dundee that would pass for Moscow, we were hard-pressed to find the Russian-speaking lookalikes he demanded as his extras. Several unproductive days were spent auditioning Scottish citizens. "She looks Russian, doesn't she?" I'd say hopefully. "No, not in the least," Schlesinger invariably replied. In the end, quite by chance, an intermediary introduced us to the Ukranian community in Dundee. We were invited to their Christmas festival, and then gallantly, in the small hours, after much feasting and drinking, one by one they agreed to assist us. These are the coincidences that can make or break a film.

Once, during preproduction, when I asked Schlesinger if he would draw some storyboards, he seriously considered the question. In the end, the storyboards never materialized, but I felt that he was open to reasonable suggestions. Like all first-class directors, he was prepared to listen to other people's ideas. There are a couple of shots in the movie that I regard as my own because, when I tentatively suggested them, he immediately saw their merit and adopted them. On another occasion, when I found a location that offered more visual potential than the one suggested in the script, he readily saw its advantages and accepted it.

Schlesinger's reluctance to storyboard suggests a relative lack of concern with formal, pictorial composition in a painterly sense. He was, above all, a storyteller, and this particular movie, with its anti-establishment undertones, greatly appealed to him. The film was about the real-life meeting between a Shakespearian actress, Coral Brown, and an exiled British spy, Guy Burgess, while her theater company was playing in Moscow. Coral Brown was to play herself because, frankly, no other actress could possibly play her better. Schlesinger was adamant from the outset that Alan Bates would play the decadent middle-aged Burgess—a controversial choice since Bates was still considered a young leading man rather than a character actor. But Schlesinger, who had worked with Bates on A *Kind of Loving* (1962) and *Far From the Madding Crowd* (1967), knew that the actor's humor and lightness of touch were perfectly suited to the role. Schlesinger also took enormous pains casting the film's secondary roles, often using quite extravagant improvisations to gauge an actor's particular quality.

Schlesinger believed in rehearsing his main actors and the major scenes before the shoot, so that no time was wasted on set. During rehearsals, he completed his shooting script and fine-tuned the performances. On the set, he knew exactly how he was going to stage the scene, and he also had suggestions about lenses. He did not fret between setups while the lights were being adjusted, as many directors do; he just sat in an adjoining room, reading his newspaper.

On the set, when he unveiled a scene to the crew for the first time, he did so with the pride of a magician performing a new trick. "Now look what the actors and I have cooked up," he seemed to be saying. But, at the same time, he displayed an element of wariness in case the trick didn't work. He told me about a scene in *Honky Tonk Freeway* (1981) that he and the crew had thought was hilariously funny while they were shooting it, but which turned out to be very disappointing in the final film. (Other directors I know have had the same experience with comedy scenes.) He was always critical of a shot while he was filming it and would do as many retakes as necessary to get it absolutely right. On the few occasions we were pressed for time and shots had to be taken quickly, he was not happy.

The camera crew remarked that they were disappointed by how few tracking shots he used and began to call his style "old-fashioned." However, when the movie was completed, it did not lack visual energy. Each shot had been well-chosen and executed, and there was plenty of movement by the characters within the frame. All the work he and his actors had done to produce lively and quirky characters had paid off.

The director's team was close to him during preproduction—especially when we were on the road, looking at potential locations. I remember some very convivial meals, as well as one dinner at which there was a heated discussion between the director and the script's author, Alan Bennett, about how the film should end. During the shoot, however, Schlesinger's attention became centered on the actors. This was partly tactical, because he realized his cast needed all the support he could give them, and it was partly temperamental, because he adored the company of actors. His appreciation of actors in general goes a long way toward explaining how he got such remarkable performances from his casts. I always felt it was a shame that he conducted rehearsals in private because I'd have loved to watch. Characteristic of him was his separating his precious actors from the rest of the crew, building a world to which they alone had the key. Julie Christie has said of him, "John almost walks along the path with the actor, but sometimes the actor runs away from him—not in a different direction, but further ahead than John. They both help each other; the actor helps by maybe introducing short cuts or more interesting routes along the path. But John is ultimately the one who knows where the path ends."[3] That seems to be a very cogent description of a good actor/director relationship.

Alan Clarke: evolving a personal vision

Alan Clarke, who was born in 1935 and died prematurely in 1990, directed a large number of television films, as well as the features *Scum* (1979) and *Rita, Sue and Bob Too* (1986).

Alan Clarke was fascinated by Hollywood, but working in it would have required too many concessions from him. He was primarily concerned with working out his own preoccupations in film, which made him, I think, one of the few true auteurs in the British industry. He was a complex man with an irresistible sense of humor—a Merseysider who retained a recognizable accent and a slightly cocky manner. (His effusive greeting to each stranger he passed

---

[3] Doug Tomlinson, ed., *Actors on Acting for the Screen* (New York: Garland Publications, 1994), p. 96.

as he walked down the impersonal, circular corridors of the BBC stunned the recipients.) The themes that fascinated him were adolescence and violence. He also had the English preoccupation with class. His excellent feature film *Scum* (1979) dealt with a group of working-class youths in a reformatory. Effective as it was, it was still a watered-down remake of a powerful TV movie that the BBC had been too nervous to air.

The two films I worked on with him were produced shortly after one of his periods of alcoholism, which had adversely affected his health. Before starting the first film, my manager warned me about Clarke's unpredictable behavior: "Be prepared to bail him out of jail at four o'clock in the morning." Luckily, by the time I worked with him, Alan had turned over a new leaf, though once or twice, late at night, his patience gave out with some upperclass English pomposity and violence would threaten. With typical self-deprecating humor, he once told a story about how he got off the London underground one afternoon and was approached by a drunk who invited him to "a place where there's a nonstop party and booze twenty-four hours a day." Following the lurching figure down the street, he was amazed to find that he was being taken to his own apartment. That was when he realized his drinking had to stop.

Humor was Alan's natural element. It polished him and made him attractive, it mitigated his constant worrying, and it defused his tendency to be aggressive. It also created a bond of affection—how can you not love someone who makes you laugh continuously?

Like all good directors, he was not secretive about his thought processes. During preproduction, as we traveled from one potential location to another, he would gaze out the car window, absorbed in thought. If we asked him what he was thinking, out would pour all his impressions of the place we'd just seen and how he was struggling to adapt it to the script. Some directors will see a location and know instantly that it is right—not Alan Clarke. Major decisions obsessed him and he would fret over them. He was very conscious of his fretting and would make fun of himself for doing it. His production team would fret and laugh with him late into the night until, one by one, we gave up and dragged ourselves to bed.

The shooting period with Alan was usually very challenging. The locations were often tricky, and there was always a conceptual component that was difficult to pull off. In the first film I worked on, we had a series of short scenes in the center of London and one major location in a very prominent building off a main street—all of which are nightmares for production managers who have to control the environment for the director.

If John Schlesinger was a master of ironically subversive storytelling, Alan Clark's terrain was violence and the strength required to resist it. He did not strive for classic visual elegance and tried to challenge orthodox storytelling. The result was that not every one of his productions was a success. The first film of his I worked on was a case in point. It explored the capitalist ties between Soviet Russia and the West by depicting all the stages of a secret deal between a Russian agent and a wealthy British entrepreneur. The problem was, no one involved in the production, including the producer, writer and director, had the faintest idea how such a deal might actually occur. Alan chose a long take, documentary style, which emphasized the complex details of the deal, but did not propel the story. More time was required for research, but the production deadline was not postponed.

In my second film with him, *Contact* (1982), he cast a group of young, half-trained actors as a platoon of paratroopers in Northern Ireland. The youths were dispatched to a training camp two weeks before shooting, where an ex-member of the Special Armed Services drilled them in military procedure. Throughout the shoot, this group lived separately from the rest of the crew, becoming increasingly restless and unruly. Those of us who had worked with Alan on more than one film recognized the pattern—great preproduction followed by a nightmare shoot.

The exclusive closeness that exists between a director and his team during preproduction cannot last into the shoot, when actors and crew also require attention. So, inevitably, we drifted slightly apart during production. As a production manager, I felt my duty was to protect Alan from as many logistical and personnel problems as I could. But problems arose during the shooting of *Contact* that were beyond my ability to handle them. (I've almost managed to expunge the horrors of that shoot from memory, but not quite. I still recall the unit funds disappearing from my car, and then being accosted at gunpoint during a night shoot by half-trained paratroopers.) Eventually, the animosity between the young actors and some of the crew became so unmanageable that I had to bring the situation to Alan's attention. He listened sympathetically to my explanation and then warned the actors that he would send them home if they did not cooperate. It was a typical Alan Clarke situation: restoring unruly adolescents to civility with his instinctive understanding of their psychology. His prompt action also won the crew's admiration.

During the period I worked with him, Alan began to experiment with form, style, and content. He often chose the subjects of the films he made and then developed them further with a professional writer. *Contact*, which was written by an ex-paratroop officer who was on set throughout the filming, was structured around the rhythms of a military patrol in Northern Ireland—long periods of dull slog contrasted with short periods of intense, deadly action. He was not interested in developing individual character portraits with his actors. The movie was about the platoon, which I think he saw as having an identity of its own. Military training and teamwork replaced formal rehearsals with actors. Almost the entire first day was spent setting up and shooting a scene in which the platoon intercepted a vehicle. The actors had to repeat the whole procedure till they understood it perfectly, and then it was shot in a series of wide shots. The film itself was comprised of a succession of set pieces, most of them shot at a distance, which gave it a detached and impassive quality.

Alan's struggle to find new ways to express his subject matter meant that each film was an experiment. I think that, like Kurosawa, he was trying to express the struggle between the individual and a violent society. (The fact that he grew up during the Second World War, on the wrong side of a powerful class divide, must have influenced his world-view.) The subjects he chose consistently explore related issues: The violent group painfully ennobling certain individuals who oppose it (*Scum*), individuals overtaken by a revolutionary society (*Danton's Death*), a platoon slowly tracing its way through a deadly, foreign no-man's-land (*Contact*). He tried to look unflinchingly and unsentimentally at both sides of the equation—the individual and the group—adapting whatever technology was at hand to express his message in a new way. In *Contact*, for example, he used military night-vision technology for the first time in a narrative drama.

During the period I worked with him, he was experimenting with the telephoto lens (or "long bottle" as he called it). The telephoto lens, with its ability to remove the viewer from the action and, at the same time, give a very close perspective, is an excellent visual expression of the dilemmas of subjectivity versus objectivity, proximity versus distance, and, ultimately, the individual versus the group, which were haunting Alan Clarke himself.

In his last period—with *Elephant* (1989) and other films—his experiments were even more radical. He had, in fact, entered a creative space that was tough, class-conscious, and highly innovative, and he was closer than ever to articulating his unique personal vision.

Roland Joffé: the power of inspiration

Roland Joffé worked extensively in British theater and television before directing his first feature film, *The Killing Fields*, in 1984. That movie brought him an Academy Award nomination as best director. His subsequent films include *The Mission* (1986), *Fat Man and Little Boy* (1989), *City of Joy* (1992), and *Vatel* (2000).

When I worked with him in the late 1970s, Joffé had already made several successful television movies and was in the midst of a remarkable burst of creativity that culminated in *The Killing Fields*. He had also had an interesting career in the theater, first at the experimental "Young Vic" theater, and later under Laurence Olivier at the Old Vic (the precursor of England's National Theatre).

Roland lived and breathed ideas. He radiated creative energy to an unusual degree. His energy level was so visceral that you could get a contact high. He was a kind of adventurer, and to work with him was to be swept up in his current visual and intellectual experiment.

I worked with him on two projects, only one of which got made. We were originally slated to do a film on the English painter Stanley Spencer. Roland had a reputation for being a radical left-wing program-maker, so this primarily artistic subject matter was a change of direction for him. (Roland's unpredictable choice of subject matter has periodically confounded his admirers.) He came in bursting with visual and conceptual ideas. Eventually he decided that the whole film was to be centered in one large suburban house through which the aged painter would ramble: As Spencer moved into each room, his imagination would transform it into a scene from his past. It was a simple, elegant, and extremely challenging concept—particularly for the production designer and lighting cameraman (DP).

Unfortunately, at the last minute, the main location fell through. British TV movies have limited budgets, and the house owner realized that he could get more money selling his property. So the location was sold, behind our backs, to a French academic couple. When we learned about the sale, Roland and I drove straight out to visit the couple and, in our hesitant French, offered them more money and pleaded with them to postpone their move. They would be happy to cooperate, they informed us, except there was a certain problem— "Nous avons des animaux très étranges" (we have some very strange animals). We offered to find the animals alternative accommodation, but to no avail. We never did find out precisely what kind of pets they had.

At a luncheon for the crew chiefs, hosted by our producer, we debated whether to continue with the project, which we had been working on for almost two months, or throw in the towel and start a new one. Eventually it was decided to flip a coin—as good a way of making a decision as any. For some reason, I was entrusted with the coin. As I flipped it high in the air, I could see that most people around the table—the set designer, wardrobe designer, makeup supervisor, and production team—had their eyes tensely shut or were holding their heads nervously in their hands. It came down tails and we went on to another production. Most directors would have been dejected, but not this one. He did not blame us for losing the location, and that made us more loyal to him than ever. Roland, the adventurer, was happy to begin a brand new project.

Initially, we had no project to go on to, so we sat by our telephones for a couple of weeks, waiting for the director and producer to come up with one. In the end, they settled on the Jacobean classic *'Tis Pity She's A Whore*, which Roland had once staged in the theater. The crew reassembled, and this time we were able to secure his first choice of location, the beautiful Chastleton House in Oxfordshire. The half dozen fine actors who had been cast in the first movie were given roles in the new one, and Nat Crosby (who also filmed Schlesinger's *An Englishman Abroad*) lit and shot the whole thing with his usual effortless grace.

Roland was very open and articulate about his concepts. He decided to set *'Tis Pity* in an indeterminate Victorian period: "Just put a huge pile of clothes on the floor and let the actors come in and choose their own wardrobe," he suggested. But this was unacceptable to British designers who were used to being given very specific historical periods and carefully matching each actor with a costume. Somehow, he eventually reached an understanding with the wardrobe department and the concept worked.

When I had asked John Schlesinger to do storyboards, he considered the idea; when I asked Roland, he actually produced them. He spent several days living and sleeping in the Jacobean location, and returned with a series of drawings that further clarified his concept. The storyboards were never actually implemented. A couple of days into the shoot he told me, "They're too straightforward. I think I can do better than that." This experience taught me that storyboards are not final images to which directors have to adhere. They offer directors a first stab at shooting, and allow them to make improvements. In this case, the rejection of the storyboards marked the departure from a straightforward, grammatically correct HCS sequence (WS-MS-MCU) to one that involved longer developing shots and actor movement and less predictable cutting.

Sometimes Roland did not finalize a scene's blocking till right before it was to be shot. I remember occasionally bringing him lunch on a tray, so that he could plan the afternoon's shoot alone in the deserted location. He enjoyed the challenge of working under pressure and often produced his most innovative solutions this way.

Shooting was preceded by a week of rehearsals in which the actors were encouraged to work in pairs to explore their relationships. Roland was particularly concerned that the seventeenth-century lines should sound natural and, at the same time, intense. I remember Kenneth Cranham and Cherie Lunghi working hard and successfully at producing a conversational tone. On the set, when an actor was about to shoot an emotional scene, Roland would take them aside and describe their state of mind—"Your husband has just left you, you feel alone and deserted, etc." Strangely enough, this was the first time I'd ever seen a screen director work intensely with an actor in this way. It was a revelation.

Unlike Alan Clarke, who would discuss his ideas and listen to anyone who happened to be around, Roland discussed his ideas simply in order to clarify them to his audience. He was absolutely secure about his vision. He was not arrogant, he simply knew what he wanted. His job was to provide conceptual and artistic leadership, and our job was to implement his vision. He was always appreciative of those who were working for him. At least twice a week, he invited the whole crew to join him at his favorite restaurant. He made no distinction between leading actor and prop man—both were equally welcome as long as they could pay their way.

Of the three directors mentioned here, Roland was the most concerned about shot composition. In 'Tis Pity, his intimate knowledge of the house enabled him to marry character and location in an exciting way. For instance, Roland placed an actor with a soliloquy in a stained-glass window recess about six feet off the ground, where he was bathed in a gentle backlight, while the camera gradually zoomed in to a closeup. I remember one rare but amicable dispute between the director and the cameraman about the framing of a 2-shot. When Nat Crosby eventually tried out his own framing, he immediately saw that Roland's was the only one that worked. The ability to produce shots of sudden beauty characterizes many of Roland Joffé's subsequent films and especially his opulent Vatel.

44. Getting Started in the Industry: Interviews with Directors

This chapter consists of interviews with five directors representing a variety of styles and approaches, who speak candidly about how they entered the industry and the routes they took to become directors. They also offer cogent advice to aspiring directors on how to prepare for the job.

Theodore Witcher

Credits include: *Love Jones* (1997)

I wanted to be a director from about age eleven and worked toward it from there. I was a working writer in Hollywood immediately prior to getting my first directing job.

What steps did you take to become a director?
The story is pretty typical. My parents bought me a Super-8 camera and a few other tools, and I began making incredibly awful short films of my own. Then I went to film school. First, the University of Iowa, which, believe it or not, had an excellent film program, and then Columbia College in Chicago, where I graduated in 1991. I had and have a love-hate relationship with film school: I don't see it as absolutely essential to becoming either a narrative feature filmmaker, given the manufacturing model of Hollywood, or a commercial/music-video filmmaker. However, familiarity with the following subjects will

almost certainly be useful to a narrative feature filmmaker: history, literature, sociology, psychology, political science, and all the other major disciplines of artistic expression. If I were to do it all over again, I'd put more of an emphasis on the stuff that is actually applicable to the task of being a dramatist.

What kind of training did you have?
For formal training, see above. Informal training: watching every movie ever made from about age ten or eleven onwards, plus as many books, interviews, laserdisc and DVD commentaries. And countless drunken philosophical conversations about the nature of cinema with enlightened, and often unenlightened, friends.

Who were your influences and role models?
A cinematography professor I had was a big influence on me. Krzysztof Kieslowski. Victor Erice. Francis Coppola. Branford Marsalis. Gabriel Garcia Marquez.

What do you find most interesting about the job?
The actual job of directing a film is constantly interesting. It is a long and difficult negotiation between the vision of the movie you'd like to make and the actualities of the physical universe you inhabit. Not to mention your own limitations as a human being and artist. What you might discover during the process about yourself or about other human beings is probably the most interesting, but often, if not always, the most painful.

And the toughest parts of the job?
Navigating the politics of Hollywood, which is to say, navigating both the politics of various multinational corporate identities and the politics of culture. That and being on your feet the whole day.

What advice would you give someone wanting to join the profession?
Run. In. The. Opposite. Direction. And if you would take that advice, you're no director.

And, to paraphrase Orson Welles, stop looking at movies and start looking at life.

Kasi Lemmons

Credits include: *Dr. Hugo* (Short, 1997), *Eve's Bayou* (1997), *The Caveman's Valentine* (2001)

I started very young as an actor. I did some off-Broadway theater, a few things on television, and by the time I went to film school I had done a couple of movies. But, being an African-American actress, I had a lot of time on my hands, and I started to really want something to fill the time.

And I had been writing. I had taken a playwriting course, had written a couple of plays, and I was writing scenes that friends of mine would do in acting class. Around that time there was a lot going on in politics—it was just after Nicaragua—and I started to get interested in documentary filmmaking. And so I went to film school to learn cinematography, and while I was there I made two documentaries. One of them was more successful than the other. With that film I really started to become a filmmaker.

There was a group in New York City at that time called Black Filmmakers, and the guys who were running it were the Hudlin Brothers. They really took me under their wing and gave screenings for me, because the film was only seven minutes long. I started to do some festival circuits with it. And I started to kind of look at my life differently.

Then I worked with Bill Cosby and he said, "Do you write as well?" And I said, "Yeah, as a matter of fact I do." So, he hired me to write a movie script for him and two other women, which was kind of based on my short film. That was in 1988, and I joined the Writers Guild.

Then I worked with this very interesting theater group in New York called "Naked Angels," and I got an audition with Jonathan Demme, which led to a part in *Silence of the Lambs*.

When I moved back to Los Angeles, I started to feel that I had a big story inside of me that I hadn't written down yet. And it got to the point where I could tell the story. So I'd be acting on these movie sets, and then taking the producers aside and telling them the story. I was in therapy at the time, and my therapist said "You know, you really should just take some time off from your acting and write this story down." And that's what I did. That was *Eve's Bayou*.

After writing *Eve's Bayou*, I became a real writer—I supported myself by writing. People read that script and hired me to write other scripts. As a matter of fact, I think I wrote four or five, maybe six, before the film *Eve's Bayou* got made.

While we were scouting for *Eve's Bayou*, we started looking for a director. We were really having a hard time. The material was very specific and strange, and people would become very interested in it and then kind of get cold feet or change their minds. Then one day, I woke up and said, "Well, you know what …

I went to film school, I'm good at directing." My producer fell over in shock, but he ended up being very, very supportive. He had this great idea—he said, "Forget these little documentaries you made in film school. Let's go out and shoot a short film on 35mm with a real crew that is a short-subject version of the feature you want to shoot." And that's what I did. We produced this short film called *Dr. Hugo*, which is actually on the DVD of *Eve's Bayou*.

So now we had this film that we could show, which was shot in the same style, using the same DP, as *Eve's Bayou*. Based on that, the actor Samuel Jackson became interested. And, once we had Sam, we had much more of a real movie, though I think it still took another year before we were finally "greenlighted."

So, you weren't driven to be a director from the start?
I was more driven to be a filmmaker. But I didn't think that at this point of my life [in 2002] I would be going into my third feature film as a director. I thought that I would act until I couldn't anymore. As an African-American woman, there was going to come a day when I was going to need something to fall back on. I thought I'd put *Eve's Bayou* in a drawer and take it out one day when I was older and wiser, and maybe star in it or produce it or direct it—but way down the line.

Your actor training and writing experience must have been great assets when it came to directing.
I think the natural by-product of acting and writing is directing. Writing is definitely a great asset, and you certainly visualize the material when you're writing. And being an actor gives you a sense of what it's like on a film set, and you know what an actor needs. When they did the EPK [Electronic Press Kit] for my second film, *Caveman's Valentine*, they asked the actors, "What makes working with Kasi different?" Every single actor replied, "Because she's an actor." So there it was in my face, the proof that it must be different working with an actor. But I don't think about it as I'm doing it.

I worked with some directors early on in my career who screamed and yelled to get a point across or were very rough. When I worked with Jonathan Demme, he was just very gentle and warm. You know, he had the Zen in his work—it was inspiring. But when you are acting in a movie, it's hard to think as a director. Directing is really a very insular skill. There's a great quote, "Directing is like sex, because you never know how the other guy is doing it." It's true—you really only have your own point of view as a director.

Are there any parts of the job that you don't enjoy as much as the others?
All jobs have their personal hell. The adrenaline of production is wonderful, exhilarating, exciting, terrifying. But there's a point at which it's almost like you have to break through the walls of physical exhaustion.

What advice would you give someone who wanted to join the profession?
There are two things that I would say. One is, if you can write at all, you should get a personal story down in some form even if you don't finish the full script. Your first film should not be just any old film. It should be something that is some sort of signature statement about you as an artist. Or find some material — maybe written by your best friend — that speaks to you on a personal level.

Then I would say, work on a set with a director to learn what it's like. I'm grateful for my years as an actor because I realized that making a film is a collaboration. You need every single person there to be working for you.

Steve Carr

Credits include: *Next Friday* (2000), *Dr. Dolittle 2* (2001), *Daddy Day Care* (2003)

My road to becoming a director was not a very common one. I had a fine arts background. I'd studied painting since I was ten years old, and my goal was to become a painter. But when you get out of art school, you kind of realize there's no job, no application you can fill in that says "painter." So I started out designing album covers for a guy called Russell Simmons in a top hip-hop agency called Def Jam, and I did that for quite a while.

Then there was this music video that they were doing, but the guy who was going to direct it was in prison. In the staff meeting, I came up with an idea and they said, "Ah, that's a great idea, who are you going to get to direct it?" And I was like, "Well, it's my idea. I want to direct it," although I had no experience in directing at all. Russell said, "You don't know how to direct." And I said, "Naw, I can do it." Of course, he knew I was lying, but he also believed I could do it. And that's how I ended up directing a music video, which is the way a lot of directors are coming up now.

And so I had no formal film background at all. I've never taken a film course. Basically, I just lied and told them I knew what I was doing, then I got onto the set and made sure that I hired the right people. And that's how I got started. At first, I directed once in a while, and then I got a little more secure and started to do it more often. And from doing music videos, I eventually decided to move out to California with the vague idea that I'd like to be a movie director, but no real plan about how to do it.

So where did you start before you went to California?
I was in New York. New York is where most of the record companies are stationed, and it's a great place for music videos. I have a commercial aesthetic. I'm not interested at this point in my life in making *Requiem for a Dream*. And so I kind of had this vague idea that if I came out to L.A. I'd have a better chance to make movies. And then I was lucky enough to have a friend named Brett Ratner, whom I knew through Russell Simmons. Brett had directed *Rush Hour*, *Rush Hour II*, and *Family Man*. I've always been lucky enough to be in the right place at the right time and form good relationships. Brett put me in touch with somebody who had a small film called *Next Friday*, a sequel to the film *Friday*. He told them, "Steve's a great guy. He's really talented …"

You gotta know that at the time I was making music videos, it was all about style. The artist was shot beautifully, and there were dancing girls and stuff like that. Initially, my instinct was to follow the pack, but my producer/partner Heidi Santelli advised me, "Don't do what everybody else is doing." So what I did, and what I ended up putting on my [show] reel, were small narratives. I utilized music videos to tell three-minute stories, which nobody else was doing. It limited me in a sense—I never became the number one video guy—but I was always in the top five because rappers tell linear stories: "I woke up. I shot someone. I went to sleep. But I got arrested." So when my opportunity came to direct a film, and they looked at all these music videos, my reel stood out because there were four little stories on it.

Did your reel drive you toward a certain kind of film?
Yeah, my first film was an urban comedy. Unfortunately for the studios, there is a shortage of black directors in Hollywood. Despite being Caucasian, I was lucky enough to have as much of an urban music and urban culture background as any white kid could. And I've always had what I hope is a fairly good sense of humor. So that, combined with my ability to show them I knew how to shoot narrative, plus the connections I had made, got me through the door and led to my first film. When I went in to meet with the producers at New Line, I was like, "Listen, I don't know anything about coming in here and pitching a film. I read the script and these are the things I think are wrong with it. Here are the

solutions I think would help," and was just very excited about the opportunity. They sent me out to see Ice Cube in Arizona, where he was shooting *Three Kings*. During lunch, I went into his trailer and he said, "How you doing?" And I was like, "Blah, blah, blah, blah, blah." And he was, like, "Okay. Get out." I waited outside for a while and then eventually flew back to L.A. And then a couple of days later, I heard, "You got the movie."

One of the things I know from having my own graphic design company and from doing those videos is that your job as a director is twofold. One is making sure you hire people who know their job and are able to support your vision. And the second is to just have the balls to agree to do it. Heidi was personal assistant to Michael J. Fox on a movie called *The Love of Money*, and so I was able to go down onto the set and meet him and hang out with him. And he gave me the best advice—"Being a director means having the balls to say, 'Follow me, I know the right way.'" I've never forgotten that piece of advice. Making a wrong decision is better than making no decision. And if you're smart and flexible, it eventually leads to the right path. Nobody wants to work with a guy who doesn't know.

What advice would you give someone wanting to join the profession?
Because my path has been kind of unique, it's hard for me to say, "Go to film school." If you are in film school, be where the films are made, be where commercials are made, be where you can get involved. I don't know how many films get made in Iowa but, if you live in Iowa and you want to be a filmmaker, you need to be a P.A. on the ones that do. And if you get the opportunity to shoot film, shoot it. Don't be afraid. If you fuck up, nobody will remember. You also need to build relationships within the community. You know, there were directors in my generation who were such prima donnas that no one hired them a second time. Being a director is about being a people person.

It's not always about getting the coolest angle or a crane shot that's going to take four hours to do and lose you your day. You probably won't use the shot anyway. It's about negotiation. It's about diplomacy. And it's about an overall vision—looking at the big picture and not worrying about the small brush stroke.

The hardest part of the job for me is just how physically and mentally demanding it is. Ron Howard said he took a counter onto the set one day and started counting the questions, from the first, like, "Do you want milk in your coffee?" to the last, "Do you want me to get your car?" And he said he answered over two thousand questions that one day. If you're doing a music video, you're doing it over the course of two or three days. But my last shoot was, like, sixty or seventy days. And when you are answering that many questions and trying to be decisive, it's mentally and physically draining. It's so funny because before I started my second film everybody said, "You know, you really need to work out. You should take yoga, you should really be physically fit." But I knew that Eddie Murphy was on what they call a twelve-hour "portal" [a strict twelve hour day]. So I said to myself, "That means I'm gonna work twelve hours. I can do that every day." First one or two days, I was fine. Third day, I was like … kill me please! Now before I start any film I'm six months in the gym.

Some actors say that working with Eddie Murphy can be exhausting because he's so quick.

I tried my hardest to prepare for the first day of shooting, because the budget for this movie was about eighty million. Basically, I had a shot list for the first twenty-five days of shooting. I knew exactly where I wanted the camera to be. So the first shot of the day on the first day of shooting is Eddie walking in and hugging his wife. I explain that to him and show him the blocking. "Start off … establishing shot here …then we're gonna do two singles … and if I have time, we're gonna do this …" Eddie's like, "Well, my character would never do that." And I'm thinking to myself, "Your character would never walk in the door?" And he's like, "No, I would never walk in that way." So I stop for a second and say, "Okay, well then this is what we'll do. You'll walk in here and my establishing shot will be a low angle, and then we'll go into …" And he goes, "Fine. Great." And then he left. And I look down at my shirt and I have sweat stains—huge! Obviously, Eddie came in and he tested me because he wanted to be sure he wasn't going to have to direct that film himself. And he never challenged me again. We had a phenomenal working relationship. I learned so much from him. But that's directing. So, if it helps anybody—if in doubt, lie. The director's creed!

Kevin Bright

Directing credits include: *The Adventures of Brisco County Jr.* (1993), *Friends* (1994 and after, also executive producer), *Veronica's Closet* (1997, and executive producer), *Jesse* (1998, and executive producer), *DAG* (2000)

My dad was in show business. He was a performer, he was a union exec and a personal manager. So I'd been around show business all my life, but I'd never really thought about it as a career. Then, when I was a first-year history major at Plattsburg State University, I took an Introduction to Film class as an elective. Studying different filmmakers and how the art evolved stimulated me academically for the first time. I knew this was something I'd unknowingly prepared myself for all my life by watching *Gone With the Wind* or *King Kong* all seven times it was the Million Dollar Movie that week, or watching every episode of *Abbott and Costello, The Three Stooges,* and *Laurel and Hardy.*

I switched to Mass Communications as a major, but at that school in those days, there was only one teacher who taught every course, and he had a theater background. It became apparent that, if I wanted to pursue this, I needed to go someplace that had professors who had worked in the industry. So the reason I went to Emerson College was Dan Lounsbery, who had made television shows I had heard of.

Then, after getting out of school, I started the way everybody does—getting coffee. I had the good fortune of working for a very small, independent producer in New York by the name of Joseph Cates, who did variety specials. I was supposed to work there for three months on two shows. Three months turned into six years, with a lot of promotion along the way.

I considered television a producer's medium, and not a director's medium, and was always far more interested in producing. I felt that the producer really had the vision of what the show was. But in order to bring that vision to life, the next step was directing. That's about as close as it gets to being an auteur in television. To write, produce, and direct is pretty tough on TV. Not many people have achieved that, but this was the next best thing. So I actually didn't start directing until I had been working in television for about thirteen years, and producing for about five or six.

When you are producing multiple projects in television, devoting a week to directing an episode is hard to do. I think most directors start out wanting to be directors. It often starts with a theater background or even a choreography background. Rob Marshall, who did *Chicago,* was a choreographer who used to do variety shows.

So how long does it take?

It takes as long as it takes. I think the thing about directing is you can approach it single-mindedly with the attitude "this is what I want to do," but sometimes it also just finds you. There is no set way to get started. You can come up the ranks, you can be a DGA [Directors Guild of America] trainee, you can be an assistant director. People have been assistants to the producer and gotten into directing.

Editing is another common way, because you have to know how to put a show together visually. Incidentally, you need to know how to deal with the bodies that go in front of the camera as well.

What advice would you give people who want to direct, particularly in the sitcom genre? Is there a way that sitcom directors come at it that's different? No. Sometimes they come from being writers. Some have been editors. Some will cross over from single-camera directing to multi-camera directing. There's nothing that's standard about situation comedy. I remember Jim Burrows telling me about how he got into television. You know, his father had been involved in the theater and he himself had directed some theater. He came out to Hollywood because he realized that with sitcoms you get to direct a play every week. And it's a new play, and when it's done you move on to the next play. And yes, it's the same characters, but it's about watching these characters grow, and also about being responsible for how that growth takes shape. So, it's a satisfaction that goes on for years. And your work lives on in reruns, so it can be tremendously satisfying.

Is there anything that you, when you are producing, look for in your directors? To me, there are two kinds of directors in sitcoms. First, there are directors who get coverage. Coverage is easy to get, especially in a multi-camera show. Whoever is talking, make sure the camera is on them. But is it a good-looking shot? Is it well-lit? Are they standing in a way that best expresses what is happening in the scene?

And then there are those who understand the story that's in the script, and know how to tell it by using all the tools at their disposal—the actors, the cameras, the sound, the editing—to their best advantage. So I think the simple answer is that you're looking for somebody who knows how to tell a story.

Jan Egleson

Credits include: *Billy in the Lowlands* (1979), *The Dark End of the Street* (1981), *Shock to the System* (1990), *The Blue Diner* (2000), and also, many television pilots, including *Orleans* (1997) and *Mind Games* (1998)

I was trained to be an actor on the stage and then acted in a few films and was very intrigued by the process. The one that really started me thinking about filmmaking was a movie called *The Friends of Eddie Coyle*, set in the Boston crime underworld. It was my first exposure to big-time filmmaking. I loved it. I had a very small part, but they made a number of technical mistakes, so we had to do it a couple of times. That was unusual but it was great for me. I earned more money and I got to see a lot more of the process.

I was involved with a group that worked with young people from the projects in Cambridge, and the kids got quite good at acting and had an appetite for it. I thought, "Gee, why don't we make a film out of their experience with this program?" So it was a very low-key, very natural way of moving over into directing film. And, because of the subject matter, it seemed appropriate to use the documentary feel of a very small crew, very light equipment—no lighting, no elaborate production values. And that's really how I began.

I had no knowledge of the language of filmmaking. I was relying on the documentary filmmakers I had befriended. I didn't have the control that I later learned. Each film that I made after that got slightly more elaborate and I began working with people who were more experienced.

Actually, the first big film I directed was shot by a cinematographer called Ed Lachman, who has just been nominated for an Academy Award for *Far From Heaven*. When he came on board, he brought with him the language and tools of larger filmmaking. He really taught me. It was very much learn-as-you-go, and Ed was very patient. I began to learn the possibilities of having a real crew, and learn some of the grammar of filmmaking. I think I was very fortunate.

Then I made a number of films for a public television series called *American Playhouse*, so I was able to work at a reasonable level of production without all the pressures of Hollywood. I think, in retrospect, I was incredibly blessed to have that. Then, the first job I was actually hired to do in the industry was a television pilot. After making four or five films, I knew something about the craft, so all I had to learn was the politics of working in the industry. That's a job in itself. I was lucky I wasn't learning both at the same time. That's hard.

Can you say something about the politics?

I think that, without demonizing it, the industry is an industry. You know, there are guilds and unions and people with expectations of what their job is, what they do, and what you should do. It's a little bewildering, particularly if you come from situations where, basically, you and your friends are making it up, and you're all buddies. If you want to move a light, you move a light, and if you want to change your mind, you change your mind. It's much harder, and, I think, rightfully so, when you're in a system in which people are used to working in a particular way.

A lot of what you're learning is the social organization: Grips are grips and they do stuff, and gaffers are gaffers. And also how to talk to fellow workers who are not necessarily your friends. That's an adjustment. It was for me. It took a couple of films to learn how to do that. A lot of it is about people skills and how you communicate. So much of it is really just how you listen and how you convey what you want to happen.

What advice would you give someone who wants to be a director?
I think everybody has their own path. I guess the first thing is—make films. It will both demonstrate your skills and also teach you. You have to learn the craft.

Try to see the industry as a place in which people have their own agendas and respect them. And try to discover how you can bring your voice to a project without being overwhelming. That's a hard thing. It is hard for people who are driven and have a real vision to find a way to work within the industry. Patience is good. As is being clear.

People in general don't like being surprised. The more you can alert people to what your vision is and what you want to do on a practical, mundane level, the better. "I want to make this shot so you see this character do that, and, yes, it's a little unorthodox, but it's going to cut to that … and, yeah, the lights will be off, but really it's going to be wonderful because you're going to hear this …" The more you can prepare people and bring them into your vision, the more they'll get on your side. It's the only underlying piece of advice that I can think of.

Can people make a living if they don't go into the Hollywood side of the industry?
I guess it depends on what you think of as making a living. I think that there are certainly plenty of people out there who have decided that they would rather work on a certain level and control what they do and be so-called "independents," and they can manage it.

The Hollywood system, unfortunately, wastes a lot of time. There are many wonderful directors sitting around waiting for projects to happen, and they've been sitting around for three or four years. Then they may get to do something with a lot of resources, but what about those four years? Big Hollywood films can take five to eight years to get going.

Small jobs can also take a long time, but at a certain point you can say, "Well, I'm going to do it." And you do it. You may not have all the things you need, but you spend more of your time making a movie. It's a trade. You have to find where you're comfortable.

Is there a difference between television and film?

In features, in general, directors really do have more authority and more control. Of course, there are gradations in it. Television in America tends to be a writer/producer medium. If you work with people who are collaborative, I think you can really bring something to it. Particularly in pilots for shows. That's one place I think is very creative. But in television, as a director, you're usually brought on board way down the line, often after casting, and often after the producers have decided what city they're going to shoot in. Many things are in place, and there are expectations about what the show will look like. I wouldn't look to TV for a lot of self-expression.

How could people prepare themselves to be directors?

Develop whatever skills you can in terms of communicating your vision. That's a good thing. Now, when I do a project, I look at areas like art history, literature, and music. I try to find pictures or fabric or music, because often describing doesn't really work. We all think differently, so it's good to find very objective things that you can point to and say, "That's the image, that's the feel, that's the music, that's the sound …" I think you can work on those skills.

Appendix: Storyboards

Academy Aperture (4x3)

Production Title

Visuals

Audio

Widescreen (HDTV) 1.78:1

Production Title

Visuals

Audio

Bibliography

Non-history chapters

Steven Ascher and Edwards Pincus. *The Filmmaker's Handbook*. Plume, 1999.

David Bell. *Getting the Best Score*. Silman-James Press, 1994.

Eugenio Barba and Nicola Savarese. *A Dictionary of Theater Anthropology: The Secret Art of the Performer*. Routledge, 1991.

Anne Bogart. *A Director Prepares: Seven Essays on Art & Theatre*. Routledge, 2001.

Michael Caine (Maria Aitken ed.). *Acting in Film* . Applause, 1990.

Simon Callow. *Being an Actor*. St. Martin's Pres, 1984.

Tom Charity. *John Cassavetes: Lifeworks*. Omnibus Press, 2001.

Michel Chion. *Audio-Vision*. Columbia University Press, 1994.

Harold Clurman. *The Fervent Years*. Da Capo Press, 1983.

——. *On Directing*. Macmillan, 1972.

Toby Cole and Helen Krich Chinoy. *Actors on Acting*. Crown Publishers, 1970 ed.

——. *Directors On Directing: A Source Book of the Modern Theatre*. The Bobbs-Merrill Co. Inc., 1963 ed.

Ken Dancyger. *The Techniques of Film and Video Editing*. Focal Press, 2002.

Bette Davis. *The Lonely Life*. Berkley Books, 1990.

Agnes De Mille. *Martha: The Life & Work of Martha Graham*. Random House, 1991.

Michael Bigelow Dixon and Joel A. Smith, eds. *Anne Bogart Viewpoints*. Smith & Kraus, 1995.

Edward Dmytryk. *On Screen Directing*. Focal Press, 1984.

Syd Field. *Screenwriting: The Foundations of Screenwriting*. Dell Publications, 1982.

Gregory Goodell. *Independent Feature Film Production*. St. Martin's Press, 1998.

Uta Hagen. *A Challenge for the Actor*. Scribners, 1991.

John Walker. *Halliwell's Film & Video Guide*. Harper Resource, 1999 + 2000.

John Irving. *My Movie Business*. Random House, 1999.

Keith Johnstone. *Impro: Improvisation and the Theatre*. Theatre Arts Books, 1979.

——. *Impro for Storytellers*. Faber & Faber, 1999.

Steven Katz. *Shot by Shot*. Michael Weise, 1991.

Jeremy Kagan, ed. *Directors Close Up*. Focal Press, 2000.

Nicolas Kent. *Naked Hollywood: Money and Power in the Movies Today*. St. Martin's Press, 1991.

Robert Lewis. *Advice to the Players*. Harper and Row, 1980.

Sidney Lumet. *Making Movies*. Knopf, 1995.

David Mamet. *On Directing Film*. Penguin, 1991.

——. *True and False*. Pantheon, 1997.

Robert Cohen Mayfield. *Acting Power*. Mayfield, 1978.

Sanford Meisner and Dennis Longwell. *Sanford Meisner on Acting*. Viking Books, 1987.

Tom Milne, ed. *Godard on Godard*. Viking, 1972.

Thomas A. Ohanian and Michael E. Phillips. *Digital Filmmaking*. Focal Press, 1996.

Gabriella Oldham. *First Cut: Conversations with Film Editors*. University of California Press, 1995.

Michael Ondaatje. *The Conversations: Walter Murch and the Art of Editing Film*. Knopf, 2002.

John Pym, ed. *Time Out Film Guide*. Penguin USA, 1999.

Karel Reisz and Gavin Miller. *The Technique of Film Editing*. Focal Press, 1995.

Brian G. Rose, ed. *Directing for Television*. The Scarecrow Press, 1999.

William Rothman. *Hitchcock: The Murderous Gaze*. Harvard University Press, 1982.

Alain Silver and Elizabeth Ward. *The Film Director's Team*. Silman-James Press, 1992.

Ed Spiegel. *The Inncocence of the Eye: A Filmmaker's Guide*. Silman-James Press, 2002.

Viola Spolin. *Improvisation for the Theater.* Northwestern University Press, 1999 (3rd ed.).

———. *Theater Games for Rehearsal.* Northwestern University Press, 1985.

Magazines

American Cinematographer. Monthly magazine with first-hand reports by prominent cinematographers. ASC Holding Corp. (published monthly). October 2003 edition has a special focus on camera movement.

The Independent. Published monthly by The Foundation for Independent Video and Film.

"Martin Scorsese's Comfortable State of Anxiety." *Movie Maker*, Vol. 9, No. 48.

New York Times Magazine, Nov. 16, 1997, p. 93.

Peter Broderick. "Moviemaking in Transition." *Scientific American*, Nov. 2000, pp. 61–69.

Colette Connor. "24P HD Ready for Primetime." *Videography*, Oct. 20001, pp.78–84.

History chapters

Steven Bach. *Final Cut: Dreams and Disaster in the Making of Heaven's Gate*. Newmarket Press, 1985.

Jean Benedetti. *Stanislavski: A Biography*. Routledge, 1988.

——. *Stanislavski and the Actor*. Routledge, 1998.

Richard Blum. *American Film Acting*. UMI Research Press, 1984.

Richard Boleslavsky. *Acting: The First Six Lessons*. Theatre Arts Books, 1949.

David Bordwell, Janet Staiger and Kristin Thompson. *The Classical Hollywood Cinema*. Columbia University Press, 1985.

Richard Brestoff. *The Great Acting Teachers and Their Methods*. Smith and Kraus, 1995.

Michael Chekhov. *To the Director & Playwright*. Greenwood, 1963.

——. *To the Actor*. Harper, 1953.

Harold Clurman. *The Fervent Years*. Da Capo Press, 1957.

Charles Davy, ed. *The Literature of Cinema*. New York, 1970.

Richard Dyer MacCann, ed. *The Stars Appear*. Scarecrow Press, 1992.

James Fisher. *Spencer Tracy: A Bio-Bibliography*. Greenwood, 1994.

Gary Fishgall. *Pieces of Time: The Life of James Stewart*. Scribner, 1997.

David Garfield. *A Player's Place: The Story of the Actors Studio*. Macmillan, 1980.

Tom Gunning. *D.W. Griffith and the Origins of American Narrative Film*. University of Illinois Press, 1991.

Leslie Halliwell. *Halliwell's Film & Video Guide*. John Walker, 2000.

Jan Herman. *A Talent for Trouble: The Life of Hollywood's Most Acclaimed Director, William Wyler*. Putnam, 1996.

Robert H. Hethmon, ed. *Strasberg at the Actors Studio*. Jonathan Cape, 1966.

S. Loraine Hull. *Strasberg's Method*. Ox Bow, 1985.

Paul Kerr, ed. *The Hollywood Film Industry*. Routledge & Kegan Paul, 1986.

Leonard J. Leff. *Hitchcock & Selznick*. University of California Press, 1987.

Robert Lewis. *Slings and Arrows*. Stein and Day, 1984.

Alan Lovell and Peter Kramer, eds. *Screenacting*. Routledge, 1999.

David Magarshack. *Stanislavski: A Life*. Faber & Faber, 1986.

Mae Marsh. *Screen Acting*. Photo-Star Publishing, 1922.

Patrick McGilligan. *Jack's Life*. Norton, 1994.

Jeffrey Meyers. *Gary Cooper: American Hero*. Morrow, 1988.

Sonia Moore. *The Stanislavski System*. Penguin Books, 1984.

Charles Musser. *History of American Cinema Vol 1: The Emergence of Cinema*. Scribner's, 1990.

James Naremore. *Acting in the Cinema*. University of California Press, 1990.

Mary Pickford. *Sunshine and Shadow*. Heineman, 1956.

Lawrence J. Quirk. *James Stewart: Behind the Scenes of a Wonderful Life*. Applause, 1997.

Richard Schikel. *D.W. Griffith: An American Life*. Limelight, 1996.

Ted Shawn. *Every Little Movement: A Book About Delsarte*. Dance Horizons, 1974.

Scott Simmon. *The Films of D.W.Griffith*. Cambridge University Press, 1993.

Donald Spoto. *The Dark Side of Genius: The Life of Alfred Hitchcock*. Little Brown, 1983.

——. *Dietrich*. Bantam, 1992.

——. *Laurence Olivier*. Harper Collins, 1992.

Kevin Sweeney. *Henry Fonda: A Bio-Bibliography*. Greenwood, 1992.

Peter Thompson. *Jack Nicholson: The Life and Times of an Actor on the Edge*. Carol Publishing, 1997.

Doug Tomlinson, ed. *Actors On Acting for the Screen*. Garland, 1994.

Geoffrey Wansell. *Haunted Idol: The Story of the Real Cary Grant*. Quill, 1983.

Edgar S. Weiner, ed. *Delsarte System of Oratory*. Wehmen Brothers, 1893.

Carole Zucker. *Figures of Light*. Plenum Press, 1995.

——. *In the Company of Actors*. Theatre Arts, 1999.

Article

"The Eyes Are Really the Focus: Photoplay Acting and Film Form and Style." *Wide Angle*, Vol. 6, No. 4, 1985 ("Actors & Acting Edition"), pp. 14–23.

Glossary

Action (or **activity**). A physical task accomplished by an actor.

"Action" is also a term used by some to mean *objective*. See also *through-line*.

Action props. See *props*.

Actors Studio. Originally founded in 1947 in New York by members of the *Group Theater* for professional scenework. It subsequently became closely associated with Lee Strasberg and his acting theories known as *the Method*.

Adjustment. (1) A new *action* that is carried out by a character to overcome an *obstacle*. (2) A note or comment given by a director to an actor that changes an underlying choice.

Anamorphic. A very wide format (such as CinemaScope) in which the image is squeezed inside the camera by an anamorphic (or reducing) lens. The image is subsequently "unsqueezed" for projection.

Animatix. A series of storyboards that are recorded and, often, edited together with readings of the associated script lines. They help a director get a better feeling for the flow of particular scenes or whole movies.

Arc. (1) The "story arc" is the way events develop over time in a story. (Visualized as an arc in space, the bottom ends of the arc would represent a story's introduction and final resolution, while a story's main climax would be represented by the arc's apex.) A story may also have "character arcs," which represent the changes that a story's character undergoes. The arc is a useful way of visually/mentally analyzing a story's form. (2) The movement of a camera in a semi-circle around its subject while maintaining a constant distance (radius) from that subject.

Art director. A person who implements the overall plan of the *production designer* by designing sets and supervising their construction. On a small-scale production without a production designer, the art director may be the most senior member of the design department.

Aspect ratio. The size of the screen in different film and television formats—frequently expressed in film as the value of its width divided by its height, with the height usually expressed as 1. For example, the ratio 1.33:1 approximates standard 35mm "Academy Aperture" and 1.65:1 or 2.25:1 and so on represent various *widescreen* formats. The standard television aspect ratio, which is also 1.33:1, is often expressed as 4x3. The aspect ratio of widescreen TV is 16x9.

Assembly. The preliminary edit of a film's individual scenes and sequences into story order.

Assistant director. Also known as the "AD" or the "first assistant" or simply the "first," this member of the *production team* is responsible for implementing the shooting schedule and maintaining a smoothly running set during shooting.

Atmosphere. Also commonly known as "atmos," this is a location's unique ambient sounds. Atmos is often recorded as a separate *wild track*, which may be used in editing to help cover discrepancies between sound takes or added as part of a scene's *soundscape*.

Automatic Dialogue Replacement (ADR). The recording (or re-recording) of an actor's dialogue after the scene has been shot. Also known as "looping" because the process usually involves playing back short loops of the original picture and audio while an actor attempts to synch his new performance to his original one.

B-roll. A term most commonly used in documentary production to describe shots that illustrate or enhance a story, but which do not carry the essential story elements (or "A-roll"). B-roll includes *cut-ins* and *cutaways*.

Backstory. That which has occurred before the events shown in a film. This usually includes details about a character's past often created by the actors and/or the director to shed light upon a particular character, scene, or story.

Beat. (1) A scene is often divided up into its component parts for analysis. Each single component is called a beat (or "unit" or " bit" or "event"). Exactly which portions of a scene constitute beats often differs for writers, actors, and directors, each of whom has a slightly different goal when analyzing a scene. (2) A term used in a script to denote a short pause in dialogue or activity.

Best boy. The assistant chief electrician. See also *gaffer*.

Bible. A record, in a long-running television series, of important events and characters' personal histories. It is used as a reference for a show's writers, producers, and directors.

Biomechanics. The very physical and stylized method of actor training developed by the Russian theatrical innovator Vsevolod Meyerhold (1874–1940).

Bit. See *beat*.

BITC. See *burned-in timecode*.

Blocking. The process of analyzing a scene and the space in which it will be played out and then assigning specific physical positions and moves to the actors and cameras.

Boom op. The person who holds a microphone on a *boompole* to record actors' dialogue.

Boompole. Often simply called a "boom," this is an extendable pole designed to hold a microphone.

Burned-in timecode (**BITC**). *Timecode* recorded on the video tracks of a tape ("burned in" to the video image), so it can be visibly displayed on a monitor. A director references this code when preparing a *paper edit*.

Bust shot. See *medium closeup*.

Call sheets. Forms on which the actors' hours are recorded (usually, by the *second assistant director*).

Camera Angle. The relation of a camera to its subject: What the camera "sees."

Camera cards. These cards, also known as "shot sheets," detail each camera's shots in a multi-camera studio production. These cards are usually distributed to the camera operators before a shoot begins.

Camera position. See *camera setup*.

Camera setup. Also commonly known as simply the "setup," it is a camera's physical position on a shooting stage, studio floor, or location, from which a number of individual shots can be taken. A scene may contain as many setups as the director chooses. When blocking the camera, the director bears in mind that each new camera setup may require an adjustment to the lighting as well.

Canted shot. A shot deliberately skewed from the horizontal plane. Also known as a "Dutch angle."

Cardioid. A roughly heart-shaped microphone *pickup pattern*. The cardioid microphone pattern, which also includes the narrower super- and hyper-cardioid patterns, is most sensitive to sounds reaching it directly from its front and to one degree or another rejects sounds emanating from behind and to the sides of it.

Cheating. The common practice of facilitating a particular shot or obtaining a particular effect by changing the physical circumstances on the set between shots in a way that will fool the camera's "eye" and, most importantly, the eye of the audience. These alterations may include moving actors, objects, or the camera itself.

Checkerboarding. The practice of splitting lines of dialogue onto alternating tracks so that individual lines may be adjusted in any number of ways during the *sound mix* without disturbing nearby lines.

Choice. A decision made by an actor about such important matters as character traits, subtext, relationship with other characters, scene and beat objectives, moments of transition, etc. An actor's choices guide his performance.

Chromakey. See *greenscreen*.

Cinematographer. See *director of photography*.

Cinéma vérité. Literally translated as "film truth," it was a documentary movement that emerged in France and America in the early 1960s as the direct result of advances in the portability of film cameras and recording equipment. Generally, it strove for a reality freed of artifice and invigorated by spontaneity. American *cinéma vérité* (also known as "direct cinema") is often distinguished from its French counterpart by its use of the camera simply to observe events, confining directorial intrusion to the absolute minimum.

Clapperboard. See *slate*.

Close shot. See *medium closeup*.

Closeup (CU). A tight single *shot* confined to the head and neck, often cutting off (placing out of frame) part of the forehead.

Conforming. See *negative matching*.

Continuity. A film's smooth shot-to-shot and scene-to-scene flow that creates the illusion of seamlessnesss. Good continuity is the product of shooting and editing choices, and attention to detail in such areas as performance, lighting, costume, and the supervision of design and props.

Continuity assistant. See *script supervisor*.

Contrast ratio. A way of describing the range of tones between black and white that can be effectively produced by particular systems (such as one film stock versus another or one video format versus another). It is often expressed as a ratio. (E.g., the contrast ratio of most film is at least 100:1—a range of approximately 7 stops— and greater than that of standard video, which is, at best, 50:1—a range of about 5 stops.)

Control room. The area of a television production studio where the director, *technical director*, associate director, producer, and other key production personnel are usually stationed, viewing a set of monitors and communicating via mics and headsets with the floor crew, during a multi-camera shoot. The control room is removed from the actual studio floor.

Coverage. (1) The number and type of shots a director chooses to shoot for a particular scene. Some directors employ a lot of coverage (i.e., shoot scenes in multiple ways) while others use more minimal coverage. (2) The evaluation of a script with a view to its possible production.

Crab. See *truck*.

Crane. (1) A device that allows the camera to move vertically (and sometimes horizontally, too) through space. (2) When used as a verb, a term describing the vertical movement of a camera through space.

Crew chiefs. The senior members or heads of the various production departments. These include the *director of photography*, the *sound recordist*, and the *production designer*.

Cue sheets. (1) Logs that show when and where a film's or a video's audio elements occur. These are prepared by the sound editor in advance of the final mix, during which they serve as a roadmap. (2) A detailed, annotated list of all music that is heard in a production. These sheets are required as part of a filmmaker's submission to any purchaser of her film. (3) Also known as "picture cue sheets," these are a description of the length and location of each picture effect (such as dissolves) in a film, which are submitted to the lab.

Cut-in. A shot that shows greater detail of a character or object within an established frame. For example, if a phone rings in a wide shot, the director may also take a cut-in close shot of the phone itself.

Cutaway. A shot of a character or object that is outside of the established frame. For example, if a character refers to a newspaper headline that is not in the current shot, the director may move the camera and take a cutaway of that headline. Cut-ins and cutaways are often used to condense dialogue (see *ellipsis*) or rearrange shots.

Cutoff. The area around the edge of a television image that does not appear on a domestic television screen.

Dailies. The unedited film footage developed by the lab each day after it is shot. This footage is screened for the benefit of the director and other crew members during the production period. Dailies are also frequently called "rushes."

Day-player. An actor on a short-term contract.

Deep focus. A shooting style in which the foreground, middleground, and background planes are all rendered simultaneously in sharp focus. See also *selective focus* and *depth of field*.

Deep shot. A *shot* in which one character is positioned in a foreground plane and another character in a background plane. The term is often used to describe a *2-shot* in which a substantial distance along the depth axis exists between the subjects.

Depth of field. The depth of acceptably sharp focus that extends in front of and behind the plane of primary focus. The combined effects of the distance between the camera and its subject, the lens's focal length, and the camera's f-stop setting determine this depth, which may be great or small or anywhere in between. See also *deep focus* and *selective focus*.

Dialogue editor. An editor who prepares dialogue tracks so that they are clean of unwanted sounds, synchronized with the picture, and ready for mixing.

Direct continuity. The situation when consecutive shots in an edited sequence contain the same on-screen elements, and therefore require as precise matching as possible. Direct continuity is especially important when the last shot of one scene and the first shot of the next contain common visual information—for example, when a character exits one room and directly enters another.

Director of photography (DP). The person responsible for a production's lighting and camerawork. As the senior member of the camera department, this person supervises the following crew members: a camera operator, a first assistant camera operator, a second assistant camera op, or "clapper loader" (see *slate*), various grips, and electricians. The DP is also known as the "cinematographer."

Director's assistant. A person who manages much of a production's paperwork, especially that generated by the director and the director's team. Also known as the "production secretary." This person should not be confused with the *assistant director*.

Director's team. The group that works closely with the director during preproduction and is responsible for organizing and subsequently managing the shoot as a whole. Members include the *first assistant director, second* *assistant, production manager, location manager, script supervisor or continuity assistant, director's assistant*, and *production assistants*.

Director's vision. A director's personal response to a film's subject matter and the screenplay. This personal response will govern many of her subsequent decisions—from actor and location choices to shooting style and much more.

Dolly. (1) A camera mount or platform that can be placed on a *track* or wheels to enable a camera to move smoothly while shooting. A "dolly shot" is a shot taken by a camera so mounted. (2) When used as a verb, a camera movement in which the camera moves toward or away from its subject while shooting, as in "to dolly in/out."

Dolly grip. A production crew member reporting to the *key grip*, who operates the camera when it is mounted on a track or wheels or a crane.

Downstage. In screen-direction terms, the part of the shooting area that is closest to the camera. The opposite of *upstage*.

Dubbers. The magnetic film playback machines that are synchronized together to play back all the audio tracks for a final mix. These are gradually being replaced in the mix today by multitrack digital recorders.

Dubbing. A broad term that can mean adding, replacing, mixing, or, most commonly, copying audio materials.

Edit decision list (**EDL**). The list of all the commands and *timecode* locations of material in a program or film made on digital software at an *offline edit*. The EDL is commonly taken to an *online edit*, where it is used as a reference for constructing the finished version.

Ellipsis. The shortening of real time into condensed, dramatic time by cutting out time during editing. "Elliptical editing"is an editing style that jumps from time to time or place to place, thereby condensing the real overall time.

Endboard. A *slate* at the end of a take rather than the beginning.

Equalization. Adjusting audio frequencies to record the cleanest sound or to achieve a particular effect.

Establishing shot. A (usually wide) shot used at or near the beginning of a scene to introduce (i.e., establish) its location.

Extra. A non-speaking player who is hired when additional characters are needed to populate a scene (to provide "background action"). Most movie and television agreements mandate that a specific number of Screen Actors Guild (SAG) members be employed as extras on a shoot. Productions contact agencies that specialize in providing extras and then specify the number and type of extras they require (e.g., five elderly men and five elderly women for a scene in a retirement home). Extras who are singled out and given specific non-speaking acting business may be upgraded to "silent bit players."

Eye light. A light that specifically illuminates an actor's eyes.

Eye-line. An imaginary line that connects one character's eyes with another character's eyes when the two face each other. This line is of considerable importance in determining both *objective* and *subjective shots* and the *180-degree rule*. The eye-line is often referred to simply as "the line."

Fill light. A light used to balance and reduce shadows cast by the key light.

First Assistant. See *assistant director*.

Flatbed editing machine. Sometimes called *"editing tables,"* these devices allow multiple reels of film (containing images) and recorded *mag stock* (containing sounds) to be synchronized and played together, with the image visible on a small screen. Despite the popularity of non-linear editing devices, some editors have not jettisoned their flatbeds.

Flats. The decorated boards placed side by side to form a set's walls. These are also known as "flattage."

Floor manager (**FM**). The individual responsible for the scheduling and smooth logistical operation of a television studio production. When a production's director is in the *control room*, the FM, who remains on the studio floor, is responsible for relaying the director's comments to the actors.

Fluff. An almost imperceptible error (such as a mispronunciation, faulty grammar, hesitation, repetition, or omission) in an actor's delivery of a line.

Focal length. The distance in millimeters between the optical center of a lens and the actual film (or video imaging element) in a camera when the lens is focused on an object at infinity. Focal length is one determinant of the size of a shot, which can have the long focal length of a *telephoto lens*, the short focal length of a *wide-angle lens*, or the in-between length of a normal lens. Lenses of differing focal lengths also have different visual properties.

Focus pull. See *rack focus*.

Foley. The art of creating sound effects, such as footsteps on gravel or rusty hinge squeaks or the sound of punching and so on, in synch with the picture. These effects are usually created on a purpose-built Foley stage and executed by Foley artists.

Fourth wall. The side of a room or set where most cameras are positioned (particularly in multi-camera television productions) to shoot the action. In this sort of arrangement, the fourth wall (which may not actually exist in certain studio sets) is rarely photographed.

Frame. (1) The borders of a screen image. See also *aspect ratio*. (2) An individual photograph on a piece of motion picture film. Film is normally recorded and projected at 24 frames per second. (3) A fully scanned video picture, which is recorded and transmitted at the rate of 30 frames per second in American NTSC video (and 25 frames per second in the PAL and SECAM systems used in Europe and the area covered by the former USSR). Variable frame rates are also increasingly available.

F-stop. A number indicating *lens aperture* size. The f-stop setting controls the amount of light admitted through the lens to the film or video-imaging element. Standard f-stop numbers range between 1 and 32, with small numbers representing large openings that allow the passage of more light than the openings represented by larger numbers.

Full-length shot. A shot that shows the whole person from head to toe. Also known as "full shot."

Gaffer. The chief (or head) electrician.

Gate. The plate mechanism in a camera or projector that holds and stabilizes film as it passes the lens.

Given circumstance. All the details about character, relationships, locations, etc., that can be gleaned from the script.

Gofer. See *production assistant*.

Greenscreen. An effect in which an actor performs in front of an evenly lit green background. The green background is then electronically replaced by selected footage or digital images in postproduction. The technique of greenscreen, and the analogous "bluescreen," are also used in multi-camera television studio work, where they are called "chromakey."

Grip. A crew member whose wide variety of on-the-set jobs may include rigging and operating tracks, jibs, and other equipment that facilitate camera movement. See *dolly grip* and *key grip*.

Group shot. A *shot* containing four or more characters.

Group Theater. A group of young actors who, under the initial leadership of Harold Clurman, Lee Strasberg, and Cheryl Crawford, brought a new level of realism to the American stage from the late 1920s through the early 1940s. See also *Actors Studio*.

Guide track. A temporary production-sound recording used during post-production as a guide for *automatic dialogue replacement*.

Hair in the gate. Common term for an unwanted strand of hair or some other particle lodged in the mechanism of a film camera that becomes reproduced on the celluloid.

Handheld shot. A shot in which a camera is held and moved by its operator, rather than a camera that is placed on a stabile support, such as a tripod or *dolly*. The often unstable motions of the handheld camera lend its shots a "documentary feel."

HDTV. See *high-definition television*.

Headshot. A (usually) 8x10 photograph of an actor, submitted by actors or agents for casting purposes.

High-concept idea. A script or proposed project's central concept expressed as a pithy slogan for purposes of *pitching* or marketing.

High definition television (HDTV). A widescreen (16x9) video and broadcast format with resolution equivalent to that of 35mm film. To record and watch HDTV requires the use of special high-definition cameras and equipment.

Hollywood continuity style. A set of storytelling assumptions and filmmaking rules that guide mainstream commercial filmmaking in Hollywood and many other places in the world. (For an indepth discussion of these assumptions and rules, see the Hollywood Continuity Style section of this text.)

Intermediate. (1) A film print that is screened by the director, editor, cinematographer, and perhaps other interested individuals to determine the quality and shot-to-shot consistency of color and exposure. Based upon their comments, further prints will be made at a film-processing lab via a process known as "timing" or "color timing" until a suitable quality print (the "release print") is arrived at. (2) A negative or positive film copy—not the original negative—that is used to make other prints.

Iso camera. A television studio camera equipped with its own separate video recorder, rather than being routed exclusively through the *switcher*, which receives signals from all the cameras and selects those that are to be recorded.

Jib arm. An adjustable crane-like attachment to a tripod or dolly that allows for smooth, extended up-and-down and side-to-side camera movement.

Jump cut. An edit that interrupts a smooth flow of visual images and draws attention to itself. While most jump cuts are infelicitous and the product of poor continuity, they have become an accepted stylistic device that can occasionally invigorate a film's pacing.

Key grip. The crew member responsible to the *director of photography* for erecting camera tracks and platforms, and rigging camera mounts. In the absence of a *dolly grip*, the key grip will also operate and maintain this equipment.

Key-light. A light, usually placed in front of a subject, that serves as that subject's primary source of illumination.

Kicker. A shaft of light that strikes its subject from the side or back.

Knee shot. See *three-quarters shot*.

Kuleshov effect. The meaning ascribed to individual shots is primarily determined by the context—the edited sequence—in which they are presented. This was demonstrated in the 1920s by Russian film pioneer and theorist Lev Kuleshov, who conducted experiments in which he juxtaposed a particular shot with a variety of other shots, and found that each new juxtaposition brought new interpretation/meaning to the original shot.

Lavaliere microphone. A small, sensitive, clip-on microphone most often used in documentary interviews. Its use in narrative drama is limited because it is visible and, if a costume comes in contact with the microphone head, a strong rustling sound ensues. Sometimes called a "clip" or "lapel" microphone.

Lead room. The space in the screen *frame* between a subject who is moving (or about to move) and the edge of the frame toward which that character is headed. (Compare with *looking room*.)

L-cut. An edit in which audio and picture elements are staggered—i.e., don't start at the same time. The audio either precedes the picture or (less frequently) follows it. This is also known as a "split edit."

Letterbox. A format for showing widescreen movies on a traditional (4 x 3) television screen without resorting to the aesthetically questionable process of *pan and scan*. To allow a film to retain its original widescreen *aspect ratio* when viewed on a television screen, a letterboxed program will black-out (like a matte placed over a photo) unused screen areas above and below the film itself. The disadvantage of the letterbox format is that a large portion of the television screen is unused, thereby reducing the size of the image and making detail harder to discern.

Lighting director. The person in charge of lighting the set. In single-camera productions, this is usually the *director of photography*.

Line, the. See *eye-line*.

Line of intimacy. The point in a scene at which the director chooses to shoot in closeup to bring the viewer into a more intimate relationship with a character.

Linear editing. Editing in a way that does not allow random access to material that has already been laid down in a sequence. Old-fashioned reel-to-reel video editing was linear because in a sequence of, for example, ten shots, shot 4 could not be replaced without removing and re-editing shots 4 through 10. Traditional film editing is somewhat linear, though shots can also be cut and pasted at any point. True *nonlinear editing* is possible with digital editing software programs.

Lip-sync. The matching of recorded dialogue with the visible movement of an on-screen character's lips.

Location manager. A member of the production team who helps locate and then contracts for the use of locations and related facilities (such as parking, costume/makeup areas, and toilets). This person also manages these during the shoot.

Lock. See *picture lock.*

Long shot (**LS**). A shot that shows the whole subject at a distance, as well as some of the area immediately above and below the subject.

Looking room. The space in the screen *frame* between a stationary subject and the edge of the frame toward which that character is looking. (Compare with *lead room*.)

Looping. See *automatic dialogue replacement.*

Loose shot. A shot framed so that there is a significant distance between the subject and the edge of the frame. (See also *tight shot* and *wide shot*.)

Magazine. The two-reel (feed and take-up) enclosed container attached to a movie camera that holds both the unexposed and exposed film.

Mag tracks. Audio tracks recorded on reels of magnetic oxide-coated film stock. During editing these tracks are synched up with the picture on a *flatbed* editing machine/table. Mag tracks are being superceded by digital audio recorders and digital audio workstations.

Magic if, the. A technique originated by Russian director/actor/teacher Konstantin Stanislavski (1863–1938) to help actors identify with a character. Utilizing this technique, an actor (or a director or a writer) asks herself, "What would I do and how would I feel under these circumstances if I were this character?"

M&E tracks. Literally meaning "music and effects," this is a production's *sound mix* without dialogue. It's used for export to those foreign-speaking countries whose audiences prefer to have their native language dubbed in instead of watching subtitles.

Mark. A position on the set where an actor is supposed to start or end a movement or perform an action or deliver a line. Often indicated by pieces of tape on the floor, this position is the exact spot on the set at which the actor will be properly in frame and in focus and will maintain continuity with other takes of the scene. Moving to a mark at the appropriate time is called "hitting" a mark.

Master shot. A single shot that covers an entire scene or a significant part of a scene. This is generally a wide shot into which closer shots will be cut during editing. (Some directors shoot a second, shorter and tighter, master shot, which is called a "mini-master.")

Master use license. A license to use a particular recording of a piece of music. (Its name derives from the fact that one licenses the use of a particular master recording.) See also *synchronization license* and *music clearance*.

MAT. See *Moscow Art Theater*.

Match cut. A cut from one shot to another in which the same subject appears in both. An actor helps achieve a match cut by positioning himself and performing an action the same way in different shots. Since the action in the outgoing shot matches that of the incoming shot, such an edit will appear invisible.

MCU. See *medium closeup*.

Medium close shot (**MCS**). See *medium closeup*.

Medium closeup (**MCU**). Also known as a "bust shot" or "medium close shot (MCS)" or a "close shot," this tight shot shows a character from the chest to the top of the head.

Medium full shot. See *three-quarters* shot.

Medium shot. See *mid-shot*.

Method, the. An interpretation of the acting theories of Konstantin Stanislavski developed by American actor/teacher Lee Strasberg (1901-1982) at the *Actors Studio* during the 1950s and 1960s. It emphasized, among other techniques, the use of emotional (or "affective") memory as a means of approaching a character. Strasberg's Method (and the many offshoots it spawned) has been the most prominent American film-acting style since the 1950s. Among the many notable early practitioners of Method acting were James Dean, Marlon Brando, Julie Harris, and Montgomery Clift.

Mid-shot (**MS**). A shot that cuts at or around waist height. (A tight MS cuts above the waist and a loose MS cuts below it.)

Montage. Telling a story or making a point through the artful juxtaposition of sounds and images during editing. In traditional Hollywood films, montage is most commonly used to show the passage of time. (Note: In various parts of the world and within various historical contexts, this often indiscriminately used term carries many specific, other connotations and meanings.) See *Russian montage*.

Moscow Arts Theater (**MAT**). Founded in 1897 by Konstantin Stanislavski and Vladimir Nemirovich-Dantchenko (1859–1943), it produced plays by Anton Chekhov, Maxim Gorki, and many others, while also serving as the principle vehicle for Stanislavski's experiments in actor training and technique.

MS. See *mid-shot*.

Music clearance. Obtaining permission to use (licensing) specific pre-existing pieces of music and particular recordings of those pieces. See *master use license* and *synchronization license*.

Narrow-angle lens. A *telephoto lens*.

Narrow-angle shot. A shot made using a narrow-angle or *telephoto lens*.

Natural sound (**nat sound**). Sounds indigenous to a particular location. These could be anything from wind-rustled tree leaves to the roar of a smelting plant.

Negative matching (or *conforming*). The frame-by-frame process of matching an original film negative to the film editor's *workprint*. This process is also commonly known as "conforming."

The New Wave (**Nouvelle Vague**). A loosely joined group of innovative French filmmakers who, working in the 1950s and '60s, sought alternatives to what they saw as overly polished studio films that were stylistically governed by long-established film industry practices, opting instead for a very personal style and fresh look that often featured handheld camerawork and location shooting. Among this group were Jean-Luc Godard, François Truffaut, Claude Chabrol, Eric Rohmer, and Jacques Rivette. The cinematic freedoms of the New Wave movement influenced filmmakers in the U.S. and throughout the world.

Nonlinear editing. Editing on a nonlinear (a.k.a. random-access) digital device, which runs editing software. Nonlinear editing, as opposed to *linear editing*, allows the user to access images and audio from any point in the material being edited and move it or delete it or duplicate it almost instantly.

Objective. That which a character strives to achieve in each beat and in each scene (*super-objective*) and in the complete story (*spine*). Objectives provide actors, directors, and writers with motivations for actions. See also *through-line* and *obstacle*.

Objective shot. A *shot* taken from a camera position that is off the *eye-line* and does not bring the audience into a sympathetic relationship with the character(s). This shot is often taken at right angles to the eye-line. See also *subjective angle*.

Obstacle. A specific object or action that provides *resistance* and thus prevents a character from attaining her goal or *objective*. An obstacle might be a wall that gets in a character's way or the threatening posture of the soldier who is guarding it.

Offline editing. Creating a first complete video edit of either a video program or a film that is being edited digitally. This may be a low-resolution digital edit from which the filmmaker can derive a list of edit points (an *edit decision list*) that will subsequently be taken to an *online edit*. An offline edit saves the producer the cost of editing preliminary versions of a project at a more expensive, state-of-the-art *online facility*. When reel-to-reel video editing was the norm, there was a substantial difference in quality between the offline and the online edits. Now, as low-level *nonlinear* editing software becomes more sophisticated, the difference in quality between the online and the offline edit is less marked.

180-degree rule. To maintain consistent *screen direction* when cutting back and forth between characters (and avoid confusing the audience), the camera must be placed on one side of *the line* or the *eye-line* running between them. And to maintain consistent screen direction for characters or objects in motion, the camera must stay on one side of the action.

Online editing. A program's final video/digital editing may be done at an *online facility*. This edit produces a high-resolution final product that contains *opticals* and other effects. Online editing usually follows the less-expensive *offline edit*. However, with today's rapid growth of inexpensive digital storage devices and greater proliferation of *nonlinear* editing systems, the distinction between online and offline editing is blurring.

Online facility. A facility for *online editing*.

Optical printer. A machine that allows for the rephotographing of either positive or negative film footage allowing for the combination of multiple filmed images and, thus, the creation of various optical effects, such as dissolves, fade-ins, split-screen images, etc.

Opticals. Optical effects, achieved either digitally or via an *optical printer*.

OS. Off screen.

Over-the-shoulder shot (O/S): a *2-shot* (usually a medium or tighter) that strongly favors one character, who is photographed over the shoulder of the second, who is positioned to the side of the frame, in the immediate foreground, with her back to the camera.

Pan. (1) To move a camera head from a central pivot-point so that it scans an area or object horizontally from left to right or right to left.

(2) A shot resulting from this camera move. (Compare with *tilt*.)

Pan and scan. A method of "reducing" a *widescreen* program for use on a normal (4x3) television screen by panning from one side of the widescreen to the other in order to include important information in the right- or left-hand sides of the frame. This process aesthetically damages much of a widescreen program's cinematography, and may even be said to rewrite the way one views a particular scene or movie. Today, due to widescreen options on certain newer television sets and the growing acceptance of the *letterbox* format, this process is waning.

Paper edit. A preparatory ordering of shots and scenes that a director takes into the edit as a guide.

Parallel storytelling. A dramatic form in which two or more plots/stories of somewhat equal importance are advanced simultaneously. In film and video this is accomplished by cutting back and forth between them. (Compare *subplot*.)

Pedestal camera. A camera mounted on a heavy, wheeled *dolly* that is designed to be navigated in almost any direction. These are commonly used in television studios.

Perambulator boom. A moveable platform on which a *boom op* sits with a long, telescoping *boompole*. These are commonly found in television studios where the boompole extends out over the top of the cameras into the set.

Pickup pattern. The area within the 360-degree field surrounding a microphone in which the microphone effectively records sound. See also *cardioid, shotgun microphone*, and *lavaliere microphone*.

Pickup shot. (1) A *shot* that re-films/re-records a problematic portion of a longer shot or provides an alternative version of a portion of a longer shot.

(2) A required shot that is filmed/recorded after the close of *principal photography*.

Picture lock. The state of a project once picture editing is completed. When a production reaches this point, work can begin in earnest on the various sound elements and the *opticals*. This is also known as "pixlock."

Pitch. The presentation of a story idea to a producer or studio executive with the hope of obtaining financial support.

Point-of-view shot (**POV**). A *shot* taken from a character's perspective, showing what that character is looking at. See also *subjective angle*.

Postproduction. The third and final stage in the production sequence (which progresses from *preproduction* to *production* to postproduction). This stage is principally taken up with editing visual elements and preparing, editing, and mixing audio elements.

POV. See *point of view*.

Preproduction. The first stage of the production sequence (which progresses from preproduction to *production* to *postproduction*). This stage is given to planning the many important tasks that will eventually provide for a project's smooth and successful realization. Among these tasks are script rewrites, research, casting of actors and location and crew, and the director's preparation of the *shooting script*.

Principal photography. The period in which the main filming/recording of actors is accomplished during a project's *production* stage.

Production. The second stage of a project's realization (which progresses from *preproduction* to production to *postproduction*). This stage is given to *principal photography* and all that is associated with that task.

Production assistant. A person who assists other members of the *production team* in a broad variety of tasks and executes a large number of assignments on the set, including organizing extras and running errands. Also called a "gofer"(or "gopher").

Production designer. A person who is responsible, in conjunction with the director and cinematographer, for the overall look of a large-scale production. Implementing this vision entails coordinating all the other design departments (such as wardrobe, makeup, and props), as well as overseeing set design and construction, and assisting in the selection of locations and then adapting them to the requirements of the film. See also *art director*.

Production manager (**PM**). The member of the *director's team* who is responsible for scheduling and budgeting. On smaller productions, the PM may double as *first assistant* or *location manager*.

Production team. All the members of a crew working on a shoot. This would include producers, the director's team, the design, camera, and sound departments (including drivers, craftsmen, and construction workers, etc.), and other miscellaneous crew members.

Property master. The person responsible for obtaining and maintaining *action props*. The property master will discuss prop selection with the designer and director, and may work with a "prop maker" (who builds props) and "prop assistants" (who help him on the set).

Prop. The physical objects that appear on a set. These include "design props" (furniture and decorations), which are selected by the *production designer* or *art director* in consultation with the director, and "action props" (objects, such as weapons, cutlery, etc., that the characters actually handle), which are often selected by the *property master* in consultation with the production designer/art director and the director.

Pull-up. A video editing term that refers to the tightening of edits between shots (especially those selected by a *technical director* on a multi-camera production). (2) In film editing, the term refers to copying sound frames from one reel and adding them to another during the mix.

Rack focus. To guide the audience's attention from one character (or object) to another by changing the lens focus from one character to another within a single shot, i.e., as an in-focus subject becomes blurred, a previously out-of-focus character comes into focus, thus pulling the viewer's attention from the first to the second character. A rack focus is easier to achieve on a film camera or a full-sized video camera with a geared mechanical focus than on certain video camcorders.

Reaction shot. A *shot* that shows a character reacting to a stimulus, which could be anything from what another character says or does to an "act of God." This is usually a fairly close and often silent shot showing the reacting character's facial expression or body language.

Recordist. See *sound recordist*.

Rembrandt triangle. A triangular spot of light just beneath a character's eye on the side of the face that is partially turned away from the primary light source. This flattering effect is created in film by the combined use of *key* and *fill* lights, though it has been used for centuries by portrait painters and photographers and in film since the days of silent movies. The lighting style that aims to reproduce this effect is known as "Rembrandt lighting."

Resistance. A force or action that opposes a character's initial attempts to achieve an *objective*. Resistance can be a concrete *obstacle*, such as a person or a thing, or an internal quality, such as fear, which a character has to overcome.

Rhythm. A temporal pattern formed by a sequence of shots of varying or similar lengths, framings, and contents. Rhythm is not only a shot-by-shot concern, it may also be considered scene-to-scene, as it defines the feel of a whole project. See also *tempo* and *tempo-rhythm*.

Rough cut. A director's preliminary edit of a scene or entire project that precedes the "final cut."

Rule of thirds. The division of the screen into thirds by imaginary horizontal and vertical lines. Figures and objects placed on these lines or on their intersecting points have particular compositional weight.

Runner. See *production assistant*.

Rushes. See *dailies*.

Russian montage. A style of *montage* that juxtaposes strongly contrasting images in an attempt to force an audience to construct particular conclusions. For example, shot 1 is of a laughing soldier. Shot 2 is of a grotesque corpse lying in the street, so the audience concludes that the forces represented by the soldier are heartless and cruel. This style is also known as "Eisenstein montage" after its early practitioner, Russian director Sergei Eisenstein (1898-1948).

Scene. A continuous event that takes place in one location. See also *shot*.

Scratch track. A temporary sound track (e.g., an imperfect dialogue track that will be replaced in *ADR* or a temporary voice-over that will be replaced by a professional actor or a temporary sound effect or music track that will be replaced by a newly-created one).

Screen direction. The direction that characters or objects move across the screen frame. Maintaining screen direction is important if one is to maintain a scene's *continuity*. See also *180-degree rule*.

Script editor. The person employed on a television series who is responsible for communicating with its writers and fielding any of the production crew's questions about script-related matters.

Script supervisor (or *continuity assistant*). The on-set person who is responsible for logging shot details for the film laboratory and editor, and for helping the director keep track of shot-to-shot and scene-to-scene continuity.

Second assistant. The member of the *director's team* who assists the *first assistant*, often giving actors their calls (i.e., telling them when to arrive at the location for costume and makeup) and keeping track of their working hours.

Selective focus. A shooting technique in which one subject is in sharp focus in a frame and another is out of focus. See also *deep focus*, *depth of field*, and *rack focus*.

Sequence. (1) A series of (usually short) connected *scenes* that can logically be thought of as a unit (e.g., a car chase). (2) A series of consecutive *shots* with a common purpose.

Setup. See *camera position*.

Shooting script. The final version of the script that is used during a production shoot. This is the version the director will mark up with his production notes.

Shot. A single continuous camera run. Also an individual pictorial unit used in editing. This may be as short as a subliminal shot (as used in *The Pawnbroker*) or as long as a continuous *master shot* (as used in *Timecode*, *Russian Arc* or *Rope*).

Shotgun microphone. Long and tubular in appearance (like a shotgun barrel), this *cardioid* microphone is the microphone most commonly used on single camera (i.e., non multi-camera studio) shoots.

Shot sheets. See *camera cards*.

Sides. Scenes or extracts from scenes that are distributed to actors who are to audition for specific roles.

Slate. Also known as the "clapperboard" or "sticks," this is a board on which the *scene* and *shot* numbers are written that is photographed by the camera at the head of each shot, thus identifying each shot with a unique scene and shot number. On top of this board is a hinged stick that the assistant camera operator snaps down to provide both a sharp sound impulse (a click) and a visual cue (the stick hitting the board), which the film editor can use to synchronize sound and picture. (Some slates that are used with video will also have a window that shows a *timecode* readout.)

SMPTE timecode. A version of *timecode* approved by the Society of Motion Picture and Television Engineers, a body that sets technical standards for the film and television industries.

Sound designer. (1) An individual who oversees a project's postproduction audio, helping to define and execute a cohesive *soundscape*.
(2) An individual who designs original sound effects using a variety of sound sources and sound processing equipment.

Sound mix. The culmination of the audio postproduction process, the bringing together and balancing of all of a production's sound elements—speech, sound effects, and music. A film sound mix today usually involves preparing a series of sound mixes, each designed for a specific presentation format.

These might include such formats as six-channel Dolby surround, 5.1 surround, three-speaker stereo, and a true stereo for television and other less-sophisticated systems, and so on. The sound mix may also separate out an *M&E* version for export.

Sound perspective. The perception of a sound's position in space, which can be near or far—"close" or "distant"—or off to one side or behind us or any combination of these positions.

Sound recordist. The person responsible for recording audio during shooting. On location she will work closely with the *boom op*. Also known as "production sound mixer."

Soundscape. (1) A sonic portrait of an environment, a space, a location at a particular point in time. (2) In filmmaking, this term is sometimes used to refer to a project's ideal or desired sound style as envisioned by the director, sound designer, and sound crew. (Also known as "sound picture.")

Soundstage. A large, enclosed, purpose-built area in which film sets can be erected, lights easily hung, and shooting carried out.

Sound track. (1) Any single audio track or grouping of channels dedicated to the recording or playing of a particular sound element—speech, effects, music—as opposed to a picture track. (2) The physical portion of *mag* film or magnetic tape or a virtual channel or channels on an audio recording device. (3) A film's completed *sound mix* of all audio elements. This usage is often as one word: "soundtrack." (4) The recorded musical portion of a film's sound. This usage is usually as one word: "soundtrack."

Source music. Music that emanates from an on-screen source (or an off-screen source implied by the location). This music might be coming from a jukebox playing in a bar or a car's radio or a polka band playing at a state fair or any other source.

Sparks. A common term for a production's electrician.

Special effects supervisor. An individual responsible for leading the visual special effects team and achieving a designated special effect during shooting.

Spine. A character's overall *objective* at the level of the complete story. See also *super-objective* and *through-line of action*.

Split edit. See *L-cut*.

Split sound. The situation in which speaking characters are so situated in a shot that a single *boom* cannot cover them all.

Spotting. Choosing locations in a *picture-locked* project for sound effects or dialogue replacement or music score, each of which is usually done separately at sessions involving the director and the person(s) primarily responsible for each field, e.g., music spotting would involve the director, composer, music editor, and music supervisor.

Square-on shot. See *symmetrical shot*.

Steadicam. A shoulder harness with an extension that holds the camera, worn by a camera operator to enhance smooth camera movement—especially in areas where it would be difficult for a *dolly* to function (such as stairways and crowded rooms, etc.). It is a popular and much-used device.

Steenbeck. A popular brand of *flatbed editing machine* that has been so commonly used that its name has become somewhat synonymous with "flatbed."

Storyboard. A visualization device. A director (or a storyboard artist) sketches the *shots* and shot manipulations (such as *pans* and *zooms*, etc.) in a scene. This set of drawings, which usually shows important dialogue lines and other audio elements beside or below each shot, provides the director with a means to test a scene's camerawork and flow, and to communicate her ideas about these to other members of the crew. See also *animatix*.

Story editor. The person working on a television series who is responsible for maintaining the overall arc and development of the series' ongoing storylines.

Subjective angle. A *camera angle* taken from close to the *eye-line* that allows the viewer to clearly read the subject's face. The degree of subjectivity increases the closer the camera gets to the eye-line. See also *objective shot* and *point of view*.

Subplot. A story that is secondary to or a subsidiary of or subordinate to a main plot. A film with one central story may have one or more subplots that come and go during the development of the central story. (Compare with *parallel storytelling*.)

Subtext. The emotions, attitudes, intentions, and meanings that underlie (and are often disguised by) what a character says. For example, the line, "I'll be back" could be read at face value as encouragement (such as, "I'll be back to see/help you") or as a thinly disguised threat (i.e., with a darker element of subtext). Actors try to understand the subtext of their lines before speaking the actual words.

Super-objective. A character's long-term *objective*. A term used to refer to a character's overall scene objective. See also *spine* and *through-line*.

Sweetening. (1) Making a scene's or a production's *soundtrack* more vivid or compelling by adding new and/or additional sounds or improving existing sounds. (2) A term sometimes used to refer to the *sound mix* stage of *postproduction*. (3) In video postproduction especially, a term sometimes used to refer to the whole audio editing and mixing process.

Swing sets. Television studio and soundstage sets that are stored for reuse.

Switcher. A device operated by the *technical director* in multi-camera production, which receives the signal from all the cameras and selects those that are transmitted or output to a master monitor or recorded onto tape. Switchers also offer a range of visual effects and other technical options.

Symmetrical shot. An *objective shot* of two or more characters who are seen more or less equally in profile.

Synchronization licence. A license to record a particular piece of music, which is negotiated with the music publisher. This license does not include the right to use a particular pre-existing recording of that piece of music. See also *master use licence* and *music clearance*.

Tail slate. See *endboard*.

Technical scout. An on-location conference among the director and various members of the crew and *director's team* (including, but not limited to, *production designer*, *director of photography*, *gaffe*r, *sound recordist*, *location manager*, and *first assistant*) shortly before shooting commences. This meeting allows the director to discuss his shooting plan with key personnel, and also allows those present to review the shooting schedule and resolve other technical and logistical issues. This is also known as a "tech scout."

Technical director. The crew member who operates a *switcher* in a multi-camera production. The technical director sits alongside the director in a studio *control room* or wherever the production is being recorded in order to implement the director's instructions. Sometimes also known, especially in the U.K., as the "vision mixer."

Technique of physical actions. An acting approach developed by Constantin Stanislavski late in his career. It emphasizes physical movement and improvisation as ways for an actor to approach a role.

Telecine. (1) A machine that is used to transfer film footage to video for television transmission or video editing. (2) The process of converting film to video using a telecine machine.

Telephoto lens. A lens with long *focal length*. It has certain characteristics, among which are the ability to sharply focus on and magnify distant subjects, and to compress the apparent distance between objects along the depth axis.

Tempo. The speed or pace or pulse at which things occur. This usually refers to the rate at which edits occur, but may also be considered on many other levels, such as a project's scene-by-scene pace or even the rate at which actions occur or dialogue is delivered. See also *rhythm* and *tempo-rhythm*.

Tempo-rhythm. Constantin Stanislavski believed that most *actions*, *beats*, *scenes*, acts, and plays contain both tempo and rhyhm, and that it is not always productive to separate these two components. Tempo-rhythm describes an event that has both tempo and rhythmic implications.

Temp score. Pre-existing music that an editor and/or director choose to put behind a project's *rough cuts* before the project's original music is recorded or completed. A temp score may help a director determine an appropriate approach for or style of music for a project. Temp scores also help early screenings feel more complete, allowing viewers to get past missing *opticals* and incomplete sound work.

Three-quarters angle. A camera angle that is halfway between fully frontal (a *subjective shot*) and profile (an *objective shot*).

Three-quarters shot. Also known as a "knee shot" or a "medium full shot," it cuts at a character's knees, showing that character from the knees to the top of the head. (Compare with *mid-shot* and *full-length shot*.)

Through-line of action. A strong *choice* by an actor that gives him the key to uniting his *actions* with his *objective* or *super-objective*. See also *spine*. Finding a through-line of action pulls a performance into focus and gives a unifying purpose to a series of individual actions.

Tight shot. A shot framed so that there is little distance between the subject and the edge of the frame. See also *loose shot* and *wide shot*.

Tight 2-shot. A *medium closeup* that shows two characters, rather than just one.

Tilt. (1) To vertically rotate a camera from a central pivot-point to scan up and/or down an area or object. (2) A shot resulting from this camera move. (Compare with *pan*.)

Timecode. An electronic system that ascribes a specific number to each frame of video and allows material to be identified and accessed with precision. A timecode readout will display a series of two-digit numbers representing hours: minutes: seconds: frames. Almost all professional video and film work uses this code at some point in the production or postproduction process to synchronize and identify sound and picture materials. See also *SMPTE timecode*.

Timeline. A nonlinear editing machine's display that graphically shows a sequence of edits in the chronological order in which they occur.

Track. (1) The rails (not unlike a miniature railroad track) on which a *dolly* rolls. (2) A smooth camera move, often following a moving subject, that is enabled by the camera's ride on a dolly. (3) A term used to describe a lateral camera movement and synonymous with *truck*.

Track-splitting. Allocating different sounds to different tracks during editing.

Transition. A moment during a performance when an actor adjusts to new circumstances.

Treatment. A detailed screenplay outline that contains little or no dialogue and which precedes the first draft. A treatment may be submitted to a producer or other funding source for approval.

Truck. A camera movement in which the camera moves to the left or to the right in its relation to a subject. This movement is also known as a *track* or a "crab." Truck may also be used as an instruction, such as in "truck left" or "truck right."

Two-shot (2-shot). A shot showing two characters. This term often implies a medium 2-shot of two people. See also *deep shot, over-the-shoulder shot*, and *tight two-shot*.

Typecasting. The practice of casting actors primarily according to their looks and/or past roles that they've repeatedly performed and become associated with in the minds of the audience.

Unit. See *beat*.

Unit production manager (**UPM**). The person who prepares the budget, authorizes expenditure, and, sometimes, drafts a preliminary shooting schedule.

UPM. See *unit production manager*.

Upstage. (1) In screen-directing terms, the area of the shooting stage or set that is farthest from the camera. The opposite of *downstage*.
(2) In acting terms, the ungentlemanly practice of one actor drawing undue attention to herself while another is supposed hold the viewer's attention.

Variable-focal-length lens. A lens that contains a series of movable fixed lenses that allow for smooth and continuous adjustments of *focal lengths* from that of a *wide-angle* to that of a *telephoto lens*. Also known as a "zoom lens."

Vector. A direction in which the viewer's eye is encouraged to move across the screen. It is often created by movement on the screen or by some other sort of strong visual indication (such as an arrow or other pointing shape).

Vertigo effect. A dramatic lens effect invented by Alfred Hitchcock (and used in his film *Vertigo*). It is created by the camera dollying either in or out while a complimentary lens *zoom* in or out is performed simultaneously (i.e., if the camera dollies in, the lens will zoom out).

Video-assist. A video system hooked up to a film camera to allow for on-set viewing of camera shots on a small monitor by the director and other interested parties. The system will also allow for a take to be immediately reviewed. Also known as a "video tap."

Walla. Background speech (murmuring and muttering and buried conversations) in which individual words cannot be clearly distinguished. Since *extras* usually mouth their conversations silently, specialists in this work—"walla groups"—can be found to provide a blanket of background voices during postproduction.

Whip-pan. An extremely fast *pan*. Most whip-pans blur everything except the images at the start and end of the maneuver.

Wide-angle lens. A short *focal-length* lens that offers a wider-than-average view and a greater-than-average *depth of field*, unlike the *telephoto lens*. One of the characteristics of a very wide (or "fish-eye") lens is that, when used to photograph objects close to the camera, it will distort these objects' proportions.

Wide-angle shot. A shot made with a wide-angle lens. This shot has a greater-than-average breadth and depth, though it is not automatically synonymous with a *wide shot*.

Wide shot. A *shot* with an angle of view significantly wider than normal. This is not necessarily the same as a *loose shot* because in a wide shot there may or may not be distance between the subject and the edge of the frame. See also *tight shot*.

Wild sound. See *wildtrack*.

Wildtrack. Any *sound track* (speech or effects or music) created on the set or location without synchronization with the picture. It might be, among other things, an *atmosphere* track or the sound of water lapping on the beach or a moment of *walla* or a performer playing a guitar.

Windjammer. A large, fluffy, specially designed coat that can placed over a microphone to reduce wind noise. In essence, this is a very heavy-duty *windscreen*.

Windscreen. A foam rubber casing that may be placed over a microphone's recording elements to reduce rumble and wind noise.

Widescreen. Any of a number of screen formats that are wider than the 1.33:1 (4x3) standard television or Academy Format aspect ratio. See also *high-definition television, letterbox,* and *pan and scan.*

Workprint. A generally low-quality copy of a production's original film footage. A workprint (rather than the original) is used during editing so that the original will not be damaged. See also *negative matching.*

Zoom. To adjust a *variable-focal-length lens* (or "zoom lens"), which can be continuously and smoothly adjusted to give a viewer the impression of moving closer to (zoming in) or farther away (zooming out) from a subject.

Index